# DIALOGIC SEMIOSIS

**Advances in Semiotics**

Thomas A. Sebeok, *General Editor*

# DIALOGIC SEMIOSIS

## An Essay on Signs and Meaning

JØRGEN DINES JOHANSEN

INDIANA UNIVERSITY PRESS

*Bloomington & Indianapolis*

The paper used in this publication meets the minimum requirements of American National Standard for Information Sciences — Permanence of Paper for Printed Library Materials, ANSI Z39.48-1984.

∞™

Manufactured in the United States of America

**Library of Congress Cataloging-in-Publication Data**

Johansen, Jørgen Dines.
    Dialogic semiosis : an essay on signs and meaning / Jørgen Dines
Johansen.
        p.  cm. — (Advances in semiotics)
    Includes bibliographical references and index.
    ISBN 0-253-33099-8
    1. Semiotics. 2. Communication. 3. Speech. 4. Peirce, Charles
S. (Charles Sanders), 1839-1914.  I. Title  II. Series.
P99. J6  1993
302.2—dc20                                          92-35668

1 2 3 4 5 97 96 95 94 93

**For Helle**

# Contents

# Part II,2 A Dialogic Model of Semiosis

# Part III Light

# Preface

This book is about semiotics. It is an essay on signs and meaning, on how signs transmit information between human agents, making understanding possible. Although in certain places (e.g., chapter IV) there is discussion of sign function in non-human agents, the main topic is intentionally produced texts, most specifically speech.

To study speech means to look at the use of signs in contexts; to do that I have in this book constructed a model of the process and presuppositions of dialogic understanding. Although I follow Peirce's insight that "thinking always proceeds in the form of a dialogue," and that "it is essentially composed of signs as its matter," this essay is not intended to be a book on Peirce's philosophy. It is an essay from a Peircean perspective.

Part I begins by pointing to the decisive, or perhaps fateful, moment when Saussure deliberately broke the circuit of speech to establish a vantage point from which it is possible to study language as a system. Despite the importance of Saussure's break, the first part of this study is not mainly on Saussure, but on the Danish linguist Louis Hjelmslev's concept of the sign and the study of semiotic systems. The reason is not to do justice to a neglected figure in semiotics, because Hjelmslev is anything but neglected. In Herman Parret's *Discussing Language* (1974), a series of interviews with outstanding contemporary linguists, he is mentioned even more often than Saussure. Hjelmslev cultivated one side of Saussure's approach to language, the formal and systematic, and tried to bring it to perfection. Consequently his glossematic theory of language — and in principle of all semiotic systems — offers another vantage point, one from which to recognize the merits and shortcomings of the structuralist concept of the sign. I am fortunate to be Hjelmslev's compatriot, and therefore have access to his work in Danish.

Because of his eminence in the field, the largest part of the book attempts to understand and expound Peirce's concepts of the process of signification, and induce readers to think semiotics with Peirce. The first section of the second part (II, 1) explains Peirce's triadic concept of the sign and his classification of signs, especially the all-important distinction between iconic, indexical, and symbolic signs. In the second section (II, 2) the subject is *signs in actu,* as Peirce would say. And after having clarified the presuppositions of dialogic communication according to Peirce, including also discussion of points of view by Roman Jakobson and Bertrand Russell, there is a summary of the arguments in the chapter that has given the name to this study (chapter VI, earlier versions in Johansen 1985 and 1988; John Deely has also expounded my model of semiosis in Deely 1990: 77-80). The last chapter of Part II, 2 deals with rhetoric and the validity claims of universal pragmatics concerning dialogic understanding, the necessarily presupposed, but in fact often flouted, preconditions for speech. Part III, the conclusion, analyzes a specific semiotic micro system from both Hjelmslevian and Peircean perspectives, and summarizes the basic features of an intentionally produced semiotic.

Since the essay expounds and confronts two different concepts of the sign it is clear that the thrust of this book is semiotics in the sense of the production, transmission, and interpretation of different kinds of signs in human communication. It is not a philosophy according to Peirce. There are several reasons why this essay is not intended as a book on Peirce's philosophy.

First, its scope is more limited than Peirce's own idea of semiotics. In a famous passage in a letter to Lady Welby of 1908 Dec. 23, he describes his view as follows:

> Know that from the day when at the age of 12 or 13 I took up, in my elder brother's room a copy of Whately's *"Logic,"* and asked him what Logic was, and getting some simple answer, flung myself on the floor and buried myself in it, it has never been in my power to study anything, – mathematics, ethics, metaphysics, gravitation, thermodynamics, optics, chemistry, comparative anatomy, astronomy, psychology, phonetics, economics, the history of science, whist, men and women, wine, meteorology, except as a study of semiotic. (SS, 1977: 85-86)

It would be fascinating, for instance, to study men and women from a semiotic point of view, but it is not done here.

Peirce was a mathematician, a logician, and a builder of philosophical systems (some think that he and not Hegel was the last of the great system building philosophers), and in his view all these areas, and the sciences, are, as it were, perfused with semiotics. Or better, they *are* semiotics. As a realist and idealist, he asked himself if the universe "is not composed exclusively of signs" (5.449). On these metaphysical subjects the reader of this book will find next to nothing.

Peirce also divided semiotics into three parts: 1) Speculative Grammar, 2) Logical Critic (or logic proper), and 3) Speculative Rhetoric or Methodeutic. About 1897 he distinguishes these three branches in this way:

> the science of semiotic has three branches. The first is called by Duns Scotus *grammatica speculativa*. We may term it *pure grammar*. It has for its task to ascertain what must be true of the representamen used by every scientific intelligence in order that they may embody any *meaning*. The second is logic proper. It is the science of what is quasi-necessarily true of the representamina of any scientific intelligence in order that they may hold good of any *object*, that is, may be true. Or say, logic proper is the formal science of the conditions of the truth of representations. The third, in imitation of Kant's fashion of preserving old associations of words in finding nomenclature for new conceptions, I call *pure rhetoric*. Its task is to ascertain the laws by which in every scientific intelligence one sign gives birth to another, and especially one thought brings forth another. (2.229)

The second part, logic proper, is not treated in this book; and as for the third part, pure rhetoric, rhetorica speculativa, or methodeutic, if it is understood in the broader sense as the study "of the necessary conditions of the transmission of meaning by signs from mind to mind, and from one state of mind to another" (1.444), then chapters V-VIII deal with this part of semiotics, but the subject is not dealt with in the way that Peirce most often understands it, namely as the study of the general characters of scientific inquiry, and especially of the relation between the three main forms of scientific reasoning, abductive, deductive, and inductive.

In Peircean terminology this study is mainly an essay on the first part of semiotics, on speculative grammar. As seen from the references to Duns Scotus and the categories in the above quotation, this term reflects Peirce interest in scholastic philosophy, but he named this part of semiotics in different ways (e.g., Universal grammar, Logical Syntax, general Physiology of Signs). Among his various definitions the following from one of the unpublished manuscripts is of special interest for the student of text theory:

It is accordingly necessary that the introductory part of Logic should examine the different sorts of Meanings of signs. Aristotle's book *De Inter-*
*pretatione,* which treats of the parts of arguments, suggests that this part
of Logic might be called *hermeneutic,* the science of Interpretations or
Meaning. Or it might be called *Universal Grammar.* The grammar of sign
in general. (Ms. 640, 1909: 7)

This definition is interesting for two reasons: It establishes a connection between the study of the formal properties of the sign and the
theory of meaning; and it explicitly connects semiotics with the problems involved in the understanding and explanation of signs, with
the signifying and interpretative processes. That is, it defines the
main concern of this study.

Moreover, Peirce himself encourages people from branches of the
humanities other than philosophy, at least from philology, to collaborate in the study of this branch of semiotics, "the different sorts of
Meanings of signs." In an unpublished manuscript, "Short Logic," from
1895 he writes:

cultivators of the art of reasoning found themselves long ago obliged to
institute a *speculative grammar* which should study *modes of signifying,* in
general. It is best regarded as separate from logic proper, for one of these
days philologists may take it in hand, for which logicians will thank them.
(Ms. 595, 1895: 23)

This study attempts to answer his invitation and to collaborate with
him from the point of view of text theory. This does not mean we avoid
philosophical questions and problems. This would be impossible for
two reasons: First, every kind of semiotics, implicitly or explicitly,
deals with questions concerning meaning, cognition, reference, truth,
and reality. Even a virginal and prudish methodological abstinence
from involvement with these questions cannot, at bottom, prevent
semioticians from taking a stance on such issues. Second, thinking
semiotics with Peirce means becoming involved with his philosophical
concerns. There are degrees of involvement, however. I do not feel
obliged to systematically expound and comment on issues such as his
tychism, synecism, and agapism, although they are essential to himself and to the study of his philosophical development. Furthermore,
many excellent studies of his philosophical position exist. A few of the
studies I have profited from reading are Buchler 1939 (2nd ed. 1966),
Goudge 1950, Thompson 1953, Murphey 1961, Potter 1967, Apel 1968,

Rescher 1981, Hookway 1985, and Fisch 1989. Concerning his semiotics, in a narrower sense, in addition to the works of Apel and Fisch I would especially like to mention works by philosophers such as Hanna Buczyńska-Garewicz, Joseph Ransdell, David Savan, and Thomas L. Short. Although Peirce is a great philosopher, and as a semiotician is unparallelled, few would wholeheartedly embrace his general philosophical position. Few would become Peirceans in the sense of defending all his points of view, which sometimes do not easily agree with each other.

Semiotics in this century has been haunted by schools, trends, and fashions. This has both helped and hindered its development: On the one hand the common points of view and the common pursuit of the scholars affiliated with the same trend or school have meant that semiotics has developed because of the amount of reflection and analysis made possible by collective endeavors. On the other hand, close affiliations have also blocked the road of inquiry because they have forced scholars to stick to questionable points of view for reasons of tenacity and authority. It would be ironic if Peircean semiotics developed into a sect-like movement idolizing his work, as if it were Scripture. I find that Peirce's concept of the sign is a better point of departure for a future semiotics than Hjelmslev's, but that does not commit me to hold what in my opinion is the rather bizarre view that "matter is effete mind" (6.24) nor does it commit me to Peirce's objective idealism. Furthermore, we should always remember that Peirce himself never thought he furnished answers to the vast variety of questions and problems that confront semiotics. He defines his role in quite another way:

> I am, as far as I know, a pioneer, or rather a backwoodsman, in the work of clearing and opening up what I call *semiotic,* that is, the doctrine of the essential nature and fundamental varieties of possible semiosis; and I find the field too vast, the labor too great, for a first-comer. (5.488)

The dialogue in this study, therefore, is not only with Peirce, although he is the main interlocutor, but also with Bruner, Eco, Goodman, Habermas, Hjelmslev, Jakobson, Piaget, Russell, Searle, Sebeok, and Tinbergen, to mention a few that play important roles in arguments about semiotic questions and problems.

The state of Peirce's writings has also made it necessary to be dialogic in another sense. The unpublished manuscripts have to be quoted, and so do his published writings, because they are not easily accessible. The monumental *Writings of Charles S. Peirce: A Chronological Edition* (Fisch, Moore, Kloesel et al., eds.), 1982ff., has only reached volume IV, and even *The Collected Papers* (Weiss, Hartshone, and Burks, eds.), 1931-1958, is hard to come by, since its fourth printing is out of print. It is proper, therefore, to quote generously from his work. It is also helpful to cite the points of view that are discussed. Not because citation guarantees fair play (it is always possible to distort the characterization of points of views and arguments), but because on principle and in actuality it gives the reader an idea why the author finds himself entitled to argue in a certain way.

Without access to Peirce's unpublished manuscripts it would not have been possible to write this book. A sabbatical year from Odense University, Denmark, and a grant from the Danish Research Council for the Humanities made possible a two-semester stay in 1982 at the Research Center for Language and Semiotic Studies, Indiana University, Bloomington, Indiana.

During my affiliation with RCLSS I had illuminating discussions with its chairman, Thomas A. Sebeok, on the nature of the sign and on topics in the history of semiotics. I am also grateful to Thomas Sebeok for his constant encouragement concerning this study. In that year I also worked at the Peirce Edition Project, Indiana University/Purdue University, Indianapolis. Anyone acquainted with Peirce studies knows the project to be a model of dedicated scholarship, and those who have visited the project know the kindness with which they receive scholars from abroad. Without generous help from Max Fisch, Christian Kloesel, Edward Moore, and Textual Editor Lynn A. Ziegler, I would never have been able to find my way through the Peirce manuscripts.

A grant from the Carlsberg Foundation and another sabbatical leave from Odense University made it possible to finish this study. Furthermore, Odense University also gave me a publication grant. I am grateful to all the scholars and institutions mentioned above.

In addition to generously accepting me as a research associate at the Research Center for Language and Semiotic Studies and at the Peirce Edition Project, Indiana University has yet another share in the completion of this book. My friend H. James Jensen of the English and Comparative Literature Departments at Bloomington has revised the manuscript to make my English more readable. I also want to thank Mss. Ulla Hansen and Gitte Storm from Odense University's typing pool for tolerance and for doing a splendid job in inserting my constant revisions into the manuscript. Floyd Merrel, Purdue University, read the book before publication, and I warmly thank him for his many valuable, scholarly comments.

Last but not least, indeed, I want to thank my wife, not only for her encouragement while I was writing this study, but also for only gently hinting that it should be finished.

# PART I. SIGNS WITHOUT WORLDS

# I. Signs without Worlds

Because this study begins with an exposition of the alternative paradigm within contemporary semiotics, with the less general theory of continental structuralism, here represented by Saussure and especially by Hjelmslev, I might be accused of preparing a scene to vindicate my own concept of semiotics: a theory of signs founded on Peirce's conception of semiotics. And because this study concentrates on certain problems raised by the structuralist and glossematic approaches, I might also be accused of stacking the deck. Consequently, I want to say that, in my opinion, the main trend of continental semiotics in this century has very much furthered the theory of signs, and that this trend has led to tremendous progress in the analysis of linguistic texts. What makes continental semiotics an efficient tool for the description of linguistic form, however, is precisely what makes it less suited to found a general theory of signs, less able to describe the process of signification, and less able to account for the factors and relations that constitute meaning.

It is important to stress that the limitations of continental structuralism are self imposed. They are not caused by naiveté. They are consciously chosen to achieve certain objectives. Whether this choice has been successful is another question. What follows attempts an answer.

## 1. The circuit of speech, the sign, and the repression of communication

All scholars and scientists are faced with questions of delimiting and order in their fields of research. Often, of course, an individual researcher accepts the contemporary map of his territory, a choice which may not prevent him from contributing significantly to the progress of inquiry within his field. Sometimes, however, scholars and scientists think it necessary to redraw the map of their areas of research, because they need to clarify what is supposed to be their proper study.

In *Cours de linguistique générale* it is obvious Saussure thought one of his main tasks was to create order, to introduce what he calls "un ordre naturel" (Saussure 1967: 25) in the heterogeneous phenomenon of language. Chapters II–V of the *Cours* are consecrated to this effort. At the same time, he describes the many different facets of the linguistic phenomenon. The first two figures presented in the *Cours* are *not* representations of the famous sign model consisting of signifier and signified; instead they represent the circuit of speech:

(Saussure 1959: 11)

Fig. 1

From this figure he extrapolates the following:

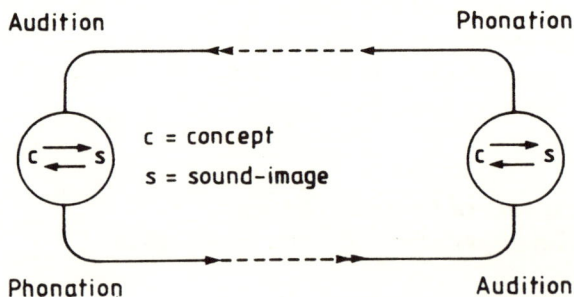

(Saussure 1959: 12)

Fig. 2

The figures represent the transmission of signs in a dialogical context, and they imply psychological, physiological, and physical dimensions. With these models of the heterogeneous speech event as the point of departure Saussure works out a set of dichotomies:

a)  outer vs. inner
b)  non-psychological vs. psychological
c)  individual vs. social
d)  active vs. passive
e)  executive vs. receptive
f)  immutability vs. mutability

Further on in the *Cours* we come across some other fundamental oppositions:

g)  substance vs. form
h)  positive vs. negative
i)  motivated vs. inmotivated, or  non arbitrary vs. arbitrary (conventional)
j)  co-ordinative/syntagmatic relations vs. associative/paradigmatic relations

Saussure proceeds to focus on *one relation* in the dialogical model of speech, namely the one between *concept* and *acoustic image* (cf. Fig. 2). For dichotomies a–g this means consciously eliminating within the dichotomies the concepts to the left of the vs.-signs, as phenomena of *speech*, or *speaking* (parole). The concepts to the right of the vs.-sign, therefore, become the differentiae specificae of *language considered as a system* (langue). Saussure says:

> Language is a well-defined object in the heterogeneous mass of speech facts. It can be localized in the limited segment of the speaking-circuit where an auditory image becomes associated with a concept. It is the social side of speech, outside the individual who can never create nor modify it by himself; it exists only by virtue of a sort of contract signed by the members of a community. (Saussure 1959: 14)

This constitution of language (langue) as the central object of linguistics is governed by a certain hierarchical relationship between the di-

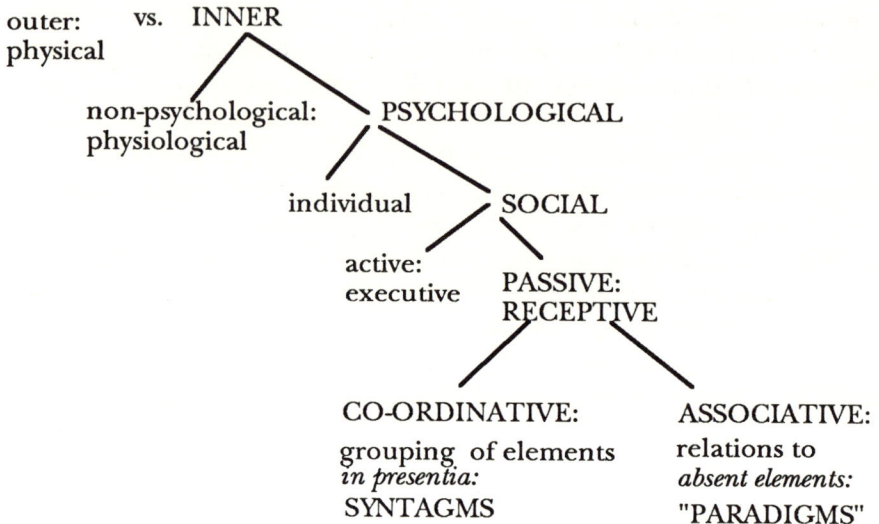

outer:      vs.    INNER
physical

non-psychological:    PSYCHOLOGICAL
physiological

individual      SOCIAL

active:
executive      PASSIVE:
               RECEPTIVE

CO-ORDINATIVE:                    ASSOCIATIVE:
grouping of elements             relations to
*in presentia:*                  *absent elements:*
SYNTAGMS                         "PARADIGMS"

Fig. 3

chotomies a–e which, at the same time, relegates half of them to the study of speech. This hierarchical order and elimination may be visualized as shown in Fig. 3. *Language* (in contradistinction to *speech*) is thus conceived as an inner, psychological, and social phenomenon literally deposited in the brains of the members of a (linguistic) community. It is further understood not as actual communicative action, *execution*, which is thought to belong to individual speaking, but as a passive competence, and this competence consists of the ability to correlate both an acoustic image with a concept and images and concept with each other by mastering two basic principles of relationships between linguistic elements: the coordination *in praesentia* of elements into syntagms and the association of present elements with absent ones, i.e., paradigmatic relations (in an inflectional language, such as German, the sentence "Die Männer sind hier" illustrates for instance both a coordination of the elements according to the rules of grammar, e.g., congruence between the plural of noun and verb, and the absent, associative relationships of the singular and the plural: Mann — Männer, ist— sind).

The dichotomy between mutability vs. immutability is linked to the one between individual vs. social, and it points to the fact — if it is a fact — that language is immune to change through individual action. The speech of an individual subject does not, according to Saussure, change language as a system. Yet, language is constantly in a state of change through collective, "unconscious" action. Saussure's remaining dichotomies are corollaries from the ones already mentioned, but are specifically relevant to his sign definition. The distinction between *substance* and *form* is analogous to the distinction between *outer* and *inner,* because *substance* is the outer manifesting material (sound-waves, ink, etc.) of linguistic *form.* The form is correlated with *negativity,* since it is conceived as *differentiality,* not as a complexus of *positive* qualities: "In language there are only differences. Even more important: a difference generally implies positive terms between which the difference is set up; but in language there are only differences *without positive terms"* (Saussure 1959: 120). Finally, the dichotomy *motivated* vs. *immotivated* (arbitrary) is related to all three of the above mentioned dichotomies, and lastly to the hierarchically highest one, *outer* vs. *inner,* because in language both the relationship between signifier and signified and the one between sign and denotation are unmotivated in the sense that while signifier and signified presuppose each other in a general way they do not specifically select each other. Furthermore, even if linguistic signs are used in speech to refer to objects and states of affairs (a fact that Saussure would not dream of denying, but which he considered irrelevant to the study of language as a system), their natures are not determined by the object or objects they refer to (for example, *horse, Pferd, cheval, hest* are equally fit to refer to one animal); and this is why, as regards languages, the sign-object-relationship is arbitrary. Consequently, at least generally, both the relationship between signifier and signified and the one between the total linguistic sign and the object lack motivation.

All the Saussurean dichotomies, and the way in which Saussure delimits the study of language (langue), are indeed problematic and certainly open for discussion, They are, however, better discussed in the context of Hjelmslev's glossematics, because he inherited these distinctions from his predecessor, and tried hard to substantiate them. Besides, Saussure's *Cours* is not devoted exclusively to the study of language as a system. Half of it is concerned with diachronic linguistics, the study of the historical development of languages (for a seminal exposition of Saussure's division of the study of language into different disciplines see Sechehaye: "Les trois linguistiques saussuriennes," in Godel 1969: 138–190).

It is interesting, however, that in undertaking his process of delimitation Saussure seems doubtful of what he is doing. In one place he conceives the relation between the theoretical and methodological approach and the subject to be studied as follows:

> Far from it being the object that antedates the viewpoint, it would seem that it is the viewpoint that creates the object; besides, nothing tells us in advance that one way of considering the fact in question takes precedence over the other or is any way superior to them. (Saussure 1959: 8)

In other places he seems to claim that his own identification and characterization of language (langue) within the facts of speech is the only sensible one. We read for instance: "As soon as we give language first place among the facts of speech, we introduce a natural order into a mass that lends itself to no other classification." And in another place he says: "In separating language from speaking we are at the same time separating (1) what is social from what is individual; and (2) what is essential from what is accessory and more or less accidental." Finally, the following patronizing remark should be quoted: "There is first of all the superficial notion [of the nature of language, JDJ] of the general public: People see no more than a name-giving system in language, thereby prohibiting any research into its true nature" (sa nature véritable).

Saussure is well aware that speech is very important, and his effort to isolate the systematic aspect of language (langue) does not make him forget the left side of his dichotomies. In fact the combination brings about his famous distinction between a *linguistics of language* (linguistique de la langue) and a *linguistics of speech* (linguistique de la parole). The relationship between these two branches of linguistics is ambiguous in the *Cours:* They are supposed to be equals and mutually interdependent. This point of view is pronounced programatically as follows:

> Doubtless the two objects are closely connected, each depending on the other: language is necessary if speaking is to be intelligible and produce all its effects; but speaking is necessary for the establishment of language, and

historically its actuality always comes first. How would a speaker take it upon himself to associate an idea with a word-image if he had not first come across the association in an act of speaking? Moreover, we learn our mother language by listening to others; only after countless experience is it deposited in our brain. Finally, speaking is what causes language to evolve: impressions gathered from listening to others modify our linguistic habits. Language and speaking are then interdependent; the former is both the instrument and the product of the latter. But their interdependence does not prevent their being two absolutely distinct things. (Saussure 1959: 18-19)

This statement is sensible; it is, however, at variance with the earlier statements quoted above, statements that give priority to the study of language as a system (langue). And what is really decisive is that the very definition of the sign is founded exclusively on the *linguistics of language,* because the notion that signs are used in communication, among other things to give names to objects, according to Saussure, prohibits "any research into its true nature."

The last remark leads directly to Saussure's famous dictum: "Le signe linguistique unit non une chose et un nom, mais un concept et une image acoustique," and to his famous system-immanent approach with its distinction between signifier and signified; its contention that language is not a substance but a form; the description of signifier and signified separately as structures that are defined relationally, negatively, and differentially; and the pivotal role played by such concepts as *valeur* and *signification.*

Thus, Saussure considers his own definition of the sign as an explicit break with a definition of the sign that is based on the sign's reference to a denotatum; instead, he chooses a definition based on the *sign relation,* that is, the internal relation between expression and content. Saussure elaborates on and substantiates this internal definition of the sign through the introduction of the terms *signification* and *valeur.* Because it has a tendency to be identified with the term *signifié* Saussure's term *signification* is ambiguous; this can be seen in the following passage:

Let us first take signification as it is generally understood. . . . As the arrows in the drawing show, it is only the counterpart of the sound-image. Everything that occurs concerns only the sound-image and the concept when we look upon the word as independent and self-contained.

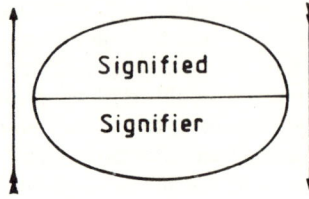

(Saussure 1959: 114)

Fig. 4

Elsewhere, *signification* seems almost to be identified with the "significance" or "meaning" which comes about through the sign's reference function:

> A few examples will show clearly that this is true. Modern French *mouton* can have the same signification as English *sheep* but not the same value, and this for several reasons, particularly because in speaking of a piece of meat ready to be served on the table, English uses *mutton* and not *sheep*. The difference in value between *sheep* and *mouton* is due to the fact that *sheep* has beside it a second term while the French word does not. (Saussure 1959: 115-116)

This example is generalized in Saussure's schematization of the interrelations that make language (langue) a system, namely the fact that all its terms are solidary in the sense of mutually delimiting and defining each other. Saussure's figure is drawn in this way:

(Saussure 1959: 115)

Fig. 5

In the English lexicon *sheep* and *mutton* are two signs that mutually delimit each other's signification, because their value, their differential position within the content system of English, is decisive. In English we might construct the following sentence: "The wolf killed a *sheep* this morning, let us have *mutton* for supper." In French we would say: "Ce matin le loup a tué un mouton, mangeons du mouton ce soir." It could be objected that it is precisely the different referential use of *sheep* and *mutton* that is decisive, and that the systematic difference between the two lexemes reflects this usage (cf. below).

Finally, by connecting it to the verb *signifie,* Saussure allows the term *signification to* function even more ambiguously:

> Now the real interpretation of the diagram of the signal becomes apparent. Thus

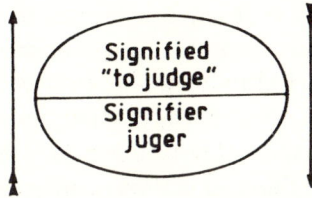

> means that in French the concept "to judge" is linked to the sound-image *juger;* in short, it symbolizes signification. But it is quite clear that initially the concept is nothing, that is, only a value determined by its relations with other similar values, and that without them the signification would not exist. If I state simply that a word signifies something when I have in mind the associating of a sound-image with a concept, I am making a statement that may suggest what actually happens, but by no means am I expressing the linguistic fact in its essence and fullness. (Saussure 1959: 117)

It is tempting to disregard the tendential identification of *signification* and *signified* as invalid, but unfortunately it seems Saussure used these two terms interchangeably (cf. also Godel 1957: 276). There is a further ambiguity left in Saussure's choice of terms. Since *signification* is partly used to denote the significance effect that arises through the coupling of *signifier* and *signified* in the sign, in part it seems to denote the total reference-function and signification, or the meaning effect's appearance in the relation sign-object. In my opinion, this ambiguity is by no means incidental.


## 2.  Hjelmslev's concept of the sign

At this point it is time to leave the Saussurean concept of the sign, and his ambiguous use of the concepts *signification* and *value,* and turn to Hjelmslev's effort to give a coherent definition of the linguistic sign.

Hjelmslev's theory of language and semiotics is profoundly influenced by Saussure. Using his predecessor's insights and points of view, he attempted to work out a stricter and – in principle – thoroughly formal approach to the analysis of sign systems. Therefore, it is interesting to follow his efforts and difficulties concerning the sign concept in general, especially the opposition between *form* and *substance* and the distintion between *signification* and *value.*

Hjelmslev's sign model is built on five terms: *Expression* which is contrasted to *content (contenu), form* which is contrasted to *substance,* and finally the concept of *level,* which has to do with substance, and denotes that the substance can be apprehended in various ways. As for Saussure, the sign for Hjelmslev is not elementary; it is built of constitutive form elements, on the expression as well as on the content plane, called *figurae.* Hjelmslev understands these in the strict sense as elements which are defined differentially, relatively, and negatively, that is, as a system of differences corresponding to Saussure's concept of *value.*

One of the most fundamental principles of the glossematic analysis of the text is the continuous partition and making of inventories of entities that can take the same "place" in the language chain, e.g., sentences, clauses, words, etc. (cf. p. 29). In these cases, the inventories will be unrestricted, although they will have a decreasing number of entities. At some point in this partition, however, the inventory will be made up of entities which are not themselves signs (i.e., do not fulfill the criterion of being a "solidarity" between expression and content), and these are called figurae:

> in order to be fully adequate, a language must likewise be easy to manage, practical in acquisition and use. Under the requirement of an unrestricted number of signs, this can be achieved by all the signs being constructed of non-signs whose number is restricted, and, preferably, severely restricted. Such non-signs as enter into a sign system as parts of signs we shall here call *figurae.* (Hjelmslev 1953a: 29)

This analysis of non-signs as figurae can be carried out on both the expression and the content planes. The expression figurae will more or less be equivalent to phonemes. On the content plane Hjelmslev claims the same principle of reduction can be used:

> While the inventory of word-contents is unrestricted, in a language of famil-

iar structure even the minimal signs will be distributed (on the basis of relational differences) into some (selected) inventories, which are unrestricted (e.g., inventories of root-contents), and other (selecting) inventories, which are restricted (e.g., inventories embracing contents of derivational and inflexional endings, i.e., derivatives and morphemes). Thus in practice the procedure consists in trying to analyze the entities that enter into unrestricted inventories purely into entities that enter the restricted inventories. (Hjelmslev 1953a: 45)

The sign, defined in short as an expression element with a connected content, is, according to Hjelmslev, thus made up of a relation between two groups of functives (i.e., figurae systems) from the expression and content planes respectively. This relation is called the *sign function,* the *semiotic function,* or in the case of language, *denotation.* We need to mention, however, that the differentiation between expression and content has *a priori* status, so to speak, and simultaneously is simply operational and formal:

We have here introduced *expression* and *content* as designations of the functives that contract the function in question, the sign function. This is a purely operative definition and a formal one in the sense that in this context no other meaning shall be attached to the terms *expression* and *content.* (Hjelmslev 1953a: 30)

This strict operative definition is followed by a subdivision of the expression plane and the content plane each into *form* and *substance,* and even if the parallelism, or isomorphism, of the two planes is maintained, the expression form and the content form are in practice defined in relation to the substances which they articulate. Hjelmslev gives several examples of this; the following formulation is typical of his point of view:

A paradigm in one language and a corresponding paradigm in another language can be said to cover one and the same zone of purport, which, abstracted from those languages, is an unanalyzed amorphous continuum, on which boundaries are laid by the formative action of the languages. (Hjelmslev 1953a: 32-33)

This is followed by an example of how the content system of the color designation divides a part of the color continuum differently in English and in Welsh (Fig. 6).

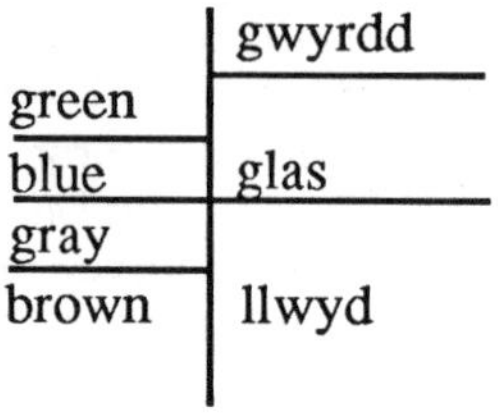

|        | gwyrdd |
| green  |        |
| blue   | glas   |
| gray   |        |
| brown  | llwyd  |

(Hjelmslev 1953a: 33)
Fig. 6

While the content system, or rather the content systems, constitute specific divisions made within a given language with regard to its referential function, the expression form of a language is the specific way in which, e.g., the phonetic zones of purport (i.e., the expression substance) are divided into different figurae (phonemes).

The parallelism or isomorphism between expression and content is clearly seen in the way in which it is possible to analyze them below the sign level. This can be illustrated as shown in Fig. 7.

|       | Expression |   |       | Content |        |
|-------|------------|---|-------|---------|--------|
|       | A          | B |       | A       | B      |
| (a)   | p          | t | (a)   | man     | woman  |
| (b)   | b          | d | (b)   | boy     | girl   |

Fig. 7

Both expression and content are analyzed in such a way that each element (phoneme and lexeme) is defined relationally, differentially, and negatively in relation to the other elements in the paradigm, and can be further divided into constitutive components. In this example, the content paradigm can be analyzed into four element (semes, or in Hjelmslev's terminology, pleremes): A: male; B: female; (a): adulthood; and (b): childhood. The expression paradigm can be analyzed into A: bilabial; B: labio-dental; (a): unvoiced; and (b): voiced.

This brief exposition should give some idea about what Hjelmslev meant by the isomorphism between content orm and expression form. The formal analysis into binary oppositions has certainly proved itself to be useful, for instance within modern structural semantics (e.g., the work of Greimas). A relatively simple example from an article by Peter

Brask, "Model Groups and Composition System," shows how the elementary componential content analysis can easily be expanded by adding more binary oppositions (Brask in Dines Johansen and Morten Nøjgaard 1979: 210), see Fig. 8:

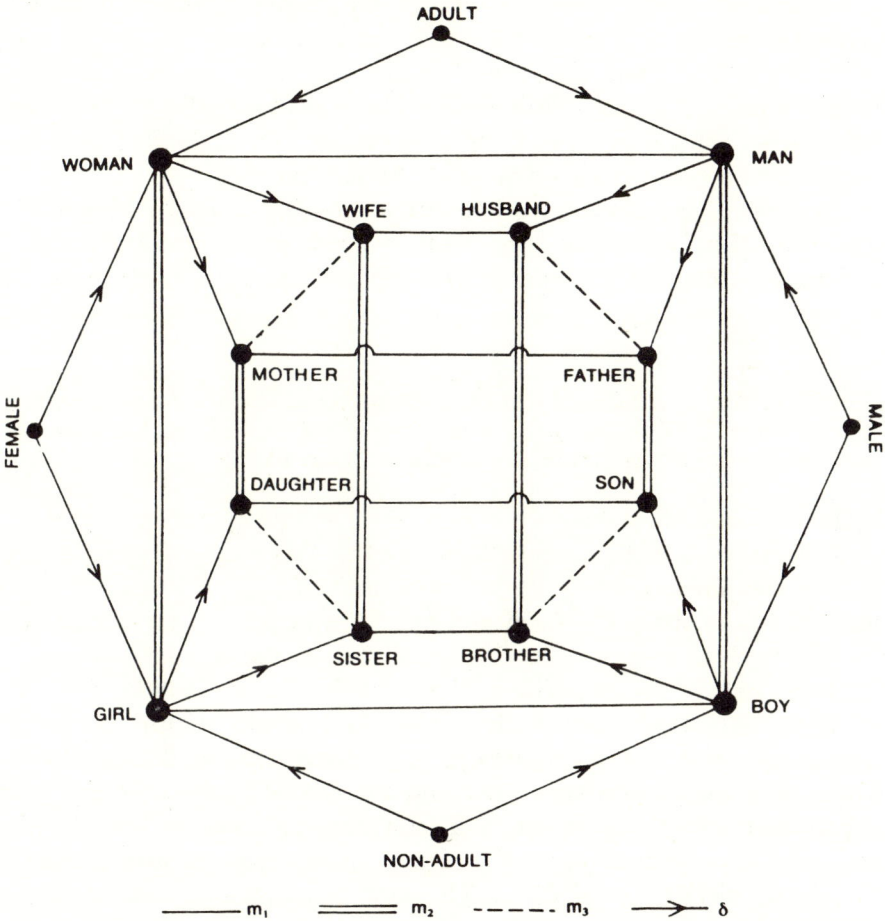

Mapping of the four-group generated by the oppositions of sexual genus $(m_1)$, and of generations $(m_2)$ upon the group with 8 elements generated by the same plus the opposition of relational roles in the kernel family $(m_3)$.

Fig. 8

The other fundamental opposition in Hjelmslev's glossematics is that of *form* and *substance*. Again, the immediate relevant source is Saussure, who says, "language is a form and not a substance" (Saussure 1959: 122). This point of view is based in the assumption that both thought and sound taken alone are unlimited and continuous like a fog, and that language as a system (langue) creates form on both planes by dividing them into systems of differences. Although the relation between expression and content in language is arbitrary (in the sense of unmotivated), the two are united in the sign like the front and the back of a piece of paper. While form on both planes is (the) articulated differences, substance is, also on both planes, the undivided continuum, either amorphous sound or amorphous meaning.

Saussure's ideas were worked out in greater detail by Hjelmslev, who states that "form is an intermediary between thought and speech" (Hjelmslev 1928: 120). Later, in *Prolegomena*, he further stresses the supremacy of form:

> Substance is thus not a necessary presupposition for linguistic form, but linguistic form is a necessary presupposition for substance. *Manifestation*, in other words, is a selection in which the linguistic form is the constant and the substance the variable. (Hjelmslev 1953a: 68)

Hjelmslev regards a linguistic sign as a solidarity between the expression form and the content form, and in this way defines the sign as a purely formal entity. In his opinion, the task of linguistics and semiotics is to study the form and not the substance, i.e., formal systems behind the usage, which is regarded a substance phenomenon.

In a later, important article, "La stratification du language" (1959: 36-81 [1954]), Hjelmslev distinguishes four strata within language: *expression substance, expression form, content form,* and *content substance.* The expression substance and the content substance are each subdivided into three levels, the expression substance into (1) the apperceptive or auditive, (2) the physiological or articulatory, and (3) the purely physical or acoustic. The content substance is divided into three parts: (1) the apperceptive level or the level of collective understanding (public opinion) or *meaning* (this level is also called the *direct semiotic substance);* (2) the social-biological level, on which is placed the social-biological conditions and psycho-physiological mechanisms, which, through natural disposition and acquired habits, allow the members of a linguistic community to create and reproduce the elements of the apperceptive level; and (3) the level of the physical. The delineation of these levels allow us to represent the language model or

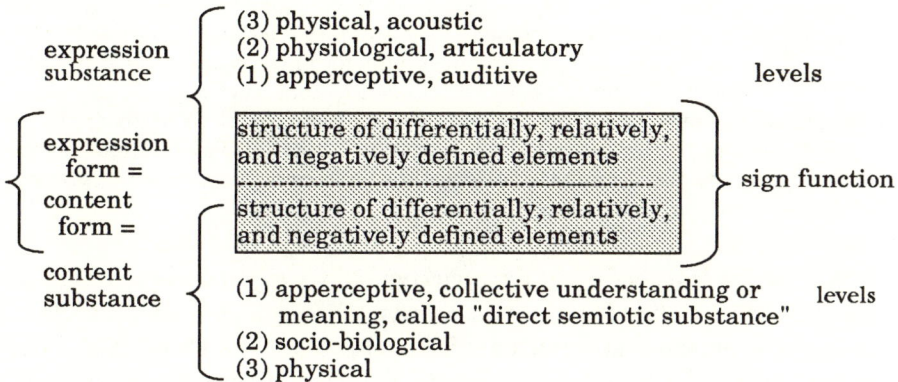

Fig. 9

the model of the linguistic sign as in Fig. 9. It is important to emphasize that when Hjelmslev talks about substance he defines it as semiotically formed substance, in contradistinction to unformed substance,
which he calls *purport* (French *matière*), i.e., matter of different kinds
which does not reflect a form.

According to Hjelmslev, a characteristic of the relation between
form and substance is that one form can be manifested in several different substances, e.g., language in the letters of the alphabet or in signal flags coded in such a way that every letter is represented by one
flag. This example shows what Hjelmslev means by semiotically formed substances, because the systems of differences (the expression
form) are projected on the manifesting substance. Whereas one substance can manifest different forms, it is, however, only true of the
semiotically unformed or amorphous substance (while the substance
ink, for example, may be used to write both English and Danish, the
latter language has letters, i.e., complex graphematic forms, unknown
in English: æ, ø, and å).

It should appear in Fig. 9 that the boundaries of the sign itself are
difficult to recognize, since the physical objects seem included by virtue of their belonging to the content substance. In Hjelmslev's work
there are, however, more definite reflections on this problem. The
starting point – as in Saussure – is a rejection of the idea that a sign is
a thing, the most important characteristic of which is that it refers to
something which lies outside it. In characterizing language he writes,
with a typical polemical sting:

Languages, then, cannot be described as pure sign systems. By the aim
usually attributed to them they are first and foremost sign systems: but by
their internal structure they are first and foremost something different,
namely systems of figurae that can be used to construct signs. The definition of a language as a sign has thus shown itself, on close analysis, to be
unsatisfactory. It concerns only the external functions of a language, its
relation to the non-linguistic factors that surround it, but not its proper,
internal function. (Hjelmslev 1953a: 29)

It is clear Hjelmslev favors a restrictive binary sign concept, where the
sign is defined (in Hjelmslev's words) through the sign function's
union of expression and content form. However, the problem of recognizing a sign's boundaries persists in the form-substance relation, and
Hjelmslev tries to solve this by affixing it to the older conception of the
sign as defined by its reference function. The definition which emanates from this attempt thus reads: *"That a sign is a sign for something means then that the sign's content form can subsume this something as content substance"* (Hjelmslev 1953a: 36). But Hjelmslev sees
this reference/projection or subsumption relationship not only as valid
for the content form/content substance relationship, but equally so for
the expression form/expression substance relationship. His final reflection on the sign therefore sounds like this:

The sign is, then – paradoxical as it may seem – a sign for a content
substance and a sign for an expression-substance. It is in this sense that
the sign can be said to be a sign for something. On the other hand, we see
no justification for calling the sign a sign merely for the content-substance,
or (what nobody has thought of, to be sure) merely for the expression-
substance. The sign is a two-sided entity, with a Janus like perspective in
two directions, and with effects in two respects: 'outwards' toward the
expression-substance and 'inwards' toward the content-substance.
   All terminology is arbitrary, and consequently nothing prevents us from
using the word *sign* as a special name for the expression-form (or, if we
wished, for the expression-substance, but this would be both absurd and
unneccessary). *But it appears more appropriate to use the word sign as the
name for the unit consisting of content-form and expression-form and established by the solidarity that we have called the sign function.* (Hjelmslev
1953a: 36, my emphasis)

We immediately see that two sign definitions appear here side by side.
But before commenting on this, we need to read Hjelmslev's reflection
on the relationship between language and thought, which throws light

on the difficulties inherent in his vacilliation between a broad and a narrow conception of the linguistic sign.

## 3. The relationship between language and thought in glossematics

Hjelmslev's broader model of the sign (Fig. 9) is constructed with the formally defined sign function at its center, i.e., as a combination of form elements from the planes of expression and content, and the expression and content substances at its periphery. The two substances are themselves divided into three levels which are each in an identical order in relation to the center.

The (hierarchical) order of the levels of the content substance leads to rather interesting problems. The content form borders on "direct semiotic substance," also named *meaning* or *collective understanding*. Hjelmslev thinks of this level as the amorphous realm of thoughts or ideas to which the content form gives definite shape (a Saussurean point of view). The relation between this level and the next, the social-biological, is not clearly defined. It seems this level functions as an intermediary system that processes an input from the third level, which is the physical world, and transforms it into a "thought mass" (the first level) which is further processed by the language form. The second level, then, might be seen as the species specific senso-motorical processing and articulation of impulses from the environment and from the organism itself. The fact that the corresponding level of expression substance is *the articulatory* supports this interpretation.

These distinctions within the two substances complicate the model, because they imply two articulatory agencies (on each plane) in the process of signification. In particular, the relationship between content form and content substance poses some difficult questions, among which is the thorny problem concerning the relationship between language and thought, a question Hjelmslev explicitly addresses in an earlier article "Sprog og Tanke" ("Language and Thought" 1936, not translated into English). He begins his argument admitting the difference between language and thought by pointing out that the same thought may be expressed in different languages. This leads him to state that "languages of different nations cannot be absolutely different; on the contrary they must have certain common features making it possible to use any of them to express the same thought" (Hjelm-slev 1936: 26). Another way of making the same classical reflection is to stress that – in innumerable cases – faithful and reliable transla-tion from one language into another is possible.

In true Saussurean spirit, Hjelmslev goes on to distinguish be-tween *articulate* and *inarticulate* language and thought, where articu-late means segmented. Roars or screams are examples of inarticulate language, or rather use of sounds. Animal behavior is, according to Hjelmslev, an example of inarticulate thought. He writes:

> In all probability what we find in animals is inarticulate thinking, just as their languages, e.g. the dog's yelp, are inarticulate utterances. The inar-ticulateness of a dog's thinking does not prevent it from being divided into some main segments. For example, a dog sees a piece of meat and runs to eat it. In doing so the dog must have thought. Afterwards it discovers that the meat does not smell good, and then it changes its mind, and refrains from eating. Once more the dog must have been thinking. Such a rough segmentation of thought will always be present, whether or not it be other-wise articulate. (Hjelmslev 1936: 27, my transl.)

Another necessary distinction, according to Hjelmslev, is between the thing in itself and its use. This leads to the well-known distinction between *language as an institution* (Hjelmslev follows Saussure in us-ing this concept), i.e., as a system governed by a set of rules, and the use of language, *speech.* Parallel to the distinction between *language* and *speech* Hjelmslev distinguishes between thought as an institution, i.e., *thought,* and the use of thought, i.e., *thinking.* Just as language, as an institution, is founded on grammatical rules, so is the institution of thought founded on the rules of logic. Language and thought can be used incorrectly, but according to Hjelmslev "language as an institu-tion is in itself a perfect instrument for thought as an institution."

Hjelmslev makes a third distinction between the *system* and the *habits* of thought and language. The language *system* is the funda-mental set of elements and rules that everybody must master to speak the language, whereas *habits* are phenomena of usage, a set of vari-ants allowed by the system, that, for instance, distinguishes two dia-lects of the same language. Hjelmslev uses a forensic metaphor saying that the *system* imposes the same *laws* within the realm of a given language, whereas the *habits* correspond to different legal usage in different parts of the realm. The same is true of thought. Thought as a system is defined as the rules of logic, whereas the habits of thought are the customary ways in which people reason. Hjelmslev's point is that even if such reasoning is incomplete (one is tempted to say in some degree inarticulate), from the strict logical point of view, it may very well derive valid conclusions from incomplete arguments.

His exemplification of this point shows certain difficulties concerning his argument. According to Hjelmslev's theory of thought, for instance, a subject-predicate proposition, which is supposed to be universally valid, will always have the same logical form: *subject – copula – predicate*. The proposition *the man is poor* is an example. In some languages the same meaning is, however, differently expressed: e.g., *the man poor,* i.e., without copula as in Russian; or *poor the man,* i.e., predicate before subject and no copula as in Hebrew and Hungarian. Hjelmslev claims that these differences are not only differences in language usage, but in habits of thought, because it is not the case that a Russian who says *the man poor* really thinks of a copula, *is,* that he does not express lingually. On the contrary, the "missing" *is* is not thought. Learning a new language, then, means learning new habits of thought. Hjelmslev says:

> Every nation has its own *habits of thought,* just as every dialect has its own habits of language. This does nor prevent, however, that many nations can build on the same *system* of thought, and many dialects on the same language *system.* The habits of thought are closely related to language. We think as we speak. (Hjelmslev 1936: 30)

Before we proceed to the last part of Hjelmslev's argument, let us summarize his reflections in the following diagram (Fig. 10). Hjelmslev's argument so far calls for some questions. One point is his treatment of the subject-predicate proposition. I doubt that logicians would consider valid his claim that its form would, or rather should, always be *subject – copula – predicate*. I suspect that the order of the elements would be regarded as immaterial. To give him the benefit of the doubt, it may be that Hjelmslev is making concessions in order to make himself understood. A second point is the distinction between articulate and inarticulate language and thought. It may rightly be objected that the distinction between articulate and inarticulate is

|  | THOUGHT | | LANGUAGE | |  |
| --- | --- | --- | --- | --- | --- |
|  | Inarticulate | Articulate | Articulate | Inarticulate |  |
| SYSTEM |  | Logic |  |  |  |
| HABITS |  | Habitual structures of thought | Language as a system |  | SYSTEM |
|  |  |  | Habitual sets of variants allowed by the system: dialects |  | HABITS |
| INDIVIDUAL USE | animal behavior considered as goal-directed action | concrete, individual thinking | concrete, individual utterances | expressive use of sounds | INDIVIDUAL USE |

Fig. 10

relative, a matter of degree, and that animals' behavior and sign use are highly patterned activities that can be analyzed into sets of habits, and it might indeed be possible to isolate a system, in the sense of an instinctual matrix, governing action and expression (cf. the *inborn releasing mechanisms* [IRM] in animals which trigger basic, genetically coded, patterns of action). I think Hjelmslev would accept this objection. He would, however, insist on the specificity of human thought and language, precisely because of their unlimited productive and creative power; and he would be justified in doing so.

A more substantial third question concerns the relationship between articulate thought and articulate language. The diagram (Fig. 10) indicates that according to Hjelmslev's argument, so far, the relationship between thought and language is incongruent or displaced. This occurs because language has no analogue to the system of thought, logic, and consequently language as a system is connected with, and influences, thought as a collection of habitual structures that organize thinking within a given language community.

One way of interpreting this point of view is to consider the system of logic as more abstract than the systems of natural languages. Such a position would make sense. It might be argued that in describing the logical form of propositions and arguments the particularities of the different natural languages may be disregarded, for instance their specific sentence structure. A corollary of this position would be that the different sentence structures of specific languages realize the same propositional structure. Hjelmslev, however, rejects this line of reasoning because, for him, it implies that language would become the expression of thought, a point of view he explicitly opposes.

Instead he argues that concepts do not exist prior to linguistic signs, and he supports his position by referring to cerebral diseases affecting the linguistic competence, or at least the performance, of patients, especially to *color word aphasia*. This language disorder makes it impossible for patients to remember and to learn the color words, but what is more, it makes it impossible for them to sort a number of samples according to the class of color to which they belong. They can pick out two identical green nuances, but cannot classify different nuances of green as species of the same color. Hjelmslev concludes:

> The concept *green* is likewise a class that contains a great number of individually different colour nuances. The interesting thing is that *by losing the word the patient has lost the concept as well*. This illustrates that concept formation is only possible by means of words, that concept formation presupposes linguistic signs. (Hjelmslev 1936: 32)

He generalizes this point as follows:

> The observations show that this very difficult achievement, the power to abstract, i.e., to sort heterogeneous individuals into classes . . ., is acquired together with language, that it is inextricably linked with language, and only possible by means of language. It teaches us that it is wrong to believe that the concept is prior to the word or that thought is prior to language. On the contrary, the concept presupposes the word, thought presupposes language as its necessary foundation.
>
> Consequently, language is indeed not only the *expression* of thought. Language is a *basis* for thought. In relation to thought language is primary. Without articulate language articulate thought could not exist. Language articulates thought, segments it, and specifies its concepts. Without language we could only divide the world into individuals, we would not be able to comprise the individuals into classes. (ibid.)

This is a beautiful example of the claims of structural linguistics – although some might say of glottocentric imperialism – and it leads to the following conclusion, which Hjelmslev does not hesitate to draw:

"The role of language is to establish fixed limits in a world which in itself consists of individuals, and in a thought which in itself is inarticulate. . . . Language measures our thought and thereby the world in which we live" (Hjelmslev 1936: 33). Consequently, *language is the form of thought,* but Hjelmslev adds that language is only *the form of thought habits, it is not the form of the thought system.* The reason is that our word concepts are sometimes vague or ambiguous, but according to Hjelmslev language itself may overcome such shortcomings because the productivity and reflexivity of language make it possible to mend ambiguity, e.g., by creating meta-(scientific) semiotics that define scientific languages (cf. Hjelmslev 1953a: 77).

The above-mentioned objection concerning the distinction between articulate and inarticulate is still valid for these conclusions. Indeed even more so, because it is questionable to link the power of classification exclusively with human language. Categorizing the relevant elements of a life-world is a necessary prerequisite for survival. Consequently, animals must possess innate discriminatory grids that allow them to distinguish their own species from others, male from female, predators from prey, edible from non-edible, etc. etc. (cf. the study by Tinbergen mentioned in III,7). Such power of classification is both rudimentary and fixed, i.e., without potential for development, but it testifies to a capability to interpret and communicate, i.e., to a limited *semiotic competence.*

What is extremely interesting in the glossematic reflection on the relationship between thought and language, and its claim that language is the form of thought, is that Hjelmslev's argumentation presupposes the interdependence between *form* and *substance,* and between *system* and *habits* or *usage,* because language as conceptualization operates on thought, e.g., on the perception of individuals, and because language as form is claimed to be equivalent to habits of thought. Such an interdependence is, however, at variance with his ideas about the formal nature of the linguistic sign and of linguistic analysis.

## 4. Signs without worlds: the formal nature of linguistic analysis

In the commentary on Hjelmslev's model of the linguistic sign (Fig. 9) we hinted it might be interpreted as picturing a process of significa- tion containing two processing agencies on each level of a plane, on the expression plane the articulatory level of the substance strata and the expression form, and on the content plane the socio-biological level of substance and the content form. According to such a point of view, the concretely manifested sign would consist of a solidarity between an expression formed by the material shaping of sound, or writing, realiz- ing the formal distinctions of the system, and a content formed by the interaction of the distinctions of the content form of language and the collateral experience of a given linguistic community processed by innate and culturally acquired ways of perceiving and acting.

Such an interpretation is not only unorthodox, but also alien to the core of Hjelmslev's thought, because it presupposes that what is called substance is considered both as theoretically important and as a dy- namic force in sign production.

In the preceding analysis (pp. 9-11) we also pointed out a certain ambiguity in Saussure's usage of the term *signification*. Hjelmslev, however, defines it only as a substance phenomenon and compare to the purely formal concept of *value*. He says:

> Does *value* belong to signification or to the content form . . . ? At first glance it might look as if *value* belongs to both of them: in contradistinction to the pure form, defined by internal functions, value might seem to represent the material form, the way in which substance complies with the pure form. We think, however, that this is a mistake that would not be in accordance with the notion of value such as it is conceived by F. de Saussure. Since it is purely differential, oppositional, and negative, value has not yet anything semantic about it. (Hjelmslev 1959: 106, Fr. orig., my transl.)

In defining *value* as a pure phenomenon of form (in contradistinction to *signification*), it is hard to see how the gap between the internal and exclusively formal sign definition and the external and referential definition can be bridged. One might, for instance, ask how meaning is analyzed and, more specifically, how the *semantemes*, or content-sub- stance elements, are determined. According to Hjelmslev (1959: 108) this is done "by uniting the specific significations which seem possible in a 'concept' or generic term *starting from a given usage from which a norm may* be *deduced."* This formulation contains important perspectives, because it is evident from it that the analysis of form is not a sufficient condition for meaning analysis (and, as I will show later, thus neither for content analysis), since the concept of and analysis of language usage *(usus)* is brought in as precondition. The term *language usage* is itself given two important definitions in Hjelmslev. In *Prolegomena to a Theory of Language* he defines it as follows in relation to the linguistic form:

> Substance is thus not a necessary presupposition for linguistic form, but linguistic form is a necessary presupposition for substance. *Manifestation,* in other words, is a selection in which the linguistic form is the constant and the substance the variable; we formally define manifestation as a selection between hierarchies and between derivatives of different hierarchies. The constant in a manifestation (the *manifested)* can, with reference to Saussure, be called the form; if the *form* is a language, we call it the *linguistic schema.* (. . .) The variable in a manifestation (the *manifesting*) can, in agreement with Saussure, be called the *substance;* a substance that manifests a linguistic schema we call a *linguistic usage* [usus, JDJ]. (Hjelmslev 1953a: 68)

In the article "Langue et parole" (1943) language usage is defined further as "l'ensemble des habitudes," that is, the regularities in the actual performed utterances acts, the actually produced texts. Hjelmslev himself gives an example of a language usage definition, and although it is of an expression figura, the French *r*, it seems to me to be clarifying and exemplary also for language usage definitions of content elements. It reads:

> Finally, the French *r* may be defined as a sonorous rolled vibrant or as a sonorous uvular constrictive.
> This definition comprises all the qualities found in the habitual pronunciation of the French *r,* and in this way it fixes it as an element of language considered as usage. This definition is neither oppositional, relative, nor negative, it exhausts the positive qualities characterizing the usage, but, on the other hand, here it stops. It leaves to occasional improvisation to vary the pronunciation within the limits prescribed by the definition. Even if the occasional pronunciation varies within these limits, the language, considered as usage, remains the same. (Hjelmslev 1959: 74)

It is important that Hjelmslev sees language usage or substance definitions as being of a kind other than form definitions, positive in contrast to the differential, relative, and negative, because the basis of the form definition is a non-interpreted system, while the substance definition rests on an interpreted material realization.

It is clear from the quotation above that Hjelmslev considers language form to be primary because it is a precondition for the substance. Substance is seen as variable, while the opposite – according to Hjelmslev – is not the case. He emphasizes this point of view at the end of his *Prolegomena*. In connection with considerations of the difference between language and games, Hjelmslev says specificially:

> Since the content-purport proves to be dispensable in the definition and description of a semiotic scheme, a formal formulation and a nominalistic description in linguistic theory is not limited to the expression form, but sees its object in the interplay between expression-form and a *content-form*. (Hjelmslev 1953a: 71)

Instead of including the content substance (meaning) as a specific characteristic of language, Hjelmslev claims language is different from games because its description necessitates the separation of two planes, expression and content form, while games are characterized as monoplanar. Hjelmslev's conception of the difference between languages and games is also interesting. Games (and individual languages as well) are certainly many different things, so let us restrict the comparison to similarities and differences between chess and the general characteristics of language as conceived by Hjelmslev. The first principal difference many would mention would be that language refers to wide-ranging states of affairs, while a game of chess is confined within the universe of the board on which the pieces move. Thus, no referential function plays any part in the definition of the game, even if the names of the pieces, and the changing of the pieces' names throughout history, together with their respective power, reflect a social organization of society. The wonder is that Hjelmslev totally disregards this difference; indeed, he explicitly denies its relevance:

> The decisive point for the question of whether or not a sign is present is not whether a content-purport is ordered to it. In view of the selection between semiotic schema and semiotic usage there exist for the calculus of linguistic theory, not interpreted, but only interpretable, systems. In this respect, then, there is no difference between, e.g., chess and pure algebra in the one hand, and, e.g., a language on the other. (Hjelmslev 1953a: 71)

This is a strong claim, and it is this claim that has both occasioned the title of this chapter and the necessity of rejecting structuralism and glossematics as points of departure for a general semiotic theory. Before attempting to show the difficulties inherent in such a position, it might be fair, however, to sketch briefly what it offers from a methodological point of view, i.e., its analytical power.

Throughout his work, and especially in *Prolegomena,* Hjelmslev attempts to give a comprehensive, albeit abstract, presentation of the basic principles which are, in his opinion, necessary to found a scientific study of language. First, language should be studied from an immanent point of view, as a structure *sui generis.* According to Hjelmslev the lack of progress within linguistics is because of the mistaken and erroneous transcendent point of view from which language has been studied (whether physical, physiological, or psychological and sociological). Only by conceiving language as a structural and functional totality can we overcome the fragmentation of language effectuated by the former viewpoint. To fulfill this objective the theory formation itself must be rigorous, it must use as few axioms, implicit premises, and indefinables as possible. Furthermore, the indefinables should be of a general epistemological kind, not specifically linguistic. Hjelmslev mentions indefinable concepts such as *description, object, dependence, uniformity, presence, necessity,* and *condition;* and the theory should consist of formal (and operational) definitions connected by implication. The objective is to construct a general calculus in which all possible combinations making up linguistic structures may be foreseen and described. Hjelmslev calls this theory formation *deduction.* His point is that the study of language should not proceed from inductively formed concepts of a "realistic" nature that are built on abstractions from usage within individual languages. On the contrary, the theory should take the form of a calculus describing the structure (i.e., the set of possible functions of language in general, whether only possible or realized in existing languages. Such a calculus might be seen as equivalent to logic [cf. pp. 22-24]). This is why Hjelmslev claims that the theory is *arbitrary* and cannot be empirically falsified. Yet the theory ought to be *appropriate,* meaning that on the basis of experience it is created with its applicability in view.

Consequently, the theory is simultaneously supposed to be *empirical* and *calculative* (cf. the scientific ideals of logical empiricism). A further theoretical requirement is expressed in Hjelmslev's so-called

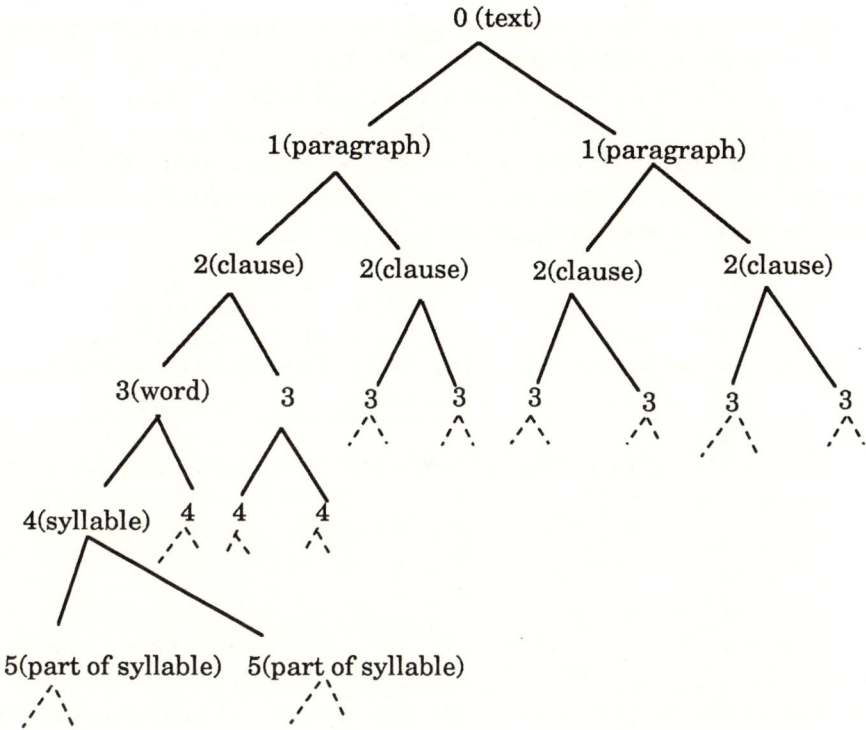

Fig. 11

*empirical principle* (it should be noted that Hjelmslev's use of the concepts *deductive* and *empirical* is controversial; he was well aware of this fact, but did not want to change his terminology). This principle states that the description must be selfconsistent, exhaustive, and as simple as possible. These three requirements mean, according to Hjelmslev, that in the future it will be possible to decide which theory of language is definitive, since among theories, all of them self consistent and exhaustive, the most simple should be preferred.

Concretely, glossematics proceeds as a text analysis, because its goal is to describe the *system* (formal and functional structures) behind the *process* (text). The procedure is *continued partition* on the basis of a functional analysis of the elements and their relations on a given level. The starting point is the text in its totality, which is conceived as a chain of elements. Using terms that, according to Hjelmslev, would have to be replaced or redefined, we can represent such a procedure diagrammatically (Fig. 11).

At each level variants are reduced, and inventories of invariants are established. The criterion of partition and establishment of inventories is the functional relationship between the elements (functives or entities) at a given level. Hjelmslev defines three functions that are pictured as follows in *Prolegomena* (Fig. 12).

| function | | relation (connexion) | correlation (equivalence) |
|---|---|---|---|
| cohesion { | determination | selection | specification |
| reciprocity { | interdependence | solidarity | complementarity |
| | constellation | combination | autonomy |

(Hjelmslev 1953a: 25)

Fig. 12

This diagram introduces some essential features of glossematics. The distinction between the two classes of functions, *correlation* vs. *relation,* corresponds to the distinction between *system* and *process.* Correlation is defined logically as *either-or* (disjunction) because a paradigm is characterized by equivalence between elements that cannot be manifested together (cf. Saussure's *principle of association*), whereas a process (e.g., a syntagma) is characterized by the function *both- ınd* (conjunction), because the linguistic chain combines elements from different paradigms (cf. Saussure's *principle of coordination,* and Jakobson's parallel distinction between *selection* and *combination).* Both within the system and within the process three functions are operative: *1) determination:* a function between a constant and a variable (in language and other semiotics the system is regarded as the constant, the process as the variable), 2) *interdependence:* a function between two constants, and 3) *constellation:* a function between two variables.

Each level of the partition of a text is defined by the functions contracted by its elements. Functions are, however, not only operative within a given level or plane but between them. Hjelmslev's conception of the linguistic sign is precisely defined as a solidarity between two planes of language, that of *expression* and that of *content*.

If we further try to summarize some of the fundamental points in glossematic analytical procedure, without using Hjelmslev's often head-splitting nomenclature, the following principles seem to be central:

1) *The principle of immanence:* Regarding the object of study as an autonomous totality of internal dependences means the decisive closure of the process of inquiry (cf. Saussure's distinction between *outer* and *inner*). For instance, isolating the linguistic sign and language considered as a system from the circuit of speech constitutes such a foundational move, through which it is decided which kinds of arguments are considered valid and which kinds of material count as relevant.

2) *The principle of continuous partition:* One of the main objectives of structural analysis is to divide the object into a hierarchy of inventories, or classes, each comprising entities identical from the point of view of formal definition. Furthermore the member of a class of a lower hierarchical order will be a constituent element of a class of a higher order (e.g., clauses are constituent elements of paragraphs, while paragraphs are constituents of texts). The objective is to continue the partition until a class is reached the members of which are constituents of a higher class, but which themselves are not constituted by members of a lower order class.

3) *The principle of binarism:* In classifying the elements at a given level the criterion used is that of binary opposition. The elements are grouped together if they can be described as having both a common or conjunctive feature, and a distinctive or disjunctive one. This dichotomic structure is claimed to be found on the different levels of analysis, from the phonological opposition between *voiced* and *unvoiced*, which (according to Jakobson) is one of the distinctive features making up the phonemes, over morphological oppositions to more complex units. And it is thought to be valid for both expression and content (cf. examples in Fig. 7).

4) *The principle of reduction:* The attempt to establish the inventories on each level means also an effort to reduce them as much as

possible by excluding mere variants, because defining the objective of structural analysis as the discovery and description of the system underlying the process means isolating the minimal elements and combination rules that can explain the generation of the text or other semiotic phenomena in question. What will count as variants and invariants is, however, dependent on how the system is defined. A description of a national language, for instance, will disregard dialect variations in pronunciation, whereas establishing the system underlying a given dialect will count such features as invariants. Even if the establishment of a given system is relative to the purpose of inquiry, it is the professed goal of glossematics to discover the most general system, that of language in general, which is thought be of the nature of a calculus permitting us to foresee and generate all languages, which will be describable as sets of specific selections from it.

The tool of reduction is the so-called *commutation test* (cf. below).

5) *The principle of correlation:* The objective of this procedure is to discern the relationships contracted between elements on and between the different levels of analysis. Disregarding the finer glossematic distinctions we can distinguish three different kinds of relationships: interdependence, determination, and constellation.

6) *The principle of transformation:* This principle is corollary to 5, but it is specifically directed to the study of the effects or changes of elements or relationships in the system as a whole. Such transformations can be observed either within a given process considered as a synchronic whole or diachronically, in the historical development of a semiotic. In a semantic analysis of a text, for instance, we may observe that a change in the signification of certain signs will imply a reorganization of the entire semantic structure to the effect that a transformation between the initial and the final state has taken place within a single text. Diachronically it means observing and explaining how a given semiotic changes during a given period of time thereby trying to discover and describe the regularities of this process.

Principles of analysis such as the above, which were in fact partly adopted from logic and the reflections of logical positivism on the general principles of scientific knowledge, meant a strengthening of stricter ideals of inquiry, not only within linguistics, which had already rather advanced methodological principles, but within the study of signification in general. Their success, manifest within humanistic studies from about the middle of this century, is explicable among other things because they are easily used as guidelines for concrete analyses: Isolate the object of inquiry and look for internal dependences, continue parsing the object considered as a process, as a concatenation of elements, until the lowest possible level is reached; in arranging the elements arrived at on each level use binarism as a classificatory principle; design a model of the research object by removing the variants by means of the commutation test; establish the combination rules of the system by analyzing the kinds of relations contracted between the elements on and between the levels; describe the regularities of changes within processes governed by the system and within the system itself during a certain period of time.

The apparent ease of such an accomplishment, when presented as above, is deceptive. For one thing, one cannot apply one principle after another in a nice and orderly fashion; a concrete process of inquiry will proceed by trial and error, in attempting to check and harmonize the provisionary results of the different procedures. More important, every concrete analytical move involves an interpretation which may be disputed, or even convincingly shown to be erroneous, because no mechanical ways of applying these principles exist, only traditions of application within different trends in structural analysis. And although they have much in common these trends may oppose each other (e.g., Hjelmslev's constant refusal to accept Prague-structuralism, and Jakobson's distinctive features-analysis in particular). Furthermore, no generally accepted structural studies of larger semiotic systems exist. Most studies describe certain parts of systems, such as aspects of natural language or certain features of different types of discourse. In fairness it must be added, however, that this state of affairs is not particular to the structuralist study of signification; other approaches to the study of systems of signification show a similar poverty as regards grand scale empirical studies covering larger subjects.

Despite the objections, the ideals, endeavors, methodological reflections, and concrete analyses of this approach have been eminently useful both by suggesting high standards for scholarship and by presenting many special studies proving the fruitfulness of its analytic procedures. Such feats, however, have been made in spite of cherished theoretical positions especially of Hjelmslev, namely that a purely formal analysis of semiotic systems such as language is possible, where formal analysis not only means treating a given subject by using a set of formal procedures, but advocates the stronger claim that it is possible to analyze form without having recourse either to properties of the manifesting substance (e.g., sound) or to the objects of the signs.

## 5.  Content form and content substance

There is a fundamental ambiguity in Hjelmslev's conception of the *content form* and its relation to the *content substance,* because sometimes it is conceived of as a purely formal system of differences, and because sometimes it is conceived of an interpreted system of differences, i.e., as semantic differences established with a view to the referential function of language (cf. below). First, it seems doubtful if the determination of whether a text under consideration (a series of signs) is language (has a connected content form) can be determined immanently. Imagine for example the situation that someone unacquainted with Arabic is shown an Arabic text. Such a person will not perceive the signs in the sense of expression elements with connected content. But we can go a step further. It must be reasonable to assert that that person will not have a chance to determine whether this is a case of a text which is lingually uninterpretable only for him or a non-meaning-bearing calligraphy. Notice further. It would be impossible for the person to connect the text with a content even through the closest analysis of the text's expression structure (which possibly could lead to setting up a [grapheme] inventory and its combination rules). This example allows us the assertion that a formal analysis never in itself would be a sufficient condition for a determination of whether a given, materially-manifested structure is a language; in other words, an analysis of the expression form cannot by itself lead to a constitution of a content form.

This limitation is also borne out by the fact that, according to Hjelmslev, the first partition we have to carry out in language analysis is that between expression and content. This immediately gives rise to the question of how it is possible to differentiate at all between the two terms. To this Hjelmslev can reply, first of all, that *the commutation test* allows such a differentiation:

> The decisive function is *commutation,* or the correlation contracted by a relation with a correlation from the opposite plane of language. Two members

of a paradigm belonging to the expression plane (or to the signifier) are said to be *commutable* (or *invariants*) if the replacement of one of these members by another may effectuate an analogous replacement on the content plane (or in the signified); and *vice versa*. (Hjelmslev 1959: 103, Fr. orig., my transl.)

Take, for example, the French lexemes, RIRE and LIRE. The justification for a differentation between expression and content — according to Hjelmslev — lies in the fact that exchange of the expression figure R for the expression figure L brings about a change in meaning (for remarks about this viewpoint, see below). In principle, the commutation test works both ways, so that a change in the content form will bring about a change on the expression plane.

To be able to make a commutation test, one must know the language in question; consequently, interpretation of meaning is a precondition for the commutation test and thereby for content analysis as well. That Hjelmslev has been well aware of this is obvious from his remarks about the commutation test in "La stratification du language." He says here that the identification of variants, through commutation, implies reference to substance phenomena, and thus, pure form analysis is insufficient as far as the research object is a natural language. This point of view is also evident in his recognition that semantic content is analyzed on the basis of usage; in his terminology, semantics would be an analysis of linguistic substance. Finally, Hjelmslev has an informative comment on the relationship between *context* and *meaning*:

> None of the minimal entities, nor the roots, have such an "independent" existence that they can be assigned a lexical meaning. But from the basic point of view we have assumed — the continued analysis on the basis of function in the text — there exist no other perceivable meanings than contextual meaning; any entity, and thus also any sign, is defined relatively, not absolutely, and only by its place in the context. From this point it is meaningless to distinguish between meanings that appear only in the context and meanings that might be assumed to have an independent existence, or — with the old Chinese grammarians — between "empty" and "full" words. The so-called lexical meanings in certain signs are nothing but artificially isolated contextual meanings, or artificial paraphrases of them. In absolute isolation no sign has any meaning; any sign-meaning arises in a context, by which we mean a situational context or explicit context, it matters not which, since in an unlimited or productive text (a living language) we can always transform a situational into an explicit context. Thus we must not imagine, for example, that a substantive is more meaningful

than a preposition, or a word more meaningful than a derivational or
inflexional ending. When comparing one entity with another we may speak
not merely of a difference in meaning but also of different kinds of meaning, but concerning all such entities we may speak of meaning with precisely the same relative right. (Hjelmslev 1953a: 28)

If we compare this quotation with Hjelmslev's claim that meaning is
described through concept construction on the basis of language usage,
it is evident that the communicative context in its broadest sense is
also a precondition for Hjelmslev, not only for meaning analysis but
also for content analysis. A nice confirmation of this can be seen in the
following, where Hjelmslev even makes a differentiation between
*meaning* and *content:*

> If we speak without thinking, and in the form of series of sounds to which
> no content can be attached by any listener, such speech is an abracadabra,
> not a linguistic expression and not a functive for a sign function. Of course,
> lack of content must not be confused with lack of meaning: an expression
> may very well have a content which from some point of view (for example,
> that of normative logic or physicalism) may be characterized as meaning-
> less, but it is a content. (Hjelmslev 1953a: 30)

What Hjelmslev does not mention, however, is which conditions must
be fulfilled to connect the expression to a content; here language usage
analysis as the precondition for semantics once again becomes decisive. In addition, the formulation is also interesting because, in a
backward way, it tacitly points out the unbreakable connection between *meaning* and *content.* Content, according to Hjelmslev, can be
determined as a differential system of figurae (content form) which is
a precondition, for example, for the categorization of phenomena of the
surrounding world; but analytically it can be described as a non-
interpreted structure. In his (1957) article "Pour une sémantique
structurale," Hjelmslev, however, complicates the question of semantic
analysis by distinguishing between *value,* which is defined on a purely
relative, negative, and differential basis, and *signification,* which is
considered as a substance phenomenon, which I take to mean dependent on usage. He also equates *signification* with what he calls
*material form* in contrast to the *pure form* of *value.*The relation between pure form and material form (formed substance) he describes in
the following way: " 'material form' means nothing but a reflection of
the pure one, projected on the substance, and feeding on its boon"

(Hjelmslev 1959: 108). Does this distinction between pure and material form suggest two different analyses or two levels of semantic analysis, or is the pure form analysis something quite different from semantics? It might seem strange to ask such questions, but it must be remembered that Hjelmslev, concerning the expression plane of language, as early as 1935 claimed that there is no necessary connection between sound and language, and the same might very well be the case for the connection between language and meaning. His answer is not totally clear, but the following interpretation agrees with his general outlook: the analysis of the pure form of content would consist in a description of the paradigmatics and syntagmatics of content figurae in the same way in which the expression figurae are analyzed. In the case of the French /r/, the pure form description contains only four characteristics: (1) /r/ belongs to the consonants; (2) /r/ belongs the sub-categories of consonants that admit of both an initial and a final position; (3) /r/ belongs to the further sub-group of consonants that are placed next to a vowel; and finally (4) /r/ is commutable with certain elements belonging to the same category (e.g., /l/). The first three points relate to the function of /r/ within the linguistic chain (its position within the syllable), and to the rules of combination that can be established without any reference to the sign function, on the plane of expression form alone. At least at an initial stage of the research process, however, they certainly presuppose taking the expression substance into account. The fourth criterion is not only paradigmatic, but implies the relation between expression and content. This means that even a form definition of a expression figure implies that the sign *in toto* has to be taken into account, and, finally, even the content substance plays a decisive role, because we cannot decide if French /l/( and /r/ are commutable without having recourse to signification.

Even if this argument makes highly improbable even the possibility of analyzing a given language as pure form, because what is presented as a formal analysis is based, implicitly, on considerations of substance, it might be of some interest to find out how Hjelmslev draws the line between *content form* and *content substance*.

In *Prolegomena,* Hjelmslev relates *content form* and *content substance* very much in the same way as Saussure. In the preceding part of this chapter (cf. pp. 14 and 19), we mentioned Hjelmslev's point that lexeme paradigms in different languages draw the distinctions differ-

ently in the amorphous thought substance; in *Prolegomena,* Hjelmslev
gives one more example that has become "classical."

This incongruence within one and the same zone of purport turns up everywhere. Compare also, for example, the following correspondences between
Danish, German, and French:

|  | Baum | arbre |
|---|---|---|
| træ | | |
|  | Holz | bois |
| skov | Wald | |
|  | | forêt |

We may conclude from this fact that in one of the two entities that are
functives of the sign function, namely the content, the sign function in-
stitutes a form, the *content-form,* which from the point of view of the purport is arbitrary and which can be explained only by the sign function and
is obviously solidary with it. In this sense, Saussure is clearly correct in
distinguishing between form and substance. (Hjelmslev 1953a: 33-34)

I suspect that no one would deny either the relevance of this point of
view or the force of the example. What can be discussed, however, is
how to interpret this phenomenon, and what the consequences should
be for the conception of the sign. In his introduction to semiotics, *A
Theory of Semiotics,* Umberto Eco comments on Hjelmslev's table as
follows:

In a table of this kind we are not concerned with "ideas," psychic entities,
nor even with referents as object; *we are concerned with values which issue
from the system.* The values correspond to cultural units but they can be
defined as pure differences; they are not defined in term of their content
(and therefore of the possibility of intentional analysis) but in terms of the
way in which they are opposed to other elements of the system and of the
position which they occupy within it. As in the case of phonemes in a
phonological system, we have a series of differential choices which can be
described by binary methods. Therefore in Hjelmslevian terms an empty
diagram like

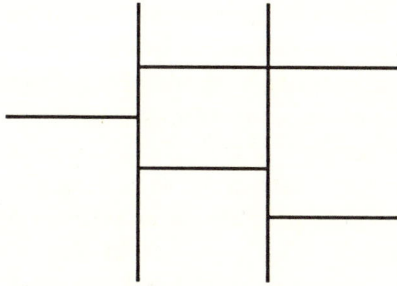

represents the content-form while such units as "Baum," "Holz," "bois" (and so on) are the content-substance. (Eco 1976: 73-74)

Eco continues, sensibly commenting on the difference between the progress made in the analysis of the expression form compared to that of the content form. What is interesting from our point of view, however, is the way he distinguishes between the empty diagram (equivalent to the content form) and the content units *Baum, Holz,* etc. (equivalent to the content substance). Eco's experimentation with Hjelmslev's iconic representation of the content form reveals that something is wrong with the conception of the content form as the constant and the content substance as the variable, a variable which for linguistic purposes is dispensable. Eco's empty diagram is first, not even a significant form but merely some lines running parallel and crossing each other, to the effect that the diagram could just as well be an iconic representation of a part of a brick wall as of a semantic field. We might object that most diagrams and iconic representations will make no sense without symbolic indications of what they are about. In this case, however, the very reason for the relative positions of the lines is the referential function of what has been left out, namely the content substances, as expressed in the words *Baum, Holz,* etc. Secondly, this particular diagram is unique, or *ad hoc:* as a form, it cannot be generalized to cover other cases of semantic differentiation within and between different languages. With regard to this diagram, all one can say is that it illustrates the different *usage* of certain concrete lexemes in Danish, German, and French. It follows, thirdly, that if we want to generalize this example, the maxim to formulate would be this: In natural languages the content form is a usage phenomenon.

The point that different languages categorize phenomena of the life-world differently is irrelevant to the question concerning the feasibility of a pure form analysis without any reference to the substance. On the contrary, this example indicates that we need an answer to the question whether a semantics that does not take the referential and the communicative aspect into account is possible at all.

Hjelmslev has tried to provide an answer to this question, and the answer is surprising. In the minutes of the meeting of the Royal Danish Academy of the Sciences of April 28, 1950, an account is given of a talk by Hjelmslev on the "Fundamental Problems of Semantics." The report was probably written by Hjelmslev himself:

> Since Aristotle, semantics (. . .) in its classical form has been founded on the doctrine that the inclusion of the *designata,* that are external to language, is a prerequisite for linguistic description. Furthermore, the analysis of the designata cannot be reduced to a single description of the surrounding world, but concerns the relationship between man and world. According to this point of view, the designata had to appear either as concepts (logistic semantics), as ideas (mentalistic semantics), or as human reactions (behavioristic semantics). It can be shown, however, that all these points of view are scientifically unsatisfactory. In contradistinction to the points of view, semantics has to be conceived as a "topistics," whose object is the syntactical combinations of a small number of constants that are defined on the basis of simple behavior-situations.[1] (Danish orig., my transl.)

This brief statement contains two interesting points. It tells us which kinds of semantics Hjelmslev is opposed to, namely those presupposing the inclusion of additional elements (mind, world) in the semantic description of language. It also tells us that the ambition of glossematic semantics is to work out a restricted inventory of elements, constants, and theircombination rules. This is certainly in accordance with the general glossematic project as it is stated in *Prolegomena,* namely to analyze the immanent structure of language on both the expression and the content planes. Then the surprising statement follows that these constants have to be defined in relation to simple behavior-situations! This means that the elements of the content form have to be defined in relation to man's relation to the world.

---

1. *Kongelig Dansk Videnskabernes Selskab, Oversigt* 1949-1950, p. 50. Unfortunately, no manuscript of this talk exists. Mrs. Vibeke Hjelmslev has been so kind as to confirm this. According to Mrs. Hjelmslev, her husband talked from notes.

## 6. Naturam expellere furca ...

To say that a certain vacillation characterizes Hjelmslev's treatment of the questions concerning *content* and *meaning* is hardly unfair, but the inclusive model of the sign put forward in "La stratification du language" (cf. Fig. 9) can be regarded as an effort to clarify the issues by introducing three different levels of content (and expression) substance: (1) the apperceptive level; (2) the socio-biological level; and (3) the physical level. In "La stratification," as in the rest of his work, Hjelmslev gives priority to the first level for the following reasons:

> Evidently, concerning the content substance it is the description by evaluation that immediately imposes itself. It is not by a physical description of the signified things that one arrives at a useful characterization of the semantic usage adopted by a linguistic community and belonging to the language that one wants to describe. On the contrary, it is [by studying] the evaluations adopted by this community, the collective appreciations, or social opinion. First of all, the description of the substance ought to consist in a juxtaposition of language with other social institutions, and it constitutes the point of contact between linguistics and the other branches of social anthropology. In this way one and the same physical "thing" may be attributed rather different semantic descriptions according to the civilization in question. (Hjelmslev 1959: 52).

This definition of the primary semiotic substance is highly interesting and useful, since it is understood as the social opinion or collective partition of the life-world as it is deposited in different semantic structures. Furthermore, it seems to agree with the description of the relationship between language and thought given eighteen years before (cf. here pp. 19-24). The question is whether this definition of semantics, which in "La Stratification" (1959: 58) is defined as a study of content substance, is so different from the mentalistic semantics Hjelmslev opposed four years earlier. Hjelmslev himself is well aware of the problem, since he asks whether the conception of the linguistic sign put forward in "La stratification" is not very similar to that of Saussure, according to which a sign unites an acoustic image and a concept. Hjelmslev rejects this point of view, but on the rather unconvincing grounds that Saussure's conceptions are equivocal, whereas his own conceptions are supposed to be strictly defined (ibid.: 56). An imagined charge of psychologism is likewise rejected on the grounds that psychology is not rigorously defined as a science (ibid.:

56). These reasons are not convincing, because in concentrating on social opinion as the primary content substance, psychological and sociological considerations ought to be taken into account, and so much the better for semantics.

Another question is the relation between content substance and content form. In "La stratification" he says this relation is the same as that between expression form and content form. Here, we will consider only two points. First, whereas the relation between expression form and content form, the semiotic relation proper, is defined as a *solidarity* (interdependence between terms in a process), the relation between form and substance within each plane is said to be a *manifestation* in which the substance selects (determines) the form. The second point is Hjelmslev's insistence on *manifestation* as due to *usage*.

Manifestation, to Hjelmslev, denotes the interstratal relations, i.e., the relations between the four planes or strata in the model of the sign. This means that the linguistic sign, as it is manifested in a given text, is a usage phenomenon. Since usage in *Prolegomena* is defined as a substance phenomenon, this may seem surprising, especially since the sign function is still defined as a solidarity. In her seminal article, "Form and Substance in Glossematics," Eli Fischer-Jørgensen (1966: 29) points out, however, that no contradiction is involved, because even if language in general presupposes the solidarity between expression and content, *no specific relation* is presupposed, and since every existing language combines expression and content differently, their concrete relation is a matter of usage. Furthermore, this definition of the concrete, manifested sign as a usage phenomenon is not really surprising considering that Hjelmslev sees the *differentia specifica* of language in the fact that it is built of non-conforming figurae systems on each plane, not in its capacity of being a sign system (cf. p. 18). Furthermore, this definition of the sign as a phenomenon of usage certainly seems justified considering the fact that both expression and content of signs may change.

Even if "La stratification" clarified the question about the relation between the three levels of content substance by defining the social opinion as the primary level (although this conception of different levels of substance is certainly not itself beyond criticism), another question remains unclear in this article and the other writings of Hjelmslev, namely the very relation between content form and content substance. It might be possible to define the primary semiotic content substance as the partition of the life-world by a linguistic community as it is deposited in the different semantic structures of a given language. The content form or the pure form of the content plane is, from the little Hjelmslev says about it, the features of a given language that are stable, analyzable into closed paradigms, and consisting of figurae or minimal sign units, which are related to each other according to combination rules in the linguistic chain and commutable within the paradigms. On the content plane, the closed classes of morphological and grammatical categories will meet these requirements, but even small closed sub-classes within otherwise open classes will do so as well (e.g., kinship terms form a rather well-structured and closed sub-class of nouns). It would certainly be tempting to illustrate the delimination of the content form from the ontent substance in glossematics by the distinction between morpho-syntactical categories and semantic categories, but there is insufficient evidence in Hjelmslev's writings to do this, even if form, in his earlier writings, is identified with grammatical, or rather functional, form. On the contrary,  one year before the publication of "La stratification du language" he published a short article called "The Content Form of Language as a Social Factor" (1953b), and his examples in it are from open classes, for instance the famous example about how *tree, wood,* and *forest* vary in different languages; in connection with the differences in kinship terms it is explicitly said that "these languages [Hungarian and Chinese] draw more distinction within the content substance than do our languages" (Hjelmslev ([1959: 91]). According to "Pour une sémantique structurale," however, such phenomena would be considered to relate to the material form of signification, i.e., to substance, whereas the *pure form* or *value* can be analyzed without taking the signification into account. As an example of pure form analysis, Hjelmslev points out that the structural isomorphism between the English, Danish, and German systems of non-composite tenses can be described without having recourse to substance. How to do it in this way remains, unfortunately, a secret.

The point is not only that Hjelmslev seems to have difficulties in making up his mind about the exact line of demarcation between content form and content substance, but also that his changing point of view stresses the general difficulty, or rather impossibility, of establishing a pure form of any given language, both on the expression and on the content plane, without having recourse to considerations of what Hjelmslev calls substance.

Hjelmslev from the fifties to his death in 1965 seems to have almost been haunted by questions concerning semantics, indeed the fundamental question: how is meaning possible? (see Hjelmslev 1961: 57). A late and little known article from 1961, "Practice and Theory in Structural Semantics," contains his final reflections on the subject. Here he reflects on learning a foreign language, and consequently on translation. Using his own broad sign model from "La stratification" (1954), he describes the pedagogy of language teaching as follows:

A pedagogical approach of the monolingual type should, incidentally, not in the least be blamed for resorting to the device of *pointing at objects, e.g., pictures, since in some way or other the "thing-meant"* must come in as one possible variant of the highest degree. On the other hand, as far as the manifestation of variants is concerned, substances are of different *levels;* there are reasons in favour of presuming that the thing-meant belongs to a very low level [level 3 of the model, JDJ], if by "low" we mean "relatively far from direct affinity with the manifestatum," and that the highest level, and the one which lends itself particularly well to manifesting linguistic forms of the content, is one of social apprehension [level 1 of the model, JDJ]. This, on the other hand, can only be attained through gradual inductive steps, and through a synthesis which must often be unconscious to the pupil, just as it mostly is to the native speaker, and which must very often be left to the pupil's intuition or to his own tentative conclusions. (Hjelmslev 1961: 62)

He praises, however, a method of language teaching, specifically The Nature Method, that proceeds by means of *explicit formulation,* which is defined as follows:

Such a formulation might be called an "internal translation," although the very term "translation" is in a way a fallacy, and theoretically a pitfall. What such a formulation really is, is a syntagmatic *definition,* corresponding to that given by a consistent monolingual dictionary, and identical with the definition actually required by the method of semantic analysis that we are advocating in glossematics [i.e., the partition of the content into figurae, JDJ]. Definitions will comprise parts that are still definable, but in the long run definitions will end in *indefinables.* It may be presumed that the last indefinables which are at the bottom of such a system of semantic definitions will be the elements of simple behaviour situations: *'I am here,'*

'*you* are *there*,' etc., which in their turn can only be made clear through
conclusions from the context of situation, for which in some cases *pointing*
may come in useful.

This is then, roughly, how Practice and Theory must meet; and if Practice is based on Theory, the reverse is equally true; both are based, ultimately, on simple behaviour situations. (Hjelmslev 1961: 62-63)

Later in this book we will see *translation* as the means to interpret
and understand signs (both in Peirce and in Jakobson). Suffice it here
to stress that, even to Hjelmslev, as far as language content is concerned, the immanent description is dependent on a pre-understood
referential function. Already in *Principes de grammaire générale*
Hjelmslev used the referential and communicative aspects of language
to give a functional definition of the articles and the pronouns (see
Hjelmslev 1928: 332-340). Furthermore, the cornerstone of Hjelmslev's
analytic procedures, the commutation test, rests on the referential
aspect of language. This test can only be undertaken because the
exchange of one expression figura for another, if such an exchange
involves commutation, denotes that the given whole (for example a
lexeme) after the exchange either will be able to enter meaningfully
into another communicative context, or no longer can be connected to
a content, this latter meaning no longer being able to enter into a
meaningful communication (cf. the series *rire, lire,* and *fire,* where the
exchange in the first case brings about a change in content; in the
other, a loss of content).

According to the preceding, it seems no accident that Hjelmslev
presents two definitions of the sign, an inclusive one based on a reference function and a restrictive one defined as the relation between
expression and content form (cf. Fig. 9). It should be evident that the
latter only comes about as a methodic extrapolation of pertinent characteristics for the given purpose from the inclusive sign conception.
What is more, as concerns semantics, the restrictive sign conception,
according to Hjelmslev's own definition, is not sufficient, since language *usage* – according to Hjelmslev, a substance phenomenon – is
the starting point for this analysis.

On the basis of the preceding there are three points concerning the
relationship between content form and content substance that need
discussions (1) the semiotic status of the so-called minimal units of
content, figurae; (2) the question concerning the restricted inventories

of such units; and (3) the relationship between negative and positive definitions in semantics, and how these relate to the concept of value.

The idea of content figurae, i.e., non-signs combined according to certain syntactical rules, thus making up the content form of a given linguistic description, has already been questioned within the glossematic milieu of the Cercle linguistique de Copenhague, where, for instance, Holger Steen Sørensen (1958: 44-47) claimed that the elementary content figurae would themselves be signs, i.e., that content analysis cannot be carried out below the sign level. I find that such criticism of the idea of elementary units of sign content that are not themselves signs is just, because if we take a lexeme paradigm like the one mentioned above (cf. Fig. 7) we are certainly able to parse it into smaller units. In the case of *man, woman, boy, girl,* the lexemes were analyzed into two binary oppositions, male vs.. female, and adulthood vs.. childhood. That these content figurae are not only sign contents, but also *signs* themselves, is simply beyond doubt. It might be objected that even if this is unquestionably true, further analysis might end up with elementary units that really are not signs. I think that even this hope has to be given up. If you try, for example, to analyze *male* into smaller units you will get something like ". . . sexual characteristics belonging to an organism distinguishing it from . . .," and if you try *sexual,* you will get something like ". . . characters connected with the reproductive function of . . . " If this phenomenon is generalized, we can formulate the dogma that *any specification of the content of a sign has to be worded in other signs.* It should be added that this *wording in other signs* is by no means accidental, since there is no way of avoiding it. Specific notations can, of course, be used and be very useful, but it is a notational dodge to claim that by using specific systems of notations one can go below the sign level, because such a system has to interpreted in language, if the notation is about language content. One more point should be mentioned in connection with the opposition between *male* and *female.* Even if they are exhaustive in their capacities as sub-divisions of semantic markers (i.e., in Hjelmslev's terminology, a restricted inventory of content figurae, since if a given sign has the semantic marker *sex* it will be either *male* or *female,* or both or neither), *male* and *female* are analyzed as signs by means of other inventories. In this sense *the distinction between restricted and unrestricted inventories is only valid at a given level of analysis.* In other words, every sign is a possible content figura of another sign, but at the same time every content figura is necessarily a sign itself. To identify a content *figura,* we must regard it as a sign; *male,* for instance, could not be identified as a content figura if it were not possible to attach a content to it (cf. below).

Because of the semiotic status of the content figurae, it is doubtful whether any finite number of them would suffice to build the content of the signs of a given language, because what this would really mean would be that the combination of a selected number of signs, or a subgroup of signs, would be sufficient to construct all other signs. The fact is that all signs function as content elements for each other. It is suggestive, however, that the French linguist and semiotician A.J. Greimas, who has done more than anybody else to carry out Hjelmslev's program of a structural semantics, and who in *Sémantique structurale* (1966) thought that such an enterprise might be feasible, changed his mind. Four years later he writes: "We begin to be aware of the illusory in the project of a systematic semantics, that in the manner of a phonology, would be able to articulate the content plane of language" (Greimas 1970: 17, Fr. orig., my transl.). Greimas has pointed out repeatedly that this does not mean it is impossible to analyze the elements of content in a limited text corpus. Because the relation between interpreted and interpreting sign is the same as the relation in conceptual analysis between *explanandum* and *explanans,* neither does it mean that the signs used to represent the content elements of the text or texts in question in their capacity of being interpretive signs do not acquire a meta-function in that particular analysis.

Sometimes there is established an opposition between regarding linguistic content analysis as *hierarchical* and viewing it as *circular.* Hjelmslevian and structuralist linguistics' model of the sign is hierarchical, since the sign is analyzed as being built up by smaller units on both the expression and content plane. Furthermore, both the partition of the linguistic chain and the construction of inventories lead to the establishment of hierarchies. If semantic analysis is conceived as the explication of the content of signs through other signs, however, a certain circularity is necessarily involved, because different signs will mutually act as content for each other. It should be emphasized that this opposition is one of epistemological attitude rather than one of practical, analytical procedure, because in analyzing texts, the sign that functions as explicatory will acquire a meta-status within the context of the analysis. Likewise, linguists favoring an immanent and hierarchical semantics have never been able to set up general content inventories (cf. the quotation from Greimas, above). Nevertheless, the choice of epistemological attitude has consequences for the general conception of the sign and for the methodological framework within which the study of semantics is placed. It is worthwhile, therefore, to argue briefly why the point of view that the content of signs is explained by and composed of other signs is the only tenable position.

The reason is that the point of departure of content analysis must be the linguistic expression, and that the specification of the content of the sign will necessarily be another linguistic expression or some special notation that can be retranslated into a linguistic expression. If the content of a linguistic expression is represented by another linguistic expression, and this is clearly the case, because *human, female,* and *adult* are just as surely linguistic expressions as *woman,* whose content figurae they are supposed to be, then it seems impossible to represent content directly in language. This is not as surprising as it may seem, since it has been argued that the content substance is necessarily implicated in the analysis of the content form. The content substance, however, is not of the nature of language, but of the nature of thought or of the nature of objects, states of affairs, events, and actions. Consequently, neither content nor meaning can be conceived and analyzed immanently, because content and meaning appear in the interplay between the structure of language and what Hjelmslev calls content substance. In other words, neither intralingual nor interlingual translation suffice to establish text meaning. An *intersemiotic translation is necessary* (cf. Jakobson, here V, 7).

One way of showing the decisive role played by the content substance in the analysis of content and meaning is to reflect on the relationship between the two kinds of definitions that are opposed to each other according to the structuralist and glossematic point of view, namely the *positive* and the *negative* definition.

Saussure proposes the differential or negative definition of language. It reads like this:

> in language there are only differences. Even more important: a difference generally implies positive terms between which the difference is set up; but in language there are only differences *without positive terms.* Whether we take the signified or the signifier, language has neither ideas nor sounds that existed before the linguistic system, but only conceptual and phonic differences that have issued from the system. The idea or phonic substance

that a sign contains is of less importance than the other signs that surround it. Proof of this is that the value of a term may be modified without
either its meaning or its sound being affected, solely because a neighboring
term has been modified. (Saussure 1959: 120)

It is, however, difficult to imagine "differences *without positive terms,"*
because a system of differences that is not manifest in some way or
another would certainly be just as nebulous as Saussure and Hjelmslev claim that the expression and the content substance are without
the formative action of the language structure. No wonder, then, that
Saussure modifies his position:

> But the statement that everything in language is negative is true only if
> the signified and the signifier are considered separately; when we consider
> the sign in its totality, we have something that is positive in its own class.
> A linguistic system is a series of differences of sound combined with a series
> of differences of ideas; but the pairing of a certain number of acoustical
> signs with as many cuts made from the mass of thought engenders a
> system of values; and this system serves as the effective link between the
> phonic and psychological elements within each sign. Although both the
> signified and the signifier are purely differential and negative when consid-
> ered separately, their combination is a positive fact. (ibid.)

It is hard to see why the combination of two differential and negative
units in itself should create a positive fact, if nothing else is added.
This seems to be the reason why Hjelmslev changes Saussure's ideas
in two respects. First, he distinguishes two different forms, that of the
expression and that of the content; this is clearly a necessary improve-
ment of the theory, since the cuts effectuated by the formal structure
of language are not made in the same places on the content and on the
expression plane. Secondly, Hjelmslev only speaks of a positive definition when considerations of substance are taken into account (cf. the
positive definition of the French /r/ (cf. p. 26). This seems sensibly to
distinguish a positive definition from a negative one, provided one is
willing to accept the dogma that *positive and negative definitions mutually presuppose each other.* That is to say, the hypothesis that certain negative definitions are sufficient to account for the existence of a
given system of differences within a phenomenon necessarily presupposes some positive definitions, and *vice versa.* With regard to content
analysis, the necessity of referring to positive definitions implies that
the study of semantics cannot be carried out immanently (and I am
confident that the same applies to the expression plane of the lan-

guage). In other words, *the concept of value is not independent of the concept of signification; on the contrary, it depends on it.*

This conclusion is similar to Saussure's original definition of the concept of value *(valeur).* He argues:

> even outside language all values are apparently governed by the same paradoxical principle. They are always composed:
>
> (1) of a *dissimilar* thing that can be *exchanged* for the thing of which the value is to be determined; and
>
> (2) of *similar* things that can be *compared* with the thing of which the value is to be determined.
>
> Both factors are necessary for the existence of a value. To determine what a five-franc piece is worth one must therefore know: (1) that it can be exchanged for a fixed quantity of a different thing, e.g., bread; and (2) that it can be compared with a similar value of the same system, e.g., a one-franc piece, or with coins of another system (a dollar, etc.). In the same way a word can be exchanged for something dissimilar, an idea; besides, it can be compared with something of the same nature, another word. Its value is therefore not fixed so long as one simply states that it can be "exchanged" for a given concept, i.e., that it has this or that signification: one must also compare it with similar values, with other words that stand in opposition to it. Its content is really fixed only by the concurrence of everything that exists outside it. Being part of a system, it is endowed not only with a signification but also and especially with a value, and this is something quite different. (Saussure 1959: 115)

This passage is celebrated, but it is also problematic. First, the terminology seems to be muddled, because Saussure here opposes *word* and *concept / signification.* Since a word is a species of sign, it is in itself a combination of *signifier* and *signified,* or *acoustic images* and *idea / concept,* and consequently it seems that Saussure is saying that *signifier + signified* is exchanged for something dissimilar, namely the *signified* in itself. (This is not due either to the English translation or to the French editing of the *Cours,* because the different variants listed in the critical Saussure edition agree on this point, cf. Engler 1968: 260-261). The problem might be explained by Saussure's rather loose use of the concept *word* (Fr. *mot*) in the sense of *signifier* in his lecture, but the problem still remains if we attempt an emendation, because saying that *value* depends both on the relationship between the signifiers as elements in a system and on their separate relations to their signified is circular, because 1) signifiers without signifieds do not exist, and 2) there would in fact be no systematic relationship between the acoustic images of separate word units without taking the content into account (e.g., *man, woman, boy, girl* are not systematically related to each other if only their acoustic images are taken into account).

If we return to Saussure's example concerning the difference between *value* and *signification* (the English lexeme *sheep* vs. the French lexeme *mouton*), it would be tempting to interpret the distinction in the light of reference and use. In fact, Saussure does it himself in saying that the main reason for their different value is that "in speaking of a piece of meat ready to be served on the table, English uses *mutton* and not sheep" (Saussure 1959: 115-116). Here he explicitly points to a referential use in a situative context. In the theoretical exposition quoted above, however, the distinction seems to relate, on the one hand, to the systematic relations between *words,* where it is uncertain whether *word* is to be taken in the sense of *sign* or of *signifier,* and on the other hand to the relation between *word (sign, signifier?)* and *concept.* Robert Godel has written a seminal study of the manuscripts to the *Cours* (Godel 1957), and he has a very interesting section on "La langue, système de valeurs" (Godel 1957: 230-251). There is not much help there concerning this question, however, because both the concept of *value* and of *signification* remain ill delimited *vis à vis* one another. What matters for Saussure is the intrasystemic relationship between values. Note the following statement in Godel: "The signified is nothing but a resumé of the linguistic value presupposing the interplay between the terms" (Godel 1957: 242). The subsuming of *signification* under *value* is not carried through, however, and, in my opinion, cannot be for the same reasons given above in the criticism of Hjelmslev.

The structuralist and glossematic endeavor to get rid of phenomena of substance, whether the manifesting substance (sound, etc.) or the manifested, consciousness, the world, when it is regarded as a methodological move, may seem reasonable, because it facilitates the foregrounding of certain properties and relationships of its objects. Such a move, e.g., Saussure's breaking of the circuit of speech, presupposes, however, what is left out, because formal analyses are carried out in chains of signs whose meaning is already known. In the only book-length study of glossematics so far, the author, Prof. Bertha Siertsema, wonders about the feasibility of such an analysis, and after having respectfully consulted Hjelmslev himself, she writes:

Although this element of *knowing the language analyzed* is nowhere mentioned explicitly by Hjelmslev, yet it is inherent in his commutation theory and is, as we shall see, the basis of all his *exclusively formal* premises. It is part of what I have called the "setting" of glossematic analysis (. . .): Hjelmslev does not mean his analysis to be applied to hitherto unknown languages, not even to hitherto unanalyzed languages. *"Process,"* in the quotations from Ch. II in OSG [i.e., *Prolegomena*, JDJ] is, as Professor Hjelmslev kindly told me, to be understood as *"analyzed process."* That is, as a process whose elements have already been distinguished and recognized (by commutation evidently). Finding (. . .) is supposed to have taken place already. (Siertsema 1954: 37)

In the light of the above, Hjelmslev's categorical claim in *Prolegomena* that "there exists for the calculus of linguistic theory, not interpreted but only interpretable, systems" should be taken *cum grano salis*. It may be that this is so for the calculus, but it works on analyzed languages, i.e., on systems that are not only interpretable, but in fact already interpreted.

What is sensible as a methodological extrapolation is, however, not sensible when reified into a theoretical position. Even if the advantage of stressing the priority of the negative and differential definitions in the immanent study of language has been proven by the progress in the formal description of language that they have set in motion and accelerated. By neglecting the referential and communicative aspects of language, structuralism and glossematics, according to the standpoint expressed here, are not able to explain how language means something. What has been lost is, to use the metaphors from economics so dear to Saussure, the use value or the purchasing power of language: just as the value of a coin is determined, among other things, by the amount of bread for which it can be exchanged, so the meaning of a linguistic sign is, to use his own examples, determined, among other things, by the bread or the mutton to which it refers.

The heroic attempt to analyze signs without worlds was, in my opinion, doomed to failure from the very beginning because it was founded on a forgetfulness, or rather a "repression," of its presuppositions. It was a valuable enterprise because it enlightened us about the intrasystemic properties of language, but in its unrelenting attempt to isolate what it regards as essential to the sign, its effort to distinguish the wheat from the tares, made it clear the price was too high. Consequently, they force us to rethink the semiotic project. In the next part, this study will expound an alternative point of departure for semiotics.

# PART II,1. SIGN, OBJECT, INTERPRETANT

# II. Sign and Object

For analytical and expository reasons, this chapter is mainly on the sign and its relation to the object. Peirce's conception of the sign is basically triadic, so if we exclude the interpretant as the third element in the sign relation, we are, according to Peirce, not justified in talking of signs. Consequently, it is important to remember that in what is here discussed the interpretant is implicitly present. Furthermore, to describe the relation between sign and object in Peirce means including something on his concept of reality, a concept dependent on his theory of cognition, which is a theory of interpretation. Before describing sign and object, and their relationships, it is, however, useful to know some general features Peirce ascribes to signs.

## 1. The general nature of the sign

> The essential function of a sign is to render inefficient relations efficient. . . . Knowledge in some way renders them efficient; and a sign is something by knowing which we know something more. (8.332)[1]

The passage states what to Peirce is most important in the study of semiotics, namely to explain the communication and growth of knowledge by means of signs. Two points should be made, however: First, Peirce is not primarily concerned with this process in its psychological aspects; on the contrary his thinking contains a strong anti-psychological vein. What interests him is the logic of the process. Second, in Peirce's view signs are not one medium among others to bring about and communicate knowledge. They are the only means of doing so. Peirce continues the above quotation as follows:

---

1. In quoting from *The Collected Papers of Charles Sanders Peirce* I–VIII, the number to the left of the decimal point indicates the volume, whereas the numbers to the right of the decimal point indicate the paragraph. So 8.332 means volume eight, paragraph 332.

With the exception of knowledge, in the present instant, of the contents of
consciousness in that instant (the existence of which knowledge is open to
doubt) all our thought and knowledge is by signs. A sign therefore is an
object which is in relation to its object on the one hand and to an interpretant on the other, in such a way as to bring the interpretant into a
relation to the object, corresponding to its own relation to the object. (8.332)

Because Peirce himself doubts the existence of a knowledge unme-
diated by signs, and because it is hard to see how such a knowledge
could be communicated both within a single mind and between minds,
we conclude that to Peirce the sign function is a necessary precondition of any knowledge whatsoever.

We understand the generality and inclusiveness of Peirce's sign
concept by the number of different phenomena considered as signs:
"Sign in general [is] a class which includes pictures, symptoms, words,
sentences, books, libraries, signals, orders of command, microscopes,
legislative representatives, musical concertos, performances of these,"
(Ms. 634, 1909: 18).[2] This inclusiveness has consequences for his approach to language. In contradistinction to the sign concept of continental structuralism (Saussure, Hjelmslev), defining the sign as an immanent solidarity between two formal entities (an element of expression and one of content), Peirce sees signs as elements in a signifying
process. One of his best (and most often quoted) definitions of the sign
runs as follows:

A sign, or representamen, is something which stands to somebody for something in some respect or capacity, It addresses somebody, that is, creates in
the mind of that person an equivalent sign, or perhaps a more developed
sign. That sign which it creates I call the interpretant of the first sign. The
sign stands for something, its object. It stands for that object, not in all
respects, but in reference to a sort of idea, which I have sometimes called
the ground of the representation. (2.228)

One of Peirce's most interesting divisions of signs for the study of
language is according to their relationship to their dynamical objects
(cf. below). He divides them into icons, indices, and symbols. An icon
characteristically  has qualities in common with the object that it de-

2. In quoting from the unpublished manuscripts the manuscript number and
date, according to the Robin-Catalogue (Robin 1967) is given. I follow the
pagination made by scholars from the Institute for Studies in Pragmatism/
(ISP), Texas Tech University, Lubbock, Texas.

notes (i.e., similarity). An index is in a real relation to its object (smoke as a sign of fire). A symbol is "determined by its object in that the thought which is determined by the symbol represents the symbol to be determined by its object" (Ms.. 612, 1908: 47). This may not be phrased elegantly, but it is a precise way of stating the conventional characters of symbols because their reference to objects is mediated by an "abstract thought," i.e., a convention of interpretation which is valid within a given linguistic community.

Language is mainly symbolic, but its indexical and iconic features are essential to its ability to convey meaning. The indexical element of language is connected to its referential function, its being about something (Peirce seems to regard self-reference as derivative and probably rightly so); and in addition to the total indexical functioning of an utterance, certain word classes, such as proper names, pronouns, and prepositions, have a specific deictic signification. The iconic element of language is double: First, Peirce regards syntax as iconic, and although it is sometimes objected that the number of different syntactical ways of expressing the same proposition makes the iconicity of language illusory, it still remains an open question whether there are basic iconic elements in language, at least in its deep structure. Second, Peirce's icons are necessary for conveying ideas, i.e., the association of a word (or utterance) with a mental image. Just as he indicates word classes are predominantly indexical, so he indicates verbs are iconic: "A verb by itself signifies a mere dream, an imagination unattached to any particular occasion. It calls up in the mind an icon" (3.459). I will return to the indexical and iconic aspects of language later, because I need to clarify five more aspects of Peirce's analysis of language in terms of signs before describing the signifying process in greater detail.

The first aspect is Peirce's insistence on language as form, as a system of types rather than a collection of tokens. In a letter he states that a "'word' is a mere possible form to which an audible sound, visible shape, or other sensible objects may conform" (L. 366, to cousin Jo, 26 June 1909). This point of view is illustrated in another manuscript:

These three lines *the* do not constitute the word the. For these quite different lines **THE** have the same relation to one and the same single word; and so do these *THE* and so do a pair of sounds that one might utter; and so do rattling sounds of lengths like this · · · · · · -

. . . These are different modes of utterance of one selfsame word. Three marks or three sounds which are but in a single place at a single instance of time is a singular instance of the word. (Ms. 280, 1905: 81)

The reason this quotation is so interesting is that it became the standard argument of structural linguistics, as seen for instance in Hjelmslev's declaration that there is no necessary connection between sound and language, and consequently that linguistics should be a study of linguistic form. In another place Peirce comes even closer to a modern linguistic point of view:

Consider, for example, the word "red." I mean the word "red" in that sense in which it is one and the same word, however often it be pronounced, and whether quite correctly or not. It has its being exclusively in governing the articulation (I leave writing out of account for simplicity) and apprehension of Anglo-Saxons. The pronunciation varies enormously, the r from the grassouillée sound that most Frenchmen give to it, or did in my day, to the sound which is attained by so much labor in the Comédie française, to the semi-articulate r of most of us, and to the "wred" of some people, the e also ranging over considerable variety, and finally the d being either of two sounds which are carefully distinguished in some languages, the dental d of the Latin races, and our aveolar d, and even an Arabic      Dhêd or      dhâ,[3] if pronounced explosively, would be tolerated. All the variation[s] are of the being of the word, for other, much smaller, departures from the average pronunciation would render the vocable quite unintelligible. (Ms. 908, 1905: 14-15)[4]

This analysis, by Peirce called logical decomposition, reads like a paragraph from a modern textbook on phonology. Compare for instance Peirce's analysis with the following from Hjelmslev:

There is in English a phoneme which I may symbolize by the letter r or by the name a:ə. In Standard English usage, this phoneme is mostly symbolized in pronunciation by one single roll or by a fricative sound produced by the tip of the tongue, and accompanied by voice. In other English usages it is symbolized otherwise, e.g. in Scotland by several rolls of the tongue, in Northumberland by a uvular fricative. These differences in usage are allowed by the English norm, because the norm allows any symbolization which does not entail confusion with other phonemes which by the English system are required to be kept apart from r. If you pronounced the English r unvoiced, saying rait, or if you pronounced it as x, saying xait, you would be able to do this without confusing it with any other phoneme, and con-

3. Peirce is probably thinking of the two Arabic letters      dâd and      za.
4. I am grateful to Christian Kloesel for giving the date of Ms. 908.

sequently you would for that reason not be in contradiction to the English norm, but only to the English usage. On the other hand, if you pronounced *r* in the same way as you pronounce the English phoneme *l* there would be confusion, and you would be in contradiction to the norm. (Hjelmslev [1937] 1973: 158-159)

Two decisive differences exist, however, between the sign concept of structural linguistics and that of Peirce, because Peirce includes the object (that to which the sign refers) in his concept, and, this is the second point, he connects form to communication. In one place he defines the sign simply  as "a Medium for the communication of a Form" (Ms.. 793, 1906: 2). A little later he explains his idea:

> That which is communicated from the Object through the Sign to the Interpretant is a Form; that is to say, it is nothing like an existent, but is a power, is the fact that something would happen under certain conditions. This Form is really embodied in the object, meaning that the conditional relation which constitutes the form is true of the Form as it is in the object. In the sign it is embodied only in a representative sense, meaning that whether by virtue of some real modification of the Sign, or otherwise, the Sign becomes endowed with the power of communicating it to an interpretant. It may be in the interpretant directly as it is in the Object, or it may be in the Interpretant dynamically as behavior of the Interpretant (this happens when a military officer uses the sign "Halt!" or "Forward march!" and his men simply obey him, perhaps automatically); or it may be in the Interpretant only representatively. (Ms. 793, 1906: 2-4)[5]

Note that the concept of form in this context (Ms. 793), although similar to the one in Ms. 280, is related to the content, not to the expression of the sign. We need not discuss the relevance for philosophical realism of the idea of the form as literally being embodied in the object, but we understand the idea of the sign conveying a form to the interpretant in relation to Peirce's analysis of the iconic element in language and other sign systems. One of his definitions of the symbol clearly brings this out: "A Symbol is a sign naturally fit to declare that the set of objects which is denoted by whatever set of indices may be in certain ways attached to it is represented by an icon associated with it" (2.295). The privileged position of the icon in Peirce's semiotics is in my opinion connected with his theory of perception (cf. below).

---

5. No doubt this quotation echoes philosophical analysis of Antiquity and the ideas of the schoolmen, cf. Boler's fine study (Boler 1963).

The defining of the sign as a "Medium for the communication of a Form" implies a third aspect of the general characters of the sign, namely its dynamic, or actional nature. Semiosis is "an action or influence, which is, or involves a cooperation of three subjects, such as a sign, its object and its interpretant" (5.494), and signhood itself does not exist outside this triadic action. This means that a sign is a dynamic and mediating relationship between at least three interdependent positions, through which it produces meaning.

The fourth and fifth features in Peirce's thinking about signs are his insistence that the uttering of signs implies a purpose, and thereby presupposes a system of values. That obliges an interpreter to expound the purposiveness of the text. Abundant evidence exists in Peirce's writings that the concept of purpose is basic to his philosophy, and it is even connected with his cosmology and religious thought.

He makes clear the relevance of purpose to this study when he defines the so-called universal law of mind: "Mind has its universal mode of action, namely, by final causation," and "being governed by a purpose or other final cause is the very essence of the psychical phenomenon in general" (1.269). Peirce's concept of mind is broad, but the same is true for human thought:

A thought is a purpose and that in order to perform the reflexion necessary to the straightening out the threads of thought and laying them orderly and parallel will consist mainly or at least first of all in defining to ourselves what the purpose is a purpose to bring about and what use, theoretical or practical, it is designed to subserve; and that is Pragmatism. (Ms. 478, 1903: 159)

Purpose entails the concept of goal or end, and implies a striving to obtain it. That is why Peirce can define purpose as "an operative desire" (1.205). The limits of this study do not allow an exposition of the relation between instinct, desire, and purpose, but the subject is important to his philosophy. One point, however, immediately bears on text interpretation, and this is that purpose, end, and desire presuppose norms and values. Just as Peirce holds that the explanation of human behavior presupposes the "law of purpose" (7.369), and consequently that meaning analysis implies reference to a purpose (5.175), he also claims that meaning and value are intimately related:

Let us note that meaning is something allied in its nature to value. I do not know whether we ought rather to say that meaning is the value of a word —

a phrase often used – or whether we ought to say that the value of anything to us is what it means for us – which we also sometimes hear said. Suffice it to say that the two ideas are near together. Now value is the measure of desirability; and desire always refers to the future. That leads us to inquire whether meaning does not always refer to the future. (Ms. 599, 1902: 24)

Purpose may of course be understood in the ordinary sense as the purpose of some particular communication, but for Peirce signs have a more general purpose which he expresses in this way:

> What we call a "fact" is something having the structure of a proposition, but supposed to be an element of the very universe itself. The purpose of every sign is to express "fact," and by being joined with other signs, to approach as nearly as possible to determining an interpretant which would be the perfect Truth, the absolute Truth, and as such (at least, we may use this language) would be the very Universe. (NEM 1976: IV, 239)

Symbols in particular, being conventional signs, are especially closely connected with the idea of purpose:

> It will be observed that an argument is a symbol which separately mon-strates (in any way) its purposed interpretant. Owing to a symbol being essential[ly] a sign only by virtue of its being interpretable as such, the idea of a purpose is not entirely separable from it. The symbol, by the very definition of it, has an interpretant in view. Its very meaning is intended. Indeed, a purpose is precisely the interpretant of a symbol. But the con-clusion of an argument is a specially monstrated interpretant, singled out from among the possible interpretants. It is, therefore, of its nature single, although not necessarily simple. (NEM 1976: IV, 244)

This conception of signs as fulfilling the purpose of expressing facts and determining the truth (of the very universe) may indeed seem impractically visionary. On second thought, however, it is reasonable, because signs are certainly means by which man structures his life-world and makes assertions about its characters, and the different ways in which they are interrelated. The objective of inquiry and argumentation is, after all, to obtain true knowledge!

According to the above a sign is a medium for the communication of a form by means of a triadic action involving purpose and value. The triad itself consists of the sign, its object, and its interpretant and their interrelations; therefore, for a clearer understanding of sign ac-tion, semiosis, we now need to analyze the element and relation of the sign itself.

## 2. The sign as representamen

Peirce uses the word *sign* in both a broad and a narrow sense. In the broad sense, which is the most important, *sign* is used to designates the triadic relation between sign, object, and interpretant; in the narrow sense *sign* denotes one element, the *sign* or *representamen* within the triad. Figure 13 illustrates the double use of the word *sign*:

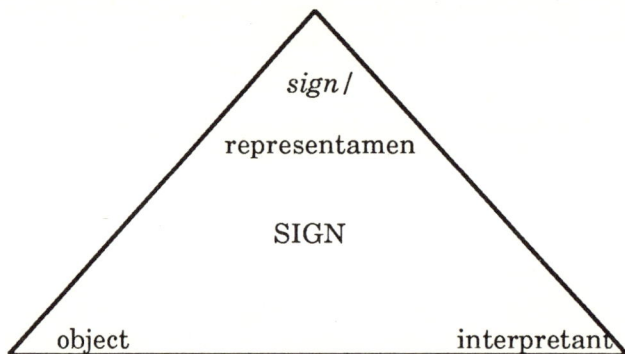

Fig. 13

SIGN denotes the relational and functional use of the word. Whereas in many respects it is similar to the term *sign-vehicle* suggested by Morris (Morris 1971: 96), *sign* is the mediating phenomenon that relates object and interpretant to itself and to each other.

Sign, in the narrow sense which concerns us here, does not denote a class of objects that have distinctive characteristics or features in common except for their *representative function*. Peirce equates the concept of *representation* with both *mind* (Ms. 477, 1903: 19) and *thought* (1.538), and, consequently, the following definition pinpoints what, in Peirce's view, is common to all signs:

> A Sign is a Cognizable that, on the one hand, is so determined (i.e., specialized, *bestimmt*,) by something *other than itself*, called its Object, while, on the other hand, it so determines some actual or potential Mind, the determination whereof I term the Interpretant created by the Sign, that that Interpreting Mind is therein determined mediately by the Object. (8.177)

Since "Cognizable" means something that can be cognized, anything that may influence a mind is, at least potentially, a sign. Page 56 quotes Peirce's enumeration of different kinds of signs (Ms. 634). Another enumeration (from "On a New List of Categories," 1867) is as follows:

> a word represents a thing to the conception in the mind of the hearer, a portrait represents the person for whom it is intended to the conception of recognition, a weathercock represents the direction of the wind to the conception of him who understands it, a barrister represents his client to the judge and jury whom he influences. (1.553)

Leaving aside for the moment questions concerning the interpreting mind (cf. chapter V), the sign's functional and relational nature becomes apparent the moment we begin to manipulate the examples :

| a word | REPRESENTS | a thing | TO | the mind |
| a portrait | REPRESENTS | a person | TO | another person |
| a weathercock | REPRESENTS | the wind | TO | the one who understands it |
| a barrister | REPRESENTS | his client | TO | the judge and the jury |

The general schema of this structure will thus be:

> A represents       B       to       C

A is a position (actually a *First*) in a triadic relation. This structure can also be written simply as a trivalent rheme:

> — represents — to —

Although Peirce's classification of signs into *qualisigns, sinsigns,* and *legisigns* (that classification will be considered shortly) distinguishes between the characters of different classes of signs, the most important feature of his sign concept is its positional character. A sign is not defined by any inherent features, but by its capacity for representation and by its position in the signifying process (cf. below p. 73).

Peirce often uses *representamen* as a *terminus technicus* for sign (in the narrow sense of the word), but in some places Peirce distinguishes the sign from the representamen, in saying that both signs and representamens convey a notion of something. Yet, he also says, "All signs convey notions to *human minds,* but I know no reason, why every representamen should do so" (1.540). In another place Peirce gives the following example of the distinction between the two concepts:

> A *Sign* is a Representamen with a mental Interpretant. Possibly there may
> be Representamens that are not Signs. Thus, if a sunflower, in turning
> towards the sun, becomes by that very act fully capable, without further
> condition, of reproducing a sunflower which turns in precisely correspond-
> ing ways toward the sun, and of doing so with the same reproductive
> power, the sunflower would become a Representamen of the sun. But
> *thought* is the chief, if not the only, mode of representation. (2.274)

The distinction is here of little practical import, because this study is
about human communication, but in general, the example is fascinating, because it illustrates the transmission of information through
a genetic coding. The distinction between representamens and signs
on the grounds that the latter convey notions to human minds can,
however, be more clearly formulated in the *icon, index, symbol*
distinction (cf. chapter III).

The quotation about the word *the* (cf. p. 58) makes another distinction essential, one between *replica* and *representamen*. The replica is
the concrete, single instance of the of the sign, whereas the sign considered as a representamen is of the nature of a rule or habit. Peirce's
distinction between replica and representamen covers the distinction
he also uses between *token* and *type,* and that between *expression
substance* and *expression form* which is used in structural linguistics.
The distinction between replica and representamen can be correlated
with the ontological distinction between two modes of being, brute
existence and habit or law, and between *Secondness* and *Thirdness*
within his categorial analysis (cf. p. 71) of element of experience. The
point, for Peirce, as well as for structural linguistics (for instance), is
that the use of most signs, and definitely of linguistic symbols, is not
essentially changed by individuals, but is a rule-governed activity
resting on acquired habits.

The scope of Peirce's sign definition, including words, libraries,
pictures, microscopes, and barristers, sets it off from the usual linguistic definition of a sign, and plays havoc with the traditional distinction between *sign* and *text*. Within linguistics a sign is normally
defined as a minimal unit of signification combining an expression
with a content. For instance, the expression "Peter's hat" is analyzed
as containing three signs: "Peter"; a sign of genitive, *in casu* "s"; and

"hat." Since a text would normally be defined as a concrete manifestation of a combination of signs, "Peter's hat" would be a text
combining three signs. Furthermore, linguistics carries out analysis of
language below the sign level. On the expression plane of language the
linguistic chain is divided into syllables, phonemes, and distinctive
features, and on the content plane linguists attempt a similar analysis
(although, in my opinion, in vain) by dividing the content into semantic markers or features (sometimes called semes). The possibility
of carrying out such an analysis is due to the specific structure of
language, its so-called *double articulation,* i.e., the first partition of
the linguistic chain divides into *significative* elements and the second
into *distinctive* elements (cf. Martinet 1964: 22-24).

Other kinds of signs are not necessarily characterized by a double
articulation: a painting or the behavior of a barrister do not allow a
logical decomposition (cf. p. 58) as rigorous as the linguistic analysis of
the constitutive elements of the expression plane. The generality of
Peirce's semiotics prevents him from transferring a conception of the
sign and a form of analysis appropriate to language to other signs or
sign systems. Even within linguistic signs Peirce calls both the word
*man* and a whole work of fiction such as Shakespeare's *Hamlet* a sign.
While he distinguishes between signs of different complexity (cf. the
*rheme, dicent, argument* distinction, IV, 5), the essential function of a
sign, of something in its capacity as a sign, is independent of its
decomposability or indecomposability, and of the nature of its constituent elements. There are good reasons for this holistic approach to
the sign concept. Although *Hamlet,* for example, is composed of words,
and even if it is decomposible in a certain sense, into less complex
signs, into words, it is nevertheless a work of literature that as a
whole represents an imaginary world, a fictional universe of discourse.

## 3. Qualisign, sinsign, legisign

Peirce divides signs or representamens into *qualisigns, sinsigns,* and
*legisigns* (the so-called first trichotomy of signs, cf. 2.243). To understand his partition it is necessary to consider briefly his categories, his
phenomenological (or as he liked to call it himself *phaneroscopic*)
analysis. The *phaneron* (or phenomenon) he defines as "the collective
total of all that is in any way or in any sense present to the mind,

quite regardless of whether it corresponds to any real thing or not" (1.284).

The origin of Peirce's categorical analysis was his study of Kant (cf. Murphey 1961: 55-97), and to a great extent his own division of the categories into *Firstness, Secondness,* and *Thirdness* is an attempt to reduce and replace Kant's twelve categories. While neither the historical relations between Peirce and Kant nor the epistemological problems concerning Peirce's own three categories lie within the scope of this book, it is necessary to describe briefly his three categories to understand his semiotics.

The different ways Peirce exemplifies the categories help define the general thrust of his division of the categories of appearance. The first category, *Firstness,* he most often identifies as *quality, but* also names *flavor* and *feeling.* The second category, *Secondness,* he often exemplifies by *reaction,* but also by *occurrence, thing,* and *subject of force.* The third category, *Thirdness,* he calls *representation, mediation, meaning,* and *mind.*

*Firstness* is "the idea of that which such as it is regardless of anything else" (5.66). Peirce's favorite example is an unanalyzed *quality,* or a feeling. Firstness is a possibility, not something actually existing, called a *may-be.* Firstness is related to spontaneity, originality, and freedom, and is also called the monadic element of the world.

The nature of Firstness makes it difficult to exemplify. One of Peirce's own examples is the invitation to imagine the perfume of a damask rose without the consciousness of smelling it and without any sense of time and change. This would amount to quality as it is in itself, or as Peirce says, quality as "self-essence, or something which is as it is by and in itself alone" (L 75, 1902: Cr 134).

*Secondness* "is the conception of being relative to, the conception of reaction with, something else" (6.32). In contradistinction to firstness, secondness is the *actual* or *existent.* It is exemplified by *force* and *resistance,* and individual things and facts are characterized by secondness. The opposition between ego and non-ego and the concept of will is related to it, and it is said to be dyadic. Firstness is an essential element of Secondness; Secondness cannot be thought without firstness.

*Thirdness* "is the idea of that which is such as it is being a Third, or Medium, between a Second and its First. That is to say, it is *Representation* as an element of the Phenomenon" (5.66). It is exemplified by *law,* and by *thought, continuity,* and *growth.* The best example of the triadic relation is, according to Peirce, the sign. Because thirdness has the existence of a *law* or a *type* it is a *would-be.* Although like firstness it has to be instanced in an object or as a relation between objects to exist, it has nevertheless real being.

Peirce uses the common sense conception of a thing as a starting point to explain the difference between the three categories:

> Remembering that by *the universal phenomenon,* I mean *everything which has got into the mind in any way whatever, including every fiction and false notion,* anyone can without difficulty see that there is an idea of a thing as it is in itself with certain qualities, however occult, which do not consist in its actual relation to anything else. In the next place, things are related to one another in pairs. That is, they are at distances from one another, attract or repel one another, etc. In the third place, finally, *there are things which represent other things to some purposing mind; that is, they act as substitutes for those other things for some purpose; that is, again, they render the object represented available for the purpose.* (L75, 1902: Cr 141-142)

The following diagram (Fig. 14) is a useful summary of Peirce's ideas about the three points of view from which to study the elements of experience. It is built on his description in the *Carnegie Application* (L 75, 1902: Cr 140-142).

A *qualisign* is related to firstness (being a sign, which is a third, a qualisign is a firstness of thirdness), and Peirce's own example is "a feeling of red in so far as it is a sign" (2.254). Since firstness is characterized by both possibility and unrelatedness (because firstness is monadic), it is not easy to see how we should ever come across a pure qualisign. Peirce admits as much: "It cannot actually act as a sign until it is embodied; but the embodiment has nothing to do with its character as a sign" (2.244). Consequently, a qualisign is a sign whose relevant aspect is a positive quality.

Suppose a person, deaf from birth, starts to study music by reading scores. Eventually, that person might in certain respects become an outstanding musicologist. Unable to hear the music performed, he concentrates on the structural features of the written texts. It might be argued that he has no experience with music at all, that he does not know the subject, because what he has studied are the *legisigns* (cf. below) of a notational system used for certain purposes by musicians and musicologists, and not music. But the tones in a performed piece

|              | Firstness                                  | Secondness     | Thirdness                       |
|--------------|--------------------------------------------|----------------|---------------------------------|
| 1) Qualities | Quality                                    | Reaction       | Mediation                       |
| 2) Subjects  | Quale                                      | Relate         | Representation                  |
| 3) Mind      | Feeling (immediate consciousness)          | Sense of fact  | Conception (Mind strictly)      |

Fig. 14

of music are embodied qualisigns, because what is relevant are their positive qualities (in addition they might also be considered replicas of legisigns, because musical notes form a conventional system). For instance, when a piano teacher plays a sequence of notes in a certain way, and the pupil tries to imitate the teacher's way of playing, the pupil is trying to play the sequence of notes in such a way that his performance embodies the same qualities as the teacher's.

*Sinsigns* are, according to Peirce "an actual existing thing or event which is a sign" (2.245). Every sign we actually experience is a sinsign. The performances by teacher and pupil mentioned above are actually sinsigns that embody qualisigns, and this is in accordance with Peirce's general notion that a sinsign embodies one or more qualisigns. The prefix *sin* is intended by Peirce "to mean 'being only once' (as in *single, simple,* Latin *semel,* etc." [2.245]). Consequently, it is debatable whether a token (or a replica), as for instance the word *the* repeated about twenty-five times on a single page, qualifies as a sinsign. The eminent Peirce scholar David Savan denies that this is the case. He says: "A sinsign's singularity as an encountered thing or occurrence must be essential to it as a sign – must be that which makes it a sign" (Savan 1976: 12). He further offers an example of what to him would qualify as a sinsign:

> The samples of moon rock being analyzed by lunar scientists are sinsigns. Every singularity and peculiarity of the moon rock is recorded, analysed, and used as a clue or sign of the structure and history of the moon, the

earth, and the solar system. Whenever some object or event is used as a clue to some other object or event past, present, or spatially at some remove, this clue is a sinsign. A clue like the moon rock is in fact a collection of clues. Every peculiarity of the rock, every molecule of it, is significant as a possible clue to the past. (Savan 1976: 12)

An objection to David Savan's moon rock example might be that the only reason why a particular rock is so interesting is its availability; otherwise, it is in fact primarily interesting as a general specimen or sample of moon rocks. Another example of a sinsign where the occurrence in itself makes it unique might be the print of naked feet in the sand on Robinson Crusoe's island. Its very appearance is the outstanding relevant fact. Peirce states:

> A *Legisign* is a law that is a sign. This law is usually established by men. Every conventional sign is a legisign (but not conversely). It is not a single object, but a general type which, it has been agreed, shall be significant. Every legisign signifies through an instance of its application, which may be termed a *Replica* of it. . . . The Replica is a sinsign. Thus, every Legisign requires Sinsigns. But these are not ordinary Sinsigns, such as are peculiar occurrences that are regarded as significant. Nor would the Replica be significant if it were not for the law which renders it so. (2.246)

This quotation justifies David Savan's plea for distinguishing between sinsigns as singular sign events, and sinsigns as just any concretely manifested signs, as replicas.

Language is the most prominent example of conventional legisigns, but there are also legisigns that are unconventional. In a brilliant article, "Life among the Legisigns" (1982), Thomas L. Short argues that the non-conventional legisigns Peirce mentions, but does not specify, might be exemplified by the genetically programmed colors and mating behavior of male birds or by the dance of the bees (Short 1982: 297-298). These exemplifications are convincing because they are law-or rule-governed signs that are not conventional, in the sense of arbitrary, acquired by learning, or like language at least partly consciously learned. Each genetically programmed communication system fulfills the two requirements essential for qualifying as legisigns: it is "a law that renders it significant"; the existent characters or behaviors are replicas of the same general type. Short points to another merit of these examples: "Consciousness and intentionality are not essential to the existence, replication, or interpretation of legi-

signs. What is essential is a purpose or goal, whether consciously
entertained or not, that is shared by sign-replicator and replica-in-
terpreters . . ." (Short 1982: 298). He goes on to compare the legisigns
of animal communication with human speech, and argues "that the
distinctive power of human speech is not a supernatural gift but is a
remarkable development of basic principles found elsewhere in nature." He sums up his argument as follows:

> There are signs throughout nature, but there are legisigns only where
> there is life, and legisigns always exist in order to serve the purposes of
> living things. Conventional legisigns, created and manipulated by indi-
> viduals in ways that constantly produce new meanings, are distinctive –
> perhaps constitutive – of the form of consciousness found in human life.
> (Short 1982: 298-299)

By arguing in favor of a continuity between natural and cultural semiosis, Short successfully fills in an empty place in Peirce's classification of signs according to the first trichotomy, and what is more important, correlates sign action with purpose and goal-directedness on a
subhuman level of semiosis. Short's examples also indicate that legisigns only function as legisigns if so interpreted. The mating colors of
the male bird become a legisign because the female bird responds to
them, or tends to respond to them, in a specific way. A legisign, therefore, is not only a rule of replication but also a rule of interpretation.
The next question, therefore, is the kind of legisign the mating colors
constitute. Are they indexical or symbolic, or both? (cf. III, 7).

The distinction between qualisign, sinsign, and legisign does not
mean actual signs can be classified exclusively under one label. First,
existing signs will be sinsigns, either in the emphatic sense, or in the
more attenuated sense of being replicas of legisigns. Second, classifying a sign as a qualisign means paying attention to the intrinsic
qualities that are embodied in the sign in question. Third, the being of
a legisign is functional. Rather than considering a legisign as existing
in some Platonic heaven, we should regard it as a dominant aspect of
an actual sign that can be replicated. In his *Logic Notebook,* Peirce has
tried to clarify the distinction. Note, however, that Peirce constantly
experimented with terminology, so, here in 1906, qualisign is called
*tuone,* sinsign *token,* and legisign *type:*

> As to the Matter of the Sign itself it is either a Tuone or a Token or a Type.
> The word Tuone is a blend of Tone and Tune. It means a quality of feeling

which is significant, whether it be simple like a Tone or complex like a Tune. But the latter is not *pure* feeling. By a Token, I mean an existing thing or an actual historical event which serves as a Sign. By a Type, I mean a general form which can be repeated indefinitely and is in all its repetitions one and the same sign. The distinction between a Type and a Token is obvious. There may be some confusion between the Tuone and the Type, they may, however, be distinguished in various ways. In the first place (a Type) is absolutely identical in all its *Instances* or embodiments, while a Tuone cannot have any identity, it has only similarity. Thus the sound of any vowel will be slightly different every two times it is pronounced and in so far it is so, it is two Tuones. But any two vowels in so far as they are alike are the same Tuone, in the only sense in which there can be any sameness to a Tuone. Anything then that could conceivably be made absolutely definite, bearing in mind that no things can be exactly alike in any quality whatever, cannot be a Tuone. Another test is that a Tuone though it may be composed of many ingredients is, like a chemical compound of many elements, perfectly homogenous and structureless in effect, while a Type, though it may be undecomposable, must be more or less complex in its relations. (Logic Notebook, entry of 1906, April 2, Ms. 339d, 1906: 533-534)

These notes from Peirce's "mental laboratory" are rich in both implications and problems. It seems to me, however, that deciding whether a sign should be regarded as a qualisign (tuone) or a legisign (type) depends on the purpose of the interpretation, whether the subjects of investigation are the invariant and repeatable characters, or the individual and variant. This implies that from one point of view an interpretation may be disregarded as a variant, and from another point of view as invariant.

Certain variants concerning the pronunciation of a given language may be considered insignificant if the purpose of an investigation is the description of the language as a system in contradistinction to other languages. If the purpose of an investigation were to describe a dialect or sociolect within a language, then those disregarded variants, or tuones might be considered as invariants, or types. Another distinction in the quotation is worth noting. The tuone is said to be homogeneous and structureless *in effect*, but complex in its *relations*. This follows Peirce's categorical analysis, because firstness is correlated with unity of quality or feeling, whereas thirdness is bound up with mediation. Peirce illustrates the first trichotomy as follows:

Take for example a given melody, say "The Last Rose of Summer." Considered as to its structure it is a Type; but considered as a whole in its esthetic effect, which is not composed of one part due to one note and another to another, it is a Tuone. As ordinarily conceived it is a Tuone, slightly different however every time it is sung, but from the point of view of contrapoint, it is absolutely the same every time it is rendered with substantial correctness (though it be a trifle out of time and tune) it is a Type. But any one singing of it is neither Tuone nor Type but a Token. (ibid. 534)

Peirce's example is significant, because he chooses an aesthetic object to illustrate the distinction between quali -, sin -, and legisign. The importance of the evanescent qualisign that is so hard to grasp lies, among other things, in its aesthetic character. Peirce explicitly defines the aesthetically good as follows:

In the light of the doctrine of categories I should say that an object, to be esthetically good, must have a multitude of parts so related to one another as to impart a positive simple immediate quality to their totality; and whatever does this is, in so far, esthetically good, no matter what the particular quality of the total may be. (5.132)

In other words the aesthetic object fuses, so to speak, the relations between its component parts into a unique and immediate quality. Peirce states, for instance, that "the tragedy of King Lear has its Firstness, its flavor *sui genesis*" (1.531). This means, according to Peirce, that the aesthetic dimension of a phenomenon is categorically a first, but since it is based on relation and mediation, it is the firstness of thirdness.

It should be clear from the presentation of the sign "in itself," that the indivisible triadic structure imposes itself even on the analysis of the pole of the representamen within the sign. Not only is the definition of the representamen positional, but also the division of the sign according to its own characters is, in fact, relational. The differences between qualisign, sinsign, and legisign, owing to their respective relational character, is monadic, dyadic, and triadic. Another outstanding feature of the Peircean description of the sign concept, which appears even in the analysis of the first trichotomy, is the importance of function and purpose. Since the sign, or representamen, is a cognizable conveyor of meaning only by virtue of its relation to an object and an interpretant, it is necessary, next, to explain these elements of the sign.

## 4. The objects of the sign

The formal definition of the object of the sign is positional, as in the case of the sign itself (or representamen). Just as the sign is a *first,* the object is a *second,* a correlate related to the representamen. Secondness, in Peirce's analysis of the categories, is characterized by the dyadic relationship of action and reaction, and so is the relationship between sign and object. On the one hand the sign indicates its object forces the attention of the interpreter to it, and on the other the object influences or determines the sign.

The object of a sign may be an almost bewildering number of different phenomena. Peirce lists the following possibilities:

The Objects – for a Sign may have any number of them – may each be a single known existing thing or thing believed formerly to have existed or expected to exist, or a collection of such things, or a known quality or relation or fact, which single Object may be a collection, or whole of parts, or it may have some other mode of being, such as some act permitted whose being does not prevent its negation from being equally permitted, or something of a general nature desired, required, or invariably found under certain general circumstances. (2.232)

This variety is explained by Peirce's use of the term *object* to denote "anything that comes before thought or the mind in any usual sense" (SS 1977: 69). From this use it follows that the object, or objects, of a sign may have any imaginable mode of being; from a certain narrow perspective ontological considerations of the object are, therefore, not worth pursuing. Considering the fact that we may use signs to refer both to mythical beings such as Zeus and Aphrodite and to members of our families this claim seems reasonable. At this point, Peirce goes on to distinguish between two different kinds of objects.

We have seen that it is necessary to distinguish between the replica of a conventional sign and the representamen, the replica as the material entity that confronts us as an existent object and the representamen as the type embodied in it. So, also, according to Peirce, it is necessary to distinguish between the *immediate object* within the sign and the *dynamical object* outside it. Immediate object means the object as it represented in and by a given sign, whereas the dynamical (or dynamic or dynamoid) object is the object which in some way determines the sign.

A portrait represents a picture of a person, and in this sense the immediate object is the object as represented *in* the sign (e.g., a face as it is represented in color and shape). If, however, the person represented exists (or has existed) independently of the picture (and the word *portrait* seems to imply that this is the case), then that person would be the dynamical object of the portrait. If the artist has any skill, the immediate object, the object represented in the portrait, will be recognizable. People who know the model personally may, for instance, recognize the portrait as a picture of that person. The portrait will, however, represent only certain characteristics of the model as the artist saw them during a definite period of time. Furthermore, the painter's artistic vision and technique will influence the representation of the model. In this case, the immediate object represented in the sign might serve as a clue to discover its dynamical object, since someone might identify the model in question by virtue of knowing the portrait.

The concept of the object is bound up with Peirce's theory of knowledge and his analysis of perception. The starting point is his reaction to his reading of Kant. As late as 1911 he says to Lady Welby: "I show just how far Kant was right though even when twisted up in formalism. It is perfectly true that we can never attain a knowledge of things as they are. We can only know their human aspect. But that is all the universe is for us" (SS 1977: 140-141). In accordance with this point of view his famous definition of reality is as follows:

> I was many years ago led to define "real" as meaning *being such as it is, no matter how you, or I, or any man or definite collection of men may think it to be;* where I use the long and awkward phrase in order to avoid all appearance of meaning *independently of human thought.* For obviously, nothing that I or anybody ever can mean can be independent of human thought. That is *real* which men *would* eventually and finally come to think to be absolutely necessary to be thought in order to understand the truth, supposing the existence and advance in knowledge of the human race to be continued without any limitation; though I cannot pretend that I have as distinct an idea of exactly what that means as I could wish. (Ms. 681, 1913: 38-39)

This definition of reality is important to the concept of the two objects of the sign. The immediate object of the sign is the object as it is represented in the context of a single signifying process; the dynamical object, in Peirce's own words, is the object "regardless of any particular aspect of it, the object in such relation as unlimited and final study would show it to be" (8.133).

Peirce holds further that the sign can only indicate the dynamical object by a hint (this hint being the immediate object), and that knowledge of it must come from collateral experience. Thus, in addition to a common universe of discourse, indexical identifications are made possible by a presupposed common universe of action. This is not to say you can only understand and make statements about a contemporary existing world (as literary scholars we would certainly be badly off if that were the case). It means that to be able to understand a text we must refer that text to something known and then must connect it to some social practice or to some natural phenomenon which we can observe or with which we can interact.

Beside the difference between the object as it is represented in a single semiosis, and the object as unlimited study would show it to be, there is another dimension to the distinction between the immediate and the dynamical object: the dynamical object exercises an influence on the sign. Peirce sometimes uses a metaphor to express this difference, saying that "The Object of a Sign is its progenitor, its father. The Dynamical Object is the Natural Father, the Objective Object the putative father" (Ms. 499s, 1906:4). Thus the relation between object and sign is double. On the one hand the dynamical object determines the sign, and on the other the sign, by means of representing the (immediate) object, indicates the dynamical one. The portrait is one example of the double relationship. Another example is the weathercock, which may be depicted in a diagram ( Fig. 15).

For the weathercock to function as a sign of the direction of the wind, it must fulfill three conditions: 1) there has to be wind, 2) the weathercock must function properly, and 3) the viewer must know the right way of interpreting the sign. In general, a sign functions as a sign when these conditions concerning the three poles of the sign hold, and for a certain subclass of indices, or *reagents* such as a weathercock, the dynamical object has to have an actual influence on the sign to make it function.

Although it might seem idle to distinguish between two objects in this case (it is the wind anyway, one could say), the weathercock illustrates an important difference between the dynamical and the immediate object, because the weathercock tells us little about the wind as immediate object. We know only the direction. The wind as

the pointing of
the weathercock

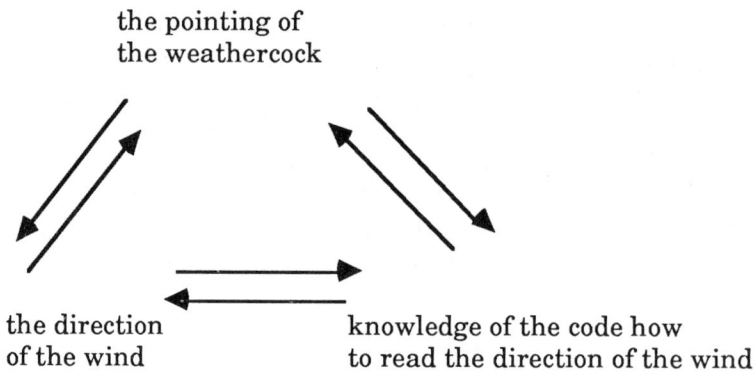

the direction                    knowledge of the code how
of the wind                      to read the direction of the wind

Fig. 15

dynamical object constitutes a subject for further inquiry, through collateral experience and observation of other characteristics such as its force and velocity.

Since Peirce in almost every place links the idea of the object with experience and observation, his ideas on perception are relevant to a more profound understanding of what is involved in this pole of the sign.

The concept immediately relevant to the question of the object of the sign is that of the *percept (res percepta)*. It is "the object perceived in a single act of perceiving" (Ms. 693b, 1904: 98). The percept to Peirce has four distinctive features: (1) it contributes something positive to knowledge; (2) it intrudes itself upon the perceiver, compels him to acknowledge its presence, and resists his attempts to dispose of it; (3) it is direct, i.e., the external object exerts a force on or acts on the perceiver: (4) and at the same time the force exerted by the object is the result of an inferential (and unconscious) synthesis. Peirce's characterization of the percept is controversial, because it is sometimes objected that (3) and (4) contradict each other or, at least, that taken together they are ambiguous. Although it is partly determined by a learning process, the development of habits, there is no contradiction, in claiming that the act of perceiving is just as well determined by external objects, i.e., that it has both a physical and a mental aspect.

The percept is regarded as the base and starting point of knowledge, because as knowledge starts from single percepts it develops to the study of single things (sometimes a thing is called a *generalized percept* or a *composite photography of percepts*), then parts, sets, collections of existent things, and finally classes of possibilities (see Ms. 693b, 1904: 113-115). Besides, the percept is said to leave the perceiver with a "powerful imaginative habit," the memory of the percept. In this way, in addition to the percept proper, our images come from imagination, memories, and modified reproductions of percepts.

Since the definition of the object of the semiosis depends on the definition of the percept, it is useful to explicate Peirce's position with regard to the mode of being of the object of perception. In a letter to Augustus Strong in 1904, he explicitly defines the percept. He writes:

> As to the direct object of perception, the percept, it is true that it does not possess fully developed reality; but it is the very existing thing itself, independent of and exterior to the mind. For to say that it *exists,* means only that it reacts. Now the percept forces itself upon me, in spite of all direct effort to dismiss it. So, it satisfies the definition of an *existent.* It is independent of the mind in as much as its characters do not depend upon my will to have them so and so. But that it is only known in its relation to my organs is obvious enough. That in no wise contradicts the independence of it, unless one were nominalist enough to deny that independent objects can be members of pairs of which pairs something is true. For a relation is nothing but a fact concerning a set of objects. That the percept is *exterior* to the mind; since, making due allowance for different points of view, another observer, or a photographic camera will show the same thing. (L 427, 1904: 20-21)

One important consequence of Peirce's position is that it is meaningless to postulate an object that has no relation whatsoever to human intelligence, and Peirce's criticism of Kant is founded precisely on reflections of that kind (as expressed in the letter quoted above).

Even if the percept is also exterior to the mind, in the sense of being created by physical activity from outside the body, unlike, for instance, a figment of imagination, it is not extra-semiotic. On the contrary, the percept is itself of the nature of a sign:

> It is easy to see that the object of sign, that to which it virtually at least professes to be applicable, can itself only be a sign. For example, the object of an ordinary proposition is a generalization from a group of perceptual facts. It represents those facts. These perceptual facts are themselves ab-

stract representatives, through we know not precisely what intermediaries, of the percepts themselves, and these are themselves viewed, and are – if the judgment has any truth – representations, primarily of impressions of sense, ultimately of a dark underlying something, which cannot be specified without its manifesting itself as a sign of something below. There is, we think, and reasonably think, a limit to this, an ultimate reality, like a zero of temperature. But in the nature of things, it can only be approached; it can only be represented. The immediate object which any sign seeks to represent is itself a sign. (Ms. 599, 1902: 35-36)

Although Peirce here seems close to admitting a *"Ding an sich,"* contrary to his general philosophical position, he draws from the description no subjectivist consequences. In another place he describes pragmatism as a thoroughgoing phenomenalism, but, he explains, this means "phenomenalism *aufgehoben."* He goes on to state pragmatism holds that the reader (of his review) actually perceives the very page itself ten inches from his eye, "and that another person, looking over his shoulder, will see the very same object [the page], although from a different angle, and although each sees the real object, not in its entirety, but only as it is related to his own view-point, literal and tropical" (8.187). The justification for his description, Peirce explains, is that it answers all human *purposes,* but (unless you prefer to part company with Peirce), two points have to be resolved. First, even if it were possible to go on dividing the object further into bundles of percepts, etc., the object as existent exerts an influence; in other words, the infinite series of supposed immediate objects have the same infinity as a line drawn upon a piece of paper, i.e., it can be divided into an infinite number of points (at least in the imagination). Second, even if it is possible to push the analysis of the object indefinitely, this does not mean it is impossible to make true statements about something at a given level (e.g., to say that two persons read the same page is true, even if its sub-atomic structure constantly changes, and even if the angle of vision is not the same). Peirce can thus claim, "The immediate object of thought in a true judgment is real" (8.17).

In other places, Peirce describes perception a little differently. The categories' firstness, as it characterizes the percepts, accounts for its positive qualities of sensation, while secondness makes up its compulsory force. In this description the percept is said to be insistent but dumb, appealing to nothing, representing nothing (cf. 7.622). The perceptual judgment, in contradistinction to the percept, contains thirdness. It represents the percept, it functions as its index or symptom, and it asserts something about it (7.630). The perceptual judgment is analytic, and it allows a certain freedom, a certain latitude of interpretation through abstraction and foregrounding of features, that in the percept appears as an unanalyzed whole.

Percept and perceptual judgment in experience are almost inseparable, however, and Peirce even invents a concept to cover them both, the *percipuum*. Furthermore, experience is certainly representational:

> Experience can only mean the total cognitive result of living, and includes interpretations quite as truly as it does the matter of sense. Even more truly, since this matter of sense is a hypothetical something which we never can seize as such, free from all interpretative working over. (7.538)

To try to reconcile these two opposing views on perception, we understand the former description of "sign under sign endlessly" as an account of the acquisition of knowledge, whereas the latter, implying a categorial distinction between the non-semiotic character of the percept and the representational character of the perceptual judgment, is a hypothetical account of the elements of the process that leads to perceptual judgments, i.e., exactly to the starting point of knowledge. Although Peirce insists on the compulsory nature of the percept, he recognizes, nevertheless, that perception (the percipuum) may be controlled by a learning process (cf. 7.648). Even if such a reconciliation might be feasible, however, a certain vacillation exists in Peirce as to the line of demarcation between the non-semiotic and the semiotic in perception.

The next diagram (Fig. 16) summarizes Peirce's view(s) on perception. Imperfect and oversimplified as it certainly is, the diagram should nevertheless give some idea of how Peirce looks on perception. He considers it first to be an inferential process analogous to critical thinking. The chain of inferences up to the formation of *perceptual facts* is, however, beyond control and criticism. The percepts themselves are instantaneously forced upon the mind, and consequently pass so rapidly they cannot be the foundation of conscious inference. The so-called perceptual facts are a kind of "stenographic report" (2.141) of the flow of percepts, and this recollection, or retention, of what has been forced on the mind enables the perceiver to make con-

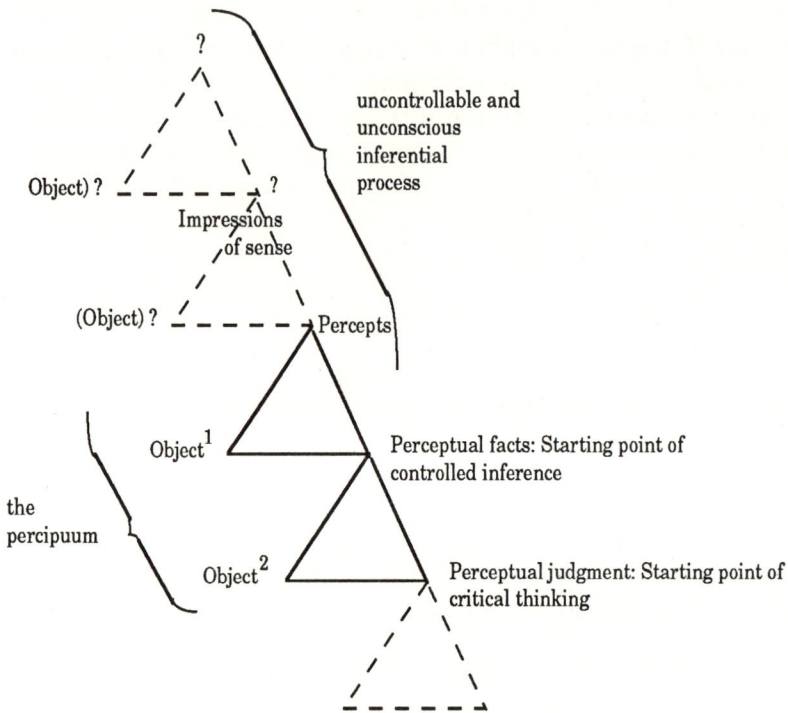

Fig. 16

trolled inferences. Although the percepts themselves are abductive, albeit unconscious, until inferences involving construction and generalization, and consequently of the nature of signs, are recollected as *perceptual facts* and interpreted in *perceptual judgments* common knowledge about the external world is impossible.

The part of the diagram that starts with the question marks and ends with "perceptual judgment" (although a continuation is indicated) constitutes a series of signs. Since each sign interprets the previous sign, each is at the same time an interpretant of the sign prior to it and a sign interpreted by a subsequent sign. The objects, starting with a question mark and provisionally ending with Object², are supposed to be the same throughout the series, because they indicate that the same dynamical object is the dynamic force (exterior to the series) that determines the concrete semiotic process. The process, as regards the immediate object, however, becomes more definite through the sign-action. A perceptual judgment is typically expressed in a proposition in the form of a sentence, such as "this is hard." This judgment is a generalization of a flow of percepts to a perceptual fact, which is interpreted in a verbal expression having subject-predicate structure, and ascribing a certain character (quality) to an object. The proposition, and especially its predicate, may in its turn be interpreted in a new sign specifying the meaning of the proposition. "Hard" could be interpreted by "is not scratched by most substances," and "this is hard" and "this is not scratched by most substances" might refer to and be true of the same object (i.e., the subject of the proposition). In this way the sign's object is specified through the interpretative action of the series of signs, semioses. From this perspective, the dynamical object is related to the sign in two ways: It is a force exerting an influence on the sign, sometimes by causation, as in the case of the weathercock, and sometimes by determination in the sense of specifying the sign (cf. 8.177), as when the relevant qualities of an icon are specified by its comparison with the object it represents. Secondly, it is the ultimate object of inquiry sought for through the continued and unlimited research process. The dynamical object stands both at the beginning and at the end (if end there be) of the process of signification and inquiry; whereas, the immediate object is the object in the aspects made apparent through a single semiosis. The two objects need not be categorically different. The dynamical object is defined and described as the body of conceptions that through final investigation are true of the immediate object. In this sense reality and truth merge in final interpretation.

Peirce pragmatically stresses the importance of perceptual acquaintance with the object of the sign for two reasons. First, he claims all knowledge is derived from perception. The important addition, however, is that the generality is perceived directly, because the predicate of a perceptual judgment is general while the subject is singular (e.g., "this is white"). Second, he believes perceptual judgment is decisive in testing the truth or falsity of propositions:

Thus a false proposition is a proposition of which some interpretant represents that, on an occasion which it indicates, a percept will have a

certain character, while the immediate perceptual judgment on that occasion is that the percept has not that character. A true proposition is a
proposition belief in which would never lead to such disappointment so long
as the proposition is not understood otherwise than it was intended. (5.569)

An important difference between an immediate and dynamical object
from the point of view of the sign is that while every sign, per definition, has an immediate object it need not have a dynamical object.
This means that the object of a sign in general is an indicated, or
designated, position that can be occupied by ontologically indifferent
units, for example both by a camel and a phoenix. Peirce makes this
obvious by the following quotation:

> A Replica of the word "camel" is likewise a Rhematic Indexical Sinsign
> being really affected, through the knowledge of camels, common to the
> speaker and auditor, by the real camel it denotes, even if this one is not
> individually known to the auditor; and it is through such real connection
> that the word "camel" calls up the idea of a camel. The same thing is true of
> the word "phoenix." For although no phoenix really exists, real descriptions
> of the phoenix are well known to the speaker and his auditor; and the word
> is really affected by the Object denoted. (2.261)

The above quotation constitutes an important addition to the idea of
the object. In the case of the phoenix, the object of inquiry is neither
some existent observable entity nor some historical being once existing, the traces of which may be found. The object is restricted to other
preexisting fictional descriptions and depictions. While the quotation
seems merely to allow fictional objects that form a part of common
knowledge to influence later uses of the signs of these objects, it actually says that meaning and existence are only mediately related,
because meaningful reference to immediate objects is possible irrespective of their reality or non-reality. This fact makes literature possible.

It might be argued that historical events and characters left to
posterity are also nothing but descriptions and depictions. On these
grounds, it is hard to substantiate in practice the difference between a
fictional being that is only supposed to exist as the immediate object of
one or more verbal and pictorial texts and a historical character who is
supposed to exist 1) independently of any single textual reference to
him, and 2) as a dynamical object to influence the signs denoting him.
Historians often cannot decide whether events and characters referred

to in ancient texts are, in fact, historical or fictional. That the reconstruction of the past is hypothetical in nature is not foreign to Peirce:

> There are certain inferences which, scientifically considered, are undoubt-
> edly hypotheses and yet which practically are perfectly certain. Such for
> instance is the inference that Napoleon Bonaparte really lived at about the
> beginning of this century, a hypothesis which we adopt for the purpose of
> explaining the concordant testimony of a hundred memoirs, the public
> records of history, tradition, and numberless monuments and relics. It
> would surely be downright insanity to entertain a doubt about Napoleon's
> existence. (5.589)

Even if it seems preposterous to doubt the existence of Napoleon,
propositions about the past are not exceptions to the fallibility of
knowledge; on the contrary, the effort to make them practically certain
is bound up with specific difficulties, because of the decisive role played by prediction in the affirmation of propositions. Peirce's idea, in the
above quotation, that the truth of a proposition consists in the appearance of a percept whose character was predicted, holds true as well in
propositions about historical events: "The truth of the proposition that
Caesar crossed the Rubicon consists in the fact that the further we
push our archaeological and other studies, the more strongly will that
conclusion force itself on our minds – or would do so, if study were to
go on forever" (5.566). How, one might ask, do studies force a conclusion upon the historian? Peirce's answer is twofold: First, the sign
forces the senses and mind of the interpreter to recognize its indications, and second, the sign itself is "compelled by its object." Peirce
continues: "This is evidently the reason of the dichotomy of the true
and the false" (5.554). An individual interpreter may be compelled by
a figment of imagination (such as Macbeth's dagger), and any limited
community of investigators may be misled by a belief in non-existent
objects. Unlimited investigation however, would be compelled only by
real objects that acted dynamically upon the signs:

> In order that a thing may be a true sign its proper significate mental effect
> [i.e., its interpretant, JDJ] must be *conveyed* from another object which the
> sign is concerned in indicating and which is by this conveyance the ul-
> timate cause of the mental effect. In order to be the cause of an effect, or
> *efficient cause,* as the old phrase was, it must either be an existent thing or
> an actual event. Now such things are only known by observation. It cannot
> be any part of the mental effect, and therefore can only be known by

collateral observation of the context or cirumstances of utterance, or putting forth. But the sign may describe the kind of observation that is appropriate and even indicate how the right object is to be recognized. The
meaning of the sign is not conveyed until not merely the interpretant but
also this object is recognized. But although the full realization of the meaning requires the actual observation, direct or indirect, of the object, yet a
close approach to this may be made by imagining the observation. If the
sign is not a *true,* but only a *fictitious* sign, it is the mere semblance of a
sign. If, however, it be so far true as to profess to be in certain respects
fictitious, the conditions of a true sign hold in slackened force. (Ms. 318,
1907: 33-35)

Although Peirce here seems to claim that the existence of a dynamical
object influencing the sign is *a conditio sine qua non* for signhood, he
recognizes fictitious signs on the condition that they in some way
announce or display their fictionality. The reason for his demand is
that signs taken to refer to an actual state of affairs, which in fact do
not do so, are misleading. Someone who lies intentionally produces
such misleading signs, but works of fiction are not regarded as lies
because by convention they are not taken to refer to the common life-
world of the parties of the dialogue. They refer to a fictional universe
of discourse, created by an author who writes a text accepted by a
reader as a sign offered for meditation and pleasure.
    One reason why Peirce claims that the conditions of a true sign
hold for a fictitious one, albeit "in slackened force," is that structurally
factional and fictional statements are indistinguishable from each
other. Peirce brings out this point beautifully: "The actual world cannot be distinguished from a world of imagination by any description."
He continues, "Hence the need of pronoun[s] and indices and the more
complicated the subject the greater the need of them" (3.363). The
indices used, together with the difference in the commitments and
obligations faced by the utterer distinguish a factual from a fictional
description. In the Peirce/Welby correspondence Peirce reflects on the
nature of assertion and lies as follows: "According to my present view
(I may see more light in future) the act of assertion is not a pure act of
signification. It is an exhibition of fact that one subjects oneself to the
penalties visited on a liar if the proposition is not true" (SS 1977: 34).
This reflection agrees with his above-mentioned definition of a true vs.
a fictitious sign. In one place, Peirce directly treats the assertive force
of fictional propositions. He says the following about the author of the
*Arabian Nights:*

It is true that when the Arabian romancer tells us that there was a lady named Scheherazade, he does not mean to be understood as speaking of the world of outward realities, and there is a great deal of fiction in what he is talking about. For the *fictive* is that whose characters depend upon what characters somebody attributes to it; and the story is, of course, the mere creation of the poet's thought. Nevertheless, once he has imagined Scheherazade and made her young, beautiful, and endowed with a gift of spinning stories, it becomes a real fact that so he has imagined her, which fact he cannot destroy by pretending or thinking that he imagined her to be otherwise. That he wishes us to understand is what he might have expressed in plain prose by saying, "I have imagined a lady, Scheherazade by name, young, beautiful and a tireless teller of tales, and I am going on to imagine what tales she told." This would have been a plain expression of professed fact relating to the sum total of realities. (5.152)

According to this passage, fiction consists of propositions, and such propositions are conceived as *real facts,* i.e., valid propositions about a certain kind of universe that neither the author nor the reader can deny. Such a universe is, however, not independent of individual imaginations; and consequently its sign character is derivative in the sense that it presupposes the sign relations of an experiential and perceptual universe of action and reaction. Peirce expresses this point of view in a critique of Hegel:

The capital error of Hegel which permeates his whole system in every part of it is that he almost altogether ignores the Outward Clash. Besides the lower consciousness of feeling and the higher consciousness of nutrition, this direct consciousness of hitting and of getting hit enters into all cognition and serves to make it mean something real. (8.41)

## 5. Remarks on Peirce's concepts of reality and truth

In the preceding sections, Peirce's concepts of *reality* and *truth* have been referred to with few comments. Peirce's concept of truth is controversial, because it seems to be partly a consensus theory, partly a correspondence theory. Here the concept will be explained briefly from the point of view of the object's role in the semiosis.

Peirce's concept of truth is embedded in his theory of inquiry. One way of looking at the process of inquiry is to see it as a striving to eliminate "the irritation of doubt," and to achieve stable and well founded beliefs about objects and states of affairs (cf. 5.374). Peirce

correlates truth and inquiry with agreement among an unlimited community of researchers, because individual persons may settle their
opinions to their own satisfaction, even if further inquiry will show
them to be wrong. In his review of Berkeley he contrasts the shortcomings of the individual with the capacity of man for discerning
truth:

> All human thought and opinion contains an arbitrary, accidental element,
> dependent on the limitations in circumstance, power and bent of the in-
> dividual; an element of error, in short. But human opinion universally
> tends in the long run to a definite form, which is the truth. Let any human
> being have enough information and exert enough thought upon any ques-
> tion, and the result will be that he arrive at a certain definite conclusion,
> which is the same that any other mind will reach under sufficiently favor-
> able circumstances. (8.12)

In "How to Make Our Ideas Clear" (1878) Peirce impressively formulates and exemplifies his point of view in his famous *principle of
hope:*

> all the followers of science are animated by a cheerful hope that the pro-
> cesses of investigation, if only pushed far enough, will give one certain
> solution to each question to which they apply it. One man may investigate
> the velocity of light by studying the transits of Venus and the aberration of
> the stars; another by the oppositions of Mars and the eclipses of Jupiter's
> satellites; a third by the method of Fizeau; a fourth by that of Foucault; a
> fifth by the motions of the curves of Lissajoux; a sixth, a seventh, an eighth,
> and a ninth, may follow the different methods of comparing the measures of
> statical and dynamical electricity. They may at first obtain different re-
> sults, but, as each perfects his method and his processes, the results are
> found to move steadily together toward a destined centre. So with all scien-
> tific research. Different minds may set out with the most antagonistic
> views, but the progress of investigation carries them by a force outside of
> themselves to one and the same conclusion. This activity of thought by
> which we are carried, not where we wish, but to a fore-ordained goal, is like
> the operation of destiny. No modification of the point of view taken, no
> selection of other facts for study, no natural bent of mind even, can enable a
> man to escape the predestinate opinion. This great hope is embodied in the
> conception of truth and reality. The opinion which is fated to be ultimately
> agreed to by all who investigate, is what we mean by the truth, and the
> object represented in this opinion is the real. That is the way I would
> explain reality. (5.407)

For scientists and scholars this "great hope" functions, or ought to function, as a regulative principle. It is founded on two assumptions: one that the process of inquiry is self-corrective, and two that the object determines the sign to the effect that the conclusions will finally force themselves upon the community of researchers. The first assumption depends on the second because the object as it appears in the process of interpretation compels the community, albeit not necessarily individual groups of researchers, to revise their theories. The object's determination makes itself felt in the the indexical force of its signs:

> Truth is the conformity of a representamen to its object, its object, ITS object, mind you. . . . What the sign virtually has to do in order to indicate its object – and make it its – all it has to do is just to seize its interpreter's eyes and forcibly turn them upon the object meant: it is what a knock at the door does, or an alarm or other bell, or a whistle, a cannonshot, etc. It is pure physiological compulsion; nothing else.
>     So, then, a sign, in order to fulfill its office, to actualize its potency, must be compelled by its object. This is evidently the reason of the dichotomy of the true and the false. For it takes two to make a quarrel, and a compulsion involves as large a dose of quarrel as is requisite to make it quite impossible that there should be compulsion without resistance. (5.554)

Peirce does not, however, regard reality as consisting in these brute compulsory forces in themselves, but rather in their semiotic processing, their becoming integrated in sign action and thereby influencing thought. He claims:

> This theory of reality is instantly fatal to the idea of a thing in itself, - a thing existing independent of all relation to the mind's conception of it. Yet it would by no means forbid, but rather encourage us, to regard the appearances of sense as only signs of the realities. Only, the realities which they represent would not be the unknowable cause of sensation, but noumena, or intelligible conceptions which are the last products of the mental action which is set in motion by sensation. (8.13)

Figure 16 above attempts to illustrate Peirce's point of view. It is designed to show that one cannot work backwards in the process, because beyond the threshold of the percept, or rather the perceptual judgment, there can be no inquiry. This does not mean, however, that there exists a fixed limit to our acquisition of knowledge, since a continuing progression in the process of interpretation may reveal new aspects of the research object, whether those aspects become possible by translating impulses radiating from the object into signs that can be perceived (cf. Bruner's idea of senso-motorical amplifiers, here pp. 143) or whether researchers ask new questions from a changed perspective of interpretation. For Peirce as a scientist, no fixed borderline between immediate and dynamical objects exists, because the influence exerted by a dynamical object may be translated into something known, namely an immediate object, by virtue of the sign process. The end of such a process of interpretation would occur at the moment new aspects of the research object ceased to be discovered. At that time a merging of dynamical and immediate objects would occur (for this see chapter IV, 4).

In a draft letter to Cantor, Dec. 23, 1900 (L 73) Peirce defines a *true proposition* – cautiously adding "if there be any such thing" – as having three characteristics: 1) it cannot be reversed permanently by anybody's effort. 2) No reasoning or discussion can prevent it from asserting itself. 3) Predictions based on it, which state that certain conditions will produce a certain experience, will be fulfilled if the conditions are met. *Reality is then defined as that which is represented in a true proposition.* However, Peirce goes on to distinguish between three kinds of reality: 1) *Positive* reality, or truth as a state to which all three criteria can be applied, although Peirce explicitly states they can be applied "of course imperfectly, since we can never carry them out to the end." Such a *positive* reality – we may surmise – would consist in an intelligible universe comprising qualities, forces, and laws. It would include the common sense notion of reality as well as the reality discovered by sciences inquiring into the nature of mind-independent universes. Another kind of reality is named 2) *ideal* reality or truth, which is defined by the applicability of the first and second criteria (although again imperfectly), but the third is *not* applicable. Peirce's own example of *ideal* reality is pure mathematics. The third kind of reality is called 3) *ultimate* reality or truth. It is defined by the applicability of the first criterion, and negatively by the fact that reasoning cannot either overthrow it or render it clearer. Furthermore no one can make predictions on *ultimate* reality alone. Peirce exemplifies *ultimate* reality in this way: "Thus, if you are kicked by a horse, the fact of the pain is beyond all discussion, and far less can it be shaken or established by any experimentation" (L 73, 1900: 3). It appears Peirce conceives of *ultimate* reality as the unavoidable reaction to the "Outward Clash," *ultimate* precisely because we cannot go behind it. This kind of reality, however, is not "fully developed" (to use Peirce's own phrase). It is simultaneously the point of departure for reaching *positive* reality, and the ultimate test for the validity of our conclusions concerning it.

Peirce's reflections on reality and truth make understandable the double role of the object in his semiotics: First, that to which the sign refers what it indicates or designates, whether it refers to an object, a state of affairs, an event, or a relation; second, it is also as a force which creates or influences the sign. In contradistinction to the once dominant trend in European semiotics, this duple conception of the object means that the relationship between signs and their denotata is dialectical. It is not conceived as a formative action whereby the sign, or rather the sign system, parses and creates an arbitrary order in an amorphous and passive substance. It is a vital and bidirectional relationship which is both determined and motivated, while taking into account the conventional features of sign and sign system. This idea — and the problems linked with it — is the subject of the next chapter on the icon, index, symbol distinction.

# III. The Icon, Index, Symbol Distinction

Peirce's distinctions of the sign in relation to its object are *icon, index,* and *symbol.* They correspond to his distinctions of the sign in itself as qualisign, sinsign, and legisign. Peirce, convinced of the importance of this classification, calls it "the most fundamental [division of signs]" (2.275); and many semioticians, myself included, agree.

It should be stressed immediately that despite its apparent self-evidence and fecundity this classification of signs generates problems. These problems concern the very nature of signhood, with the features and relations that make it possible for a sign to mean and represent something. They lie at the very heart of semiotics; and thus the discussions and sometimes lively debates they provoke are understandable. What is at stake here are issues such as the relative weight of the positive and the negative features of the sign, new versions of the time-honored debate between realism and nominalism, and the concepts of nature and culture, their borderlines and interrelations.

Before addressing directly Peirce's classification, and its problems, we should look at another distinction between two concepts in Peircean semiotics, the one between *ground* and *interpretant,* because its very existence tells us something about Peirce's way of conceiving the distinction between icon and symbol, and because its dispensability as a concept make us aware of the problems connected with it.

## 1. Ground and interpretant

The last chapter quoted one of Peirce's most well-known definitions of the sign (cf. p. 56). The relevant paragraph concerning the sign in its relation to its object is this: "The sign stands for something, its *object.* It stands for that object, not in all respects, but in reference to a sort of

idea, which I have sometimes called the *ground* of the representation" ◢
(2.228). Although the concept of *ground* plays no role in Peirce's later
writings (whereas it is important in "On a New List of Categories,"
1867), the idea of the tripartition of the sign in its relation to the object
remains the same. In "On a New List . . ." the concept of *ground* is
defined as "a pure abstraction, reference to which constitutes a quality
or general attribute" (1.551). At this time Peirce thought this concept
to be indispensable, "because we cannot comprehend an agreement of
two things, except as an agreement in some *respect*" (1.551). But later
he preferred the concept of interpretant.

Everything that appears to a mind, by Peirce called the *phaneron,*
is, according to his analysis of the categories, either a *quality,* or concretely a *quale* (that which refers to a ground); a *relation,* or concretely
a *relate* (that which refers to a ground and to a *correlate,* the correlate
being the object of a sign); or a *representation,* or concretely a *representamen* (that which refers to ground, correlate, and interpretant
[1.555–1.557]). If we keep in mind that the sign is an indivisible triad,
consisting of the relation between representamen, object, and interpretant, then the distinction between a sign that refers only to a
ground, one that refers both to ground and correlate, and another that
refers to ground, correlate and interpretant has to be one of its
predominant modes of signification and reference, and *not* a distinction between, monadic, dyadic, and triadic signs. The sign pole of the
sign, therefore, can be considered as to its non-relative characters, its
inherent qualities: as a *quale* in its dual relationship to a correlate; as
a *relate,* and as trirelational, as a *representamen.* A diagram of these
relations (Fig. 17) indicates the reference to a ground by a dotted line,
the reference to a ground and a correlate by a solid line, and the
reference to ground, correlate, and interpretant by a thick line:

This diagram depicts the predominantly monadic, dyadic, and
triadic relationships of the sign pole of the sign as described in "On a
New List . . . ," but at the same time it illustrates that something
might be at odds with Peirce's general concept of the sign as triadic,
because what we have is, in fact, a four term structure. The reason is
that Peirce here uses two different mediating concepts, both *ground* ◢
and *interpretant.* In "On a New List . . ." an *interpretant* is defined as
a mediating representation relating relate (sign) and correlate (object)
by means of *imputed* qualities or characters whereas *ground* signi-

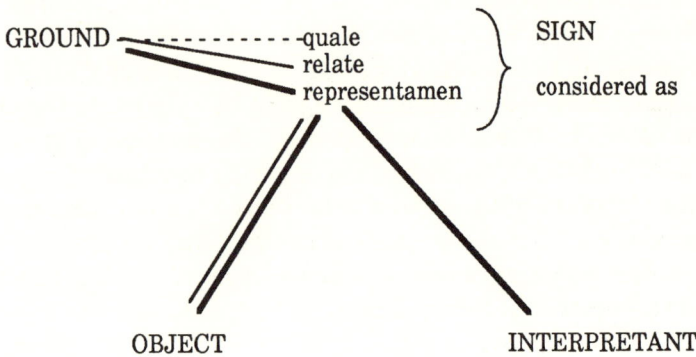

GROUND ----------- quale          } SIGN
                    relate
                    representamen  } considered as

OBJECT                              INTERPRETANT

Fig. 17

fies qualities, or characters, *inherent* in the sign. This means that in addition to the predominantly dyadic relationship in fact, i.e., by some kind of *contiguity* between sign and object, we have a relationship between sign and object mediated by their inherent qualities, i.e., *similarity,* by virtue of possessing common inherent properties, and a relationship between sign and object founded on *conventionality,* by virtue of characters *arbitrarily* attributed to the sign by the interpretant. Figure 18 illustrates this way of thinking:

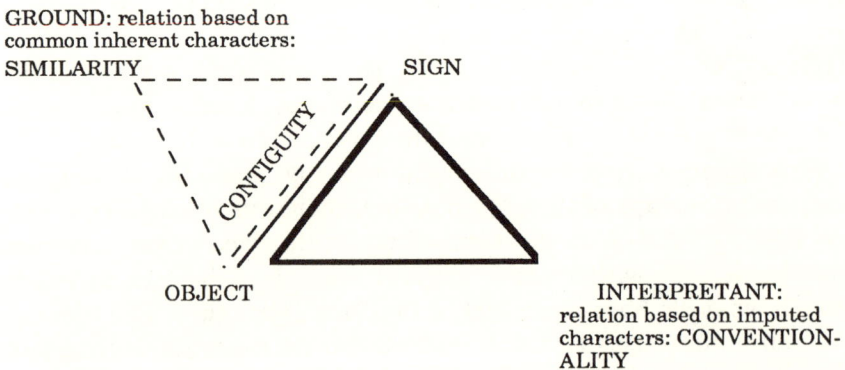

GROUND: relation based on
common inherent characters:
SIMILARITY - - - - - - - - SIGN

CONTIGUITY

OBJECT                              INTERPRETANT:
                                    relation based on imputed
                                    characters: CONVENTION-
                                    ALITY

Fig. 18

The diagram also makes evident that in all important respects ground and interpretant are two aspects of the same mediating function that correlates sign and object; and since the sign, according to Peirce, "is only a sign *in actu* by virtue of receiving an interpretation" (5.569), we may subsume the concept of ground under that of interpretant. This attempt to clarify the relationship between ground and interpretant, indicating a possible explanation for the disappearance of the former, should at the same time have cleared the ground for an exposition of the distinctions between icon, index, and symbol.

## 2. The pure icon and the iconic sign

The concepts of the icon and iconicity are among the most debated and contested notions within semiotics. In *A Theory of Semiotics* (1976) Umberto Eco asks himself and his readers if it would not be better to get rid of the notion of the iconic sign altogether (Eco 1976:216); and in the background of any contemporary discussion of this subject looms the awe-inspiring archangel of conventionalism and nominalism, Nelson Goodman. Despite objections, however, the concept of iconicity seems so eminently useful and enlightening that it is worth preserving, even if some of its traditionally attributed characteristics have to be given up or redefined.

As a first approximation, an icon is a sign by virtue of its similarity to the object it denotes. In Peirce, the concept of the icon is, however, rather complicated and not always altogether clear. Consequently a step by step explanation is useful. A general, and important, definition of the icon is as follows:

> An icon is a representamen of what it represents and for the mind that interprets it as such, by virtue of its being an immediate image, that is to say by virtue of characters which belong to it in itself as a *sensible object,* and which it would possess just the same were there no object in nature that it resembled, and though it never were interpreted as a sign. It is of the nature of an appearance, and as such, strictly speaking, exists only in consciousness, although for convenience in ordinary parlance and when extreme precision is not called for, we extend the term *icon* to the outward objects which excite in consciousness the image itself. A geometrical diagram is a good example of an icon. A pure icon can convey no positive or factual information; for it affords no assurance that there is any such

thing in nature. But it is of the utmost value for enabling its interpreter to study what would be the character of such an object in case any such did exist. Geometry sufficiently illustrates that. (4.447, my italics)

In this quotation a pure icon is given a series of interesting characteristics: It is said to be "an immediate image," to be of "the nature of appearance," and to "exist only in consciousness." Here, a definition of the pure icon is close to the definition of the phaneron itself, i.e., every thing that may appear to the mind. The relatedness of the pure icon to the phaneron is further emphasized if we compare another formulation about the pure icon (in the strictest sense): "even an idea, except in the sense of a possibility, or Firstness, cannot be a icon. A possibility alone is an Icon purely by virtue of its quality" (2.276). What Peirce attempts to isolate in his concept of the pure icon is the monadic aspects of quality and possibility, i.e., its unrelatedness to anything else. Consequently, a (pure) icon can be defined as "a sign by virtue of its own quality and it is a sign of whatever partakes of that quality" (L 75, 1902: c145). The potential being of a pure icon is stressed by its absolute indeterminacy as regards its relation to its possible object, because given the fact that everything has properties in common with everything else, then any appearance may be an icon of any other appearance (for a fuller discussion of the pure icon, and especially of its role within aesthetics, see L. Santaella Braga, "From pure icon to metaphor: Six degrees of iconicity," forthcoming).

Furthermore the pure icon is said to convey no positive or factual information because it does not point to a given object. This means a pure icon does not signify by denoting an object. Peirce describes its mode of signification by saying that an icon "serves as a sign solely and simply by exhibiting the quality it serves to signify" (NEM 1976: IV, 242).

The definition of a pure icon may seem rather weak, since an icon can be summarized as an appearance in the mind that by exhibiting or representing its own qualities may function as a possible sign of everything else that appears and exhibits an identical quality. That is, it represents or exhibits concretely everything of which the same characteristics can be predicated. When we spoke about the qualisign, we said a qualisign *sui generis* never existed, and the same is true of the pure icon. This being so, we might ask why Peirce is so eager to isolate and describe these potential, in a sense non-existing, entities. The answer is in two parts: first, Peirce's theory of knowledge commits him to make his categorical analysis thorough, so even if firstness in isolation from secondness and thirdness remains a possibility which is not empirically realized, the category loses none of its systematical and analytical necessity. Second, by isolating these may-bes in their purity, Peirce calls attention to what is, so to speak, not only essential to but is also the generative power of this kind of sign. Since nothing prevents anything from being an icon of anything else, icons may be created freely by scientists, scholars, authors, and artists. By exploring the field of possible likenesses through unbridled iconic imagination, they may discover important properties and relations of the mental constructions on which the semiosis works, properties and relations that might hold true of some possible object of the icon.

The passage from the (stipulated) pure icon to the *iconic sign* requires three changes: First, the quality has to be embodied, just as the passage from qualisign to sinsign. Second, an actual functioning sign will never be pure. In addition to its predominant iconic features, indexical and symbolic features will play a role in the sign. Third, for an actual sign to function as a predominantly iconic sign, some principle of selection is needed. This condition may seem strange, because the ground of the relation between iconic sign and object is defined as *similarity*. But according to Peirce everything in some respect is similar to everything else; consequently, similarity by itself does not suffice. A further principle to select the relevant common properties is needed.

In "Seven Strictures on Similarity" (1970) Nelson Goodman gives the following example of what difficulties might be involved in using unspecified similarity as a criterion of classification. Goodman presents the following three figures (Fig. 19).

# B B O

Fig. 19

Goodman's point is that figure two is not topologically equivalent to figure one, but to figure three (Goodman 1972: 439). If we are less interested in geometrical topology than, for instance in deciphering a handwritten manuscript we would probably take figures one and two to be replicas of the legisign 'B', rather than figures two and three to be replicas of the legisign 'O' (Goodman would prefer to say 'replicas of each other,' but to discuss this would take us too far afield). Goodman's example proves unequivocally that similarity, which as in Peirce is understood as the possession of common characteristics, is always similarity for a purpose.

Peirce's position is the same, because starting to state that an icon is a sign by virtue of its quality as thing "that renders it fit to be a Representamen," he goes on, saying: "Thus anything is fit to be a *Substitute* for anything it is like. (The concept of "substitute" involves that of a purpose, and thus of genuine thirdness)" (2.276). As regards the iconic sign this means that the mediation through the ground is itself mediated through a relevant frame of reference.

Peirce stresses the relationship between iconic signs on the one hand and perception and experiential observation on the other. Not only are icons (i.e., iconic signs) said to be "percepts minus the insistency and percussivity of percepts" (Ms. 293, 1906: 9), but Peirce also identifies with an iconic sign the idea excited by an external reacting upon the brain (2.276). Although iconicity alone is certainly insufficient to make up perception, since an indexical element that represents the insistency of the object is needed, and although iconic signs need not be bound to actual perception, since they can be representations of memory or fantasies, iconicity and perception presuppose each other. What we perceive are iconic signs of the surrounding world selected and structured by our species' specific capacity for processing stimuli. This capacity in mankind has both a natural and a cultural side, because human intelligence has created devices that translate impulses and stimuli that are beyond the limits of man's sensory capacity into perceptual facts that can be interpreted according to the nature of the devices and hypotheses about the impulses themselves. In theory, there are no limits to the creation of such devices translating impulses into perceptual facts, and consequently no limit to the acquisition of new information about nature.

It will be remembered that Peirce considered perception simultaneously to be direct and inferential. This belief implies that iconic sign and object may coalesce, may be indistinguishable. The eminent Peirce scholar Joseph Ransdell has repeatedly asserted this point (see Ransdell 1979 and 1986), and as one example among others points to the famous review of the works of Berkeley (1871) in which Peirce states his realist position:

The realist will hold that the very same objects which are immediately present in our minds in experience really exist just as they are experienced out of the mind; that is, he will maintain a doctrine of immediate perception. He will not, therefore, sunder existence out of the mind and being in the mind as two wholly improportionable modes. When a thing is in such relation to the individual mind that that mind cognizes it, it is in the mind; and its being so in the mind will not in the least diminish its external existence. For he does not think of the mind as a receptacle, which if a thing is in, it ceases to be out of. To make a distinction between the true conception of a thing and the thing itself is, he will say, only to regard one and the same thing from two different points of view; for the immediate object of thought in a true judgment *is* the reality. (8.16)

Ransdell speaks about the self-representation of the sign (in distinction to its other-representing capacity) when an iconic sign exhibits its own qualities. If, however, perception is direct, then a partial identity exists between those aspects of the object represented in the percept and those external to the perceiving mind. According to Ransdell, Peirce's concept of the iconic sign means a fusion of two distinct theories of perception, the theory of representative and the theory of direct perception. The theory of representative perception has the merit of being able to account for error, for non-veridical perception: however, it leaves the object as an unknowable entity. The theory of direct perception accounts for veridical perception, but makes it hard to explain errors and diversity of perception (for this see Ransdell 1986: 73-74). Ransdell is correct. It is beyond reasonable doubt that Peirce attempted a fusion of the two points of view, and also that even if his theory of perception has great merits (e.g., its accordance with common sense), it leads to problems of its own.

The important thing to recognize in the fusing of the two points of view is the reciprocity of the relationship between perception and iconicity. An icon is defined as a mental image, and, accordingly, every percept is, among other things, iconic. Yet, the concept of iconic signs is not limited to percepts but includes signs intentionally produced as signs exhibiting some of the same qualities, structural relationships, forces, or effects as the generalized or standarized percept of the object that they are intended to denote. What we call things are, according to Peirce, generalized percepts, or composite photographs of percepts, and in so being are themselves the result of a chain of perceptual judgments involving structuration and abstraction. Iconic signs, if intentionally produced, are built on existing perceptual schemata, inborn or acquired (Peirce regards, in fact, association by resemblance as an inborn neural capacity, cf. 7.498).

## 3. Images, diagrams, and metaphors

Peirce distinguishes between three kinds of iconic signs, or hypoicons as he terms actual iconic signs: *images, diagrams,* and *metaphors.* Images are characterized by having simple qualities in common with their object. If a piece of a red carton is used as a sign exhibiting the color of the paint you want to buy, then it functions as a simple iconic sign, an image, of the desired color. A producer of after-shave lotion may claim that his product functions as an olfactory icon, an image, of a certain scent characteristic of human maleness. An actress's scream may function as an auditory image of an expression of horror. The photographs posted by the police of wanted criminals are supposed to exhibit enough pictorial resemblances to the people in question to enable the public to recognize them by such means.

A diagram is characterized by depicting relations analogous to those of the represented object. A map, for instance, is a diagram, because the relations between its differents parts are analogous to those between the parts of the geographical area it depicts. A city map of Copenhagen is in certain respects a specific iconic representation of this particular city. It is useful for finding one's way in Copenhagen; it would be of no use in any other city. Peirce points out, however, that a diagram need not look like its object, and he offers the following simple example of an iconic sign of this kind:

$$\text{Signs:} \left\{ \begin{array}{l} \text{Icons,} \\ \text{Indices,} \\ \text{Symbols.} \end{array} \right.$$

This is an icon. But the only respect in which it resembles its object is that the brace shows the classes of *icons, indices,* and *symbols* to be related to one another and to the general class of signs, as they really are, in a general way. (2.282)

This example is valuable, because it shows that Peirce's concept of iconicity is not tied down to shared properties of a sign and an existent, individual object. The above diagram functions rather as a concretization, a visualization, of intelligible relationships (cf. 4.531). Furthermore, without losing its *motivated relationship to its object*, diagramming enjoys a rather extensive freedom. The point in Peirce's diagram could, for instance, be expressed like this:

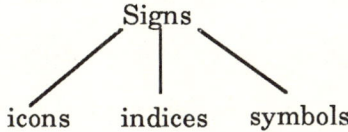

Signs

icons    indices    symbols

Fig. 20

or like this:

Signs: (icons, indices, symbols)

Fig. 21

It is a mistake to regard the freedom exemplified here as an argument for the looseness of the concept of the iconic sign; it merely shows that there are several ways of exhibiting relationships, and that the one someone uses is to a certain extent a matter of choice (cf. below).

Peirce considers diagrams (and iconic signs in general) to be of the utmost importance, because they are visual, or better yet perceptual, exhibitions of relationships. What counts in a diagram are the relationships of its parts to each other. Besides, diagrams are iconic signs created in the imagination that we can observe and experiment with. Thus, according to Peirce, observation of and experimentation with diagrams are the main if not the only way we acquire new knowledge of relationships. Peirce so stresses the part played by diagrammatic reasoning in mathematics and logic that he often characterizes all necessary (i.e., deductive) reasoning as diagrammatic:

All necessary reasoning without exception is diagrammatic. That is, we construct an icon of our hypothetical state of things and proceed to observe it. This observation leads us to suspect that something is true, which we may or may not be able to formulate with precision, and we proceed to inquire whether it is true or not. (5.162)

He also says that the truth of deductive and mathematical reasoning is derived "from observation of creations of our own visual imagination, which we may set down on paper in form of diagrams" (2.77).

The puzzle that on the one hand mathematics is purely deductive in nature, and that on the other it offers a seemingly unending series of surprising discoveries, just as any other observational science, is, according to Peirce, explained by its predominantly iconic nature:

> The truth, however, appears to be that all deductive reasoning, even simple syllogism, involves an element of observation; namely, deduction consists in constructing an icon or diagram the relations of whose parts shall present a complete analogy with those of the parts of the object of reasoning, of experimenting upon this image in the imagination, and of observing the result so as to discover unnoticed and hidden relations among the parts. For instance, take the syllogistic formula,
>
> All M is P
> S is M
> S is P.
>
> This is really a diagram of the relations of S, M, and P. The fact that the middle term occurs in the two premisses is actually exhibited, and this must be done or the notation will be of no value. As for algebra, the very idea of the art is that it presents formulæ which can be manipulated, and that by observing the effects of such manipulation we find properties not to be otherwise discerned. (3.363)

The role of iconic signs (e.g., diagrams) is, however, not confined to the formal reasoning of logic and mathematics. Everyday reasoning includes, most often subconsciously, the use of diagrammatization, as when people observe a hypothetical or imaginary state of affairs. Even in scrutinizing our own desires, we use, according to Peirce, an iconic mode of reasoning. Peirce describes a man who asks himself if he really wants something as performing the following mental operation:

> He makes in his imagination a sort of skeleton diagram, or outline sketch, of himself, considers what modifications the hypothetical state of things would require to be made in that picture, and then examines it, that is, *observes* what he has imagined, to see whether the same ardent desire is there to be discerned. (2.227)

From this example it follows that phenomena such as dreams and literature, in important respects, may be regarded as exercises of iconic imagination.

The third kind of iconic signs are *metaphors* which are defined as those signs "which represent the representative character of a representamen by representing a parallelism in something else" (2.277). The poetic images we term metaphors within the study of literature are also metaphors in Peirce's sense, except that because of their expression in language (i.e., by symbols) the iconic quality is not direct but is mediated. Peirce's concept of metaphor is, however, broader and a little different from the linguistic and literary one. It covers, for instance, many devices and gauges used for measurement. A thermometer may exemplify a metaphor in this extended sense, because the rise of the pillar of mercury signifies the rise of temperature. Since the rise of the mercury pillar is an effect of the rise of the temperature, the thermometer has strong indexical aspects, but here we are considering only its iconicity. The parallelism exhibited by the thermometer and the temperature consists in the fact that heat is translated into a visual sign where the pillar's height indicates the temperature's "height." Another kind of thermometer, very popular with children, is placed on the forehead of a person suspected to be febrile, and it changes color according to the person's temperature. A kind of chemical reaction is operative here, but from the point of view of iconicity a parallelism exists between sign and object.

Although the distinction between image, diagram, and metaphor may seem congruent, it is difficult to draw the distinction in practice. The three catchwords, *quality, relation,* and *parallelism,* may direct the attention of the interpreter to relevant features of the iconic signs in question, but even if a portrait for instance in a certain sense may be said to have qualities in common with its dynamical object, it seems obvious that diagrammatization is also salient.

The neatness of the line of demarcation between diagram and metaphor depends, among other things, on whether *spatialization* of non-spatial relations is considered to be metaphorical. An example is a non-metaphorical diagrammatic sign in the hallway of a four-story appartment building:

4th. Smith
3rd. Jones
2nd. Brown
1st. Williams

Fig. 22

This sign has all-important symbolic features, but in its iconic character it represents by its own spatial relations a factual spatial relationship, the flats being one on top of the other. It would be rather
farfetched to look upon such a sign as a metaphor; it is better classified as a relatively simple diagram.

Consider, however, the following list:

> general
> colonel
> lieutenant colonel
> captain
> lieutenant

Fig. 23

Here military rank is represented spatially, but the relationships between the commissioned officers are certainly not spatial. They are,
rather, of power and dominance. In this case it could be argued, by
using a *parallelism in something else* (power represented by spatial
position), that such a simple list is metaphorical. If this view is accepted, many other diagrams will also contain metaphorical elements.

It might be worthwhile briefly to inquire into the reason why such
a diagrammatic/metaphoric representation of military rank seems so
"natural" or "convincing." The Danish linguist Holger Steen Sørensen
illustrates his concept of *relation* by the following example:

Suppose we want to divide the class of soldiers into subclasses. That we
could do on the basis of a relation sign R (and "a soldier"). Suppose the
class of soldiers consists only of privates, lieutenants, colonels, and gene-
rals. And suppose R = "gives orders to" ("does not give orders to"). We can
then define in the following way:
1. "A private" = "a soldier who does not give orders to any soldier."
2. "A lieutenant" = "a soldier who gives orders only to a private (= a soldier
who does not give orders to any soldier)."
3. "A colonel" = "a soldier who gives orders only to a lieutenant (= a soldier
who gives orders only to a private (= a soldier who does not give orders to
any soldier)) and a private (= a soldier who does not give orders to any
soldier)."
4. "A general" = "a soldier who gives orders to a colonel (=a soldier who
gives orders only to a lieutenant (= a soldier who gives orders only to a
private (= a soldier who does not give orders to any soldier)) and a private

(= a soldier who does not give orders to any soldier))." (Holger Steen Sørensen 1958: 29)

By choosing a pertinent criterion as a basis for the relationship between the subclasses of soldiers, he succeeds in defining them unambiguously, and this definition in itself imposes an order of representation. Note, however, that the above order is the opposite of the one used in my own list of commissioned officers; and that both ways of listing are equally valid.

The above lists illustrate that diagrammatic representation allows a certain latitude of manner of exhibition. Nevertheless, they also illustrate that even the representation of such simple lists puts constraints upon what can count as a proper representation. Diagrammatic representation such as the following must be counted invalid:

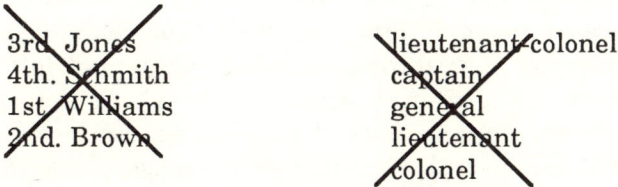

3rd. Jones             lieutenant-colonel
4th. Schmith           captain
1st. Williams          general
2nd. Brown             lieutenant
                       colonel

Fig. 24

The first is invalid because the numerical and the spatial order conflict, the second because the listing is random, contrary to the ordered series of rank which is, in fact, effective within the army. If the listing of military rank by spatialization is defined as metaphorical, then the invalid version represents an ineffective and invalid metaphor.

Questions concerning metaphor and spatiality are fascinating. Man exists and moves in space, but this concrete dimension of his being is in different ways within different cultures at the same time metaphorical. This is brought out beautifully in van Gennep's classic ethnographic study *The Rites of Passage* (1977, Fr. orig. *Les rites de passage,* 1909). Although van Gennep's study is about the ritualistic and symbolic division of the life-*time* in different cultures (the rites of pregnancy, childbirth, childhood, initiation, betrothal, marriage, death, and funerals, etc.), the basic concept is spatial, namely that of the *territorial passage*. He explains its importance in this way:

it seems important to me that the passage from one social position to another is identified with a *territorial passage,* such as the entrance into a village or a house, the movement from one room to another, or the crossing of streets and squares. This identification explains why the passage from one group to another is so often ritually expressed by passage under a portal, or by an "opening of the doors." These phrases and events are seldom meant as "symbols"; for the semicivilized the passage is actually a territorial passage. In fact, the spatial separation of distinct groups is an aspect of social organization. The children live with the women up to a certain age; boys and girls live separated from married people, sometimes in a special house or section or in a special kraal; at marriage one of the two spouses, if not both, changes residence; warriors do not keep company with blacksmiths, and sometimes each professional class has its assigned place of residence. (Van Gennep 1977: 192)

The point is that it is hard to separate the literal from the metaphorical, or symbolic, in the social division of space. If acquiring a new status, at a certain age, within a culture means changing residence, either momentarily (e.g., during initiation) or permanently (e.g., at marriage), then the territorial passage is literal. At the same time, however, the very design of social space seems to be governed by principles that are metaphorical in Peirce's sense of "representing a parallelism in something else." van Gennep says: "Two primary divisions are characteristic of all societies irrespective of time and place: the sexual separation between men and women, and the magico-religious separation between the profane and the sacred" (ibid., p. 189). Even if one could not reduce the division of any concrete social space (e.g., a village) to being governed by just these two principles, there is little reason to doubt that those and similar principles are decisive for the design and division of cultural space. Whereas the division of space in animals is mainly governed by instinct (combat and mating behaviors are related to territory), in man space is appropriated, designed, and shaped by structuring principles taken over from systems of significations that are non-spatial. The reason is that space, as one of the two dimensions of our being (the other is time), functions as a canvas on which we project important cultural (and natural) distinctions:

> The heavens themselves, the planes, and this center
> Observe degree, priority, and place,
> Insisture, course, proportion, season, form,

> Office, and custom, in all line of order.
> And therefore is the glorious planet Sol
> In noble eminence enthroned and sphered
> Amidst the other; whose med'cinable eye
> Corrects the influence of evil planets,
> And posts, like the commandment of a king,
> Sans check, to good and bad. But when the planets
> In evil mixture to disorder wander,
> What plagues, and what portents, what mutiny,
> What raging of the sea, shaking of earth,
> Commotion in the winds, frights, changes, horrors,
> Divert and crack, rend and deracinate
> The unity and married calm of states
> Quite from their fixure? O, when degree is shaked,
> Which is the ladder of all high designs
> The enterprise is sick. (*Troilus and Cressida,* I, III, 85-104)

Ulysses' famous speech certainly testifies to man's semiotic appropriation of space, here the entire known universe. It would be a mistake, however, to regard human space as semiotic in contradistinction to animal space, because the latter is semiotic as well. Every species, man included, inhabits a sign-space the nature of which is primarily dependent on its senso-motorical and instinctual capacities, but only man creates part of his space by concretely realizing metaphors (for further information on this subject see Edward T. Hall's seminal study in spatial semiotics, *The Hidden Dimension,* 1966).

## 4. Features of the iconic sign

The preceding analysis shows that Peirce's concept of iconic signs and iconicity is complex and far-reaching. It is useful, therefore, before proceeding to the index, to summarize some of the main points of his reflections on the subject:

a) According to Peirce's categorial analysis, the concept of the icon is linked to the category of firstness. This means that it is bound up with quality and possibility. Consequently, a pure icon does not exist other than as an idea conceived of as a qualitative possibility.

b) Because an iconic sign exhibits its embodied qualities, but does not assert them, a latitude, or indeterminacy, of applicability and interpretation is one of its characteristics.

c) Peirce's concept of the iconic sign (in contradistinction to the pure icon) is closely related to perception. Where Peirce regards the percept as representational (e.g., Ms. 599) he considers it as an iconic sign physiologically excited by an external object exerting influence on the brain, logically analyzable as a series of (subconscious and uncontrollable) inferences. Where Peirce regards the percept as non-representational (7.597-7.687), the iconic sign, image, is distinguished from the percept precisely because of the latter's representational character (7.619).

d) Perception rests on both inherited and acquired habits. Peirce regards *association by resemblance* to be inborn, but also points out the difficulty of distinguishing between species' specific dispositions and what is due to early learning processes. In both cases, however, iconicity is founded on senso-motorical schematas. Hence the possibility of the intervention of perceptual stereotypes.

e) The concrete functioning of something as an iconic sign is a judgment that the sign is similar to (i.e., having properties in common with) its object.

f) Since everything has properties in common with everything else, a further principle of selection (in addition to similarity) must be operative to distinguish the relevant properties of both sign and object.

g) The additional, necessary principle of selection can be specified as the (supposed) purpose of the iconic representation. This means that relevance and usefulness are intervening factors in deciding iconicity. Peirce speaks sometimes of *association by interest* (7.499). This means that an iconic sign is *motivated*.

h) The *image, diagram, metaphor* distinction signifies different modes of iconic representation. In a certain sense there are differences in the level of abstraction between them, but they are first distinguished by different criteria of pertinence concerning the object's relevant features. Removed from the sensuous qualities of its object, the iconic sign, however, remains for its function dependent upon its own material and relational properties, and their motivated relationship with the object's properties.

i) Because of its possible indeterminacy (cf. b) and its potential for abstraction (cf. h), it follows that the iconic sign may attain a certain generality. Thus, it may denote classes of objects, in addition to individual objects (an anatomical map exhibits what characterizes species rather than individuals; whereas, a road map shows the relational properties of a specific network of roads according to some principle of projection and proportion).

j) From its generic characterization as a possibility (cf. a), an iconic sign despite its close relation to perception (cf. c, d, and e), need not be a sign of anything existent. On the contrary, an iconic sign may depict or exhibit imaginary objects, relations, or states of affairs.

k) An iconic sign's potential for generality (cf. i) and its ability to represent imaginary objects (cf. j) leads to the iconic sign's utility both in hypothetic-deductive reasoning and in the arts and literature.

l) Since the iconic sign itself is a perceptible object whose material and relational properties are significant, it may be observed and experimented on to the effect that hitherto unknown features of the object may be hypothesized.

m) In exhibiting its properties, and especially the relationships between them, the iconic sign offers a kind of evidential experience of the truth of the inference of which it is a part.

Let us, for the moment, leave the concept of the iconic sign with this resumé of its (supposed) characteristics. Not because this exposition is sufficient to convince skeptics of its coherence and usefulness, but because further discussion is better postponed until after we expound Peirce's description of the symbol.

## 5. The indexical sign

Although the indexical sign has provoked less controversy than the iconic sign, the consistency of the definition of this class of signs has also been contested. In an important article Thomas Goudge has claimed "that while Peirce says important things about some of these signs [i.e., the different kinds of indices, JDJ], his attempt to formulate a comprehensive, general theory of identification based on the index is not successful" (Goudge 1965: 53).

As a curiosity it should also be mentioned that within the Greimasian semiotics of "l'école de Paris" the index is even denied signhood. Greimas and Courtés in the *Sémiotique: Dictionnaire raisonné de la théorie du langage* say:

> If we admit, following the linguistic tradition of Saussure, that the ex-
> clusion of the referent is a necessary precondition for every semiotic en-
> terprise, then one has to accept that the index . . . enters into the category
> of non-sign (Greimas and Courtés 1979: 186, my transl.)

This book will disregard the above position because it seems obvious
that indexicality lies at the very core of the process of signification,
because ostension is bound to enter at some point in this process (as
even Hjelmslev realized [cf. pp. 45-46).

For Peirce indices belong to the category of secondness, and  he
distinguishes an index, or better an indexical sign, from iconic and
symbolic signs because it is

> a sign, or representation, which refers to its object not so much because of
> any similarity or analogy with it, nor because it is associated with general
> characters which that object happens to possess, as because it is in dy-
> namical (including spatial) connection both with the individual object, on
> the one hand, and with the senses or memory of the person for whom it
> serves as a sign, on the other hand. (2.305)

It is further defined as follows:

> Indices may be distinguished from other signs, or representations, by
> three characteristic marks: first, that they have no significant resem-
> blance to their objects; second, that they refer to individuals, single units,
> single collections of units, or single continua; third, that they direct the
> attention to their objects by blind compulsion. (2.306)

In the discussion of the iconic sign and perception, main features of
the index, or rather the indexical sign, have already been described,
even if the concept has only been mentioned in passing. According to
Peirce's categories, indexicality is bound up with secondness, and consequently with the dyadic aspect of experience, with force, and with
action and reaction. This is why Peirce distinguishes between genuine
and degenerate indices in the following way:

> An *Index* or *Seme* is a Representamen whose Representative character
> consists in its being an individual second. If the Secondness is an exist-
> ential relation, the Index is *genuine*. If the Secondness is a reference, the
> Index is *degenerate*. A genuine Index and its Object must be existent in-
> dividuals (whether things or facts), and its immediate Interpretant must
> be of the same character. (2.283)

In a fragment he specifies this distinction:

An *index* represents an object by virtue of its connection with it. It makes no difference whether the connection is natural, or artificial, or merely mental. There is, however, an important distinction between two classes of indices. Namely, some merely stand for things or individual quasi-things with which the interpreting mind is already acquainted, while others may be used to ascertain facts. Of the former class, which may be termed *designations,* personal, demonstrative, and relative pronouns, proper names, the letters attached to a geometrical figure, and the ordinary letters of algebra are examples. They act to force the attention to the thing intended. Designations are absolutely indispensable both to communication and to thought. No assertion has any meaning unless there is some designation to show whether the universe of reality or what universe of fiction is referred to. The other class of indices may be called *reagents.* Thus water placed in a vessel with a shaving of camphor thrown upon it will show whether the vessel is clean or not. (8.368, note 23)

This quotation admirably states what is specific to the indexical sign, or to the indexical aspect of signs. If we remember that the icon, index, and symbol distinction is founded on the relation of the sign to its dynamical object, the concept of *reagent* properly names a sign directly influenced by the action of the object on it.

Most of the examples of signs in the preceding sections on the object and the icon have had strong indexical aspects. A portrait, for instance, is influenced by its object, the model. If it is a photograph, the influence is *direct* and physical, namely the action of the light waves upon the film. At the same time, however, the action is also *mediated* by the properties and function of the camera and the film, by environmental conditions (chiefly distance, angle, and light), and by the techniques used for developing the negative and the picture. In case the portrait is a painting, an influence of the object upon the painting is still operative, even if the mediation effectuated by the artistic imagination of the painter may be complex.

In accordance with his categorial analysis, Peirce points out that an indexical sign may within itself contain an iconic sign. This is the case as regards the portrait. Ransdell has elegantly demonstrated the difference between the iconic and the indexical aspects of such a sign by a photograph of an identical twin. This photo may serve as an iconic representation of either twin, but it is only an indexical sign of the one who was photographed (Ransdell 1979: 56).

A pure icon, and even an iconic sign with negligible indexical aspects, remain, according to Peirce, a possibility; whereas, indices, and especially reagents, are said to be used in ascertaining facts (although indices do not by themselves assert anything). This is due to the double relationship between object and sign characterizing the reagent. This birelational character of the genuine index has already been exemplified by the weathercock (cf. Fig. 15) which indicates the direction of the wind, because it is determined by it. In this respect all genuine indices are the same.

The other characteristic of an indexical sign is shared by reagents and designations, namely the fact that they force the attention of the interpreter towards the designated object. In the quotation from the note to 8.365 Peirce's examples include linguistic shifters, i.e., deictical expressions that either link together the parts of the verbal text (e.g., relative pronouns) or link text and context with each other (e.g., demonstrative pronouns). The indispensability of an indexical sign in discourse is due to its power to identify its topic. Designations are, however, not confined to linguistic shifters; their prototype is rather what is caught in the anatomical sense of the word *index,* the pointing finger. Ostension is essential to designations making possible collateral observation, or as Russell would say, *knowledge* by *acquaintance* (Russell 1948: 87 passim), thus relating speech to a universe of discourse, experiential or fictional. On pages 83-84 Peirce's claim was quoted, in that "the meaning of the sign is not conveyed until not merely the interpretant but also this object is recognized," and this recognition of the object is precisely what the indexical aspect of a sign brings about. Just as the iconic sign, or the iconic aspect of signs, is characterized by being in some way similar to its dynamical object, so is the indexical sign characterized by what Peirce calls e*xperiential associations of contiguity* (3.419). This contiguity between sign and object is obvious as regards the reagents, since they came into being as reactions to the object. But designations are also characterized by connection by contiguity, or at least by the attempt to effectuate such a connection. Since, however, the routes of reagents and designations are opposite, the former going from object to sign, the latter from sign to object, in important respects they are different.

These differences may be illustrated by the following example. If, for instance, we interpret smoke as a sign of fire, we claim that fire is the dynamical object causing the smoke. Smoke is a natural phenomenon that functions as a reagent, but if we say, 'Look at the smoke there to your left, there must be a big fire,' then we are using linguistic signs (including designations) to refer to and to give directions for identifying the subject of the communication, which is the 'smoke as a sign of fire.' Evidently, the perception of the smoke has not caused the use of the word 'smoke' in the same sense as the fire is supposed to have caused the smoke, because even if the percept is forcing itself upon the mind of the utterer, it is not forcing him to utter these words. He could remain silent or say something else, for instance, 'Look at that big grey cloud over there.' Thus, we, with Peirce, have to distinguish a sign standing in a causal relation to its object from the referential function of the sign being used to designate something. It could be argued, however, that the perception of the phenomenon determined the utterance in another and much weaker sense, because his having this percept was the reason why he uttered the sentence. This means, however, that we are talking about acceptable reasons for saying something. We can further imagine that the other party in the dialogue answers: 'That is not smoke, that is fog.' In this case they will be referring to the same phenomenon, but in naming it differently they will ascribe different characteristics to it, because they do not interpret it in the same way. To speak of some object or state of affairs thus implies interpretation, but it certainly does not imply either that both are right or that there is no way of deciding what type of phenomenon the subject of their discourse really is. To decide this question Peirce suggests an experimental procedure involving some propositions in the conditional mood. He would say, for instance: 'If the cloud over there is smoke, we should expect to find fire or traces of fire in investigating the place.' If, upon investigation, we found a fire burning, then it would be reasonable to conclude that the word 'smoke' applies to the phenomenon. The word 'fog' does not.

It is tempting to distinguish between reagents as natural signs characterized by a causal relationship between object and sign on the one hand, and conventional signs, such as designations, on the other. Such a distinction cannot be made, however, outside an interpretative framework. According to Peirce, a causal relationship between two phenomena may exist regardless of its being known, and scientific inquiry consists, among other things, precisely in discovering and explaining such relationships. For such a causal relationship to assume sign function, however, it must be interpreted: Just as a designation can denote nothing unless the interpreting mind already is acquainted with the thing it denotes, so a reagent can indicate nothing unless the mind already is acquainted with its connection to the phenomenon it indicates (8.368, note 23). By pointing out that even reagents, as signs, are dependent on interpretation, Peirce makes clear that the third kind of relationship between sign and dynamical object, the symbolic, is indispensable in any sign action.

Nevertheless, there is certainly a considerable difference between reagents and designations, among other things, because reagents presuppose existing dynamical objects, and it is even tempting to say mind-independent objects, whereas this is not the case concerning designations.

Thomas A. Goudge (Goudge 1965: 66) indicates an important point in Peirce's reflections on designations. In discussing propositions Peirce writes:

> Every subject partakes of the nature of an index, in that its function is the characteristic function of an index, that of forcing the attention upon its object. Yet the subject of a symbolic proposition cannot strictly be an index. When a baby points at a flower and says, "Pretty," that is a symbolic proposition; for the word "pretty" being used, it represents its object only by virtue of a relation to it which it could not have if it were not intended and understood as a sign. The pointing arm, however, which is the subject of this proposition, usually indicates its object only by virtue of a relation to this object, which would still exist, though it were not intended or understood as a sign. But when it enters into the proposition as its subject, it indicates its object in another way. For it cannot be the subject of that symbolic proposition unless it is intended and understood to be so. Its merely being an index of the flower is not enough. It only becomes the subject of the proposition, because its being an index of the flower is evidence that it was *intended* to be. (2.357)

This example is parallel to the utterance, used above, about "smoke as a sign of fire." Both examples make it obvious that most designations are degenerate indices, and if they are to function presuppose intentional acts; whereas reagents, genuine indices, do not, because the object-sign relationship would exist even if it were not recognized.

A literary work of fiction is full of indices, i.e., designations (including the proper names of fictional characters and places), but their indicative and identificatory function is restricted to the author's fictional universe. They are guides to a mental landscape. One further problem becomes apparent by taking fictional designations into account, namely whether the dynamical objects of indices need to be mind-independent.

We normally think of reagents as the outcome of physical processes taking place and being observed in the world around us. It is
obvious that they also take place within our bodies; and symptoms of
diseases qualify as such intrabody reagents. Thomas Sebeok has suggested we treat symptoms and signals as separate classes of signs
distinct from the index (cf. Sebeok 1976: 117-142), but they are better
conceived as subspecies of the index, because their essential characters seem to be the same (cf. 5.474). Sebeok defines the symptom as
follows: *"A symptom is a compulsive, automatic, nonarbitrary sign,
such that the signifier is coupled with the signified in the manner of a
natural link. (A syndrome is a rule-governed configuration of symptoms with a stable designatum.)"* (Sebeok 1976: 124). Red spots of a
certain kind count as symptoms of measles, because they are naturally
linked with this disease. In fact they function, to the interpreter, as a
*pars pro toto,* as a synecdoche for the disease, because they *are objec-
tively* a part, and the easiest recognizable part, of it. This link between
sign and object is physical and, we presume, mind-independent; although we cannot in principle exclude further research that might be
able to point to psychosomatic elements in this desease.

The case is, however, more complicated concerning mental phenomena. Peirce treats this question in Ms. 200 (1907). He writes about
narrative as follows:

> A true narrative is true if the events described are *real.* Why real? because
> they are not figments, or "make-ups," whether intentionally or uninten-
> tionally; they remain true whatever I say about them, so that should I
> have stated them otherwise than I did, my assertions would be false. (Ms.
> 200, 1907:174-175)

Peirce then goes on to describe dreaming: "The dream itself was a real
occurence, a real hallucination, although the things dreamed of were
figments of the sleepy brain. What I say about my dream is true, if my
brain really did play such tricks. But the dream is not real" (ibid.,
175). This seems a sensible way of looking at such phenomena, but it
implies that figments of the brain may function as dynamical objects
generating reagents.

Obsessional behavior is a fairly clearcut example of this kind of
reagent, and being compulsive, automatic (or at least quasi-automa-
tic), and nonarbitrary it fits Sebeok's definition of a symptom very
well.

Like the red spots of measles, a given obsessional behavior pattern is a part, and the easiest recognizable part, of the mental disorder. It is thus synechdochially related to it, and determined by it. It makes little sense, however, to describe this relationship as physical; and more important, even when it makes good sense, it is by itself insufficient, although it is necessary, to trace the history of the disorder and to attempt to find the real events or states of affairs that played a part in the development of the illness. It is insufficient because something intervenes in the mental processing of interpersonal interaction, namely that the patient endows real events with specific significations and combinations. Such a patient suffers from "figments" of his own creation, because they mean something to him, whereas they are more or less void of significance for others. Freud has a beautiful semiotic description of a case of paranoia of jealousy. He writes about attacks of jealousy experienced by a young, married, and paranoic man as follows:

> These attacks drew their material from his observation of minute indications, by which his wife's quite unconscious coquetry, unnoticeable to any one else, had betrayed itself to him. She had unintentionally touched the man sitting next her with her hand; she had turned too much towards him, or she had smiled more pleasantly than when alone with her husband. He was extraordinarily observant of all these manifestations of her unconscious, and always knew how to interpret them correctly, so that he really was always in the right about it, and could furthermore call in analysis to justify his jealousy. His abnormality really reduced itself to this, that he watched his wife's unconscious mind much more closely and then regarded it as far more important than anyone else would have thought of doing. (Freud [1922b] S.E. XVIII, 1955, 225-226)

A discussion about the validity of the psychoanalytic interpretation of jealousy and paranoia would certainly take us too far afield; here, the importance of Freud's case history is his description of the self-created hell of significations in which his patient is living. For the patient, his wife's every action, when directed towards other men, became an infallible index of her infidelity, whereas his interpretations of her behavior were symptoms or indices of his own mental disorder.

Cases like the above are examples of genuine indices, because they exist, persist, and insist as nonconventional and nonarbitrary sign relations outside the control of rational throught. They are, however certainly not mind-independent; indeed, they depend on individual minds, and they are certainly mediated by symbols, because they are based on characteristics imputed to actions by the patient's use of language (inner speech).

According to Peirce, we all inhabit two worlds, the external world of facts and the internal world of fancy. He normally distinguishes between them by claiming that we are masters of our inner world, because it obeys our creative *fiat*. In one place, he recognizes that "the greater part of the reader's labor is expended on the world of fancy" (1.321), but even this statement does not take into account the inner compulsions described above. He recognizes, however, that mental constructions contain indexical signs and allow a degenerate form of observation:

> But the imaginary constructions of the mathematician, and even dreams, so far approximate to reality as to have a certain degree of fixity, in consequence of which they can be recognized and identified as individuals. In short, there is a degenerate form of observation which is directed to the creations of our own minds - using the word observation in its full sense as implying some degree of fixity and quasi-reality in the object to which it endeavours to conform. (2.305)

By its very definition the pure icon is a theoretical construct we will never encounter (cf. p. 94); as regards indexicality it belongs to second-ness, and thus implies existence. From the point of view of categorical analysis, a pure index is thus conceivable as an actually existing sign. It is highly interesting, therefore, that Peirce seems to doubt the actual existence of the pure index. He writes:

> But it would be difficult if not impossible, to instance an absolutely pure index, or to find any sign absolutely devoid of the indexical quality. Psychologically, the action of indices depends upon association by contiguity, and not upon association by resemblance or upon intellectual operations. (2.306)

This statement does not in the least detract from the importance and usefulness of his description of this sign function; it substantiates, however, the suspicion that the distinction between iconic, indexical, and symbolic signs is a distinction in the predominant mode of function of different signs and not a classification according to which any sign can be univocally fit into a single category.

## 6. The symbolic sign

In relation to the iconic and the indexical sign, the symbol, or the symbolic sign, is defined negatively. It is neither a sign by virtue of its inherent perceptible qualities, nor by virtue of some real relation with its object, but, as Peirce says, "simply because it is interpreted as a sign in another sign" (L 75, 1902: Cr 146). The following quotation sums up this difference:

> A chalk mark is like a line though nobody uses it as a sign; a weather-cock turns with the wind, whether anybody notices it or not. But the word "man" has no particular relation to men unless it be recognized as being so related. That is not only what constitutes it a sign, but what gives it the peculiar relation to its object which makes it significant of that particular object. (L 75, 1902: Cr 149)

Positively, the symbol is characterized by two ideas: 1) the relationship between sign and object exists only by virtue of a habit, and 2) the relationship is mediated and made explicit by means of another representation, an interpretant. This means that the symbol points to its own interpretation in other signs.

Saussure and Benveniste see the negative aspect of the relationship between sign and dynamical object (as regards the symbol) as a lack of motivation. Saussure states:

> The idea of "sister" is not linked by any inner relationship to the succession of sounds s-ö-r which serves as its signifier in French; that it could be represented equally by just any other sequence is proved by differences among languages and by the very existence of different languages: the signified "ox" has as its signifier b-ö-f on one side of the border and o-k-s (Ochs) on the other. (Saussure 1959: 67-68)

Benveniste objects that it is not the internal relationship between signifier and signified which is arbitrary (according to him it is necessary); rather, it is the relation of the total sign to its signified object that is arbitrary, i.e., unmotivated (cf. Benveniste 1966: 50). Whether Benveniste is right in his emendation of Saussure's argument is a question for Saussure philology and need not concern us here (for another view of this problem see Ege 1949).

To Peirce there is no doubt that the conventionality of the symbol (in structuralist terminology *sign*) lies in its relation to the object, because its denotative function is governed by convention. Using the example *man* once more, Peirce reflects on the linguistic symbol:

> The word itself has no existence although it has a real being, *consisting* in the fact that existents *will* conform to it. It is a general mode of succession of three sounds or representamens of sounds, which becomes a sign only in the fact that a habit, or acquired law, will cause replicas of it to be interpreted as meaning a man or men. The word and its meaning are both general rules; but the word alone of the two prescribes the qualities of its replicas in themselves. (2.292)

Peirce, here, is close to a linguistic way of thinking by his distinction between two kinds of rules, the "word-rule" governing the combination of the expression plane (sounds, letters) on the one hand, and the "meaning-rule" governing the application of the word on the other. The conventionality of symbols exists, because "word-rules" and "meaning rules" do not influence each other. In other words the rules governing, or generating, the sign as a perceptible entity offer no indication as to its applicability and interpretation.

Its rule-governed character (that its significant character is due to habit) is the first positive aspect of the symbol's definition, but to accept this as the symbol's distinctive characteristic in contradistinction to the icon and the index, is problematic. The first reason, according to Peirce's own analysis of iconicity is, that the iconic sign functions as such only if it is related to a concept of a purpose (cf. p. 96). This means that as the ground of iconic representation we do not have similarity *tout court,* but *similarity for a purpose.* In other words, conventions specifying the relevant frame of reference govern iconic signs. The conventionality of an iconic sign has been argued, for instance, by Douglas Greenlee:

> In order for a sign to designate an object through a likeness or similarity, the sign must have been APPOINTED, as it were, to serve as a representative of the sort that it does. A convention or rule must have been established to the effect that the sign should be interpreted to signify in a certain way, which it does through some respect of resemblance. A CONVENTION OR RULE OF INTEPRETATION MUST ESTABLISH THE GROUND OF THE REPRESENTATION (AND ACCORDINGLY SIGNIFICATION) OF THE ICON. (Greenlee 1973: 77-78)

Greenlee concludes that the distinction between iconic and symbolic signs is on the verge of collapsing, and that "symbolism thus begins to emerge as one of the key concepts of a general theory of signs" (ibid). The second reason, according to Peirce's statement about the index (here quoted p. 109) that even "a reagent can indicate nothing unless the mind is already acquainted with its connection with the phenomenon it indicates," makes obvious that all three kinds of signs in order to function as signs require a mediating representation relating sign and object. Consequently, what is claimed about the symbol, that it is interpreted in another sign, is true for all signs; or more specifically, what is left to characterize the symbol is its negative characteristic, that neither being like nor influenced by its object.

Greenlee may seem justified in claiming that symbolism is a key concept of sign theory, but I, for one, am unwilling to give up the icon, index, symbol distinction (and neither is Greenlee for that matter), because it describes different modes of signifying. Since a close look at iconic and symbolic signs (especially) brings them close to each other, it might therefore be useful to return to the list of the iconic sign's characteristics (pp. 105-107) to see which are specific to the iconic sign itself, and which are also valid for symbolic signs.

| *Iconic sign* | *Symbolic sign* |
|---|---|
| a) Categorized as firstness (of thirdness); characterized by quality and possiblity. | a) Categorized as thirdness (of thirdness); characterized by mediation and necessity. |
| b) Exhibition of embodied qualities and relations crucial to the referential function of the sign. | b) Referential function independent of the sign's inherent qualities and relations. |
| c) Exhibition of qualities related to perception of significant forms and qualities. | c) Manifestation of intrasystemic distinctive features. |
| d) Utilizes senso-motoric schematas and perceptual stereotypes to signify. | d) Utilizes acquired senso-motorical patterning to differentiate. |
| e) Similarity with its object is the ground of sign function. | e) Dissimilarity with other signs within the semiotic ground of sign function. |

| f) Similarity for a purpose. | f) Distinguishability for a purpose |
| g) Relevance and usefulness. | g) Relevance and usefulness. |
| h) Criteria of pertinence hold between sign and object. | h) Criteria of pertinence hold among the signs themselves. |
| i) Potential for generality. | i) General signs. |
| j) Sign of possibility as well as of the existence. | j) Sign of possibility as well as of the existence. |
| k) Usefulness for deductive and creative reasoning. | k) Usefulness for deductive and creative reasoning. |
| l) Allows inferences through observation and experimentation. | l) Allows inferences through combination into propositions and arguments. |
| m) Allows evidental proofs. | m) Allows discursive reasoning. |

The distinction of a) is categorical. In the analysis of concrete signs it may only serve as a point of departure, because existent signs, and semioses that really happen, contain all three modes of signification (cf. below). The differences noted from b) to f) and in h) may be summarized as concerning 1) the frame of reference within which the qualities of the signs are important, and 2) the exhibition of similarity for a purpose vs. distinction allowing identical replication. As regards material and relational qualities, the frame of reference relevant for predominantly iconic signs is the sign-object relationship; whereas, for predominantly symbolic signs it is the sign-sign relationship, i.e., the intra-systemic differences of substance and form. The difference, therefore, is not that iconic signs, unlike symbolic signs, utilize perceptual schematas, because symbolic sign systems, such as natural languages, are dependent on users' acquisition of certain articulatory and auditory patterns (for instance, a Dane needs much training to learn to pronounce and even to recognize Polish sound patterns and sound differences that distinguish between significations). Despite certain dogmas of structuralism, the articulation and differentiation of positive qualities lie at the very heart of symbolic systems. Even if the articulation by differentiating between elements of expression makes denotation and signification possible, the decisive reason is that the specific articulation of a symbolic (linguistic) sign has no relation to its referential potential. The difference, therefore, between iconic and symbolic signs is in the direction of what could be called *articulatory fit*. If this fit concerns the object, the sign will be predominatly iconic, if it concerns the sign system, it will be predominantly symbolic.

Peirce is aware that a concrete sign may, and often does, have a double, or bifocal, fit, meaning that its material and relational properties are determined both by its referential and by its systemic character. A certain tension in his different reflections on paintings and portraits illustrates this point:

> We say that the portrait of a person we have not seen is *convincing*. So far as, on the ground merely of what I see in it, I am led to form an idea of the person it represents, it is an Icon. But, in fact, it is not a pure Icon, because I am greatly influenced by knowing that it is an *effect*, through the artist, caused by the original's appearance, and is thus in a genuine Obsistent relation to that original. Besides, I know that portraits have but the slightest resemblance to their originals, except in certain conventional respects, and after a conventional scale of values. (2.92)

In addition to stressing the role played by indexicality in portraits, here Peirce points to this kind of picture's conventionality. Elsewhere, he tries to isolate what is specificly iconic about representational paintings:

> Icons are so completely substituted for their objects as hardly to be distinguished from them. Such are the diagrams of geometry. A diagram, indeed, so far as it has a general signification, is not a pure icon; but in the middle part of our reasonings we forget that abstractness in great measure, and the diagram is for us the very thing. So in contemplating a painting, there is a moment when we lose the consciousness that it is not the thing, the distinction of the real and the copy disappears, and it is for the moment a pure dream — not any particular existence, and yet not general. At that moment we are contemplating an *icon*. (3.362)

If the painting of the quotation is a portrait, the moment Peirce is speaking about will be the one in which the interpreter concentrates on the articulatory fit between sign and object, overlooking momentarily the style and conventions of the painting as a work of art. It would be odd to deny that certain classes of signs (portraits, paintings, photos, etc.) function in this way; consequently, statements such as "this portrait represents a remarkable likeness to the way he looked at that time of his life" are meaningful. Other statements, such as "This portrait represents very well his style of painting during that period of his career," are also meaningful, but here the articulatory fit is directed from the particular sign (the painting) to other signs (other paintings).

Since the senses are not innocent, because perception itself is bound up with learning processes within specific cultural frameworks, it is impossible to disregard the intrasystemic articulatory fit of any sign. Internal articulation and differentiation also necessarily regulate and stereotypify predominantly iconic signs from the very beginning, so that likeness is experienced through conventions (*through* here meaning both *by virtue of* and *disregarding*). Consequently, *similarity* and *conventionality*, although differently directed, are co-present in iconic signs. These kinds of signs are, however, distinguished from other signs (e.g., symbolic) by their perceptually motivated relationship to the object. This motivation depends on a complex, culturally determined horizon of expectations governed and specified by the probabilities of the situational context. The following two signs may serve as examples:

Fig. 25

Placed on doors in public buildings their information value is, for somebody who knows the code, immediate and unambiguous (except of course for the perennial question: at what age should a boy go with his mother and at what age with his father?). They exemplify the co-presence of iconicity and symbolicity. Their articulatory fit is, indeed, bifocal; the internal differentiation between the figures is certainly just as important as their relation to their respective object. They are iconic in exemplifying a culturally determined perceptual stereotype which is valid and motivated despite of its highly conventional character; and although they are culture bound, they are not language bound, because in most industrialized countries they communicate to people. The utility of such signs, that may be termed *symbolic icons,* will be immediately recognized if confronted with the following symbolic signs:

MIEHET                                           NAISET

Unless one knows Finnish, it is hard to decide which door to use, or even hard to know whether the rooms behind the doors are, in fact, lavatories (*miehet* means *men, naiset women*).

The borderline between predominantly iconic and predominantly symbolic signs is difficult to draw in practice. If, however, the iconic sign is defined as exhibiting a relevant, perceptually motivated articulatory fit directed towards its object, then it is possible to point out the part played by iconicity in individual signs or texts.

Peirce also points out the closeness of iconic and symbolic signs to each other when speaking about the origin of symbols. He says:

> Symbols grow. They come into being by development out of other signs, particularly from icons, or from mixed signs partaking of the nature of icons and symbols. We think only in signs. These mental signs are of mixed nature; the symbol-parts of them are called concepts. (2.302)

Peirce is also indicating what symbols, or symbolic signs, contribute to semiosis (the signifying process), namely conceptualization detached from any individual image, diagram, or metaphor. The limitations of iconic signs are due to their articulatory fit directed towards the object. However stereotyped, that fit is conceived and exhibited in the sign. Iconic signs have a certain potential for generality (as pointed out on p. 107 and exemplified by a map of human anatomy), but being tied down to the exhibition, however rarified, of a senso-motorical recognition of the objects, their strength, to exemplify by exhibiting, becomes their weakness as well, since they cannot assert anything, and consequently cannot express and hypothesize about general facts, rules, and laws.

Commenting on the maxim, to which he subscribes, *Nihil est in intellectu quod non prius fuerit in sensu,* Peirce criticizes Berkeley:

> Berkeley and nominalists of his stripe deny that we have any idea at all of a triangle in general, which is neither equilateral, isosceles, nor scalene. But he cannot deny that there are propositions about triangles in general, which propositions are either true or false; and as long as that is the case, whether we have an *idea* of a triangle in some psychological sense or not, I

do not, as a logician, care. We have an *intellectus*, a meaning, of which the triangle in general is an element. (5.181)

Although the Berkeley criticism is of no concern here, Peirce's point that true propositions about triangles in general exist illustrates the contribution of symbolic signs to the thought process. Peirce does not think an unbridgable gap exists between perceptual judgments and general, intellectual judgments. On the contrary, perceptual judgments contain general elements that allow the deduction of universal propositions from their particular propositions (cf. 5.156-5.157). This claim is, of course, controversial. Semiotically speaking, it would be impossible to express general judgments by nothing but iconic signs, not only because iconic signs, if uninterpreted in symbols, have no assertive power, but also because by themselves they allow neither generalizations nor certain relevant limitations and specifications.

The point may be illustrated by returning to our symbolic icons, the stereotyped lavatory signs (fig. 25). Because of a culturally determined learning process, we do, in fact, translate the

iconic signs into symbolic ones. We read ![sign] as *men's restroom* and

![sign] as *women's restroom,* a coded response, that, strictly speaking, is unwarranted by the iconic signs themselves. Let us suppose it is only known that the rooms behind the doors are lavatories. In this case, a possible reading might be:

![sign] : *lavatory for people wearing slacks,* and: ![sign]

:*lavatory for people wearing dresses* (or skirts). If one knows Finnish, *miehet* and *naiset* will have the great merit of indicating the general and relevant classification. If somebody, despite norms of decency, were to insist that the message could be made iconically unambiguous by choosing a stereotype of a naked man and a naked woman, it could be objected that such signs, contrary to intention, might be interpreted as a *lavatories for naked men and women.*

The power and vital necessity of symbols, symbolic signs, come from their generality. Peirce holds that the symbol does not indicate individual things. It "denotes a kind of thing" (2.300), and it is "applicable to whatever may be found to realize the idea connected with it"

(2.298). This is why Peirce sometimes considers symbols such as *the moon* and *the sun* as degenerate, because they denote a singular object.

Generality and conventionality seem inextricably bound up with each other. The intrasystemic character of the signs' articulatory fit allows the necessary detachment from concrete objects in order to select, combine, foreground, and disregard the elements of experience without taking into account the accidental contingency of any particular environment. Furthermore, symbols, such as natural and artificial languages, incorporate elements such as quantifiers and operators that state relations hardly expressable in iconic signs (cf. Freud's analysis, in *the Interpretation of Dreams* [1900], of the difficulties of rendering logical words iconically). Finally, we should mention the reflexivity of symbolic sign systems (most importantly natural language). This is an outstanding feature. It is possible to think about symbols in symbols, because a symbol's meaning is given in its translation into another symbol, its interpretant. This is why symbolic signs alone afford the means of discursive reasoning, being combinable into propositions and arguments, and finally into discourse. Through their higher level of generality, symbolic signs part company with the iconic ones with which they have so much in common (cf. the list of comparison between the iconic and symbolic sign, pp. 118-119).

The above does not mean that the symbol, the genuine sign as Peirce calls it, in contradistinction to the two degenerate classes of signs, the icon and the index, alone suffices for acquiring knowledge. Semiosis, the signifying process, requires the collaboration of all three classes of signs. This chapter concludes by comparing Peirce's classification to findings within the study of animal behavior (what Thomas Sebeok has named zoosemiotics) and developmental and cognitive psychology.


## 7. Logical and developmental features of the icon, index, symbol distinction

There is contiguity between nature and culture (between zoosemiotics and anthroposemiotics). Even if human sign production and sign interpretation are different from the limited, genetically encoded sign systems of other species, human communication is built on and has developed from their sign processing capacities. A famous study of animal behavior, Niko Tinbergen's observations of and experiments with the Three-spined Stickleback (this study also attracted the attention of E.H. Gombrich, cf. Gombrich 1960:87, and Hall, cf. Hall 1966: 16-18), poses interesting questions about animals, concerning the function and kinds of signs in mating and combat behavior related to this contiguity.

During breeding season the male Three-spined Sticklebacks isolate themselves and select territories:

> They assume brilliant nuptial colours. The eye becomes a shining blue, the back, instead of dull brownish, becomes greenish, the underparts become red. Whenever another fish, and particularly another male, enters the territory, it is attacked. (Tinbergen 1953:9)

The male then builds a nest for the female Stickleback to spawn and to protect the fertilized eggs. The actual mating is described in this way:

> The nest is now finished. At once the male changes its colour. The red becomes still more intense, and all the black colour cells which are found on the back contract to minute dots. Thereby the underlying glittering bluish crystals of guanin which are situated in a deeper stratum of the skin are exposed, and the back now becomes a shiny whitish blue. The light back and the dark red underside, together with the brilliant eye, now make the male extremely conspicuous. Displaying this attractive dress, the male parades up and down its territory.
>
> In the meantime the females, which have not bothered about nest building at all, have developed a brilliant silvery gloss, and their bodies are heavily swollen by the bulky eggs which have developed in the ovaries. They cruise about in schools. In a good Stickleback habitat, they pass through occupied territories repeatedly during the day. Each male, if ready to receive a female, reacts to them by performing a curious dance towards and all around them. (Each dance consists of a series of leaps, during which the male first turns as if going to swim away from the females, then abruptly turns towards them with its mouth wide open. Sometimes it may hit a female, but usually it stops just in front of it, and then turns away for a new performance. This zigzag dance frightens most of the females away, but a single one may be sufficiently matured to be willing to spawn, and such a female does exactly the opposite from fleeing: it turns towards the male, at the same time adopting a more or less upright attitude. The male now immediately turns round and swims hurriedly towards the nest. The female follows it. Arrived at the nest, the male thrusts its snout into the entrance, turning along its body axis, so that it lies on its side, its back towards the female, which now tries to wriggle into the nest. With a strong

beat of her tail she manages to penetrate into the narrow opening, and slips in. She remains in the nest, her head protruding from one end, the tail from the other. The male now begins to prod her tail base with his snout, giving series of quick thrusts. After some time the female begins to lift her tail, and soon she spawns. This done, she quietly pushes through the nest, while the male enters it and, slipping through in his turn, fertilizes the eggs. Then he chases her away. . . . This is the end of the whole mating ceremony. There is no "marriage," no personal relationships, and the female's whole task in reproduction is just to provide the eggs. The whole care of eggs and young is the male's job. The association between male and female therefore is just a series of quick reciprocal reactions. (Tinbergen 1953:10-11)

Unfortunately we must omit Tinbergen's fascinating account of the male Stickleback's parental care and turn to a short description of the male's combat behavior. Here the interesting point is neither the actual fighting technique nor the peculiar threat behavior. Actual fighting is rarer than threat. What is interesting, in this context, is what releases fighting or threatening behavior in the male during mating season.

First, whether a male Stickleback attacks, shams an attack, or flees depends on where two male Sticklebacks encounter each other. If male Stickleback B enters into the territory of male Stickleback A, then as a rule A will attack and B will flee; if A enters B 's territory, B will attack and A will flee (Tinbergen has shown this to be the case using the same pair of Sticklebacks by moving them from one territory to another, Tinbergen 1953: 62-64).

Second, although a male Stickleback will fight or threaten to fight in a variety of different situations and against a variety of other animals, e.g., to protect the young during mating season, it will almost invariably attack another male Stickleback that enters its territory, whereas it will court a female.

Tinbergen sums up these factors as follows:

Stimuli from the territory to which the animal reacts either innately or as an added result of conditioning, makes the animal confine its fighting to the territory.

The gross timing of the attack is again a matter of outside factors. As in mating, the first, very crude timing depends on sex hormones. Fighting appears as a consequence of gonadal growth which, in its turn, through the pituitary gland, depends on rhythmic factors such as day lengthening in the case of many animals of the northern temperate zone. The more accurate timing however is again a matter of reaction to signals. Signals from the rival release fighting when the latter comes too near the territory, or whatever the defended object may be. These signals always have a curious double function. When displayed by a stranger, they draw the attacker to it. When displayed by an attacker on its own ground, they intimidate the stranger. (Tinbergen 1953: 64-65)

According to Tinbergen, the signal releasing fighting behavior in a male Three-spined Stickleback during mating season is the sight, display, of the intruding male's red belly. Tinbergen describes his beautiful experiment in this way:

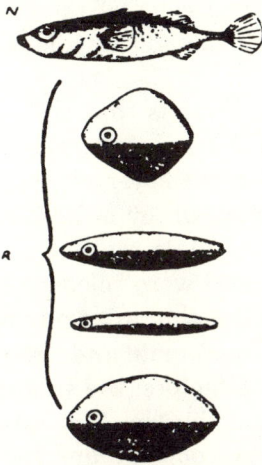

FIG. 40.—Models used in experiments on the release of fighting in male Three-spined Stickleback. A perfectly shaped silvery model (N) is rarely attacked, while crude models with red undersides (R) are strongly attacked (after Tinbergen, 1951)

Models of males release the same response, provided they are red underneath. A bright blue eye and a light bluish back add a little to the model's effectiveness, but shape and size do not matter within very wide limits. A cigar-shaped model with just an eye and a red underside releases much more intensive attack than a perfectly shaped model or even a freshly killed Stickleback which is not red. . . . Size has so little influence that all males which I observed even "attacked" the red mail vans passing about a hundred yards away; that is to say they raised their dorsal spines and made frantic attempts to reach them, which of course was prevented by the glass wall of the aquarium. When a van passes the laboratory, where a row of twenty aquaria were situated along the large windows, all males dashed towards the window side of their tanks and followed the van from one corner of their tank to the other. (Tinbergen 1953: 66-67)

A few other points should be added. First, a red painted model not only releases fighting behavior in a male Three-spined Stickleback, but also during mating season a mature female will follow that model to the nest, if the model is made to make the appropriate movements. She will even spawn, if she is touched by quivering movements. Furthermore, such release signals have been found in other animals. An impressive case is reported by Tinbergen: During mating season a male Robin will not attack a mounted immature Robin which has a brown breast, while an isolated tuft of red feathers will release the fighting behavior (Tinbergen 1953: 67).

Even more semiotically interesting is the study of Herring Gull chicks' responses to different models of the bill and head of adult Herring Gulls. Tinbergen found that the most prominent releaser is "a red colour patch which stands out quite conspicuously against the yellow background of the bill itself." The chicks' response to a model without a red patch was only one-fourth the number of responses to a model with the patch. The shape and general color of the model's bill and head made no difference; even a model of a bill without a head released about the same number of responses. If the model represented a bill without any patch, a red bill released twice as many responses as any other color, while a yellow bill, the natural color of the bill, released no more responses than a white, blue, or black (for this see Tinbergen 1953: 79-80).

There are three more significant points. The first is that the response of the male Three-spined Stickleback to the red underside of another male and to the appearance and behavior of the female, both during breeding season, is innate. This has been shown by isolating a male Stickleback from the egg stage on. When the male reached maturity, fighting and courtship behavior occurred and were released in the same way as in non-isolated males. The second is that after having fertilized the eggs the male Stickleback attacks the female and drives her off. According to Tinbergen, this is due to two factors: the sudden drop of the male's sex drive after ejaculation, and the fact that after having laid her eggs, she "has no longer a swollen abdomen and thus fails to provide one of the releasers evoking the male's sexual response. She now offers mainly attack-releasing stimuli" (Tinbergen 1953: 108). The third is the answer to the question why hybridization in closely related species is rare. The answer seems to be that mating behavior constitutes a complex pattern of actions and reactions; even if a specimen of the opposite sex from a related species may release some responses, it will normally fail to release the whole necessary interactional series that leads to copulation. A Three-spined Stickleback might, for example, be expected to interbreed with its near relative, the Ten-spined Stickleback, but is prevented by the different mating colors and behavior. In Spring the Ten-spined Stickleback male develops a pitch black color that attracts the females of its own species, but not the Three-spined females.

The relevance of these ethological observations both to semiotics in general and to questions concerning Peirce's second trichotomy of signs are twofold: These observations prove, if anybody doubts it, the existence throughout the animal kingdom of rather complicated, innate communication systems. The existence of such systems stresses the continuity between nature and culture. Second they abundantly confirm Thomas Short's claim that legisigns are everywhere life exists (cf. p. 70). The question is rather this: to which kind of signs do these releasers, and the ensuing sequences of actions and reactions, belong? It seems reasonable to claim they are predominantly indexical signs. Given the appropriate context they exert a compulsive influence in the species-specific interpreter, and they elect a specific response. Furthermore, such signs are synecdochical. The red underside of the male Stickleback, for instance, *is* a part of its male sexuality, and the part that most conspicuously displays it. Thus, a relation of contiguity exists between this particular aspect and its total sexuality. To fit it more exactly into Peirce's ten classes of signs, we would classify it as a *dicent indexical legisign*. It functions as a sort of advertisement saying both "Come, here is a male Three-spined Stickleback ready for sex!" and "Beware, here is a male Three-spined Stickleback ready for aggressiveness!"

The above interpretation, as far as it goes, seems to the point. It is necessary to reflect a little more on the specific signs themselves, e.g., the *red underside* of the Stickleback and the *red breast* of the Robin. Remembering that Peirce claims that "a genuine Index may contains a Firstness, and so an Icon as a constituent part of it" (2.283), it is tempting to claim that the red underside and red breast are iconic signs, or better yet, iconic aspects embedded in predominantly indexical signs. The only trouble is that it cannot be right. In defense of such a classification it might be said that *redness* constitutes a positive quality, and this quality is the specific releasing factor. This is, of course, true and important. An iconic sign, however, presupposes a comparison that brings out a similarity (or better yet, shared properties) between sign and object (Peirce's *ground*). Consequently, we have to ask ourselves to what is the red underside of the Stickleback and the red breast of the Robin similar? The answer has to be "to nothing" or if we would prefer, "to itself," stressing that the red color constitutes a case of self-representation. We could say that the redness represents the male sexuality of the species in question in the same way as the word "sails" in the expression "fifty sails" is taken synecdochically to represent "ships." The "sails" are, however, not in any way similar to the "ships." They are a significant part of (certains types of) ships; and this analogy is true as well of the mating colors.

The models of the male Stickleback Tinbergen used in his experiments are iconic signs, because they represent a significant likeness with the object embedded in varying degrees of dissimilarities. And throughout nature iconic signs exist, as Thomas Sebeok has shown convincingly. One of Sebeok's example should be quoted here in full. He writes:

Aphids are small, soft-bodied insects, very vulnerable to predator attack, protected and tended by ants with which they communicate by an alarm pheromone that functions to stabilize their association. Their blissful liaison is further reinforced by the fact that the ants "milk" the aphids by vibrating their antennae against an aphid's back: the aphids then secrete droplets of honeydew which are consumed by the ants. Kloft insightfully realized that this congenial bond must rest on a "misunderstanding," in view of which he proposed, as a working hypothesis, that the hind end of an aphid's abdomen together with the kicking of its hind legs constitutes, for an ant worker, a compound sign vehicle, the icon, signifying, from its perspective, the head of another ant together with its antennal movement, the model: "so bemerkt man," says Kloft of the observer, "eine geradezu verblüffende Ähnlichkeit" (see Fig. 1-3). In other words, in an act of perversion of the normal trophallaxis occuring between sisters, the ant identifies the replica (the rear end of the aphid) with the model (the front end of her sister), and then proceeds to solicit on the basis of this misinformation, treating a set of vital releasers out of context, viz., in the manner of an icon (or, to be more specific, an effigy). The multiple resemblances between this icon and the object for which it stands are so striking, subtle, and precisely modulated that they can hardly be explained away as an evolutionary coincidence. In loose adherence to Uexküll's terminology introduced above, the aphid can thus be regarded as an iconic releasing (auslösende) scheme that sparks off the ant's chain of behavior pattern, thus bringing the ethological analysis (Lorenz 1965: 268) into a common from frame with the semiotic analysis.

(Sebeok, 1979: 13-14)

Since Sebeok's example involves a kind of mimicry, we are confronted with iconic signs. It should be added, mimicry in nature seems to be a survival factor.

To explain the problem concerning the classification of the Three-spined Stickleback's nuptial colors, it is useful to make a schematic, componential analysis of the relevant features (Fig. 26).

| | Outside mating season | | In mating season | |
|---|---|---|---|---|
| | Three-spined Stickleback | | | |
| Colors and form | Male: brownish back | Female: slim | Male: shining blue eye, from greenish to shining with-ish-blue back, red underside | Female: silvery gloss, swollen abdomen |
| Behavior | | | First "lead," then "attack" female | |
| | Ten-spined Stickleback | | | |
| | Male: | Female: | Male: | Female: |
| Colors and form | | | pitch black | |
| Behavior | | | First "attack," then "lead" female | |

Fig. 26

The Three-spined Stickleback's nuptial colors function as releasers to which the female is genetically programmed to respond. They do not attract the female of the closely related Ten-spined Stickleback's. Their absence means no response is released in the female. The schema can therefore be read as a table of differences, where the decisive factor is the presence or absence of certain marks or distinctive features. To fit them into Peirce's classification, it seems most sensible to classify them as symbolic signs. This may at first seem strange, because normally we associate Peirce's symbol with human language and artificial sign systems. His concept of the symbolic sign is, however, explicitly designed to cover cases as the above. In his entry in *Baldwin's Dictionary* he defines a symbol as follows: "A Sign which is constituted a sign merely or mainly by the fact that it is used and understood as such whether the habit is natural or conventional, and without regard to the motive which originally governed its selection" (2.307). When he comments on the Renaissance logician Burgersdicius' term *thema,* he says it seems to be a sign which is "connected with its object by a convention that it shall be so understood, or else by a natural instinct or intellectual act" (2.308). He continues, saying this definition is equivalent to his definition of the symbol. In 1895 he explictly says that earlier: "I restricted symbols to conventional signs, which was another error" (2.340). Finally, in "Prolegomena to an apology for pragmaticism" (1906), he defines a symbol as a sign that denotes the object in consequence of a habit, and adds, "which term I use as including a natural disposition" (4.531).

Releasers, such as the male Stickleback's red underside and the red patch on the Herring Gull's bill, agree admirably with the concept of the symbol as being related to its object (and interpretant) by a natural disposition, i.e., an innate habit. The force exerted by these signs makes them predominantly indexical, but the sign vehicle, to use Morris' happy expression, is symbolic rather than iconic, even if it is a positive quality.

The point of making this excursion into ethology is twofold: First, ethological findings stress that classification of a given sign as iconic, indexical, or symbolic is a matter of foregrounding its predominant mode of function. Second, from an evolutionary point of view the different types of signs do not replace each other. There is a vast difference between the nuptial colors of the Stickleback and human speech, but this is not due to the former being iconic, which it is not, and the second symbolic. It is rather due to the difference on the one hand between an innate, limited, and inflexible instinctual semiotic competence, and on the other a learning capacity that makes habit-changes possible.

My second example explaining Peirce's classifications is from cognitive and developmental psychology, specifically from the works of Jean Piaget and Jerome S. Bruner. Piaget has been analyzed from semiotic points of view by Krampen (1986) and Uexküll (1986): furthermore, Bouissac (1986) has pertinent observations on iconicity and biology). In exploring their views I will concentrate on matters of principle, however tempting it would be to do justice to their rich empirical material. An important part of these two psychologists' work focuses on the growth of representation in the child. According to Bruner there are three ways in which we may be said to know something; "through doing it, through a picture or image of it, and through some such symbolic means as language" (Bruner 1966: 6). Piaget says:

> Representation thus occurs as a result of the union of "signifiers" that allow of evocation of absent objects with a system of meanings by which they are related to present objects. This specific connection between "signifier" and "signified" is typical of a new function that goes beyond sensory-motor activity and that can be characterised in a general way as the "symbolic function." It is this function that makes possible the acquisition of language or collective "signs," but its range is much wider, since it also embraces "symbols" as distinct from "signs," *i.e.*, the images that intervene in the development of imitation, play and even cognitive representation. It has in particular frequently been observed in cases of aphasia and in the development of children, that there are certain connections between the use of language and spatial representation. The symbolic function is thus essential for the constitution of representative space as well as of the other "real" categories of thought. (Piaget 1962: 277-278)

In the developmental psychology of Jean Piaget the criterion for the presence of the sign function, or semiological function, is the absence of the object or state of affairs referred to (Piaget 1962: 277-278). This does not mean, however, that before being able to refer to absent objects the environment and its objects and persons do not signify anything to the child. Characteristic of the pre-semiotic (as Piaget calls it), kind of signification is, according to him, that it is a precondition for something to be attributed sign function that the significatum (object) is co-present with the object that assumes the position of significator (sign). This means that at this stage a perceived continuity is necessary between sign and object. As examples of kinds of signs not separated from their objects, Piaget mentions an aspect of something (whiteness for milk), the visible part of something which has been partly hidden, the apprehension of something as an effect or consequence of something co-present within the perceptual field (a spot as a sign of something spilt). All these signs Piaget calls *indicia* or *indices*. They are characterized by perceptual, or senso-motorical, continuity between significator and significatum. At this stage the child is also well able to imitate something present, i.e., to accommodate its movements or posture to the likeness of a model within its field of perception.

In all these cases the predominant sign function in Peirce's terms would on the surface seem to be the indexical. It is, however, more complicated, because as imitation iconicity seems to be the substance of the child's activity. Because imitation is triggered by the presence of the model, then it may be reasonable to say iconic activity does not exist independently of indexical relationships. Furthermore, it should be noticed that the child's body is the medium which expresses the sign. Piaget says that imitation on the pre-representational stage of development in contradistinction to *imitation in thought* is an *imitation in action*. Imitation is an early phenomenon. It appears in the child at the age of one month. About the fourth month it is the so-called *echopraxis,* e.g., the repetition of simple sound patterns communicated by another person to the child. That early it almost seems to be triggered involuntarily and unconsciously.

Until the age of about eighteen months the development of the signifying process seems to be characterized by a lack of differentiation, or separation, between the constituting elements of the semiosis. It is triadic, but either the apprehended sign is not differentiated from its object, or it is not differentiated from the interpreter. Interpreter and interpretant seem to be one, not two, distinct factors (see Fig. 27 and Fig. 28).

According to Piaget, the semiotic (or in Piaget's term "semiological") function is established when the utterer is able to use signs to represent absent objects. The first stage of the semiotic function proper is the so-called *deferred imitation* (about eighteen months) which presupposes the storage and recall of imitative schematas. Consequently, the contiguity between sign and object characteristic of the

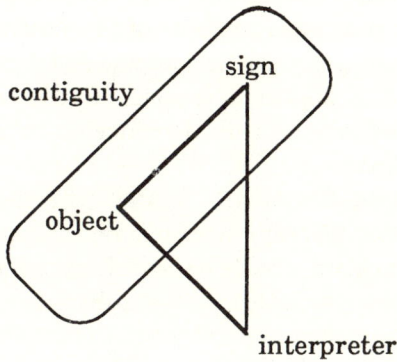

Fig. 27

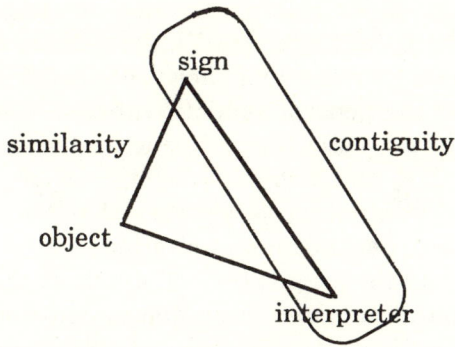

Fig. 28

indexical mode of representation has been broken and replaced by internalized coding, which in Peircean terms would constitute the immediate interpretant of the sign.

Next in order is the so-called *symbolic play*. It differs from *deferred imitation* by introducing an object, used as a sign, an object different from the object referred to (e.g., a child uses a tablecloth as a pillow while pretending to fall asleep). Consequently, there is both a separation in time between signifier (sign) and signified (object) and a marked material difference between signifier and signified. The result is the creation of a complex sign combining the deferred reenactment of the child's or another person's action with the use of a substitute object standing for the signified object. Furthermore, at this stage there is a clear indication the child is conscious that its behavior is a representational imitation.

According to Piaget the *mental image* (the deferred imitation of which is a sign) precedes representational imitation, and is established as an interiorization of the external imitation in action. In the perspective of Peircean semiotics the establishment of deferred imitation indicates that the strict dependence of iconicity on indexicality is broken. The relationship of signifier (sign) and signified (object) mediated by similarity acquires an independent function, and in this way the child also takes the the first step towards the acquisition of symbolicity in the sense of conventionality.

Whereas the mental image is individual and private, because it is bound up with the child's individual experience, with its own perceptual activity, speech is collective, since language is a social institution. I do not intend to go into Piaget's description of language acquisition. It should be mentioned, however, that Piaget regards language as a part of the general semiotic function and that its acquisition seems to start a little but not much later than deferred imitation, symbolic play, and mental imagery, all of which are iconic representations. Furthermore, he stresses that language acquisition at least in part is also dependent on imitation.

It is logical that the acquisition of a conventional sign system presupposes a separation between similarity and contiguity, because without a discrimination between sign and object (i.e., an object functioning as signifier and an object signified by means of the first object) no conventional sign could ever succeed in signifying anything. Since the indices that function as signs at the pre-representational stage are directly and metonymically attached to the object within the context of a semiosis, they do not exist as a part of the child's semiotic competence outside the sign situation itself. As soon as the attachment of signification to a specific situation is broken, the possibility of substituting different kinds of signs for other signs will be open. No wonder the iconic aspect of the sign gets an intermediate position between the indexical and the symbolic aspects. After all, iconicity is intimately related to the child's perceptual activity, as the child explores its environment. Peirce defines the iconic signs akin to percepts, but "minus the insistency and percussivity of percepts" (Ms. 293, 1906: 9). His definition points exactly to what according to Piaget and developmental psychology constitutes the priority of the indexical aspect of the sign in relation to the iconic.

It is tempting to view the transition from the indexical relationship of contiguity to the iconic relationship of similarity as the most decisive step in the ontogenetic development of a semiotic competence, because in using an iconic sign there takes place a double operation of identification and discrimination. Also remember that within semiotics the notion of similarity is broader than in ordinary language use. This is borne out both by Peirce's distinction between image, diagram, and metaphor (cf. III, 3) and by Gombrich's analysis of representation which shows that iconicity may be functional rather than pictorial (Gombrich 1963: 6). The reason why the transition from the predominantly indexical to the predominantly iconic mode of signification seems to be decisive is twofold: First, the spatio-temporal continuity characterizing the predominantly indexical sign's relation to its object is broken. Second the boundary between the iconic and the symbolic is not clear cut. Peirce took this fact into account by saying that "any material image, as a painting, is largely conventional in its mode of representation; but in itself, without legend or label it may be called a *hypoicon*" (2.276).

We now should distinguish between natural and conventional signs. Likely candidates for natural signs are indices of a certain type called by Peirce *reagents,* but as claimed on pp. 111-112 even reagents *must be interpreted* to function as signs. This kind of sign would constitute a rather heterogenous class. It would, for instance, include the symptoms of a disease, the movement of trees indicating wind direction, and a weathercock. In a certain sense, a member of parliament or a senator are also signs of this type, and so are the postholes revealed by archeological excavation. The point is that the existential relation between sign and object need not be natural in any ordinary sense of the word, and especially not as opposed to cultural or conventional.

The distinction between natural and conventional is inapplicable in predominantly iconic signs. This does not mean a pictorial representation of a hamburger is less like a hamburger than it is a hot dog, because most of us, for good reasons, would identify it as a hamburger-representation and not a hot dog-representation. We would do so because we select certain features such as shape and color and compare them with an actual hamburger and hot dog, or what is more likely, with some kind of stereotyped image of them. Identifying something as a pictorial representation of something else means selecting features and perceiving, i.e., constructing, them in such a way that they represent something else which is similarly constructed. This may seem a circuitous way of expressing what at first glance looks simple. It is, however, necessary to put it in this way to emphasize the part played by habit in the interpretation of iconic signs.

The part played by learning processes and habit formation in the interpretability of iconic signs is also substantiated by ethnographical evidence. In *Languages of Art* (1969) Nelson Goodman quotes the following illuminating passage from Melville J. Herskovits:

> Concerning the fact that one has to learn to read pictures in standard perspective, Melville J. Herskovits writes in *Man and His Works* (New York: Alfred A. Knopf, 1948), p. 381: "More than one ethnographer has reported the experience of showing a clear photograph of a house, a person, a familiar landscape to people living in a culture innocent of any knowledge of photography, and to have the picture held at all possible angles, or turned over for an inspection of its blank back, as the native tried to interpret this meaningless arrangement of varying shades of grey on a piece of paper. For even the clearest photograph is only an interpretation of what the camera sees." (Goodman 1969: 15)

This claim is supported by evidence from unexpected quarters. In *My Life and Loves* (1925) Frank Harris relates the following observation from his African adventures:

> I was content with my Kodak to take snapshots of the prettiest girls and the finest young men, and here I made some remarkable discoveries.
> . . . I soon found that these girls did not recognize themselves in their photos. One of our leaders was a Negro with perfectly white hair. When we showed the girls this Negro and his photoed likeness, they all exclaimed with delight: they could recognize him, but not themselves. (Harris 1963: 743)

The interpretation and use of iconic signs depend both on the ontogenetical development of the child and learning. They are, at least partly, culture specific, because the learning of sign systems in general is a part of learning to know and becoming integrated in a specific life-world. Photographs are an important part of the life world of industrial societies in our time. They are predominantly indexical signs containing an iconic sign, and they are physically related to their object. They are only readable, however, by virtue of learning processes. It should be noticed, however, that some contemporary research indicates that the reading of color pictures may not be culture specific (Sonesson 1989: 251-262).

We seem, however, to have a problem, because according to the cognitive development described by Piaget and Bruner we have a learning series: predominantly indexical signs, then predominantly iconic signs, and finally predominantly symbolic signs. In Peirce's semiotics and pharanoscopy a distinction between firstness, secondness, and thirdness is fundamental, and although Peirce, to my knowledge, has paid little attention to developmental aspects, at least logically seems to give priority to iconicity. Consequently, the question arises whether his views and those of cognitive psychology are really opposed to each other or whether a way of reconciling them exists. The latter is the case, and furthermore, it is really a variation of the question of which comes first, the chicken or the egg.

Empirically and superficially the psychologists have a strong case, because contiguity between sign and object seems to be a precondition in the young child for the development of the semiotic function.

If Piaget is right in stressing the importance of imitation, however, iconicity lies at the very core and at the very beginning of the acquisition of the semiotic function. The early phenomenon of echopraxis is a clearcut example of enacted iconicity. It is, however, possible to ask whether symbolicity is not also a prerequisite even for the most embryonic semiotic function. The answer to this question depends on where we draw the line between the iconic and the symbolic. Here (p. 122) I have argued that the distinction between iconicity and symbolicity lies in the fact that iconicity is bound up with the sharing of perceptible properties between sign and object. Even if these are stereotyped or merely relational, some principle of translation exists that relates the qualities and structures of the sign-vehicle to those of the object, and *nota bene* a principle of translation that makes evident they share these properties. In other words, the important *articulatory fit* is between sign and object. If, however, symbolicity, in a very general sense, is understood as a principle of differentiation that decides whether two features are identical or different, then symbolicity as a principle of discrimination is operative within iconicity; as a precondition for the comparison of sign and object, it is indeed at the very basis of signhood.

Symbolicity in the above sense is thought as negativity or differentiality, the operation of which has from Saussure to Hjemslev to Derrida been regarded as constitutive of any kind of signification. It is well known that according to Saussure language and all other semiotic systems are negatively defined as a system of differences.

It is important to realize, however, that even Saussure was well aware that a semiotic system considered as a totality is positive as well as negative (Saussure 1959: 120). Peirce, in his description of firstness, stresses its positive character. In his reflection on feeling this is brought out as follows: "there is no resemblance at all in feeling, since feeling is whatever it is, positively and regardless of anything else, while the resemblance of anything lies in the comparison of that thing with something else" (1.310). To discover possible iconic features of a sign means that we focus on the comparative and common positive qualities of sign and object, which includes necessarily a mediative principle of discrimination and identification. The following passage from "On a New List . . ." certainly testifies to Peirce's awareness of this process. He writes:

> Moreover the conception of a pure abstraction is indispensable, because we cannot comprehend an agreement of two things, except as an agreement in some respect . . . . Such a pure abstraction, reference to which constitutes a quality or general attribute, may be termed a ground. . . .
> Empirical psychology has established the fact that we can know a quality only by means of its contrast with or similarity to another. By contrast and agreement a thing is referred to a correlate, if this term may be used in a wider sense than usual. The occasion of the introduction of the conception of reference to a ground is the reference to a correlate. (1.551-1.552)

Here we seem to have it the other way around, namely that the dyadic relationship between two objects embodies certain qualities as a precondition for discerning the monadic qualities in themselves. I don't think a contradiction exists between this statement and Peirce's categorial distinctions between firstness, secondness, and thirdness, precisely because the latter is a categorical, a logical, analysis of the phaneron, in contradistinction to the empirical study of the modes of functions of concrete signs in our life-world, (bearing in mind that signs are always thirds, i.e., governed by a principle of mediation and of differentiation).

Peirce's curious remark concerning origins helps clarify the issue. In his speculations on cosmology he describes the difficulties which confronted him when he tried to account for the origin and development of the universe:

> Metaphysics has to account for the whole universe of being. It has, therefore, to do something like supposing a state of things in which that universe did not exist, and consider how it could have arisen. However, this statement needs amendment. For time is itself an organized something having its law or regularity; so that time itself is a part of that universe whose origin is to be considered. We have therefore to suppose a state of things before time was organized. Accordingly, when we speak of the universe as "arising" we do not mean that literally. We mean to speak of some kind of sequence, say an objective logical sequence; but we do not mean in speaking of the first stages of creation before time was organized, to use "before," "after," "arising," and such words in the temporal sense. But for the sake of the commodity of speech we may avail ourselves of these words. (6.214)

Cosmology is certainly not the subject of this book (for this see the study by Turley, Turley 1977), but the difficulty of expressing logical operations and presuppositions in a narrative ordered by time applies to certain aspects of the icon; index; symbol distinction. On the one hand, the three aspects seem always to be integrated, infolded. Whenever one begins to analyze both sign use in general and concrete signs, sooner or later all three aspects, or modes of function, will be encountered either as manifested or presupposed (e.g., the photograph). On the other hand, there is also a story, or rather a number of stories, that legitimately ought to be told about the development of sign systems and about the ontogenetic development of the semiotic competence in the different species, especially in man.

The studies in cognitive development by Piaget and Bruner point to important changes and growth in the semiotic competence of the child, because even if it is sensible to hold that all three aspects of the sign function must be present in an embryonic state for a sign to represent, then it makes a decisive difference if only one way of signifying and interpreting is developed, e.g., enactive representation, or if the child, later, masters iconic and symbolic systems of representation. Sign systems with different dominant modes of representation do not replace each other. Even if they are unfolded and made operative at different times, they supplement and support one another.

So far, it appears 1) that all living organisms possess a semiotic competence in the sense they are able to process information and react accordingly, and that this competence serves purposes of survival; 2) that a continuity exists between innate habits, i.e., instinctual behavior and genetically programmed sign processes, and the use of so-called conventional sign systems. Consequently, Peirce's concept of the symbol as a sign type that cuts across the nature-culture distinction is worth considering. That iconic and indexical signs do not respect this borderline is a matter of course. Although the difference between animal communication (e.g., the role of releasers) and human speech and artifical sign systems is vast, it is due not so much to a difference in the kinds of signs used, but rather to the relative autonomy of sign users and interpreters *vis-à-vis* sign systems within the purview of mankind. And it is also due to the fact that man can develop and refine new and existing systems.

When, in mating season, a male Three-spined Stickleback shows its nuptial colors, e.g., its red underside, neither the sign nor the reaction is a result of its own doing. It simply cannot help what it does, and given the appropriate context neither can the female help responding to it in a predetermined way. When a young woman, or man for that matter, shows her/his colors and attempts to attract the opposite sex, she or he has probably spent a fair amount of time in front of the mirror choosing, arranging, and painting. The mating colors are, to a certain extent (cf. below), of her/his own doing. And as those who have teenagers in their families know, often nobody, or at least not the right one, responds to the message. Bruner sums up and generalizes this difference in a pertinent way:

> We depend for survival on the inheritance of acquired characteristics from the culture pool rather than from a gene pool. Culture then becomes the chief instrument for guaranteeing survival, with its techniques of transmission being of the highest order of importance. (Bruner 1966: 57)

Teenagers' mating colors are, so to speak, fished out of the culture pool, or to be more precise out of one specific culture pool among others. This fact makes the idea of individual choice somewhat illusory, since the range of possibilities is constrained by norms, conventions, and values of the culture in question. Nevertheless, customs and conventions may change within a longer or shorter time span, and their change is, among other things, due to actions by groups and individuals. In other words habit changes, and changes in sign and communication systems, become, at least to a certain extent, subject to the control of the species.

One interesting way of looking at cultural evolution is to see it as a consequence of the invention and use of so-called *amplifiers.* Bruner mentions three kinds of such amplifiers: 1) *amplifiers of human motor capacities,* ranging from the invention of the axe to nuclear power, and from the wheel to the space craft. 2) *Amplifiers of sensory capacities,* ranging from the magnifying glass to electronic microscopes, but, according to Bruner, also culturespecific perceptual "software." Although Bruner is not specific on this point, we presume that culture-specific perceptual "programs" for searching or "scanning" the environment would count as such. Finally 3) *amplifiers of human ratiocinative capacities,* ranging from language to theory formation. Bruner claims that all such forms of amplification are more or less conventionalized and transmitted by culture. He continues:

> Where representation of the environment is concerned, it too depends upon learned techniques; and these are precisely the techniques that serve to amplify our motor acts, our perceptions, and our ratiocinative activities. We know and respond to recurrent regularities in our environment by skilled and patterned acts, by conventionalized spatioqualitative imagery and selective perceptual organization, and through linguistic encoding which, as so many writers have remarked, places a selective lattice between us and the physical environment. In short, the capacities, that have been shaped by our evolution as tool-users are those we rely on in the primary task of representation.
>
> The consequence of the development of such a representational system, as psychologists and anthropologists alike have pointed out, is to make possible a kind of integration over space and time, that approaches the conditions necessary for dealing with past and future in the present and for dealing with the distant as if it were near. (Bruner 1966: 56-57)

Motor, sensory, and ratiocinative capacities are necessarily intertwined, and so are the different modes of representation.

Most of the criticism of Peirce's icon, index, symbol distinction is due to the assumption that pure instances of the different categories of signs exist. Having made this assumption his critics then proceed to demonstrate that this is not the case by pointing out that likeness *tout court* cannot function as a criterion, because similarity is always similarity under a certain description and for a certain purpose. This critical observation is true, but most of the time misfires (although as conceptual analysis it is valuable), because neither Peirce nor most contemporary semioticians make this assumption. The usefulness of the icon, index, symbol distinction, which in my opinion can hardly be overrated, lies in its adjectival use, i.e., in pointing out iconic, indexical, and symbolic features or aspects of signs. It seems fair to assume that any sign system will possess all three aspects although in a variable proportion. Peirce writes as follows about this distinction, and about the perfect sign:

> The value of an icon consists in its exhibiting the features of a state of things regarded as if it were purely imaginary. The value of an index is that it assures us of positive fact. The value of a symbol is that it serves to make thought and conduct rational and enables us to predict the future. It is frequently desirable that a representamen should exercise one of those three functions to the exclusion of the other two, or two of them to the exclusion of the third; but the most perfect of signs are those in which the iconic, indicative, and symbolic characters are blended as equally as possible. (4.448).

When Peirce talks about the exclusion of one or two modes of function of the sign, it should be remembered that the genuine sign, the symbolic one, subsumes the function of the two other classes of sign. Consequently "excluded" in the above passage ought to be interpreted as "disregarded" for specific purposes of inquiry. If this interpretation is correct, it follows that not only "the most perfect of signs," but all signs, indeed semiosis, the signifying process, require the collaboration of all three classes of signs; or better, at least in the view presented here, of all three modes of signification, *exhibition, ostension* or *indication,* and *conceptualization.* Their collaboration in "the most perfect of signs," in human speech, will be sketched in chapters V and VI.

# IV. The Interpretants

The interpretant has cast a large shadow in the background of the preceding chapter. The images on the lavatory doors function as signs because they are interpreted as meaningful statements, the red underside of the male Stickleback owns its signhood to the female's responding properly to it (and from our perspective to the studies of zoologists such as Tinbergen), and human speech signifies because it communicates by means of socially shared symbols. Now it is necessary to confront directly the problems concerning the interpretant part of the sign, because even if the basic idea of the interpretant, that of an *interpretation* or translation of one sign into another sign, is easy to state and even if it seems to have immediate plausibility, it is difficult to explain specifically, and difficult to make clear its consequences for a theory of meaning.

## 1. Extension, comprehension, information

In Peirce's Lowell Lecture VII from 1866 we witness the origin of the concept of *interpretant*:

> Indeed, the process of getting an equivalent for a term, is an identification of two terms previously diverse. It is in fact, the process of nutrition of terms by which they get all their life and vigor and by which they put forth an energy almost creative since it has the effect of reducing the chaos of ignorance to the cosmos of science. Each of these equivalents is the explication of what there is wrapt up in the primary — they are the surrogates, the *interpreters* of the original term. They are new bodies, animated by that same soul. I call them the *interpretants* of the term. And the quantity of these *interpretants,* I term the information or implication of the term. (WP 1982, I: 464-465)

The *interpretant,* at least in this place, is more or less equivalent to *information* (this latter concept being the quantitative aspect of the interpretant), and therefore by explicating the idea of *information,* we will begin to clarify what Peirce means by *interpretant.* First, however, we need to explain the relationship of information and symbol.

*Information* is related to two other concepts that apply to symbols: *denotation* and *connotation.* While the concepts of *denotation* and *connotation* are familiar in traditional logic, they are essential to an understanding of Peirce's concept of the *interpretant. Denotation* refers to the objects to which a symbol applies. It is considered as a quantity, and is called the *extension* of the symbol. The *connotation* is the quantitative aspect of a symbol's *content* (sometimes called *meaning*), i.e., the attributes or qualities that can be predicated of a symbol. In his early works Peirce calls these the symbol's reference to a form or to a ground. He states: "The pure abstraction reference to which constitutes a *quality* may be called a ground, of the character of the substance which has the quality" (WP 1982, I: 522). An example of his way of analyzing symbols along the lines just mentioned helps to make clear what Peirce means. Here is an excerpt from an unpublished manuscript (1911) that shows that Peirce's way of thinking is consistent in his writings, even with the early material from 1865-66. In this manuscript he reflects on the *object* and the *interpretant* of the sign, offering as an example the word *dog*:

> [The] word dog – meaning *some dog;* implies, the knowledge there is some dog, but it remains indefinite. The *Interpretant* is the somewhat indefinite *idea* of the characters that the 'some dog' referred to has. . . . As to the characters we know it has four legs, is a carnivorous animal etc. and here we must distinguish first the essential characters which the word implies – the essential interpretant. Second the idea it actually does excite in the particular interpreter. Third the characters it was intended specially to excite – perhaps only a part of the essential characters perhaps others not essential and which the word now excites though no such thing has hitherto been known. (Ms. 854, 1911: 2-3)

Peirce's point of view, which transcends this particular manuscript, forces us to conclude that the comprehension and the interpretant of a symbol are, at least partially, equivalent, and we confirm this hypothesis by turning to his concept of *information.* In his early writings he analyzes *information* in two respects: as the product of the *denotation* and the *connotation* of a symbol, and as a state in a process of knowledge acquisition. The relation between *extension, comprehension,* and *information* is expressed in the following equation: extension x comprehension = information (WP 1982, I: 465 and 2.419), which says that information is the product of both denotative and connotative aspects of the symbol. It is, however, important that Peirce, with regard to the symbol (or *term* within logic), gives priority to connotation, because denotation in this case presupposes connotation. Peirce claims priority for connotation because the sum of a symbol's characters governs its applicability. In a late manuscript from 1910 he expresses the idea: The meaning of most common nouns and ordinary adjectives consists in their not being applied to objects that lack any of a number of characters, and to their being applied to whatever there may be that has all of these characters (Ms. 664, 1910: 21). This means that a precise definition of *information,* although considered to be the product of both *extension* and *comprehension,* is more closely connected with *comprehension* than with *extension,* since it is defined as the 'amount of comprehension a symbol has over and above what limits its extension' (WP 1982, I: 287).

Information, then, is that part of the comprehension of a symbol which exceeds what is necessary to delimit its extension. In an article from 1867, "Upon Logical Comprehension and Extension" (printed with additions in Peirce 2.391-2.430), Peirce distinguishes between the symbol's *essential, informed,* and *substantial breadth* (extension), and *depth* (comprehension). The *informed breadth* of a symbol is all the things of which it is predicable in a supposed *state of information;* the *informed depth* is all the real characters that can be predicated of a symbol in a supposed *state of information.* The *essential breadth* and *depth* of a symbol is the breadth and depth that it would have in an imaginary state of information where the only facts known would be the meaning of words. The *substantial breadth* and *depth* of a symbol, would be an imaginary state in which the information would amount to a complete knowledge of all there is (cf. 2.409-2.415). An example, taken from a later manuscript, could be that of the word *woman.* Peirce writes:

Now I call any acquistion of knowledge "information" which has logically required any other experience than the experience of the *meanings of words.* I do not call the knowledge that a person known to be a woman is an adult, nor the knowledge that a corpse is not a woman, by the name "information," because the word "woman" *means* a living adult human being having, or having had, female sexuality. Knowledge that is not informational may be termed "verbal." (Ms. 664, 1910: 20)

When we apply the 1867 terminology to the 1910 manuscript, the *essential depth* of "woman" would be "living adult being having or having had female sexuality." The *informed depth* of "woman" would be all the real characters that, for instance, at this time could be predicated of the word, and the *substantial depth* would be all the characters known in a perfect state of information.

One way to define *information* is this: the set of characters which can be predicated of a symbol minus the characters contained in its verbal definition. Another way of looking at this concept has already been touched on, namely *information* as a process of knowledge acquisition. This aspect, prominent in Peirce's treatment of the so-called *inverse proportionality of breadth and depth* (proposed by Kant), states that an increase in one of the quantities will imply a decrease of the other. Peirce accepts this "law" within any given state of information, but he denies its validity if the state of information changes. As an example, Peirce mentions *rational animal* which can be divided into *mortal rational animal* and *immortal rational animal;* and he continues:

> But upon information we find that no *rational animal* is *immortal* and this fact is symbolized in  the word *man. Man,* therefore, has at once the extension of *rational animal* with the intension of *mortal rational animal,* and far more beside, because it involves more *information* than either of the previous symbols. (WP 1982, I: 188)

In this context the expression *upon information* means through experience or through the process of inquiry, and this is in agreement with Peirce's distinction between *verbal* and *informational* knowledge, as quoted above. This distinction together with the one between essential, informed and substantial breadth and depth points to the problems involved in defining the difference between analytic and synthetic statements.

Before going into the analytic-synthetic distinction, we have to stop for a moment to explain a seeming inconsistency, because it seems that Peirce in this period (1865-1867) is working with a *four term structure* and not with a *triadic sign concept*. To explain, let us choose Peirce's own example from "On a New List . . ." (1867):

> Suppose we look up the word *homme* in a French dictionary; we shall find opposite to it the word man, which, so placed, represents *homme* as repre-

senting the same two-legged creature which *man* itself represents. By further accumulation of instances, it would be found that every comparison
requires besides the related thing, the ground, and the correlate, also a
mediating representation which represents the relate to be a representation of the same correlate which this mediating representation itself
represents. Such a mediating representation may be termed an *interpretant*, because it fulfills the office of an interpreter, who says that a foreigner
says the same thing which he himself says. (1.553)

Here we see four terms: 1) related thing: the sign; 2) ground; 3) correlate: object; and 4) interpretant. It has already been argued, however, that *ground* and *interpretant* may be considered two aspects of
the same mediating factor (cf. p. 93), and, if this is accepted, we can
construct this example diagrammatically in the usual triadic fashion:

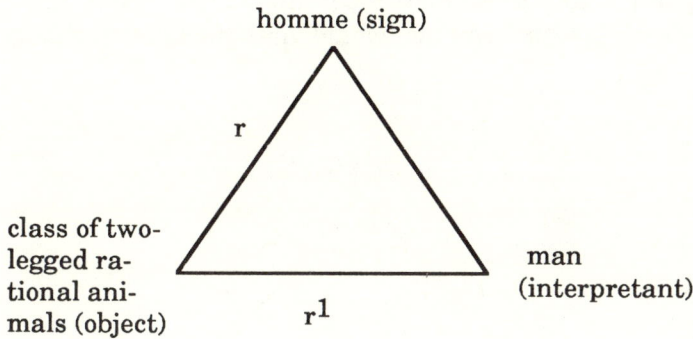

homme (sign)

r

class of two-
legged ra-
tional ani-
mals (object)                                      man
                                    (interpretant)
                          $r^1$

Fig. 29

In the quotation (1.553) the condition for one sign (here symbol) being
another sign's (symbol's) interpretant is claimed to be the signs' identical representative function in relation to the object. In Fig. 29 this is
indicated by r and $r^1$. If these two relations are identical, then the two
signs may serve as each other's interpretant, because they are ex-
tensionally equivalent ($r = r^1 \rightarrow S = I$, or $S = I \rightarrow r = r^1$).

   If we construct the same example according to "Upon Logical Comprehension and Extension" (1867), we have to take into account Peirce's insistence on the *triple reference* of the symbol. He says:

A symbol, in its reference to its object, has a triple reference:

First, Its direct reference to its object, or the real things which it represents;

Second, Its reference to its ground through its object, or the common characters of those objects;

Third, Its reference to its interpretant through its object, or all the facts known about its object.

What are thus referred to, so far as they are known, are:

First, The informed *breadth* of the symbol;

Second, The informed *depth* of the symbol;

Third, The sum of synthetical propositions in which the symbol is subject or predicate, or the *information* concerning the symbol. (2.418)

The concepts of *depth, breadth,* and *information* have been commented upon above, and we have seen that as late as 1910 Peirce distinguishes between *verbal information* and what may be termed *experiential information.* The important thing is that a construction of *man* as the interpretant of *homme* according to the triple reference to breadth, depth, and information would yield the following diagram:

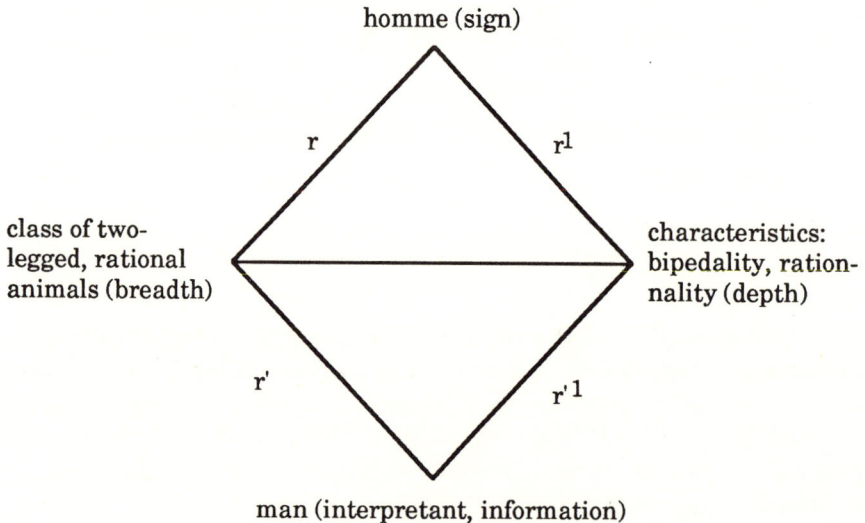

homme (sign)

r                    r$^1$

class of two-legged, rational animals (breadth)          characteristics: bipedality, rationality (depth)

r'                    r'$^1$

man (interpretant, information)

Fig. 30

Instead of the sign being related to object and interpretant (as shown on Fig. 29), here (Fig. 30) the sign is related to its extension (its denotative potential) and to its comprehension. The interpretant of the sign, its translation into another sign, presupposes that the interpretant sign has the same extension and comprehension as the the the interpreted $(r + r^1 = r' + r'^1 \rightarrow \quad S = I$, or $S = I \rightarrow \quad r + r^1 = r' + r'^1)$.

## 2. Translation, synonymity, and use

There are two slightly different ways of expressing the relationship between *homme* and *man* in the diagram (Fig. 30). One is to say that, according to its verbal definition, the word *homme* has a certain breadth and depth, and that both together contain information that may be expressed in other interpretant signs, one of which is the English word *man*. It can be argued that the proposition, *"The French word 'homme' may be translated into 'man' in English,"* is indeed synthetical, because the predicate is not contained in the subject. Another way of expressing the contents of the diagram would be simply to say that two terms (here words) are equivalent, if their breadth and depth are identical (here differences in fact between the depth and breadth of *homme* and *man* are disregarded). In the latter case, however, it seems doubtful whether *homme* and *man* should be regarded as each other's interpretants or simply as replicas of the same term or concept. Peirce wavers on this question. In "On a New List . . ." the interpretant is identified with the translation of a symbol into another language. Although in some places Peirce uses this or similar examples, it is an interesting fact that in other places this point of view is disputed. In the *Harvard Lectures* (1865) Peirce says: "When both terms are objects of information as when I say *homo* is *man*, the phrase is only of grammatical import" (WP 1982, I: 278). This point of view is repeated in 1904 when he states, "Replicas need not be alike as things *homo, man* . . . are the same signs" (Ms. 9, 1904: 2). In the famous Ms. 517 from the same year he explains that "(for logical purposes) a whole book is a sign and a translation of it is a replica of the same sign" (NEM 1976, IV: 239). He explicates this later in the same manuscript:

> A sign has its being in its adaption to fulfill a function. A symbol is adapted
> to fulfill the function of a sign simply by the fact that it does fulfill it; that
> is, that it is so understood. It is, therefore, what it is understood to be.
> Hence, if two symbols are used, without regard to any differences between
> them, they are replicas of the same symbol. If the difference is looked upon
> as merely grammatical (as with *he* and *him*), or as merely rhetorical (as
> with *money* and *spondesime*), or as otherwise insignificant, then logically
> they are replicas of one symbol. (NEM 1976: IV, 255)

It is not surprising that a logician, who carefully distinguishes between a proposition and its expression as a sentence in a given language, sometimes will define terms in different languages as replicas
of the same symbol, and at other times will treat them as distinct
symbols belonging to different sign systems. From one point of view
*man* and *homme* are equivalent because they occupy the same, or almost the same, position within two different systems, but they are
certainly not substitutable within the same system, since there will be
a considerable difference between saying 'he is a *man*' and 'he is an
*homme.*' The reason for this being so is that within a natural language
a part of a symbol's comprehension is to signify that it belongs to a
specific language. The only difference, then, between a given text and
its ideal translation into another language would be that they signify
they belong to two different languages, their extension and comprehension otherwise being exactly the same. For Peirce, however, synonymity (or as he preferred to call it, equivalence) between symbols is
connected to their function, i.e., their being used for some purpose.
Accordingly, Peirce defines absolute equivalence as follows:

> The latitude of interpretation which constitutes the indeterminacy of a sign
> must be understood as a latitude which might affect the achievement of a
> purpose. For two signs whose meanings are for all possible purposes equi-
> valent are absolutely equivalent. (5.448)

This definition of equivalence makes it difficult to speak of totally
synonymous symbols within natural languages, since it is hard to
imagine that the meaning of two symbols would not, at least in some
context, differ however slightly, but often so would different uses of
the same word, i.e., the same expression. Conversely, this definition
certainly implies that symbols can be used synonymously if their latent difference in meaning potential is of no consequence to the accepted purpose of the message. According to Peirce, then, equivalence,

or synonymity, is context-bound and relative to a purpose, and it is possible to define it as two symbols having the same breadth and depth. This, however, means only that they are identical in the respects relevant to the topic of a given text.

The questions concerning interpretation as a process of translation will be treated later (chapters V and VI). Here I return to two problems posed by the different concepts of the relationship between sign and interpretant that are illustrated in Fig. 29 and Fig. 30. One problem is the four term structure of the latter figure which seems to belie Peirce's dogma that the sign is triadic. Compared with Fig. 29 it becomes clear that the problem arises from the differentiation between comprehension (or depth) and interpretant, since the place occupied by the interpretant in Fig. 29 has been taken over in Fig. 30, by comprehension. The interpretant in Fig. 30 is added as a fourth term, an independent sign, related to the interpreted sign because of their equivalent extension and comprehension.

In analyzing dyadic relations within logic, Peirce himself in 1903 comments on this question. He says:

> The dyadic relations of logical *breadth* and *depth,* often called denotation and connotation, have played a great part in logical discussions, but these take their origin in the triadic relation between a sign, its object, and its interpretant sign; and furthermore, the distinction appears as a dichotomy owing to the limitation of the field of thought, which forgets that concepts grow, and that there is thus a third respect in which they may differ, depending on the state of knowledge, or amount of information. (3.608)

As regards semiotic analysis, Peirce's solution to this problem is to differentiate between several interpretants of a sign (e.g., the distinction between *immediate, dynamical,* and *final* interpretant, cf. below). This distinction is by no means just a terminological one, as I hope to show later; it is bound up with his categorical analysis, and it characterizes important features of the signifying process, semiosis.

## 3. Infinite interpretation

The second problem, already touched on, concerns the equivalence (or synomymity) between sign and interpretant. Peirce advocates the thesis that the process of signification is infinite. One of his more spectacular statements runs as follows:

A sign stands *for* something to the idea which it produces, or modifies. Or, it is a vehicle conveying into the mind something from without. That for which it stands is called its object; that which it conveys, its *meaning;* and the idea to which it gives rise, its *interpretant.* The object of representation can be nothing but a representation of which the first representation is the interpretant. But an endless series of representations, each representing the one behind it, may be conceived to have an absolute object at its limit. The meaning of a representation can be nothing but a representation. In fact, it is nothing but the representation itself conceived as stripped of irrelevant clothing. But this clothing never can be completely stripped off; it is only changed for something more diaphanous. So there is an infinite regression here. Finally, the interpretant is nothing but another representation to which the torch of truth is handed along; and as representation, it has its interpretant again. Lo, another infinite series. (1.339)

Besides expressing a distinction between *meaning* (comprehension?) and *interpretant,* as commented on above, the quotation makes it obvious that despite such a distinction both the series of meanings and of interpretants could be infinitely prolonged. If, absolute equivalence between sign and interpretant really existed, however, then the process would stop short. In both Fig. 29 and 30 and in the comments on them we have pretended that such absolute equivalence is at least possible. There are good reasons, however, to believe that sign and interpretant are never absolutely equivalent. In three Mss. from 1904 Peirce makes this point clear. In one he says:

It is equally essential to the function of a sign that it should determine an *Interpretant,* or a second correlate related to the object of the sign as the sign is itself related to that object; and this interpretant may be regarded as the sign represents it to be, as it is in its pure secondness to the object, and as it is in its firstness. (Ms. 914, 1904: 3)

In Ms. 517 (1904) Peirce further points out that "the interpretant is a sign which denotes that which the sign of which it is interpretant denotes. But being a symbol, or genuine sign, it has a signification and therefore represents the object of the principal sign as possessing the characters that it, the interpretant, signifies" (NEM 1976, IV: 244). Further on in the same Ms. Peirce also characterizes the interpretant, or rather the interpretant symbol:

An *entire* interpretant should involve a replica of the original symbol. In fact, the interpretant symbol, so far as it is no more than an interpretant *is* the original symbol, although perhaps in a more developed state. But the interpretant symbol may be at the same time an interpretant of an independent symbol. (NEM 1976, IV: 260)

Finally, in a letter to Matthew Curtis from the same year Peirce expresses the same point by distinguishing "between 1st the interpretant as it is intended to be determined by the sign, 2nd, the interpretant as it is related to the object, and 3rd, the interpretant as it is irrespective of the peculiarities of the sign and the object" (L 107, 1904: 31-32). Another important point in this letter is the coupling of a formal definition of the sign with the idea of an endless series of interpretants:

A sign is anything, A, in a relation, $r$, to something, B, its *object,* this relation, $r$, consisting in fitness to determine something so as to produce something, C, the *interpretant* of the sign, which shall be in the relation $r$ to B, or at least in some analogous relation. Thus, the sign involves the idea of a possible endless series of interpretations. (L 107, 1904: 25-26)

If we visualize diagrammatically what is stated in the two quotations, we get the following figure:

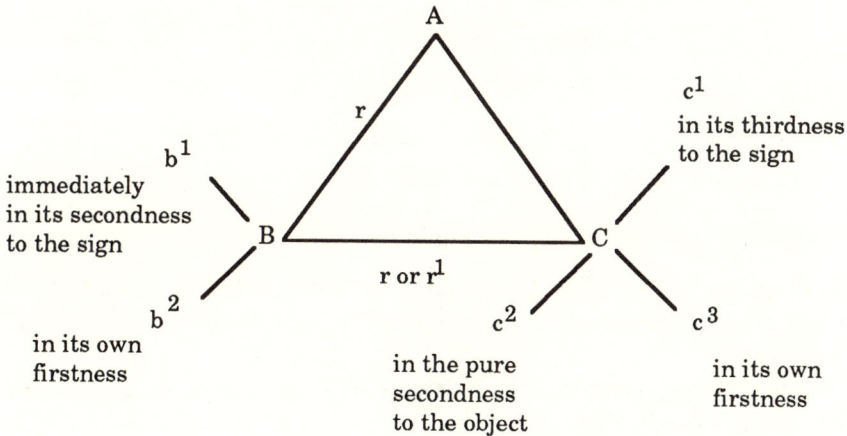

Fig. 31

This determination of the interpretant is threefold. The sign determines a given symbol functioning as an interpretant in the sense that
the selection of the interpretant is determined partly by the "grammar," or structural constraints of the sign, partly by its own potential
of reference, and partly by the interpretants which by itself it calls up.
It also shows how the endless series of interpretations becomes possible because of the threefold determination of the interpretant which
is itself a sign. The double status of the interpretant as the inter-
pretating sign of a previous sign and as a sign in its own right means
also its reference to two, at least topically different objects: objects:

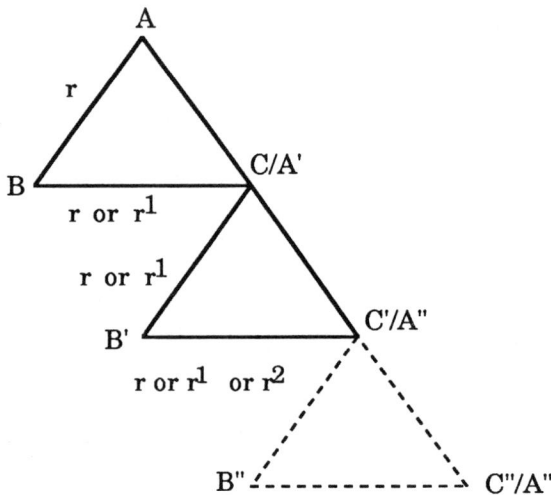

Fig. 32

This diagram shows that by starting at some arbitrary point in the
process of signification we get a series of interpretations, each by itself
a semiosis.

    This diagram confronts us with several questions and problems.
First, what exactly does it mean that a sign A' is simultaneously an
interpretant, C, of another sign, A, and a sign in its own right? One
way of understanding this is to see the different interpretants in a
chain of semioses as a series of predicates related to the same subject

(i.e., the object of the sign). This interpretation accords with the general outline of Peirce's division of signs and with his propositional analysis. In discussing the object of the thought-sign in "Some Consequences of Four Incapacities Claimed for Man" (1868) he exemplifies it in the following way:

> Let us suppose, for example, that Toussaint is thought of, and first thought of as a *negro*, but not distinctly as a man. If this distinctness is afterwards added, it is through the thought that a *negro* is a *man*; that is to say, the subsequent thought, *man*, refers to the outward thing by being predicated of that previous thought, *negro*, which has been had of that thing. If we afterwards think of Toussaint as a general, then we think that this negro, this man, was a general. And so in every case the subsequent thought denotes what was thought in the previous thought. (5.285)

Diagrammatically the sequence of thought-signs would look like this:

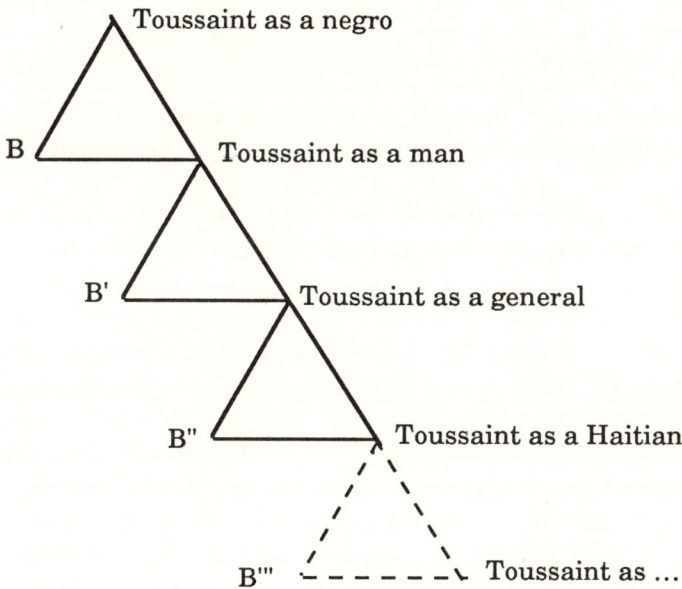

Fig. 33

B, B', B'' are the immediate objects of the three semioses, in this case
constituting aspects of the dynamical object, and the three interpretants are predicates attached to the same subject. Furthermore, the
signs and interpretants stand in the same relation to the object, and
the interpretants function as specifications of the object's attributes or
characteristics. If the object was an existent, historical figure such as
Toussaint or Richard III, it has a double function: It determines the
sign (it is its cause), and it is the final outcome of the process of
interpretion. In taking Richard III as an example Peirce imagines a
discussion between two parties, distinguishing two objects in the following way:

> Thus if a person [ . . . ] remarks that Richard III appears to have been an
> able ruler, it is a hundred to one that he never read any first hand tes-
> timony concerning Richard [ . . . ]. He refers merely to the current notional
> Richard. The real object [ . . . ] is that figure of Richard which we should
> ultimately have in our minds as the result of sufficient information and
> reflexion. But in any case the reference of a sign to its object merely serves
> the purpose of identification; namely, the identification of the actual or
> supposed previous experience with which the new meaning, conveyed in
> the sign, is to be attached. (Ms. 318, 1907: 342-43)

The statement accords with Peirce's concept of truth, and means that
the real object is eventually correlated with the final or ultimate interpretant.

It is basic that the concept of the interpretant is related to the
object in the same way as the sign itself, but even if the interpretant
meets this requirement, it is at the same time a sign in its own right,
and therefore may not be an exact equivalent of the sign. First, the
interpretant may only denote and signify a part of what the sign does
(cf. NEM 1976, IV: 239), and this means that the interpretant represents a certain aspect of the object referred to by the principal sign.
Secondly, the interpretant of a given symbol may at the same time be
an interpretant of another sign (cf. ibid.: 260). Thirdly, as a sign the
interpretant may denote other objects besides the object denoted by
the principal sign. It will be remembered that the basic definition of
the interpretant has a certain duplicity, because the interpretant is
said to be an equivalent or perhaps a more developed sign of the same
object as the original sign (cf. for instance, NEM 1976, IV: 261). If the
interpretant does not possess more information, at least in the sense

of making explicit what is implicit in the principal sign, it could not furnish an explication of what is wrapped up in the sign in question.

It is useful to remember, in this connection, that Peirce makes no distinction between sign and text (as is usual within structural linguistics). As a logician Peirce uses instead the distinction between term or rhema, proposition and argument. It is also useful to remember that one of the important definitions of the interpretant of a sign is that it is "the sum of synthetical propositions in which the symbol is subject, or predicate, or the information concerning the symbol" (2.418). To Peirce the process of interpretation means the insertion of a term into a proposition, the formation of propositions into an argument, and the linking of arguments into a discourse: ". . . discourse consists of arguments, composed of propositions, and they of general terms, relative and nonrelative, of singular names, and of something that may be called copulas, or relative pronouns, etc., according to the family of speech to which one compares the discourse" (Ms. 939, 1905: 27).This means a steady expansion of the sign, because it becomes embedded in an interpretative discourse. Through this embedding, the denotation of the sign, its object, becomes an element within the universe of a given discourse, and thus its interpretation necessitates a description of its interaction with the other elements within the universe. The interpretant of the indexical expression *Toussaint,* for instance, will include his role in Haitian, Latin American, and French history. This example shows that the limits of the universe of discourse denoted by a given sign as well as the number of elements within it are hard to fix exactly, because in this case a whole book, a historical biography, or even a library to which new volumes are added, would be the interpretant of the indexical expression *Toussaint.* Furthermore, through the experiental relationship with the object the state of information about the the sign is changed, and this means that we — always in principle and very often in fact — face an unstable state of information concerning any field of inquiry.

The instability of the state of information effectuated by the chain of semioses also affects the distinction between the essential and the informed depth of a symbol, and consequently the analytic-synthetic distinction as well, because these distinctions make sense only within a stable state of information. This is not the place to discuss the analytic-synthetic distinction; it should be noted, however, that it cuts across the concept of depth and thereby across that of the interpretant as well. I will comment on three points. First, since the depth of a symbol is explicated in its interpretants it follows that the characters implied in a given symbol must be expressed in other symbols. Peirce says explicitly: "Extension and Comprehension can only be reckoned by the interpretants, each interpretant measuring either the one or the other (WP 1982, I: 479). One may still distinguish between the essential and the informed depth and choose to name the latter the interpretant and the former the depth, but, second, such a strict distinction between the *essential* and the *informed* depth of a symbol seems to be untenable. Take, for instance, Peirce's analysis of the word "woman" (cf. p. 147-148). Although it is difficult to imagine that the essential depth of this word would ever cease to include the character "human being having, or having had, female sexuality," it is not even just a possibility, but a fact, that the concept of female sexuality itself has changed and will change. This means that the essential characters have characters themselves, or in other words, that a character constituting a part of the essential depth of a symbol has itself an informed depth which is liable to change. That Peirce was of the same opinion is verified by the following passage from an early manuscript: "Every word is to be regarded as the embodiment of all that we believe about that symbol" (Ms. 731, 1865: 7). Furthermore, he repeatedly points out that words have a capacity for learning. In his "Ethics of Terminology" (1903) he advocates exact meanings for scientific vocabularies, but at the same time thinks it illusory to believe we arrive at absolute exactitude (cf. also 5.312):

> For every symbol is a living thing, in a very strict sense that is not mere figure of speech. The body of the symbol changes slowly, but its meaning inevitably grows, incorporates new elements and throws off old ones. But the effort of all should be to keep the *essence* of every scientific term unchanged and exact; although absolute exactitude is not so much as conceivable. (2.222)

Third, it is difficult to point out the difference between the *depth* considered as the "characters common to the objects of a symbol" and the *information* considered as "the sum of synthetical propositions in which the symbol is subject or predicate." At first glance the difference might seem obvious, because depth concerns the partition of the content of a symbol into characters, while *information* relates to the possibility of placing the symbol in the context of different propositions. At second glance, however, it is not that obvious, and what is more, it is possible to base the following objection to this view in Peirce's own writings because of his division of symbols into *terms, propositions,* and *arguments.* A term is equivalent to a symbol in the way it has been used till now, i.e., as a sign that can be the subject or the predicate of a proposition. A *proposition* is a symbol that separately indicates its object and prescribes its characters. An *argument* is a symbol that separately indicates its interpretant. According to Peirce, the "end of a term is to be introduced into a proposition" (Ms. 316, 1903: 3), and a proposition itself is characterized as a "truncated argument" (L 237, 1902). This means he bases even the content of terms on the process of inference. To indicate of how this position could be argued, we return to Peirce's analysis of the symbol *rational animal.* Logically, Peirce claimed, the term could be divided into mortal and immortal rational animal, but *information* tells us that immortal rational animals do not exist. Therefore *mortality* certainly forms a part of the essential depth of the symbol *rational animal.* But the inclusion of mortality under the constitutional characters of *rational animal,* according to Peirce, seems to be based on a kind of inductive argument stating that no member of the class *rational animal* has, until now, been known to live forever, and this is certainly a synthetic statement about what goes on in the world. It is worthwhile to make this point because making it casts doubt on the absolute distinction between the *essential* and the *informed* breadth of a symbol. We remember that information has been defined as superfluous comprehension, i.e., the characteristics a symbol possesses over and above what determines its extension. Essential depth, however, has to be defined with regard to: (1) the purpose of the sign, and (2) the information available. That is why Peirce believes that a state in which we know only the meaning of words is an imaginary state of knowledge.

Up to now the concept of interpretant has been presented without taking into account Peirce's different divisions. We have seen how this concept from the beginning is affiliated with the traditional philosophical distinction between *extension* and *comprehension,* and with their product, which Peirce calls *information.* The duplicity of the interpretant is explained by this affiliation. On the one hand, the interpretant is the third term in the sign's triadic structure, and in this capacity it is more or less equivalent to *comprehension* determined by the sign as the first term and by the object as the second term. It is also a sign in its own right, denoting an object and determining an interpretant of its own. Bound up with this duplicity is the dialectic of identity and difference in the relationship between a sign and its interpretant, or rather its interpretants (since there is normally more than one translation of a sign). This dialectic may lead to a potential infinite series of interpretants, because a sign's interpretant may only partially realize the meaning potential of the principal sign (*principal* is only used in a positional sense, the *principal sign* is the sign which is interpreted by an interpretant), while simultaneously manifesting significations of its own. This process is repeated in a new interpretant, and so on. Note, however, that this latitude of translation is only one, and to Peirce not the most important, reason for the ongoing interpretation. Another reason is the growing acquisition of experiental information about the object (i.e., through direct or indirect perceptual acqaintance with the object as it appears in a series of semioses) as it is interpreted in a corresponding series of interpretants which add to the distinctness of its concept.

The perspectives and problems concerning the interpretant are one of the main reasons for Peirce's incessant preoccopation with the differentiation and division of the concept. That is the subject of the next section.

## 4. The divisions of the interpretant

Peirce has three main principles in the division of the interpretant. The first is that of his phenomenology and his theory of the categories (cf. here pp. 66-67). This is central to Peirce's semiotics. It is explicitly used in the definition of the sign itself, for: A REPRESENTAMEN is a subject of a triadic relation to a second called its OBJECT, for a third, called its INTERPRETANT. This triadic relation is such that the RE-PRESENTAMEN determines that its interpretant stand in the same triadic relation to the object for some interpretant" (1.541). The second principle, according to which the interpretant is divided, was explained in the previous part of this chapter, namely, a division based on the distinction between the *essential,* the *informed,* and the *substantial* breadth and depth of a symbol. This division has two aspects, since the interpretant can either measure the amount of information in a given state of knowledge or can signify a process whereby we acquire further knowledge. Often, however, it is difficult to make a strict distinction between this division's static and dynamic aspects. The third way Peirce divided the interpretant is determined by its place in the process of communication. This is especially important with regard to the linguistic sign, because Peirce holds that the linguistic sign can only be understood within a communicative context, saying: "The only way to get a sufficient understanding of a proposition is to imagine one person communicates in some language to a second" (Ms. 1408A, ca. 1910: 38).

The difficulties in explicating Peirce's statements about the interpretant and his different ways of dividing it are twofold: he used these three main principles of classification, and to complicate matters further he was not always careful to keep them apart from each other.

The division of the interpretant according to the categories of *firstness, secondness,* and *thirdness* in a way pervades Peirce's whole concept of the subject, at least in the sense that his divisions always are trichotomic. But several divisions are explicitly connected with main characteristics of these categories.

One important way in which the categories are used to analyze not only the sign in its triadic totality, but also the three elements of the sign, has already been described on pp. 155-157. Another more substantial classification of the interpretant, which is directly dependent on the categories, is the well-known division into the *emotional,* the *energetic,* and the logical *interpretant.* One of Peirce's better definitions of this division runs like this:

> It is now necessary to point out that there are three kinds of interpretants. Our categories suggest them, and this suggestion is confirmed by careful examination. I term them the Emotional, the Energetic, and Logical Interpretants. They consist respectively in feelings, in efforts and in habit-changes. . . . The majority of signs, in their significative capacity, provoke efforts, whether these be active efforts in the outer or inner world, or whether they be efforts of inhibition, or self-restraint, which make so large a part of the effort to pay attention. (Ms. 318, 1907: 35-37)

Peirce goes on to illustrate the energetic interpretant by the soldiers' reaction to the command, "Ground arms!" The *emotional* interpretant is said to be their familiarity with the words, and the *energetic* interpretant is the bringing down of the rifle butts to the ground. The *logical* interpretant embodies and conveys "thought proper, whether in the form of a concept, or in that of the meaning of a proposition, or in that of the force of a reason, or argument" (Ms. 318, 1907: 334-335). Whereas the *emotional* and the *energetic* interpretant are not, strictly speaking, signs, themselves, the *logical* interpretant is to be understood as the transformation and development of the sign into other signs.

Peirce distinguishes, furthermore, between the *first,* the *second,* and the *third* logical interpretants. The *first* logical interpretant consists of conjectures called up by the sign suggesting them. These conjectures are built on voluntary performances of the inner world by imagining different situations and alternative lines of conduct. A slight modification of the conjectures make them more carefully defined, and in this process we reach, according to Peirce, the *lower second logical* interpretant. By noting certain relations between the modified conjectures "we are led to generalizations and to abstracting the forms of conjectures which (with much else) will constitute the *higher second logical interpretant"* (Ms. 318, 1907: 169-170). This interpretant constitutes "the ultimate, normal and proper mental effect of the sign taken by itself" (Ms. 318, 1907: 171). Peirce identifies this interpretant with the *meaning* and describes it a *"habit of internal imaginary action."* Even if the *second higher logical* interpretant is the normal outcome of the thought process, Peirce discovers one more interpretant, the *third logical* interpretant, one constituted by the process of external experimentation or quasi-experimentation.

What Peirce describes here as *first, second (lower and higher),* and *third logical* interpretant, are evidently steps in the process of inquiry. These steps bring us close to his pragmatic concept of meaning. This is indicated by the fact that *meaning* is defined as a *habit.* Accordingly, in the same manuscript (and in 5.476, where parts of Ms. 318 are published), Peirce also talks about an *ultimate logical* interpretant consisting in a *habit-change.* Generally, Peirce defines the *logical interpretant* as the "intellectual *apprehension of the meaning of a sign"* (Ms. 318, 1907: 176), but the resulting logical interpretant will itself call forth a logical interpretant, and so forth *ad infinitum.* Therefore, Peirce concludes, the *ultimate logical* interpretant, cannot be of the nature of a sign, but must be a *habit,* which he defines in the following way:

> By a habit I mean any modification of a person's disposition or tendency, when actuated by certain desires, to respond to perceptual conditions by conduct of a certain kind, such modification resulting from previous external experience and from certain previous voluntary actions of effort on the part of the same person. (Ms. 318, 1907: 285)

Compare this passage with the following formulation of the *Pragmatic Maxim* from the *Monist* article "Issues of Pragmaticism" (1905):" The entire intellectual purport of any symbol consists in the total of all general modes of rational conduct which, conditionally upon all the possible different circumstances and desires, would ensue upon the acceptance of the symbol" (5.438). Clearly, the pragmatic definition of the intellectual purport of a symbol is close to the description of the habit which constitutes the *ultimate logical* interpretant.

That the division of the interpretant into *emotional, energetic,* and *logical* depends on the categories should have been made obvious from the above arguments because it is related to the main characteristics of the three categories: feeling, reaction or effort, and thought or law. This division is without doubt central to Peirce's philosophy, but even so it is not unproblematic as a tool within linguistic and textual analysis, and maybe even within philosophy. One of the problems, of which Peirce himself is well aware, is how to isolate the *emotional* and the *energetic* interpretant from each other. Another question is the following: if the energetic interpretant is a reaction to a linguistic sign, for instance the sign to obey an order, then, it might be argued, this reaction must also involve a logical interpretant, because the right execution of what is demanded presupposes an understanding of the propositional content of the order.

The clearest example of the division of the interpretant with regard to the concepts of the *essential,* the *informed,* and the *substantial* breadth and depth of a symbol has been quoted earlier (p. 146), namely, the distinction between (1) the idea of the *essential characters,* (2) the characters realized in a given state of information, and (3) the characters the symbol was intended to excite, including characters of the symbol hitherto unknown, i.e., the adding of information to a symbol, and thus through this increase in depth (or breadth) the process of approaching the *substantial* depth of the symbol. Communicational considerations play an important part in this division, and I will return to this aspect later. Here, we note how basic is the idea of the growth of knowledge.

The most important division that emanates from the early concept of the interpretant, however, is the distinction between the *immediate,* the *dynamical,* and the *final* interpretant. A problem, debated among Peirce scholars, is the relation between the two triadic classifications of the interpretant: one is the *emotional,* the *energetic,* and the *logical;* the other is the *immediate,* the *dynamical,* and the *final.* Some think the former is a subdivision of the *dynamical,* interpretant (John J. Fitzgerald, and David Savan), whereas others (as Douglas Greenlee) think they are almost identical. In *The Logic Notebook,* entry of Oct. 23, 1906, Peirce defines the *immediate,* the *dynamical,* and the *final* interpretant as follows:

> The *Immediate Interpretant* is the immediate pertinent possible effect in its unanalyzed primitive entirety. In the case of a sign interpreted by a mind, that idea (in a very extended sense) which must be apprehended in order that the sign should fulfill its function, this idea being presented whole and unanalyzed. It may be a quality of feeling, more or less vague or an idea of an effort . . . or it may be the idea of a form or anything of a general type. The *Dynamical Interpretant* is the actual effect produced upon a given interpreter on a given occasion in a given stage of his consideration of the sign. This again may be 1st a feeling merely, or 2nd an action, or 3rd a habit. . . .
>
> The *Final Interpretant* is the ultimate effect of the sign, so far as it is intended or destined, from the character of the sign, being more or less of a habitual and formal nature. . . . (Ms. 339d: 546-547)

From this it seems clear that the distinction between the *emotional,* the *energetic,* and the *logical* interpretant is a subdivision of the *immediate, dynamical, final* trichotomy, but this subdivision is not confined to the *dynamical* interpretant. It is also explicitly connected with the *immediate,* and we presume that it might be valid for the *final* interpretant as well (cf. chapter VIII). The quotation above is, however, only one of many places where Peirce tried to work out his concept. We could multiply the quotations, but it is more feasible to summarize the characteristics of the three interpretants.

The *immediate interpretant* has three related but distinct definitions throughout Peirce's writings: (a) The interpretability that a sign has before it gets an interpreter; and also a vague possible determination of consciousness, or a possibility consisting in an abstraction effected by the semiosis of which it is an element; (b) the meaning that the sign is calculated to produce, the intended meaning; (c) the first unanalyzed, total effect of the sign upon the interpreter. His diversity of definition is understandable because the intentions of the utterer are presupposed, at least vaguely, by the interpreter, and are often recognizable in the structure of the utterance itself. Moreover, in a perfect transmission of meaning there will be no difference between intention and immediate effect. There are, however, problems with (b) and (c), and I prefer definition (a), according to which the immediate interpretant of the sign is its specific interpretability understood as a set of strictures (because the sign belongs to a given sign system) that determine what can count as an interpreting sign.

The *dynamical interpretant* is the actual effect of the sign upon some interpreter. Peirce also says it is a "determination of a field of representation exterior to the sign (such a field is an interpreter's consciousness) which determination is affected by the sign" (Ms. 339c, Oct. 8, 1905: 504). This interpretant will then be the concrete interpreting sign (or the actual emotion or effort) produced by/in some interpreter.

The *final* (also called normal) *interpretant* is the interpretant the sign ought to produce as a result of sufficient study. Another related definition is the interpretation that would be agreed on after unlimited research by the scientific community, i.e., a dynamical interpretant accepted by this community. To illustrate the difference between the three interpretants we can place two quotations, side by side, each divided into the constituent parts:

I. Take, for example, a witness in court.

A word has meaning for us in so far as we are able to make use of it in communicating our knowledge to others and in getting at the knowledge that these others seek to communicate to us. That is the lowest grade of meaning.

II. His story is told without the slightest idea that it can be doubted. He contemplates and asks uncritical acceptance of it, as the very vestige, or footprint of the Truth,

The *meaning* of a word is more fully the sum total of all the conditional predictions which the person who uses it *intends* to make himself responsible for or

necessarily conformed to the real
Object in so far as the testimony
is determinate. That is the Immediate, Naive or Rogate Interpretant.

III. The dynamical interpretant is
the judgment of the fact which
listening to the witness's testimony
actually produces on the minds of
the jury.

intends to deny. That conscious
or quasi-conscious *intention* in
using the word is the second
grade of meaning.

But besides the consequences to
which the person who accepts a
word knowingly commits himself to, there is a vast ocean of
unforeseen consequences which
the acceptance of the word is
destined to bring about not merely consequences of knowing,
but perhaps revolutions of society. One cannot tell what power
there may be in a word or a
phrase to change the face of the
world; and the sum of these consequences makes up the third
grade of meaning. (8.176)

IV. The normal interpretant is the
modification of the verdict of the
jury in which this testimony ought
logically to result. (Ms. 499, 1906:
47-48)

The two quotations show that Peirce analyzes textual meaning as
something dynamic, as an ongoing signifying process, the starting
point of which is the public, relatively stable meanings that words
have acquired through application at a certain time, and which are a
part of the utterer's (and hopefully the interpreter's) *competence*.

Here, we should stress that Peirce's description of infinite semiosis
does not mean he considers the meaning of linguistic signs to be in
constant flux. On the contrary, the reality of words consists, according
to Peirce, precisely in their relatively stable significations (the interpretative habits attached to words):

any word that has been in use in even a tolerable definite sense, is itself
real. For the predicate "conveys such and such meaning" is true of it,
whatever any man may think. It is a solid historical *fact* that it has many
times conveyed that meaning, as it undoubtedly will do in the future. The
word is then *real*. (Ms. 200, 1907: 178)

This does not mean significations are unchangeable, because the signification of words grow, and furthermore in this historical process they may also lose previous meanings. Peirce formulates the idea beautifully: "The type of a sign is memory, which takes up the deliverance of past memory and delivers a portion of it to future memory" (Ms. 599, 1902: 37). This dynamic and historical character of the interpretation process leads directly to the third principal way in which Peirce conceived the interpretant, as a dialogical form of communication.

Before turning to the third major principle of partition, we need a further comment on the immediate, dynamical, final distinction. I have given three of Peirce's important but different definitions of the immediate interpretant. For several reasons I recommended the first definition: (a) the interpretability a sign may have, before it gets an interpreter, i.e., the significative power of the sign in itself. One reason is that such a definition is in accordance with Peirce's categorial analysis and his metaphysics, in which firstness is characterized by *possibility*, secondness by *actuality*, and thirdness by *law* or *necessity* (for a further treatment of these distinctions, and for the relationship between Peirce's phenomenology and metaphysics see Feibleman 1969: 183-195). In his analysis of possibility, Peirce distinguishes a special kind which he gives the traditional philosophical name *potentiality*, and which he defines as "indeterminate yet capable of determination in any special case" (6.185). The *immediate interpretant* of a sign can be seen as a possible field, or a potential, of signification which is realized through actual interpretation. The outcome is the *dynamical interpretant*.

Another reason for the acceptance of the first definition is that the distinction between immediate and dynamical interpretant might have replaced the earlier distinction between comprehension and interpretant (cf. here pp. 149-152), since the concept of immediate interpretant and that of comprehension are closely alike. Both concepts are intrinsic to the triadic structure of the sign, because they indicate its potential translation or interpretation (its interpretability), something which has to be actualized in another sign, i.e., a dynamical interpretant. This idea of potential signification is by no means empty, because it functions as a constraint on what can count as a valid (dynamical) interpretant of a given sign. The double status of the interpretant as something which is simultaneously intrinsic and extrinsic to the sign is conceptualized in the distinction between the immediate and dynamical interpretant. This does not mean that Peirce does away with the duplicity of the concept of the interpretant, because this duplicity is inherent in the process of interpretation. What he does is maintain it and make it articulate.

A brief comparison with a classical structuralist position (for instance, the positions of Hjelmslev and Greimas) shows the superiority of Peirce's concept. It is a dogma of structural linguistics that, at least, linguistic signs can be defined and analyzed as being built up of elements of a lower order, which are not themselves signs. As regards the content, such elements Hjelmslev calls *pleremes,* or simply *content figurae,* and Greimas calls *semes.* A paradoxical situation arises, however, from the fact that whenever such non-signs are pointed out they are manifested as signs (cf. chapter I, pp. 46-48). By distinguishing between the immediate and the dynamical interpretant of a sign, Peirce succeeds in taking into account two ideas: that a sign has an intrinsic signification (a *content* in structuralist terminology) and that this signification is always realized by translation into other signs. The intrinsic signification of a sign, i.e., its immediate interpretant(s), is precisely its power to (partially) determine its translation (or interpretation).

The third major principle, according to which he divides the interpretant, Peirce bases on a dialogical or conmunicational view. In one of the drafts in the Peirce/Welby correspondence we see a division of the interpretant that he explicitly connects to a communicational point of view: The relevant part of the text is this:

> There is the *Intentional* Interpretant, which is a determination of the mind of the utterer; the *Effectual* Interpretant, which is a determination of the mind of the interpreter; and the *Communicational* Interpretant, or say the *Cominterpretant,* which is a determination of that mind into which the minds of utterer and interpreter have to be fused in order that any communication should take place. This mind may be called the *commens.* It consists of all that is, and must be, well understood between utterer and interpreter at the outset, in order that the sign in question should fulfill its function. (SS 1977: 196-197)

This classification differs from those proposed in Ms. 499 and the *Collected Papers* (8.176) in its rather limited scope. Here, Peirce explicitly focuses on the dialogical situation, and here the third interpretant, the *communicational,* means the agreement between utterer and interpreter based on the explication or tacit presupposition of what Peirce often calls the common ground, or "a well understood common experience" (SS 1977: 197). This point of view is limited because the task of sign interpretation seems to end when two parties in a single act of communication have reached mutual understanding and agreement. Despite its limitation, however, it can be argued that this division of the interpretant constitutes the nucleus of Peirce's theory of linguistic interpretation.

It can be the nucleus of Peirce's theory because it is possible to arrange the other two divisions of the interpretant in relation to the communicational point of view. There are two reasons. First a division based on different states of information is in itself, based on communicational considerations. Second, even if the division of the interpretant into *emotional, energetic,* and *logical* is directly dependent on the categories, it can be (and is often by Peirce) interpreted as different aspects or stages in the process of understanding the sign. We risk a paradox, however in trying to frame the interpretants according to the communicational point of view, because it seems to be the most narrow, focused as it is on a single act of communication. We avoid the paradox by choosing, as the point of reference, the widest concept of the process of interpretation, and the widest concept of the process of interpretation is the distinction between the *essential,* the *informed,* and the *substantial* breadth and depth of a symbol. At one imaginary limit the concept is defined as a minimum state of information, and at the other imaginary limit as a maximum state. The minimum state of information is purely imaginary because, according to the concepts of denotation and comprehension, even the smallest amount of comprehension of a symbol would serve to govern its applicability. This implies that meanings of words cannot exist without, at least, some crude distinctions between different objects or facts. The maximum state of informations, the other limit, seems to be just as unattainable and imaginary, since it presupposes a state of perfect knowledge. This does not mean these states are useless as a delimitation of the process of interpretation. They define the extremes: therefore, every given interpretation will be situated somewhere between these extremes.

The division of the interpretant into *immediate, dynamical,* and *final* is to be situated somewhere midway between the extremes of the former classification and the communicational since it, in some versions, possesses some of the characteristics of the former. In other versions it comes close to the *communicational* classification. This last classification will constitute the dialogic nucleus of the interpretative process. In this way we will obtain nine different concepts (shown in the list below) of the interpretant, as seen in its relation to the process of communication and to the acquisition of knowledge:

1. Minimal state of information: The essential depth of a symbol. Designation: *Essential Interpretant.*

2. State of information prior to any given single semiosis. The informed depth and breadth of a symbol (or parts of a symbol) at a given time. Sometimes in Peirce's writings the term *Immediate Interpretant* seems to be used in this way, but normally it is used to designate the interpretability, or potential meaning, of the sign in a given actual semiosis (cf. 4). It is closest to what Peirce designates as the *lowest grade of meaning of a word* (cf. 8.176).

3. The interpretant in the intention of the utterer, i.e., the state of information the utterer intended to result from the semiosis, including the purpose of the communicative act as it is conceived by him and the information for which he will assume responsibility. Designation: *Intentional, Intended, Objective, Naive, Rogate* Interpretant.

4. The interpretant as expressed by the sign itself, i.e., the interpretability of the sign as a function of its internal structure, and of the constraints placed on its interpretation by its grammar (e.g. phonological, syntactical, and semantical features). Designation: *Immediate, Expressed, Initial* Interpretant.

5. The interpretant in the Interpreter's intention, i.e., its effect in an exterior semiotic field and the resulting actual interpretation. Designation: *Dynamic(al), Actual, Existential, Middle, Effectual* Interpretant.

6. The interpretant common to both utterer and interpreter, i.e., the interpretation of the sign agreed on by both parties of communicative act. This agreement is based on the explication or tacit presuppositions of a common experience. Designation: *Communicational* Interpretant, *Cominterpretant.*

7. The habit produced by the sign, i.e., the interpretant defined as a disposition to act in a given way under certain circumstances; since the interpretant in this case is a disposition to act it is best expressed as a proposition in the conditional mood. Designation: *Final, Habitual, Logical* Interpretant.

8. The rational effect the sign ought to have on the proper logical outcome of the semiosis. Whereas the communicational interpretant only presupposes an agreement between utterer and interpreter without any reference to a norm, and whereas the habitual interpretant designates a habit formation, this interpretant includes a normative aspect according to which it is possible to judge the dynamical, communicational, and habitual interpretation. Designation: *Rational, Normal, Final* Interpretant.

9. Maximal state of information: The substantial depth and breadth of a symbol. A state in which there would be no difference between the sign's object and interpretant, that there would be no gap between reality and our concept of it. This is a state of *perfect knowledge* and would lead to the establishment of *habits* that would never be modified. Designation: *Eventual, Final, Normal, Ultimate Logical* Interpretant.

Between the two imaginary extremes of 1 and 9, a language without a world and the total merging of reality and meaning into truth, we can apply the concept of the interpretant to seven different cases. Here, these cases are arranged so they can be seen as successive stages in the semiosis.

The most important divisions of the interpretant are the immediate, the dynamical, and the final. If there are used recursively on the above nine stages of the process of inquiry, or interpretation, the result will be the following tripartite division: I) stages 1-4, II) stage 5, III) stages 6-9:

| | |
|---|---|
| I   IMMEDIATE INTERPRETANT | 1) Essential interpretant |
| | 2) Lowest grade of word meaning |
| | 3) Intended interpretant |
| | 4) Immediate interpretant |
| II  DYNAMICAL INTERPRETANT | 5) Dynamical interpretant |
| III FINAL INTERPRETANT | 6) Communicational interpretant |
| | 7) Final interpretant |
| | 8) Rational interpretant |
| | 9) Ultimate logical interpretant |

We see, thus, 1-4 as different specifications of the concept of the *immediate interpretant*, and 6-9 as specifications of the *final* interpretant. The point of subsuming the four first of the interpretants under immediate and the four last under final interpretant is that they function respectively as antecedents and consequences of a given actual act of interpretation, the objective content of which is contained in the *dynamical interpretant*. A dynamical interpretant occupies a middle position, Janus-like looking back at the sign that (partly) determined it by its meaning potential, and forward towards its fate in the further chain of semiosis (acception, rejection, or modification).

Four important questions concerning the interpretant remain: 1) The varieties of the concrete process of interpretation in a dialogic context; 2) the interplay between the iconic, indexical, and symbolic signs in the acquisition and communication of knowledge; and 3) the thorny question of final interpretation; and 4) the question concerning the termination of the process of interpretation in habit formation. These questions are, however, better discussed later. The following chapter will explain points one and two in the context of interpretation as dialogue. Points three and four will be the main theme of the last chapter. First before concluding this chapter on Peirce's interpretants, we have to understand his third trichotomy of the sign, his classification of signs, and his division of arguments.

## 5. Rheme, dicisign, argument, and the ten classes of signs

Although Peirce constantly worked on revising his classification of signs, he never completed his study. In a letter to Lady Welby (1908 Dec. 23, in SS 73-86) he mentions a classification of signs based on ten trichotomies yielding sixty-six classes of signs; and in the Mss. from the later part of his life (e.g., in his *Logic Notebook)* we find tables in which he attempts to specify these classes. It has even been possible to give sensible reconstructions of the sixty-six classes, although scholars disagree about their order (Weiss and Burks 1945: 383-388, Lieb 1953: 51-55, reprinted in SS 160-166, and Gary 1970: 3-16). In Peirce's own opinion his most important trichotomy is the icon, index, symbol distinction. Having claimed in the preceding chapter that I find this trichotomy eminently enlightening if used adjectivally, it is not surprising I have doubts about the fruitfulness of his elaborated classification. It might be harmful to semiotics to concentrate excessively on the fine art of pigeonholing signs. Consequently, I will stick to his ten classes of signs, and begin with the third trichotomy.

The third trichotomy concerns the sign's relation to the interpretant. Analogous to the second trichotomy based on the relation of the sign to its object (in which an icon is a possible sign of everything which is like it in some respect, an index is a sign of an actual relation with an object, and a symbol is related to its object by habit, or convention), the third trichotomy distinguishes between *rheme, dicisign,* and *argument,* among other things, on the basis of the difference between possibility, actuality, and law.

The *rheme* (or *rhema,* also named *term* and even *seme*) is "a Sign which, for its interpretant, is a sign of a qualitative possibility" (2.250). It also "represent[s] its object in its characters merely" (2.252). The editors of the *Collected Papers* note that in modern logic what Peirce calls a rheme is normally known as a *propositional function* (2.95). Its status as a possibility is stressed in Peirce's definition of a *term,* which is said to leave "its Object, and a fortiori its Interpretant, to be what it may" (2.95).

The best way to understand a rheme is to work downwards from argument to proposition: An *argument* is a representamen which separately shows which interpretant it is intended to determine. A *proposition* is a representamen which is not an argument, but which separately indicates what object it is intended to represent. A *rhema* is a simple representation without such separate parts (5.139). Leaving aside the argument for the moment, we may exemplify a proposition by the statement,

"These beans are white."

If the subject is erased from the proposition, we get "– are white," and "– are beans," which are both predicates with one blank, and these are examples of *non-relative,* or *monadic* rhemes. A *relative, dyadic rheme* may be exemplified by "– loves –" where there are two blanks, and a *plural relative rheme,* or *polyad,* may be exemplified by "– gives – to – ," or by "– represents – to –" (cf. 3.465).

The validity of Peirce's claim that a rheme leaves its interpretant (and its object) to be what it may should be apparent from the above examples, because expressions such as "is white," "is mortal," and "is a man," are open to a variety of interpretations governed only by the minimal depth of the rheme in question. If we hear the exclamation "are white," or, more likely, just "white!" we will not know what object is meant, and consequently are left with an indefinite number of possible interpretants. To delimit the number of possibilities, an interpreter will have to find out the object (subject) to which the predicate applies. He may, for instance, interpret the rhematic expression in the following sentence: "Oh, yes, these beans are white." In so doing he has completed the expression by adding a subject, containing an indexical sign *(these)* to the predicate, thus transforming the rheme into a proposition.

As mentioned above, a rheme may be exemplified by a *term*, or a propositional function within logic. It is important to realize, however, that the concept of a rheme is much broader (cf. 4.538). This is made evident by the classification of signs worked out by Peirce about 1903 (cf. 2.233-2.271). This classification is based upon the three trichotomies, which, according to Peirce, yield ten classes of signs:

> Rhematic Iconic *Qualisign*
> Rhematic *Iconic Sinsign*
> *Rhematic Indexical Sinsign*
> *Dicent* Indexical *Sinsign*
> Rhematic *Iconic Legisign*
> *Rhematic Indexical Legisign*
> *Dicent Indexical Legisign*
> *Rhematic Symbol* Legisign
> *Dicent Symbol* Legisign
> *Argument* Symbolic Legisign (cf. 2.264)

This table of the sign classes indicates that no less than six out of ten classes are rhematic signs (I, II, III, V, VI, and VIII), and by characterizing these six classes a double purpose may be served, both to introduce and comment upon this classification, and to exemplify the different species of rhematic signs.

I. A *qualisign* is defined as a quality that is a sign. Peirce's own example is "a feeling of red" (2.254). Since a quality is monadic, something which is such as it is in itself, a qualisign can only be iconic, in case something else shares its positive quality, and since it is a possibility, it can only be rhematic. In this case, as in all ten cases, the sign class is characterized by labels from all three trichotomies, so the name of the first class of signs is really Rhematic, Iconic *Qualisign*. Since being a qualisign also implies being iconic and rhematic, the determining factor is being a qualisign. Furthermore, it should be remembered that, to exist, a qualisign has to be embodied in a sinsign.

II. A *rhematic iconic sinsign* embodies a qualisign (cf. I), and may be a sign of anything possessing the same qualities. Since it has no inherent indicative power, it is a possibility, and thus is rhematic. A blotch on a wall may be a rhematic iconic sinsign of anything that it is taken to represent by virtue of its own qualities (cf. Hamlet's cloud at the end of *Hamlet*, III, ii, with which he ridicules Polonius). Peirce's own example is an individual diagram (cf. 2.255).

III. A *rhematic, indexical sinsign* directs the awareness of an intention to the object that causes it. Peirce's own example is a spontaneous cry, because it directs the attention (of the interpreter) to its utterer without giving any definite information about its signification (of course, even a concrete spontaneous cry may often vaguely indicate its signification).

V. A *rhematic iconic legisign* may be exemplified by the lavatory signs presented on p. 121. Each instance (itself an iconic sinsign) is a replica of a general type. That these signs are rhematic, iconic legisigns has already been made obvious in the previous discussion (cf. p. 123), where an observer realizes their signification by reading them as propositions according to a code. In themselves, however, they are rhemes.

VI. A *rhematic indexical legisign*. It is worth citing Peirce on this subject since as examples of this class he mentions demonstrative pronouns. That means his classification of signs cuts right through the class of linguistic signs. Most linguistic signs are, also according to his classification, symbols, but such linguistic signs as *this* or *that*, whose primary deictic function is to correlate text (or sign) and context, are prime examples of indexical signs that are conventional, i.e., are legisigns. The rhematic character of such signs is obvious. *This* in itself, for instance, is incomplete, drawing its signification from the co-text or context it points out. Certain classes of gestures are non-linguistic equivalents in so far as a given society codifies them. A universal human gesture such as pointing is a rhematic indexical legisign, since it functions as a demonstrative pronoun, and like a pronoun it is in need of completion.

VIII. The *rhematic symbol,* being a symbol, is by definition a legisign, and most important is exemplified by common nouns. Peirce defines a rhematic symbol in this way:

a sign connected with its Object by an association of general ideas in such a way that its Replica calls up an image in the mind which image, owing to certain habits or dispositions of that mind, tends to produce a general concept, and the Replica is interpreted as a Sign of an Object that is an instance of that concept. Thus, the Rhematic Symbol either is, or is very like, what the logicians call a General Term. (2.261)

The definition indicates this kind of sign's dependence on its interpretant, since its object is interpreted as an instance of the general concept of the sign, i.e., through its interpretant. The rhematic character of a common noun should be obvious, because its indeterminateness leaves open various possibilities of interpretation, among which one cannot choose because of lack of information. The dictionary's listing of a range of partly equivalent terms reflects the rhematic character of insulated nouns and other words. Here I should mention that to Peirce the importance of common nouns (and general terms within logic) is exaggerated within traditional studies of grammar (and within classical logic, see, for instance SS 1977: 33-34). In non-relative monads, rhemes (functioning as one place predicates), common nouns, and adjectives play a prominent role (e.g., – is a man, – is mortal). Relative rhemes (dyadic and polyadic), however, are made up by verbs and prepositions (e.g., – loves –, or – represents – to –), although certain verbs may even function as non-relative rhemes (– blooms, – dies).

The two salient features of a rheme are its status as a possibility and its lack of determination. In contradistinction to the rheme, a *dicent sign,* or a *dicent* (also called *dicisign* and *pheme),* is characterized as a sign, "which, for its Interpretant, is a Sign of actual existence" (2.251). A little later Peirce thought it better to distinguish more rigidly between a sign and the assertion of it, and consequently, in 1904, he modified his definition in this way: "I define a dicent as a sign represented in its signified interpretant as if it were in a Real Relation to its Object (Or as being so, if it is asserted)" (SS 1977: 34). We might want to add "asserted about a certain universe," bearing in mind fictional assertions, such as those about Scheherazade (cf. p. 85).

The most prominent class of dicents, but certainly not the only one (cf. below) is *propositions*. Propositions contain rhemes, but complete them, making them capable of being asserted, if the blanks are filled out. The two rhemes, – are beans, and – are white, may be used to form the following proposition: *these beans are white*. What is added to a rheme to form a proposition is an indexical sign functioning as subject to the predicate and indicating the object of the sign. This is why Peirce, in 1903, defines a dicent as a sign of actual existence for its interpretant.

Within the ten classes of signs, three are dicent signs (IV, VII, and IX):

IV. A *dicent indexical sinsign* is exemplified by the weathercock which has already been used here to illustrate a real, in this case causal, relation between object and sign. (cf. Fig. 15). Peirce's own definition of this kind of sign is worth quoting, because in addition to specifying the character of this class of signs, he offers insights about his general way of conceiving the nature of signification. He says:

> A Dicent Sinsign [*e.g.*, a weathercock] is any object of direct experience, in so far as it is a sign, and, as such, affords information concerning its Object. This it can only do by being really affected by its Object; so that it is necessarily an Index. The only information it can afford is of actual fact. Such a Sign must involve an Iconic Sinsign to embody the information and a Rhematic Indexical sinsign to indicate the Object to which the information refers. But the mode of combination, or *Syntax,* of these two must also be significant. (2.257)

Three aspects of this definition are of general importance: 1) the relationship between experience and signhood: for Peirce, any experience, that which points to something outside itself and is interpreted in another sign (e.g., a thought), constitutes a sign action, a semiosis. 2) The embedding of signs within signs to make up complex signs that for their function are dependent upon their parts, and their different significative powers. According to Peirce's categorical analysis, a higher category presupposes and contains a lower as a part of itself, and accordingly, an index may incorporate an icon (as here), and a symbol both an index and an icon. It is not necessary that the lower sign category, or sign function, should be materially present in the sign of a higher order. This may be the case, for instance, when a photograph, which is predominantly indexical, contains an iconic representation within itself. Instead of being incorporated, the subsumed sign function may be associated with the more complex sign as necessary partial interpretants of it (this is the case as regards symbols). This leads to the third aspect. 3) If, however, as here, the dicent sinsign directly involves both an iconic sinsign and an indexical sinsign, then, as Peirce says, their combination, the sign's syntax, becomes "significant." His statement indicates two interesting features of Peircean semiotics. First, the scope of the concept of syntax, since it is applicable to reagents (a weathercock is a reagent) as well as to propositions. Second, syntax can be operative within signs, relating their different significational functions to each other, and not only between signs (note that Hjelmslev also conceived a syntagmatic analysis operating within words, Hjelmslev 1953a: 27).

VII. The difference between a dicent indexical sinsign (IV), and the seventh class of signs, a *dicent indexical legisign,* is that the latter being a legisign is a general type or law (cf. 2.260). Being indexical, it is still affected by its object, but being a legisign it is at the same time an instance of a type. Peirce's own example is a street cry, because it both calls attention to its utterer, and, by its traditionally established signification, informs the interpreter about what object is offered for sale.

IX. A *dicent symbolic legisign,* or an *ordinary proposition.* Since a legisign need not be a symbol in the sense of being conventional (cf. the red underside of the Three-spined Stickleback), this kind of sign is distinguished from the preceding class (VII on Peirce's list). The proposition has already been characterized in its relation to the (symbolic) rheme (on p. 175).

The fact that a dicent indexical sinsign and a dicent indexical legisign may be translated into a proposition makes evident the affinity of the three classes of dicent signs Peirce considers. The pointing of a weathercock may be represented in symbols by a proposition such as "the wind is easterly," and a characteristic street cry may be translated "fish for sale." Conversely, if propositions are asserted, and their claim that something is the case is supported by appeal to facts, the proposition will be translated into dicent indexical legisigns and/or sinsigns. The proposition, "The wind is easterly," will be justified by referring to the direction in which the weathercock is pointing.

X. The tenth and last class of signs is the *argument* (also called a *delome*). It is defined as "a representamen which separately shows what interpretant it is intended to determine" (5.139). A typical example of an argument is a syllogism:

> All the beans from this bag are white.
> These beans are from this bag.
> These beans are white.

This example shows that the intended interpretant, the conclusion, is represented within the sign itself. An argument means the bringing together, the *colligation* as Peirce names it, of the premises in such a way that the conclusion can be inferred from them: "Every inference involves the judgment that, if such propositions as the premisses are true, then a proposition related to them, as the conclusion is, must be, or is likely to be, true" (2.462). This quotation should be compared with the one on diagrammatic reasoning on p. 100, because, as far as semiotics and logic is concerned, the important thing about the argument is not the material, or factual, truth of the conclusion, but the compellant and lawlike nature of its form. In "Prolegomena to an Apology for Pragmaticism" Peirce distinguishes what he calls "the familiar logical triplet, Term, Proposition, Argument," by defining the rheme (in this context called seme) as "anything which serves for any purpose as a substitute for an object of which it is, in some sense, a representative or Sign" (4.538). This definition clarifies the rheme's status as an indeterminate possibility. A dicent sign (here called pheme) is defined as "a Sign which is equivalent to a grammatical sentence, whether it be Interrogative, Imperative, or Assertory" (ibid.). He further says about the dicent that *"such a Sign is intended to have some sort of compulsory effect on the interpreter of it"* (ibid., my italics). Here he stresses the role played by indexicality in the dicent, the compulsory aspect of this kind of sign means the direction of the attention of the interpreter towards its supposed object (and this is the reason why dicents are associated with secondness and actuality).

In contradistinction to the dicent, the influence of an argument (here called *delome*) on an interpreter he defines as follows: "It is a Sign which has the Form of tending to act upon the Interpreter through his own self-control, representing a process of change in thoughts or signs, as if to induce this change in the Interpreter" (4.538). According to this point of view, the action of an argument is directed towards its own interpretation, because the arrangement of its parts (rhemes and dicent signs) forces a thought process upon the one who interprets it. It might be assumed that an argument constitutes a self-sufficient unity in no need of further interpretation, since its conclusion, its intended interpretant, is contained within the sign itself. For three important reasons this is, however, not the case. First, the trivial, but fundamental point is that to function as a sign an argument (as any other sign) has to be realized through interpretation, for instance in the mind of an interpreter. Second, according to Peirce, an argument, such as a syllogism, does more than "distinctly represent the Interpretant, called its Conclusion, which it is intended to determine" (2.95). In addition to the specific material import of a given argument, it also functions as an example of a general way of reasoning, as a specimen of a certain kind of inference. Peirce says: An Argument is a sign whose interpretant represents its object as being an ulterior sign through a law, namely, the law that the passage from all such premises to such conclusions tends to the truth (2.263). In its formal aspect, then, an argument will be interpreted, and judged, according to its logical truth or falsity, and thus, it will be accepted or rejected as a general figure of thought. Third, in its material aspect, the premise of any argument rests on presuppositions which are not expressed, but supposed to be well understood, and valid, in order for it to have any force. Consequently, any argument is, at least implicitly, linked to a certain universe of discourse acting as frame of reference by virtue of which it is thought to be indubitable or probable. Since the pragmaticist Peirce believes the basic universe is perceptual, but only given through interpretation, this process adds what Peirce calls adjunctions to the perceptual universe, until, at least at an ideal limit, the highest of all universes, that of Truth, is reached through the operation of self-controlled thought, i.e., through the process of inquiry (for this see 4.539).

In the process of inquiry the linking together of different kinds of arguments, each supporting the others and fulfilling a specific function, is of highest importance. This is not the place to go into Peirce's logical work (in the technical sense), but his basic trichotomic division of arguments needs to be briefly outlined because it shows the continuity of his thought in linking the classification of signs with the logic of inquiry.

## 6. The division of arguments: deduction, induction, and abduction

Peirce wrote a series of six papers for the journal *Popular Science Monthly* called "Illustrations of the Logic of Science." The last of these papers, "Deduction, Induction, and Hypothesis" (1878), serves to introduce his fundamantal distinction between these three kinds of arguments, in a comparatively simple analysis of the syllogism. According to his analysis, a syllogism is an inference operating with three propositions, *rule* (major premise), *case* (minor premise), and *result* (conclusion). The deductive argument is exemplified by a syllogism in *Barbara*:

## DEDUCTION

*Rule* - All the beans from this bag are white.
*Case* - These beans are from this bag.
*Result* - These beans are white.                                   (2.623)

In Peirce's view, all deductive reasoning consists in applying general rules to particular cases. Inductive and abductive (*hypothetic,* also sometimes called *retroductive*) reasoning can be exemplified by changing the order of *rule, case,* and *result.* Accordingly, an induction is illustrated as follows:

## INDUCTION

*Case* - These beans are from this bag.
*Result* - These beans are white.
*Rule* - All the beans from this bag are white.    (2.623)

Abduction (hypothesis, retroduction) is illustrated thus:

## HYPOTHESIS

*Rule* - All the beans from this bag are white.
*Result* - These beans are white.
*Case* - These beans are from this bag.              (2.623)

Starting from the archetype of the classical syllogism of the first figure, Peirce inverts the deductive inference to obtain the two other modes of inference. As shown in the above examples, in inductive and abductive reasoning the conclusion does not necessarily follow from the premises. In Induction, it might happen that the next sample drawn from the bag contained black beans, thus proving the generalization of the induction to be invalid. As regards the abductive inference, it is, as explicitly stated by Peirce, an extremely weak kind of argument (in this particular case the storeroom may contain a hundred bags of white beans, and the beans in question may as well be from one of the other ninety-nine bags).

In contradistinction to deductive reasoning, however, inductive and especially abductive reasoning add to the knowledge of the universe in question. Their difference is explained as follows:

> Induction is where we generalize from a number of cases of which something is true, and infer that the same thing is true of a whole class. Or, where we find a certain thing to be true of a certain proportion of cases and infer that it is true of the same proportion of the whole class. Hypothesis is where we find some very curious circumstance, which would be explained by the supposition that it was a case of a certain general rule, and thereupon adopt that supposition. Or, where we find that in certain respects two objects have a strong resemblance, and infer that they resemble one another strongly in other respects. (2.624)

A substantial part of Peirce's writings is consecrated to reflections and technical tracts on induction, the logic of probability, and abductive reasoning, and they constitute an important contribution to the philosophy and logic of science. They are, however, not the subject of this study (Nicholas Rescher in an interesting study has expounded and questioned Peirce's logic of inquiry, i.e., his methodeutic, cf. Rescher 1978). One last point should be mentioned, however: according to Peirce, the process of inquiry involves a certain sequential order of the three basic kinds of arguments, namely abduction, deduction, and induction. The course of inquiry may, simply, be described like this:

1) A curious, unexpected phenomenon is discovered. In order to account for it some general rule is assumed that would explain the appearance of the phenomenon in question. This constitutes the abductive step in the process of inquiry. 2) The deductive step consists in deducing which consequences would necessarily follow, if the general rule, admitted hypothetically, were valid. Finally, 3) the inductive step consists in testing whether the consequences inferred by deduction are in fact present. Peirce gives the following simple example of the abductive step in the process of inquiry: "Fossils are found; say, remains like

those of fishes, but far in the interior of the country. To explain the phenomenon, we suppose the sea once washed over this land" (2.625). If we try to add the two subsequent steps to this example (asking forbearance for not being geologists), the second, deductive, step would consist in analyzing what would follow from the ancient presence of sea water. Presumably, different things would follow from this hypothesis. Let us, however, grossly simplify matters, and surmise that the rocks containing fossils should contain salt as well. Although this deduction would not be as simple as it is stated here, it may serve as an example of a deduction letting itself be used as a prediction. This prediction would then, in the inductive phase of inquiry, be tested by analyzing samples from the rock formation in question. If it, in fact, contains salt, the initial hypothesis has been supported by inductive evidence. It is important to stress, however, that to confirm the hypothesis many more deductively inferred consequences would have to be tested inductively.

Furthermore, according to Peirce, knowledge is fallible. Beliefs that are initially thought indubitable may, through the process of inquiry, be doubted, modified, or rejected. This does not mean, however, that Peirce is easily enrolled in the lists of skeptics and relativists, since he believed in the progress of knowledge, and the self-correctiveness of scientific inquiry (cf. his famous *principle of hope* quoted on p. 86).

What is impressive in Peirce's work with the classification of signs is its all-encompassing character. There exists an unbroken interconnection. from the iconic rhematic qualisign, which remains a possibility, to the division of arguments, and their different functions in the process of inquiry, this means he endeavors to analyze semiotically the process of interpretation from the percept to theory formation, showing how different kinds of signs interact and make up different parts of discourse.

This is, indeed, an accomplishment. It does not mean, however, that there is an easy solution to questions concerning the interpretations of speech and written texts, i.e., to questions asked by *hermeneutics* (according to Peirce an equally valid name for the part of semiotics he himself chose to name *speculative grammar*). In the following chapter some of these problems will be treated from the perspective of the concept of semiosis.

# PART II, 2. A DIALOGIC MODEL OF SEMIOSIS

# V. Elements of Human Communication

Socrates: Excellent. And do you define thought as I do?
Theaetetus: How do you define it?
Socrates: As the talk which the soul has with itself about any subjects which it considers. You must not suppose that I know this that I am declaring to you. But the soul, as the image presents itself to me, when it thinks, is merely conversing with itself, asking itself questions and answering, affirming and denying. When it has arrived at a decision, whether slowly or with a sudden bound, and is at last agreed, and is not in doubt, we call that its opinion; and so I define forming opinion as talking and opinion as talk which has been held, not with someone else, nor yet aloud, but in silence with oneself. (Plato: *Theaetetus,* 1961: 179)

Thinking always proceeds in the form of a dialogue – a dialogue between different phases of the *ego* – so that, being dialogical, it is essentially composed of signs, as its matter, in the sense in which a game of chess has the chessmen for its matter. Not that the particular signs employed *are* themselves the thought! Oh, no; no whit more than the skins of an onion are the onion. (About as much so, however.) One selfsame thought may be carried upon the vehicle of English, German, Greek or Gaelic; in diagrams, or in equations, or in graphs: all these are but so many skins of the onion, its inessential accidents. Yet that the thought should have *some* possible expression for some possible interpreter, is the very being of its being. . . . (Peirce 4.6)

The quotations testify to the time-honored origin of considering the development of thought as the dialogue of the soul with itself and to the importance of the concept of *dialogue* in Peircean semiotics. Here Peirce at least seems to echo Plato. It is necessary to inquire into Peirce's presuppositions of speech and dialogue before beginning to expound a dialogic model of semiosis based on his theory of signs. In the preceding part (II,1) of this study I have hinted many times at Peirce's dialogic concept of the process of signification, and have stressed the dynamical nature of his sign concept. Both his published work and especially the manuscripts contain much material concerning the presuppositions of speech and dialogic understanding, so much that he might almost be counted a forerunner of speech act analysis as it was developed by Austin and Searle (Austin 1962, Searle 1969 and 1979; for this aspect of Peirce's thought see Brock 1981), except that Peirce did not develop his insights systematically. Furthermore, we find in his work, especially after the turn of the century, a constant preoccupation with the role of indexicality in the setting of dialogue, with its grounding in a presupposed context, and reflections concerning the role of the parties of a dialogue, the utterer and interpreter.

This chapter compares Peirce's reflections to some aspects of Roman Jakobson's analyses of the presuppositions of communication. The main reason for this is not historical, although Jakobson was an admirer of Peirce, and he did much to make Peirce's work known. More important is that Jakobson's work represents a fascinating and fruitful attempt to analyze linguistic phenomena from a semiotic point of view.

## 1. Utterer and interpreter

> Thought is not necessarily connected with a brain. It appears in the work of bees, of crystals, and throughout the purely physical world; and one can no more deny that it is really there, than that the colors, the shapes, etc., of objects are really there. Consistently adhere to that unwarrantable denial, and you will be driven to some form of idealistic nominalism akin to Fichte's. Not only is thought in the organic world, but it develops there. But as there cannot be a General without Instances embodying it, so there cannot be thought without Signs. (4.551)

Without accepting or rejecting Peirce's position, which implies there is thought in crystals, note the extraordinary scope of the concepts of thought and sign within his semiotics. This scope bears on our present subject, because it raises the question whether utterer and interpreter are necessary elements of semiosis or whether it is possible to analyze sign action without taking into account both positions. The distinguished Peirce scholar, Joseph Ransdell, expresses his view on the problem as follows:

> Peirce believed that, for theoretical purposes, it would be both possible and desirable to omit from the conception of the sign relation in its generic form any reference either to an interpreting agent or to an act of interpretation; (without thereby denying that it might be pertinent in some special discipline or area of application to include these further conceptions, because

the subject-matter of investigation therein is specially conceived in such a way as to require it). In so conceiving the sign relation in its generic form, Peirce enormously broadened the scope of possible application of a theory of signs; for there are many phenomena which may be amenable to a semiotic that does not assume any interpreting agent but only makes available a way of describing analytically the various forms and possible modifications of such processes: for example, there are the various intra-organismic processes, which biologists tend to think of in terms of the transmission of information; there are socioeconomic-political processes, to which the idea of individual interpreting agents and their individual acts of interpretation may be impertinent; and one may even speculate on the possibility of a semiotic analysis of some puzzling physical phenomena. (Ransdell 1986: 53)

In principle, Ransdell is right both in stressing the generality of Peirce's concept, and in pointing out the applicability of semiotics to a wide range of research areas that are better described without reference to utterers and interpreters. It is fair, and important, however, to signal that throughout his writings Peirce seems to waver between eliminating and integrating the two positions.

Peirce is fairly confident that the position of utterer is not always necessarily presupposed in order to describe sign action. In a letter to Lady Welby (1909) he points out that "natural Signs and symptoms have no utterer; and consequently have no Meaning, if meaning be defined as the intention of the utterer" (SS 1977: 111); and in another famous passage Peirce even seems to deny the relevance of the interpreter:

I define a Sign as anything which is so determined by something else, called its Object, and so determines an effect upon a person, which effect I call its Interpretant, that the latter is thereby mediately determined by the former. My insertion of "upon a person" is a sop to Cerebus, because I despair of making my own broader conception understood. (SS 1977: 80-81)

Note, however, that it is rather the concept of an individual person than that of an interpreter which is here repudiated. A continuation of the quotation from 4.551 with which we began this part of the study confirms this. Peirce says:

Admitting that connected Signs must have a Quasi-mind, it may further be declared that there can be no isolated sign. Moreover, signs require at least two Quasi-minds; a *Quasi-utterer* and a *Quasi-interpreter;* although these two are at one (i.e., *are* one mind) in the sign itself, they must nevertheless be distinct. In the Sign they are, so to say, *welded.* Accordingly, it is not merely a fact of human Psychology, but a necessity of Logic, that every logical evolution of thought should be dialogic. (4.551)

These quasi-minds, however, are positions in the development of thought, and are void of individuality.

In the all-important Ms. 318 (1907) we can follow in detail Peirce's wavering. This is not the place to do so, but we should briefly mention one line of thought presented in that manuscript. Admitting that most sign action involves an utterer and an interpreter, or at least the latter, Peirce asks himself whether it might not be possible to eliminate them, but at the same time integrate their essential characteristics in the concept of the sign itself. The "essential ingredient of the utterer" is, according to Peirce, the function of "standing for," or "representing," the object of the sign, because the utterer indicates what universe and object he refers to. As regards the interpreter, Peirce says that that "which the sign in its significant function essentially determines in its interpreter I term the 'interpretant' of the sign. . . . If a sign has no interpreter, its interpretant is a 'would be,' i.e., is what it would determine in the interpreter if there were one" (Ms. 318, 1907: 79-80). An example of a sign without an interpreter, in the sense of nobody qualified to interpret it, is a language resisting deciphering, e.g., Linear A. In a case such as Linear A, philologists are for many reasons confident that the remaining fragments are not just calligraphy but writing supposed to manifest a system of signification. These fragments are "would-bes." They are reasonably believed capable of determining interpretants in a future community of scholars.

Peirce's idea of subsuming utterer under object, and interpreter under interpretant, as regards the abstract level of semiotics, is interesting for several reasons. One is that it brings out the elements of *sequentiality* and *force* in sign action. These elements may be exemplified by a semiotic consideration of the unconditioned and the conditioned reflex:

1) Some strong-smelling food is present, but hidden. The smell triggers the production of saliva in a dog. Here, the *object,* food, produces a *sign,* smell, which triggers an *interpretant,* saliva, in an *interpreter,* a dog. The dog cannot, of course, be reduced to a saliva-producing machine (it may also be somebody's best friend), but, as far as this semiosis is concerned, the saliva is the significate effect deter-

mined by the sign, and as far as this sign is concerned, this interpretant is the "essential ingredient" of the interpreter.

2) The master of a dog pronounces the word "food," and the dog begins to produce saliva, to wag its tail, and to run towards the kitchen door. Here, an *utterer* has been added to the sign action. To the dog the master represents, or "stands for," the food; and so it is reasonable to say that the utterer represents the object. Furthermore, a replica of a rhematic symbolic legisign (the word "food") has been substituted for a rhematic indexical sinsign (the smell), to the effect that the sign no longer emanates from the object. An utterer directs the attention of the interpreter towards the possible existence of the object.

Leaving aside the complexities of the dog's learning process that make this sign action possible, we see that the elementary sequence of 1) is object → sign → interpretant, and that the sign exerts an influence on the interpretant due to the instinctual responsiveness of the interpreter. In 2) the sequence is utterer → sign → interpretant → object, because it is by interpreting the sign that the object is constituted within the sphere of the sign action. To this it might be objected that the object must have been in the utterer's mind before he emitted the sign. This objection is valid, but it also proves Peirce's point that the object can be seen as "the essential ingredient" of the utterer. If we add the interpreter to the sequence as the "environment" both determined by but also determining the interpretant, we get the following sequence:

object → utterer → sign → interpreter → interpretant → object

Fig. 34

No wonder that Peirce was tempted to put utterer and interpreter within parentheses:

object (→ utterer) → sign (→ interpreter) → interpretant → object

Fig. 35

By doing so we get in, fact, the indivisible triadic sign action:

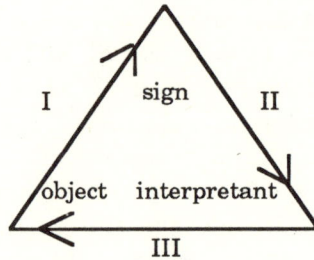

Fig. 36

The anti-psychological and anti-individualistic strain in Peirce's thought is one reason, maybe the most important one, why Peirce's tries to eliminate utterer and interpreter from general semiotics. This antipathy may be explained by a concept of science which leaves no room for individuality and personal opinions. He says, "there is nothing which distinguishes my personal identity except my faults and my limitations" (4.672). Ideally, utterers and interpreters would be negligible, incidental circumstances in the process of semiosis by virtue of which knowledge progresses.

## 2. Individuality and the ethics of inquiry

According to Peirce, logic, i.e., semiotics, is one, the lowest, of the three normative sciences, and so it is connected with ethics and aesthetics. It is necessary to sketch his argument for the linking together of these three sciences. While Peirce's reflections on the three normative sciences are also closely connected with his religious thought and with his cosmology, these are not the subjects of this study. Peirce defines aesthetics as the science of ideals, the object of which is to define the *summum bonum* (ultimate good), namely, that which in itself is admirable regardless of any ulterior reason. As Peirce says:

The one thing whose admirableness is not due to an ulterior reason is Reason itself comprehended in all its fullness, so far as we can comprehend it. Under this conception, the ideal of conduct will be to execute our little function in the operation of the creation by giving a hand toward rendering the world more reasonable whenever, as the slang is, it is "up to us" to do so. In logic, it will be observed that knowledge is reasonableness; and the ideal of reasoning will be to follow such methods as must develop knowledge the most speedily. (1.615)

Here, Peirce indicates how ethics and logic are connected with and subordinated to aesthetics. It should be added that since the two sciences are normative, purpose is an essential ingredient of both, and purpose only exists with a view to an end (defined by aesthetics). Ethics and logic also are closely related in another respect, that they are controlled conduct:

The phenomena of reasoning are, in their general features, parallel to those of moral conduct. For reasoning is essentially thought that is under self-control, just as moral conduct is conduct under self-control. Indeed reasoning *is* a species of controlled conduct and as such necessarily partakes of the essential features of controlled conduct. (1.606)

From Peirce's concept of the *summum bonum,* and from his concept of truth as the "opinion which is fated to be ultimately agreed to by all who investigate" (5.407), there follow certain ethical and logical consequences. If the ultimate good consists in making the universe more rational, and if truth (and reality) is what is agreed on by a scientific community after sufficient (maybe endless) investigation, then it follows that the principle on which man acts cannot be confined to the promotion of his personal interest, or to the satisfaction of his desires. According to Peirce, truth is thus attained by means of inductive approximation, which is self-corrective. Consequently, no one can reasonably hope to reach it through the finite, limited chain of inferences of which a single person is capable. This forces Peirce to argue in the following way:

It seems to me that we are driven to this, that logic inexorable requires that our interests shall not be limited. They must not stop at our own fate, but must embrace the whole community. This community, again, must not be limited, but must extend to all races of beings with whom we can come into immediate or mediate intellectual relation. It must reach, however vaguely, beyond this geological epoch, beyond all bounds. He who would not sacrifice his own soul to save the whole world, is, as it seems to me, illogical in all his inferences, collectively. Logic is rooted in the social principle. (2.654)

Peirce thus bases the sacrifice of self-interest on the individual's recognition that his interest and goal ought to be identical with that of
the community; because the perfection of knowledge may be obtained
only by an (unlimited) community (of researchers) (cf. 5.356).

Peirce's definition of the *summum bonum* gives rise to a new dimension of his concept of the so-called *communicational interpretant*
as "the determination of that mind into which the minds of the utterer
and interpreter have to be fused in order that any communication
should take place" (cf. here p. 170), and is even related to his cos-
mological and metaphysical reflections:

> The real universe began in many individual minds, strangers to one an-
> other, but gradually [it] becomes the common thought of the whole com-
> munity. Furthermore, the pragmaticistic analysis, like that of Kant, makes
> the sum of reality itself to consist in thought, since thought can think
> nothing but thought. (Ms. 288b, 1904: 251)

Here, the evolutionary and idealistic core of Peirce's philosophy is
certainly prominent. It should be noted, however, that even if Peirce
speaks about his *social theory of reality* founded on *consensus* (e.g.,
6.610), his concept of truth (and reality) can by no means be described
as a mere consensus theory of truth (cf. II, 5). He defines truth most
often as the *correspondence* between propositions and reality: "There
would not be any such thing as truth unless there were something
which is as it is independently of how we may think it to be" (7.659).
Without going further into the controversial questions concerning
Peirce's theory of truth (cf. Apel 1975, 1980, and 1982 and Hookway
1985), no contradiction is necessarily involved in claiming on the one
hand that truth consists in the conformity of a proposition to something which has the characters it has independently of any particular
proposition ascribing this or that character to it, and conversely that it
is void of meaning to postulate a concept of truth that does not imply
the agreement on the applicability or non-applicability of terms and
propositions (cf. that Peirce in a letter to Lady Welby of 23 Dec. 1908
claims that the truth should "be recognized as *public!*" SS 1977: 73).

Peirce's attempt to eliminate utterer and interpreter on the basis
of fusion, on the level of general semiotics, should not be carelessly
disregarded, since it expresses an *ethos* of inquiry and scientific and
scholarly ideals that are both presupposed and operative within research. Careers, vanity, material awards, and personal well-being are,

in practice, not negligible factors within academia, or other communities of researchers, a lesson taught by history and experience. However, even the most vain scholar, and even the scientist who falsifies evidence may, in moments of reflection, realize a certain *mauvaise foi* within themselves; and even during the constantly ongoing fights for power and funding, the soundness of arguments may be taken into consideration. If these things sometimes happen, then Peirce's idea about the logicality of scholarly and scientific collaboration, and the individual scholar's identification with the purpose and objectives of his field, may even have a *fundamentum in re.*

Peirce's negative attitude, sometimes even hostility, towards concepts of individuality is lodged in the context of his view on scientific norms and ideals. He also says, as regards persons, that uniqueness and individuality in any absolute sense are illusory:

> a person is not absolutely an individual. His thoughts are what he is "saying to himself," that is, is saying to that other self that is just coming into life in the flow of time. When one reasons, it is that critical self that one is trying to persuade; and all thought whatsoever is a sign, and is mostly of the nature of language. The second thing to remember is that the man's circle of society (however widely or narrowly this phrase may be understood), is a sort of loosely compacted person, in some respects of higher rank than the person of an individual organism. It is these two things alone that render it possible for you — but only in the abstract, and in a Pickwickian sense — to distinguish between absolute truth and what you do not doubt. (5.421)

From this we see how the repudiation of individuality is bound up with an ideal concerning the progress of knowledge through inquiry, that leads to the attainment of truth. Truth is not to be identified with personal beliefs, however indubitable they may seem; it is the outcome of a critical dialogue, not of the individual soul with itself, but between the members of an unlimited community of researchers. Furthermore Peirce breaks up the common sense concept of the unquestionable unity of the individual person, because dialogism is a constitutional relation of the self, and because dialogical relationships with others are of the same nature as the dialogue within a single person. Consequently, dialogism necessarily transcends individuality, and, as far as inquiry is concerned, the difference between intrapsychic and interpsychic dialogue is negligible, void of interest.

## 3. The contract of dialogue

From what has been said so far concerning verbal communication between persons, it would be wrong to conclude that we can neglect the positions of utterer and interpreter. Even scientific inquiry and the progress of knowledge depends on the community's acceptance of values and standards, shared goals and purposes. Furthermore, the classification of the interpretant according to the communicational point of view (cf. here IV, 4), and the different examples of interpretants given by Peirce, show that the parties participating in symbolic action are not exterior to the analysis of meaning. One of his best illustrations of thirdness stresses this point:

> Now let us consider the triad, A makes a contract with C. To say that A signs the document D, and C signs the document D, no matter what the contents of that document, does not make a contract. The contract lies in the intent. And what is the intent? It is that certain conditional rules shall govern the conduct of A and of C. There is no positive fact in this; it is only conditional and intentional. . . . A psychical fact is involved; but there is no intent unless something be intended; and that which is intended cannot be covered by any facts; it goes beyond anything that can ever be done or have happened, because it extends over the whole breadth of a general condition; and a complete list of the possible cases is absurd. (1.475)

It is not accidental that Peirce chooses the contract as an example of triadic relations because it illustrates five points that are central to his concept of communication: purpose, intention, responsibility, future action governed by rules, and the indeterminacy of linguistic texts.

Peirce conceives the act of uttering a verbal sign as a deed or action, which does not add a new thought to the propositional content of the utterance but in a certain way commits the utterer. Peirce says, "One and the same proposition may be affirmed, denied, judged, doubted, inwardly inquired into, put as a question wished, asked for, effectively commanded, taught, or merely expressed, and does not thereby become a different proposition" (NEM 1976, IV: 248). As a logician Peirce is mainly interested in the act of affirmation (or assertion), and his favorite way of analyzing it is by comparing it to the legal act of going before a notary public and making an affidavit to the content of a proposition. This action has penalties attached to it;

swearing to the truth of something may move an interpreter to act accordingly and at his expense because he believes in it. The only difference between swearing to a proposition and merely affirming it is that the commitment and the penalties in the latter case are less. Peirce sums up his analysis in the following way:

> A *belief* in a proposition is a controlled and contented habit of acting in ways that will be productive of desired results only if the proposition is true. An *affirmation* is an act of an utterer of a proposition to an interpreter, and consists, in the first place, in the deliberate exercise, in uttering the proposition, of a force tending to determine a belief in it in the mind of the interpreter. Perhaps that is a sufficient definition of it; but it involves also a voluntary self-subjection to penalties in the event of the interpreter's mind (and still more the general mind of society) subsequently becoming decidedly determined to the belief at once in the falsity of the proposition and in the additional proposition that the utterer believed it to be false at the time he uttered it. (NEM 1976, IV: 249-250)

Here Peirce opens up the whole field of speech act analysis. He goes further, however, when he points to the fact that the utterer, besides being responsible for the consequences bound up with the mode of utterance that he selects, is also determining the *deixis*, or deictic system, of the utterance. Consequently the interpreter has to follow the directions of the utterer to be able to identify the topic of the discourse.

It should also be mentioned that Peirce explains the use of *selectives* (quantifiers) within a dialogical context, since he claims that by using the universal selective (e.g., *all* men sin) the utterer transfers the right of selecting an instance to falsify the proposition to the interpreter. Using the particular selective (e.g., *some* men sin), the utterer reserves the right of choosing an instance, which proves his argument, for himself. In the use of a proposition with a singular selective (*this* man sins), neither the utterer nor the interpreter has freedom of choice.

Since the utterer chooses the mode of the utterance, gives the directions for identifying the topic of discourse, and decides the range of the utterance's applicability, what is then left to the interpreter? First, the interpreter plays an important role in the capacity of being the *addressee* in the intention of the utterer. This is clear from the description of what is involved in the act of affirmation, and in a less formal manner Peirce describes the dialogical character of uttering something as follows:

> The purpose of a sign is to supplement the ideas of the life of which I, the interpreter, am a part — ideas which I have drawn directly from my own life — with a copy of a scrap torn out of another's life, or rather from his panorama of all life, his general view of life, and I need to know just where on my own panorama of universal life I am to insert a recopy of this copied scrap. (Ms. 318, 1907: 194)

This states the problem from the interpreter's point of view, and Peirce goes on to state it from the point of view of the utterer:

> But the utterer has no ideas but his own ideas. . . . Let him try to specify a place on the interpreter's panorama, and he can only look over his own panorama, where he can find nothing but his own ideas. On that panorama he has, however, no difficulty in finding the interpreter's life, that is to say, his idea of it, and among the interpreter's panorama to which he conceives this scrap should be attached and this he expresses in his sign for the interpreter's benefit. The latter has to go through a similar round-about process to find a place in his own life that seems to correspond with his idea of the utterer's idea of his life and with all these changes of costume there is such imminent danger of mistake. . . . (Ms. 318L, 1907: 198-199)

Peirce goes on to suggest that the utterer should express his own ideas clearly and leave it to the interpreter to make up his mind. This advice seems to be sensible, but does not do away with the problem, and Peirce's description of the hermeneutics of dialogue is precise
    Besides figuring as a mental construct, as *addressee,* in the intentions of the utterer, the interpreter plays an active role in constructing the meaning of an utterance, because no utterance is completely determinate as to its meaning:

> Honest people, when not joking, intend to make the meaning of their words determinate, so that there shall be no latitude of interpretation at all. That is to say, the character of their meaning consists in the implications and non-implications of their words; and they intend to fix what is implied and what is not implied. They believe that they succeed in doing so, and if their chat is about the theory of numbers, perhaps they may. But the further their topics are from such presciss, or 'abstract,' subjects, the less possibility is there of such precision of speech. (5.447)

If honesty and a common purpose is essential to the communication of meaning between utterer and interpreter, we have the problem of determining the purpose and testing the trustworthiness of the utterer. Since people sometimes knowingly utter false statements motivated by the desire to achieve some purpose, the interpreter, in principle and in fact, has to distinguish between the utterer as he is presented in the utterance (e.g., because the utterance expresses a familiar and, as it were, 'codified speech act'), and the utterer as the producer of the utterance. Let us call the utterer as an element within the signifying process the *addresser* and reserve *utterer* for the producer.

In distinguishing between a proposition and the act of asserting that proposition, Peirce implies another distinction - that between the truth of the proposition and the veracity or trustworthiness of the utterer (cf. the quotation from Ms. 517 on p. 199). In his part of the entry on "Truth, Falsity and Error" in *Baldwin's Dictionary,* Peirce distinguishes between *logical truth* ("concordance of an abstract statement with the ideal limit towards which endless investigation would tend to bring scientific belief" [5.565]) and *ethical truth* ("conformity of an assertion to the speaker's or writer's belief" [5.570]). Even if ethical truth, as defined above, is a rather narrow concept, it is basic to the understanding of utterances as regards their purpose, and in order to use them as evidence it is necessary to assume that utterances conform to a writer's or speaker's belief (cf. p. 283).

It might seem we are far from our subject, the semiotic interpretation of the linguistic text, but this is not the case; we are right in the middle of it, because the relationship between utterer and interpreter in the semiosis depends on the right understanding of the utterer's intentions by the interpreter. Without this understanding it would be impossible for the interpreter to analyze the utterance as a deed or action even if he understands the text's propositional content. Whether a given text is ironic or sincere, for instance, is certainly fundamental to the understanding of it; and to decide this question, we need to make an assumption about the intention of the utterer, because an ironic and a naive utterance may be identical as to their linguistic expression, but opposed to each other with regard to their mode of enunciation, since each is a different speech act.

Intentions imply purposes, because intending something means attempting to attain something with a view to an end. Even the most casual conversation fulfills some purpose, perhaps nothing more than serving to establish contact, secure the lines of communication, and ensure social interaction. This means that to interpret a given text a semiotic text analysis ought to establish its purpose; and since purpose implies the concept of an end, the analysis ought to incorporate this as well. It might be objected that by including intentions, purposes, and ends as a part of text interpretation, one commits the error known as "the intentional fallacy"; but since it is impossible to understand the meaning of a text without determining its mode of enunciation, an analysis of intentions is a necessary prerequisite for text interpretation. In Peircean terms you could say that an interpretation means the adding of a dynamic interpretant to a sign referring to the same object, action, or state of affairs that the sign itself refers to. A linguistic text is an expression of a belief, a wish, a command, a question, a request, etc. That is why an utterance not only refers to some object, action, or state of affairs, but also indicates its own mode. Mode, however, has to be analyzed as a relationship between utterer and interpreter with regard to the object of discourse, and this means that an interpretant that does not reflect the mode, or modes, of a text, at best, can be regarded as a partial interpretant; by leaving out the modal aspect of a text, the danger of misinterpretation becomes imminent. It should be noted that an analysis of the modal aspect and the intentions and purposes of a text does not necessarily imply a psychological analysis of the producer of the text (but can be the point of departure for such an analysis), because stating the intention or purpose of the text does not mean looking inside the head of the utterer but rather determining the kind of deed or act of which the utterance is an instance. Otherwise the utterance would make no sense. In other words, the primary frame of reference is linguistic rules, rules of social interaction, norms, values, and ideals. The psychological state of the utterer is only the secondary frame of reference, albeit an important one.

Understanding of the modalities of a given text is, however, bound to the understanding of the communicative and referential context in which it is placed. Consequently, to narrow the latitude of interpretation inherent in linguistic texts, we need a certain amount of shared knowledge and common presuppositions between utterer and interpreter. Because of the indeterminacy of linguistic signs, interpretation always means contextualization. The question, however, is to determine a text's proper context.

## 4. Universes of discourse

No object can be denoted unless it be put into relation to the object of the *commends*. A man, tramping along a weary and solitary road, meets an individual of strange mien, who says, "There was a fire in Megara." If this should happen in the Middle United States, there might very likely be some village in the neighborhood called Megara. Or it may refer to one of the ancient cities of Megara, or to some romance. And the time is wholly indefinite. In short, nothing at all is conveyed until the person addressed asks, Where? — "Oh about half a mile along there" pointing to whence he came. "And when?" "As I passed." Now an item of information has been conveyed, because it has been stated relatively to a well understood common experience. Thus the Form conveyed is always a determination of the dynamical object of the *Commind*. By the way, the dynamical object does not mean something out of the mind. It means something forced upon the mind in perception, but including more than perception reveals. It is an object of actual *Experience*. (SS 1977: 197)

Here Peirce himself points to the necessity of embedding the sign (or text) in a communicative and referential context to make it understandable. What is going on in the fictitious dialogue is a narrowing down and specification of a common universe in relation to which the text becomes informative. The concept of *universe of discourse* is in Peirce, and in general, bound up with logic in the more formal and technical sense, which is of no concern in this study. Viewed in relation to the triadic sign concept, and to the idea of the dialogical nature of the semiosis of speech, the universe of discourse is related to the object pole of the sign. Peirce states the relation between object and universe as follows:

If the Sign be the sentence "Cain killed Abel," in which Cain and Abel are equally Partial Objects, it may be more convenient to say that that which determines the Sign is the Complexus, or Totality, of Partial Objects. And in every case the Object is accurately the Universe of which the Special Object is member, or part. (8.178n)

According to this definition the universe is a kind of space, or rather a spatio-temporal network, within which the specifically mentioned objects are situated. Suppose we read the following text on a wall:

## ROMEO LOVES JULIET

Although most of us would take the utterance to be a (true) proposition about the characters of Shakespeare's play, it does not, as it stands, warrant this interpretation, because it does not contain sufficient information to link it univocally to Shakespeare's fictional world. The utterance might refer to two teenagers in the neighborhood. As in Peirce's own example, what is brought out is an important aspect of the problem of contextualization, namely, the embedding of the objects represented by the sign within the totality, or total object, which is identified with the universe of discourse.

The importance of establishing the relationship between sign and universe is pointed out in Peirce's entry, "universe of discourse," in *Baldwin's Dictionary*. He writes: "In every proposition the circumstances of its enunciation show that it refers to some collection of individuals or of possibilities, which cannot be adequately described, but can only be indicated as something familiar to both speaker and auditor" (2.536). Here the concept, *universe of discourse*, is negatively defined as what is presupposed, not what is described in the sign, in order that it may convey information. This means that to identify and understand the universe of discourse, experience other than the one mediated by the sign itself is necessary. That is what Peirce calls *collateral experience*, or *collateral observation*. He carefully distinguishes this experience, or observation, from the interpretant of the sign:

> All that part of the understanding of the Sign which the Interpreting Mind has needed collateral observation for is outside the Interpretant. I do not mean by "collateral observation" acquaintance with the system of signs. What is so gathered is *not* COLLATERAL. It is on the contrary the prerequisite for getting any idea signified by the sign. But by collateral observation, I mean previous acquaintance with what the sign denotes. Thus if the Sign be the sentence "Hamlet was mad," to understand what this means one must know that men are sometimes in that strange state; one must have seen madmen or read about them; and it will be all the better if one specifically knows (and need not be driven to *presume*) what Shakespeare's notion of insanity was. All that is collateral observation and is no part of the Interpretant. But to put together the different subjects as the sign represents them as related — that is the main [i.e., force] of the Interpretant-forming. (8.179)

Interpretation, or "interpretant-forming," means realizing the significance of the specific way in which the sign represents the object, e.g., through the relation of the sign's parts to each other. Thus the semantic texture of the play in its relation to the relevant semantic codes of English at the time of Shakespeare will determine the interpretant of Hamlet's madness. In this case, the collateral experience necessary to perceive the significative structure of the text is the ability to indicate the kind of objects, events, states of affairs, etc. to which the utterances of the play are applicable and to embed them within the experiental network presupposed, but not explicitly stated, by the text. Consequently, a universe of discourse can be analyzed from two closely allied, but different points of view, ontological and epistemological (in a state of perfect knowledge, according to Peirce, these two views would merge).

From an ontological point of view the universes of discourse are differentiated according to the ontological status of the elements contained within them. Not surprisingly, in accordance with his categories, Peirce distinguishes three different universes of discourse defined by their modality of being: 1) the universe of ideas or *possibles*, 2) the universe of *existents*, and 3) the universe of *necessitants* (habits and laws) (for this distinction see SS 1977: 81-83).

In addition to the categorical distinction between the three classes of universes of discourse, Peirce concretely lists the following different universes: the physical universe, the imaginary world of some play or novel, and a range of possibilities (2.556). In another place he lists a universe of non-distinct individuals, i.e., of continuity (e.g., the collection of drops of water in the sea), and a universe consisting of completed and objective common experiences, in which "the units retain each its distinct identity." One of Peirce's examples is a universe consisting of the great tragedians that, at the point in time he is writing, i.e., 1897, have acted in New York in the last ten years. He claims that he can draw up a definite list, containing the relevant proper names. One wonders whether that would be an easy task? Another universe consists of possibilities, which are of a general nature, e.g., the number of people committing suicide in New York City two years from now. Even if the number can be fairly accurately predicted, their distinct identity is unknown. Finally, Peirce mentions a fictional universe of discourse, which he characterizes as follows:

> When the universe of discourse relates to a common experience, but this experience is of something imaginary, as when we discuss the world of Shakespeare's creation in the play of Hamlet, we find individual distinction existing so far as the work of imagination has carried it, while beyond that point there is vagueness and generality. (4.172)

Elsewhere Peirce gives an amusing example of the limitations as to what questions can be asked of a work of literature:

> When we busy ourselves to find the answer to a question, we are going upon the hope that there is an answer, which can be called the answer. It may be there is none. If any profound and learned member of the German Shakespeare Society were to start the inquiry how long since Polonius had had his hair cut at the time of his death, perhaps the only reply that could be made would be that Polonius was nothing but a creature of Shakespeare's mind, and that Shakespeare never thought of the point raised. (4.61)

Few scholars would care about Polonius' haircut. The point is that because of lack of information many questions about a fictional universe of discourse can never be answered. We are not able to obtain additional information.

We have to make inferences *per analogiam* from our experiental and historical universe to answer many questions concerning a fictional universe of discourse If nothing else is stated, we make presuppositions and inferences for a given fictional universe of discourse we believe to be valid concerning objects, states of affairs, or events in a historical universe of discourse, because such beliefs are either supposed to be operative at the time of the production of the work of fiction or eternally valid (cf. Johansen 1989). Consequently, even if the concept of a universe of discourse is ontologically neutral, the understanding of different kinds of universes is based on acquaintance with an experiential universe (for a full and interesting study of fictional discourse see Pavel 1986, for Peirce's view of the fictional see the interesting article by Jerry Bozorete, Bozorete 1979).

Another problem is that the number of discursive universes must necessarily be infinite, because it is always possible to construct a new universe of discourse by producing a text that contains new, never before encountered, indexical signs. In this way a separate universe of discourse, a new possible world, is established which is marked off from other universes by containing the elements designated by the new indexical signs. It is essential, however, that the indexical signs are produced, or invented, by the individual text itself, that they owe their existence to it, because otherwise we would have to admit as many different universes as there are texts, and for several reasons this would lead to unintended and inappropriate conclusions.

Suppose we have two historical biographies, one about the Duke of Wellington and one about Napoleon, written by two different authors. It would be probable that both texts would contain indexical signs (e.g., proper nouns) that could not be found in the other, although they would share many such signs. Since the inventories of the indexical signs in the two biographies would be different, it might be argued that they refer to two different discursive universes: the former to a universe containing, say, the Duke of Wellington's great grandmother but not Napoleon's, the latter to one containing Napoleon's great grandmother but not Wellington's. To hold such a point of view would, however, lead to a radical fragmentation of the representation of our historical universe, and of our life-world. Carried to its logical conclusion it would imply solipsism. Another way of analyzing the relationship between the two texts is to claim they are partial representations of a common universe, namely the historical universe of man. The principal reason why such a viewpoint is preferable is cogently stated by Paul Ricoeur:

> we can expect that the facts dealt with in historical works, when they are taken one at a time, interlock with one another in the manner of geographical maps, if the same rules of projection and scale are respected, or, yet again, like the different facets of the same precious stone. Whereas there is no sense in placing stories, novels, and plays side by side, it is a legitimate and unavoidable question how the history of a given period interlocks with that of some other period, the history of France with that of England, for example, or how the political or military history of a given country at a given time dovetails with its economic history, with its social history, and its cultural history. A secret dream of emulating the cartographer or the diamond cutter animates the historical enterprise. Even if the idea of universal history must forever remain an Idea in Kant's sense of this term, since it is incapable of constituting a Leibnizian geometral, the work of approximation that brings the concrete results attained by individual or collective inquiry ever closer to this idea is neither useless nor meaningless. To this desire to tie things together on the side of historical facts corresponds the hope that the results reached by different investigators can be combined, due to their complementarity, and that they can mutually correct one another. The credo of objectivity is nothing other than

this twofold conviction that the facts related by different histories can be linked together and that the results of these histories can complete one another. (Ricoeur 1984: I, 176)

The reason why discursive universes of stories, novels, and plays do not interlock is because it makes no sense to place them within a time-space continuum, and because they do not supplement and complete each other. This might seem a strange statement coming from a literary historian, because, for literary scholars, it seems obvious that the reading of Ben Jonson's comedies in a certain sense adds to our knowledge of Shakespeare's. I think this is true; but the reason why is either that they are analyzed as separate universes and then compared as to their similarities and differences, or that they are conceived as mind-dependent signs, figments of the imagination, produced within the same historical life-world. In the latter case the time-space continuum is important. The relationships is not, however, between their fictional universes, but within the historical universe of their production.

Ricoeur's ideas concerning the interlocking and mutual completion are important. It is also interesting that his formulation of the *ethos* of history writing is analogous to the *principle of hope* advocated by Peirce as regards the sciences (cf. p. 86). It is not surprising, however, since they both presuppose the co-referentiality of both scientific and scholarly texts. This co-referentiality exists because such texts are supposed to be partial and incomplete representations of a single universe. The history of man is supposed to be of the nature of a multilayered and heterogeneous network of processes that are related to and influence each other in different ways; and no text will be able to represent the total network.

If different history texts are different discursive representations of a common universe, it means, from a semiotic perspective, that they are different semioses representing immediate objects, each revealing different aspects of the dynamical object: history in its totality. To view global history as a dynamical object seems justified if it is remembered that 1) a dynamical object is only known through immediate objects, and that 2) history as a dynamical object is supposed to influence the texts, as when for instance new historical evidence, indices, change the interpretation of a given course of events.

Our two historical biographies mentioned above are claimed to represent a common universe because they are supposed to relate either the same states of affairs, actions, and events, or that they relate such that exist within the same time-space system of coordinates. Furthermore, they are also supposed to be ontologically compatible.

Regardless of the ultimate ontological status of a given universe of discourse, it functions (or fails to function) as a presuppositional network common to the parties of a dialogue, as to what is familiar and well-understood by both. This is why Peirce, in another place, talks about the universe of discourse as *a continuity of experiential appearance,* or a *field of attention.* This field, however, is not specifically singled out for being scrutinized. It is "the Universe of discourse — where it only receives *general* attention as that Universe — that is to say of the continuity in experiential appearance of the Universe, relatively to any objects represented as belonging to it" (4.561n). In its capacity both as a presuppositional network and as a field of general attention, other parts of it may be attended to and analyzed by being represented in subsequent, successive semioses, but the sum of all presuppositions or the whole field of general attention cannot be stated either in a single semiosis or in any finite series of semioses, at least only in a state of total knowledge. Furthermore, what is implicit and presupposed, and what is only the subject of general attention, remains vague, and thus the universe of discourse will include elements, although familiar and well-understood, which are indefinite, neither questioned nor analyzed by the parties of the dialogue.

It may seem strange to describe a universe of discourse both as a complexus of objects within a field of general attention and as a presuppositional network, because these two descriptions applied to the same phenomenon seem to blur the distinction between the object pole and the interpretant pole of the semiosis. This apparent merging of the two poles is, however, in accordance with a seeming contradiction in Peirce's concept of the relationship between them. Clearly he holds that the distinction between object and interpretant is of the utmost importance:

Pragmatism looks upon a concept as a mental sign or medium between the object to which it is molded and the "meaning," or effect which the object is enabled by the concept to produce; and in all general inquiries about signs nothing is of more lively importance than maintaining a clear and sharp distinction between the object, or proposed cause of the sign, and the meaning, or intended effect of it. Now experiences seem to me to be rather the object of a conception than its meaning, for they are too external to the mind to be meanings. (Ms. 320, 1907: 9)

Two years later, still maintaining the relevance and importance of this distinction, he qualifies his position concerning object and interpretant:

The determination by a Sign of its Interpreting Mind, — i.e., the idea that mind gets, or the feeling it sets up, or the action it stimulates, I call its "Interpretant"; and there is all the difference in the world between the Object of a sign of which the interpreter must have some collateral experience, immediate or mediate, or he won't know at all what it is that the Sign represents (and whoever questions that point simply fails to understand what I mean by the Object, and confounds it with the Interpretant). The latter is all that the sign conveys. The Object is the otherwise known something concerning which what it conveys relates. The distinction is a real distinction and yet it is purely relative, in the sense that the line of demarcation between the two can just as well be drawn in one place as another; just as if there is a long island in a river,

it is a real fact that there are two parts of the river; for one must carry a dam from one shore to another to cut the river in two where it passes the island; although at the same time, if we neglect the flow of the water & suppose it to be a lake not a river, the line of demarcation between the two can be drawn almost wherever one likes. By "the two" here, I mean that part where there are two branches of the water and that part where there is only one.

The point is that the artificiality of a line of demarcation does not prove that the twoness of the parts that the line of demarcation may be regarded as separating does not correspond to any twoness in re. (L 36, 1909)

In my opinion, no contradiction is involved in maintaining the distinction between object and interpretant and pointing out its relativity. Peirce's analysis of perception and experience makes this qualification necessary, because given that he describes perceptual judgment as inferential, as a special kind of abductive inference forced upon the perceiver, then the perceptual universe is a universe partly constituted by interpretation. Such a universe is, however, beyond the control of the perceiver and not reducible to what he wills it to be;

consequently, its objects determine signs independently of his expectations and predictions. This power to produce signs that determine interpretants regardless of any individual will and comprehension belongs to the object (i.e., the dynamical object). Since the object is always apprehended within a semiosis, however, it is always a part of a triadic action involving interpretation, and, thus, any given universe of discourse is always partly interpreted.

Another reason why the distinction between object and interpretant is relative is because it is *positional,* because nothing prevents a given entity from functioning as an object in one semiosis, and as an interpretant in another, or to assume both functions simultaneously. If, for instance, while a mother is walking with her child, a cat suddenly appears, and she points to the animal and says "cat," then, assuming that the child has neither heard the word nor seen a cat before, the animal will almost simultaneously function as object and as interpretant of the word "cat." Obviously, this particular cat is the object of the mother's utterance (in fact a one-word sentence), but for the child it functions as an interpretant of the word as well, because (the mental image of) the cat explains the meaning of the symbolic sign, cat, albeit this explanation is partial and perfunctory.

## 5. The common ground

The double status of the universe of discourse, and especially of the perceptual universe, as interpreted and interpretable, but also resisting interpretation and forcing interpreters to modify beliefs, makes it the most important part of what Peirce terms the *common ground* shared by the parties of a dialogue. According to Peirce, every successful dialogue between two parties presupposes that both parties possess six requirements: (1) Knowledge of the specific language used, (2) knowledge of the rudiments of universal grammar, (3) the most important attributes of the genus *homo,* (4) a similar experience of life concerning elementary items of experience, (5) control of body and of thought, and (6) the knowledge that the second party takes this for granted in the first party, and vice versa, together with the knowledge that both parties know the other party knows it (cf. Ms. 612, 1908: 2-3). These preconditions of understanding may seem trivial, but are fundamental, and they seem to cover almost every aspect of the se-miosis. Points one and two have to do with the relationship between sign and interpretant, since a common language is a precondition for attaching interpretants to signs and thus for being able to ensure understanding by making the propositions more determinate. Point two refers to a more general precondition of translatability, a kind of linguistic deep level structure that despite their different surface structures ensures the identity of the utterances as regards both refe-rence and syntactico-semantic features. Point three indicates that to reach mutual understanding the parties must have the same potential of acting and reacting, e.g., of perception and motility. From a semiotic point of view, this precondition can be stated in the following way: To reach mutual understanding in dialogue both parties must be able to receive, store, interpret, and emit signs in a structurally identical way, and to do this presupposes the same neuro-physiological apparatus and capacity for learning in both parties. Point four stresses that a minimal universe of action must be common to both parties. When speaking of a cultural barrier we refer to the difference in the life-world of two persons, classes, or cultures, a difference that makes dialogue difficult. Peirce, however, points to the fact that, at an ele-mentary level, some experiences are cross-culturally shared (e.g., ex-periences of needs), and even if they are culturally embedded, i.e., endowed with a social and a symbolic signification and significance specific to each culture, nevertheless, they constitute a common stock of knowledge that makes interpretation possible. Point five is parallel to point three, but stresses the functional and developmental aspect of human nature. It should be noted that the concept of self-control is basic in Peirce's thought, because his definition of logic is self-con-trolled thinking, and conduct is often defined as self-controlled action. It is sensible to presuppose this control because without this pre-supposition the parties could not share even a minimal universe of action. Their potential for action would be different. The last point con-cerns what could be called the *reciprocity* of *reflexivity* of dialogue (he knows that I know that he . . . and I know that he knows that I . . .). This reciprocity is important because the ability to change position within the semiosis both in imagination and in reality, to the effect that utterer becomes interpreter, interpreter utterer, is a necessary precondition both for agreement on sign interpretation and for the equality of the parties of the dialogue. Without the presupposition of this knowledge it would, so to speak, make no sense to "negotiate" the interpretant; the parties could try to make each other react in certain ways to given signs, but these signs would rather function as signals, as fixed sequences of stimuli and responses. This is why this knowledge is essential to the equal status of the parties as well, because only if the other party is recognized as a partner in the process of interpretation (and as at least a potential utterer in his own right) is dialogue possible; otherwise speech would be the privilege of power.

Let us designate these six factors together as making up the *semiotic competence* (a term coined in analogy to Habermas' *communicative competence*, cf. p. 261, which is itself an analogy of Chomsky's *linguistic competence*) of an utterer/interpreter. Obviously, the mere listing of these factors is not sufficient to indicate how dialogical understanding is possible, since it is not their sum but their product that matters. Indications of one way of answering the questions raised by the interaction of these factors (in fact these questions are the thorny epistemological ones concerning the relationship between language and reality) are given by the *icon, index, symbol* distinction. Peirce indicates their different offices in the thought process, in a general way, as follows:

> all thinking is conducted in signs that are mainly of the same general structure as words; those which are not so being of the nature of those signs of which we have need now and then in our converse with one another to eke out the defects of words, or symbols. These non-symbolic thought signs are of two classes: first, pictures or diagrams or other images (I call them *Icons*) such as have to be used to explain the significations of words; and secondly, signs more or less analogous to symptoms (I call them *Indices*) of which the collateral observation by which we know what a man is talking about are examples. The Icons chiefly illustrate the significations of predicate-thoughts, the denotations of subject-thoughts. The substance of thoughts consists of these three species of ingredients. (Ms. 200, 1907: 43-44)

As a logician Peirce is mainly interested in symbols, but he recognizes that thinking demands the cooperation of all three, and he says that the logician "must not confine himself to *symbols* since no reasoning that amounts to much can be conducted with [sic, this is clearly an error, the context demands *without*, JDJ] *Icons* and *Indices*" (SS 1977: 118).

Chapter III characterizes *iconicity, indexicality,* and *symbolicity,* respectively, by *exhibition, ostension,* and *conceptualization.* Language, of course, is mainly symbolic (cf. the introduction to chapter II), but according to Peirce's analysis of the categories, symbolicity (being the the thirdness of thirdness) subsumes iconic and indexical aspects. This is why he gives the following absolutely essential definition of a symbol: "A symbol is a sign naturally fit to declare that the set of objects which is denoted by whatever set of indices may be in certain ways attached to it is represented by an icon associated with it" (2.295). Peirce goes on to exemplify his definition thus:

> To show what this complicated definition means, let us take as an example of a symbol the word "loveth." Associated with this word is an idea, which is the mental icon of one person loving another. Now we are to understand that "loveth" occurs in a sentence; for what it may mean by itself, if it means anything, is not the question. Let the sentence, then, be "Ezekiel loveth Huldah." Ezekiel and Huldah must, then, be or contain indices; for without indices it is impossible to designate what one is talking about. Any mere description would leave it uncertain whether they were not mere characters in a ballad; but whether they be so or not, indices can designate them. Now the effect of the word "loveth" is that the pair of objects denoted by the pair of indices Ezekiel and Huldah is represented by the icon, or the image we have in our minds of a lover and his beloved. (2.295)

This example shows clearly the collaboration of the three modes of signifying in the establishment of meaning. To understand a linguistic utterance, we identify its objects within a universe of discourse by means of its indexical elements and realize what is predicated about them by mentally iconizing its symbols.

From the above the reasons for Peirce's factors 3-5 (cf. p. 212) of the common ground of dialogical understanding become evident, since they are concerned with a cross-cultural but species specific potential for experiencing the life-world. Does this mean, however, that Peirce's concept of the relationship between language and world can be reduced to a mixture of two rather simplistic points of view, namely that words are names for things, and that language simply offers a picture of a given state of affairs in the world, both through the iconic character of its syntax and by calling forth mental pictures in the mind of the interpreter? I think not. His work shows he is fully aware of the complexities haunting the word-world relationship. His dictum that facts "are fluid extracts of events carrying away so much of them as a proposition will hold" (Ms. 478, 1903: 155) stresses that there exists no natural and univocal bond between any language and the surrounding world. He believes, however, both in the interdependency between a language and a socio-material life-world and in the possibility of transgressing at least some of the limits and imperfections that a given language at some point in time imposes upon its users. He is well aware that any language categorizes the life-world in its own way, but he thinks that such categorizations can be modified, and their shortcomings amended, through interpretation and translation, because the word-world fit is bidirectional and reversible, and because language is itself an instrument for reasoning.

The basic point, for man, in which language and world interact is in the perceptual judgement. It will be remembered that Peirce even coined a term to cover the totality of the percept and the perceptual judgment taken together: the *percipuum* (cf. p. 80). The perceptual judgment, expressed in a proposition, and the percept are, however, very different. In addition to the four characteristics of the percept, 1) positive qualities, 2) compulsiveness, 3) directness, and 4) unconscious inferential synthesis (cf. pp. 76-77), two more of its features are important here, its singularity and its definiteness:

> The percept, however, exhibits itself in full. These two kinds of definiteness, first, that the percept offers no range of freedom to anybody who may undertake to represent it, and secondly, that it reserves no freedom to itself to be one way or another way, taken together, constitute that utter absence of "range" which is called the *singularity*, or singleness, of the percept, the one making it individual and the other positive. The percept is, besides, whole and undivided. It has parts, in the sense that in thought it can be separated; but it does not represent itself to have parts. In its mode of being as a percept it is one single and undivided whole. (7.625)

Its definiteness is owing to the compelling nature of the positive qualities that it forces upon the perceiver, i.e., its embedment of firstness within secondness. If the percept is considered a sign, because of its being the result, or conclusion, of an unconscious and uncontrollable inferential process, then it is a predominantly indexical sign containing iconic elements.

The perceptual judgment stands, according to Peirce, almost in the same relation to knowledge and belief as the percept. They are close to each other in many respects, as Peirce says: "If one *sees*, one cannot avoid the percept; and if one *looks*, one cannot avoid the perceptual judgment. Once apprehended, it absolutely compels assent. Its defect in forcefulness is thus excessively slight and of no logical importance" (7.627). Peirce's statement gives the reason why he characterizes the perceptual judgment as an index, or true symptom, of the percept (7.628), although it falls short of the full forcefulness and unreasonableness of the former.

Nevertheless, the perceptual judgment is unlike the percept in important respects. According to the categorical analysis, what distinguishes the perceptual judgment from the percept is the prominent part thirdness, or representation, plays in it: "In a perceptual judgment the mind professes to tell the mind's future self what the character of the present percept is" (7.630). Furthermore, as concerns the world-word fit, five differences between percept and perceptual judgment are significant. Using the proposition "this chair is yellow" as an example, Peirce points out the differences as follows (the arrangement and wording are mine, JDJ):

|  Percept | Perceptual judgment |
|---|---|
| 1) The qualities are prescribed in perceiving the percept; they leave the interpreter no freedom of choice. | 1) The perceptual judgment: "This chair is yellow" is dependent on a choice between a range of color words signifying different nuances. |
| 2) The percept is explicit and definit as to shade, hue, and purity. Singling out this particular yellow from other percepts of yellow. | 2) "— is yellow" is general. It represents the percept as belonging to a more or less well-defined class of intersubjectively shared distinctions between qualities. |
| 3) The percept directly contains elements of sensation. | 3) "— is yellow" has only elements of sensation attached to it by association, and not even elements of sensation *sensu strictu*, because they are, or may be, associated through imagination. |

4) The percept presents itself whole and undivided.

4) "This chair is yellow" represents the percept as a subject-predicate relation, i.e., certain features are prescinded from the totality of the percept and predicated of the subject.

5) The percept has no separate indication or division of the subject.

5) When expressed in language the subject of a perceptual judgment is divided into an indexical (the quantifier *this*), and a symbolic aspect (the general term *chair*).

It should be stressed that having a percept and forming a perceptual judgment are most often not separate activities. We normally do not see something yellow and then form the judgment: "This chair is yellow." Rather, we see a yellow chair. In other words we see (or hear, or smell, etc.) our percept *as* something, because we "know," or rather assume, that we perceive such and such objects as having these or those qualities. In a sense we learn to perceive our life-world by the formative influence of linguistic categories used in others' perceptual judgments. There is a limit to this, however, because we also form linguistic expressions to conform to our perceptions, if we chance to see things differently; furthermore, even if the above perceptual judgment has been represented by a linguistic proposition, it need not be tied up with language. Animals, in all probability, make perceptual judgments governing their purposive action, instinctively prescinding relevant features from their sense impressions. Infants not yet possessing language, and people who can never learn it because of some physical disability, may be supposed to make perceptual judgments of some kind.

It is not, however, an unwarranted identity between perceptual judgments and linguistic propositions that matters concerning the question of the common ground of understanding. It is the fact that perceptual judgment may be expressed by linguistic propositions without being identical with them. Because perceptual judgments are so closely allied to the percepts, they serve as indices, or symptoms, of

them, and because they are expressible in language, utterer and interpreter may reach agreement about the applicability or non-applicability of propositions expressing perceptual judgments to the parts of
the perceptual universe singled out for attention. Of course, for this to
occur both parties must possess the common characters of the genus
*homo*, have physical and psychical self control, and have elementary
experiences in common.

Elsewhere, Peirce sums up what characterizes an act of judgment:

> This act [. . .] is a peculiar act of the will whereby we cause an image, or
> *icon*, to be associated, in a peculiar strenuous way, with an object re-
> presented to us by an *index*. This act itself is represented in the proposition
> by a *symbol*, and the consciousness of it fulfills the function of a symbol in
> the judgment. (2.435)

In the Carnegie Application he exemplifies this kind of act:

> An assertion is an *act* which represents that an icon represents the object of
> an index. Thus, in the assertion, "Mary is red-headed," "red-headed" is not
> an icon itself, it is true, but a symbol. But its interpretant is an icon, a sort
> of composite photograph of all the red-headed persons one has seen.
> "Mary," in like manner, is interpreted by a sort of composite memory of all
> the occasions which forced my attention upon that girl. The putting of these
> together makes another *index* which has a force tending to make the icon
> an index of Mary. (L 75, 1902: 323d)

To Peirce, then, a symbolic sign subsumes the denotative function of
the index and the significative function of the icon, and he sees this
subsumption illustrated in a judgment or in a proposition. Even if
symbolic signs, such as linguistic signs, have acquired a relative autonomy, their meaning is, nevertheless, dependent on the iconic and
indexical modes of signification.

This point may be illustrated by the analysis of word meaning. In
the first chapter I sketched the structuralist analysis of word paradigms, and quoted on p. 147 Peirce's own comments on the information contained in the word *woman*. Peirce would say that a linguistic expression such as /woman/ has signification because it can be
applied to a class of objects and because it signifies a set of characters,
or qualities, its indexical aspect being its extension and its iconic
aspect its comprehension. This can be represented graphically:

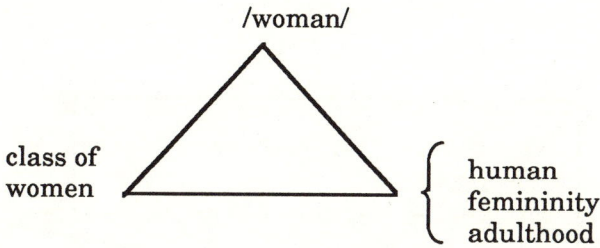

Fig. 37

If we object that this interpretation suppresses what is peculiar to language, namely its systematic and differential nature, it can easily be shown that this is not the case, because we can analyze the whole paradigm in the same way. Designate the three oppositional qualities that make up the distinctive characters of the paradigm by the numbers 1 to 3. The first opposition is human: 1 vs. animal: 1̄, the second femininity: 2 vs. masculinity: 2̄, and the third adulthood: 3 vs. childhood: 3̄. The significative, or iconic element, will be the combination of these characters attached to the four expressions in question, and the indexical or denotative element will be the reference to the collection of objects that possesses these characters. Graphically, the paradigm can be presented as in Fig 38.

According to this analysis the characteristic feature of the paradigm is that it unites three kinds of oppositions: the symbolic non-systematic difference of the four conventional linguistic expressions, the systematic iconic opposition of characters, and the indexical opposition between the objects to which the words apply. We might object that what is here called the iconic aspect is simply the content form of the words in question analyzed according to the principle of structural semantics. As an observation this is true, but it is no objection. It is precisely the point. According to structural semantics the content form of language can be viewed as a collection of minimal form elements arranged into different content paradigms of a relative, negative and differential nature. Peirce would, without doubt, have approved of this analytic procedure, if only for the reason that it is hard to distinguish this procedure from the traditional logical analysis of the connotation

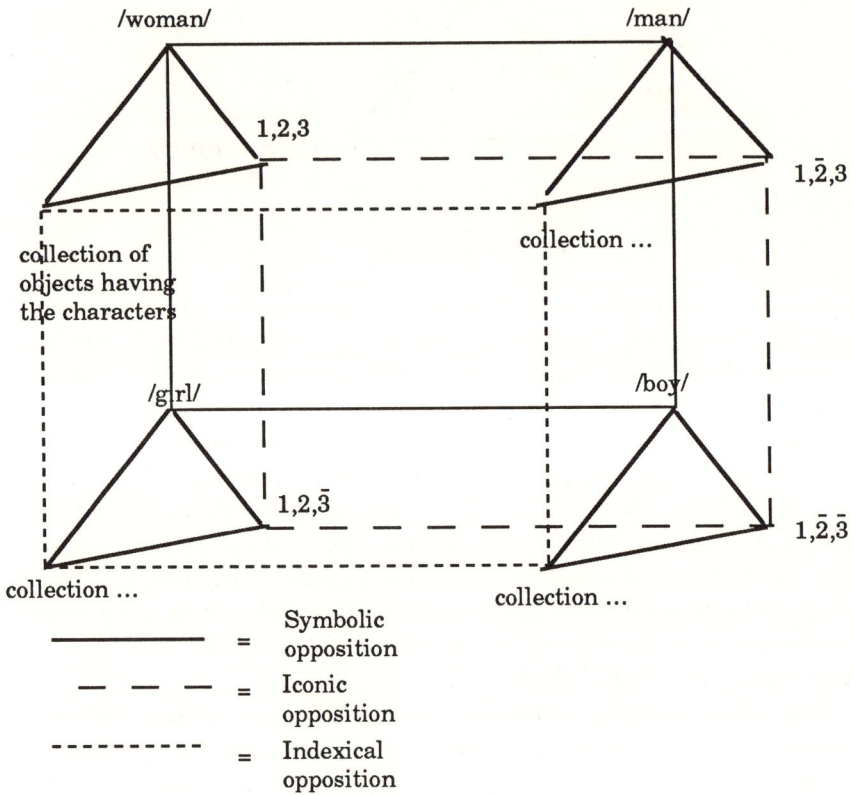

/woman/                                      /man/
                        1,2,3
                                                                 1,$\bar{2}$,3

collection of
objects having
the characters                collection ...

              /girl/                           /boy/

                    1,2,$\bar{3}$
                                                              1,$\bar{2}$,$\bar{3}$

collection ...                      collection ...

——————  =  Symbolic
                        opposition
— — — —  =  Iconic
                        opposition
- - - - - - -  =  Indexical
                        opposition

Fig. 38

of a term. He would say, however, that this componential interpretation of the sign's signification is of an iconic nature. This is why in one
of the entries in his *Logic Notebook* he defines the symbol as follows:
"Symbols are signs which bring about ideas like their objects in
certain definitely designated respects" Ms. 339b: 298, about June 11,
1898). This quotation points to an important difference between the
predominantly iconic sign and the predominantly symbolic sign: in the
former the iconic aspect of the sign is based on common properties

between *sign expression* (sign vehicle) and object, whereas in the latter the iconic aspect is based upon common properties between *the interpretation of the sign* and the object.

We might also object that the semantic characters *human, femininity,* and *adulthood* are themselves symbolic, and not iconic, signs. This is, of course, true, but there are three reasons to call this interpretative specification iconic: First, these constituent content elements serve as directions for an iconic representation, strictly speaking, because they specify a few number of pertinent characters that, for instance, a pictorial representation has to possess in order to count as a woman-picture, i.e., species, sex, and age must in some way be discernable. Secondly, the interpretant sign names the characters, or qualities, that the object must possess to count as a member of the collection designated by the expression /woman/, and this means that the same characters are, or are supposed to be, present in the object and in the interpretant sign. In the object they are entitatively present, in the interpretant they are, in this case, representatively present, as Peirce would say. Thirdly, the specification of the elements of the paradigm is itself of iconic nature, because it is built up as an alternation between oppositional elements. For this reason it is easily represented by a diagram.

There is another, rather fundamental objection. Why insist on the iconic and idexical aspects of the symbolic when you can effectively analyze linguistic semantics without bothering about them?

Semantics is based in the analysis of language use, and in ordinary language use the indexical and the iconic aspects of language are presupposed, even if the parties of a dialogue are seldom aware of these aspects, or conscious of them only in a fragmentary way suited to the purpose of their dialogue. If you ask your way, you will be acutely aware of the indexical aspects of language, whereas if you seek information to identify an object by means of description, you will explore the iconic aspects. In ordinary language use, language and the psychic, social, and physical realities are related in many different ways, according to the goals and desires of speakers and hearers. Furthermore, the elements of language are endowed with standard significations, which are social, not individual properties, that form a part of the speaker's competence and makes mutual understanding possible. Consequently, it is reasonable to assume that the understanding of language is made possible by the interplay between the

generality of standard significations of the signs and the occasionality
which governs the indexical and iconic aspects of the individual utterance. The point is that even the so-called standard signification of the
linguistic signs, which is the object of semantics, has to be explicated
finally by reference to its iconic and indexical elements.

We might object that symbolic systems, such as language, are
means for categorizing the surrounding world, and that, consequently,
the borderlines of signification between different symbols, e.g., between the signs of a paradigm, determine the iconic and indexical
aspects of the signs in question. This objection might be admitted,
provided that two other caveats be equally admitted: first, that without differences in iconicity and indexicality there would be no borderlines at all, and second, that since man's relationship with the
surrounding world is experiential as well as symbolic. Even if the
experiential relationship is mediated by the symbolic, it follows that
changes in the experiential relationship will also cause changes in the
categorization. In other words, even if we admit that the way in which
content systems within a given language are structured is a matter of
convention, in the sense that distinctions are drawn differently in
different languages, nevertheless these distinctions are meaningful
only because the signs are applied to and signify different objects,
states of affairs, events, and actions. This means that within semantics conventional distinctions are founded on iconicity and indexicality.

## 6.  The utterance and the icon, index, symbol distinction

The unity of Peirce's semiotic concept should be apparent from the
analysis of perception to the analysis of what is involved in making an
assertion. From the point of view of epistemology, and from the broad
perspective of general semiotics, his analysis of the interaction of the
iconic, indexical, and symbolic aspects of signs is highly important,
and it is a promising point of departure for a further development of a
general theory of signs. One of the greatest linguists of this century,
Roman Jakobson, testifies to its specific importance for the study of
linguistic texts.

Jakobson has repeatedly, and with admiration, written on Peirce
(cf. for instance Jakobson 1977), stressing the fruitfulness of the Peir-

cean approach in overcoming the narrowness of certain tendencies within classical structuralism. His unqualified praise of Peirce deserves to be quoted:

> Half a century of Peirce's semiotic drafts are of epochal significance, and if they had not remained for the most part unpublished until the 1930's, or if at least the printed works had been known to linguists, they would certainly have exerted an unparalleled influence upon the international development of linguistic theory. (Jakobson SW, II: 346)

This section will expound and comment on two of Jakobson's observations on Peirce's theory of signs: his exemplification of the icon, index, symbol distinction within linguistics, and his reflections on meaning as translation.

According to Jakobson the importance of Peirce's distinction for linguistics is that it brings into focus the somewhat neglected indexical and iconic aspects of language and speech. In his seminal paper "Shifters, Verbal Categories, and the Russian Verb" (Jakobson 1957), Jakobson distinguishes, on the basis of the fundamental opposition between *message* (M) and *code* (C), four elementary two term combinations: 1) M/M, e.g., reported speech. 2) C/C, proper names (because they cannot be understood without reference to a code in which they are themselves mentioned [*Jerry* means a person named *Jerry*]). 3) M/C, intra- or interlingual translation (*pup* means *young dog, homme* means *man* in French). Finally, 4) the relation C/M designates code units that cannot be defined without reference to the message, the so-called *shifters* (a term coined by the Danish linguist Otto Jespersen). The prime examples of this relation are the first and second person personal pronouns.

Explicitly referring to Peirce, Jakobson defines the pronouns *I* and *you* as indexical symbols (Peirce also calls them *designations*, cf. here III, 5). Symbols, because they possess a general meaning (*I* means the addresser, *you* means the addressee); indices, because they cannot represent their objects without being in an existential relation to them. To borrow a happy phrase from Ducrot, "*I* and *you* signify the irruption of speech (or discourse) into the interior of language" (Ducrot & Todorov 1972: 323). This irruption of speech as a communicative event referring to addresser and addressee is not confined to the personal pronouns, as Jakobson's article shows.

He points out that simple utterances may contain all four two term relations (M/M, C/C, M/C, and C/M), and he gives and comments on the following example:

> *Jim told me "flicks" means "movies."* This brief utterance includes all four types of duplex structures: reported speech (M/M), the autonomous form of speech (M/C), a proper name (C/C), and shifters (C/M), namely the first person pronoun and the preterit, signaling an event prior to the delivery of the message. In language and in the use of language, duplicity plays a cardinal role. In particular, the classification of grammatical, and especially verbal, categories requires a consistent discrimination of shifters. (Jakobson SW II: 133)

This complexity makes Jakobson claim the necessity of analyzing verbal categories with regard to two basic distinctions: 1) speech itself vs. narrated matter (topic), and 2) the event itself vs. its participants. From these distinctions he points out four basic items of speech: 1) a narrated event ($E^n$); 2) a speech event ($E^s$); 3) a participant of the narrated event ($P^n$); and 4) a participant of the speech event ($P^s$), i.e., addresser and/or addressee (see Jakobson 1971: II, 133). This is not the place to follow Jakobson's further analysis. The point is that shifters, indexical expressions that cannot be defined without reference to the message, pervade linguistic utterances in multiple ways. As regards verbal categories the following features have to be analyzed as shifters: person, mood, tense, and what Jakobson calls, evidential, i.e., that relation between a speech event, a narrated speech event, and a narrated event ("Have you heard, it is said, that it happened in this way?").

The indexicality of speech, and of language considered as a system, is much wider than indicated here. It includes, among other things, relations of time and space, the whole deictic dimension of speech. Important here, however, is the fact that as regards the interpretation of linguistic utterances the indexical dimension of speech and language cannot be left out of account. It attaches utterances to a context without which they would become incomprehensible: and that dimension is an integrated part of the very structure of speech and language. After discussing problems raised by the idealization, standardization, and decontextualization of language done by linguists, John Lyons concludes:

Here we are concerned to emphasize that the grammatical and semantic coherence of text-sentences and text-fragments within a text is but one aspect of the global problem of contextual appropriateness; and that it cannot be handled without taking into account situational factors and the non-linguistic features of utterances and their co-text.

If linguistic semantics is taken to be that branch of semiotics which deals with the way in which meaning (of all kinds) is conveyed by language, it must be accepted that a comprehensive theory of linguistic semantics will need to be based upon, or include, a theory of contextual appropriateness. (Lyons 1977, II: 590)

Lyons defends micro-semantics studies because a full scale semiotically founded semantics may at the moment be too ambitious a task, but he recognizes that, in the long run, semantics and pragmatics cannot be separated.

Besides the fact that symbols have iconic signs for their interpretants, Peirce's idea that language contains an iconic dimension essential to it is founded on his claim that it is a special kind of diagrammatization, a kind of *algebra* (cf. 3.419, this paragraph contains one of his most pertinent descriptions of language). Taking his clue from this statement, Jakobson, in a brilliant essay with the telling title "Quest for the Essence of Language" (Jakobson 1965), shows the iconic nature of speech and language on different levels.

Syntax, according to Jakobson, is diagrammatic, because the relations between the different parts of the sentence reflect, or reproduce, the order of events or rank. He writes:

The chain of verbs — *Veni, vidi, vici* — informs us about the order of Caesar's deeds first and foremost because the sequence of co-ordinate preterits is used to reproduce the succession of reported occurrences. The temporal order of speech events tends to mirror the order of narrated events in time or in rank. Such a sequence as "the President and the Secretary of State attended the meeting" is far more usual than the reverse, because the initial position in the clause reflects the priority in official standing. (Jakobson SW II: 350)

He also points out, following J. H. Greenberg, that a near-universal feature of all languages is that the subject precedes the object in declarative sentences. It is important to realize this is certainly not the only possible order. In an inflectional language, such as Russian, the sentence "Lenin cites Marx" all six combinations of subject (S), verb (V), and object (O) are possible and occur (SVO, SOV, VSO, VOS,

OSV, and OVS). Jakobson points out, however, that only the first, "Lenin citiruet Marksa" (SVO), is stylistically neutral, while the others are felt by native speakers to imply shifts of emphasis (cf. Jakobson 1971: II, 584). The iconic character of this feature is due to the importance alloted to the agent, the doer, in language, and in interaction. The iconicity of syntax is much more thorough than indicated by these two examples (for a fuller treatment see the seminal study by Roland Posner, Posner 1986), but here they will have to suffice. As a student of literature, I would, however, add one comment, that sentences which from the point of view of linguistics are semantically equivalent are, from the point of view of poetics, radically different. If a story begins with the sentence, "Jill was loved by Jack," the expectations of most readers will differ greatly from those elicited by "Jack loved Jill."

In morphology Jakobson also sees clearly iconic features. The relation between roots and suffixes reflect their semantic contrast, and the restricted inventory of phonemes of which they are built up (in contrast to the roots) mirror their grammatical and semantical functions. Furthermore, in many Indo-European languages the positive, comparative, and superlative degrees of adjectives is expressed by an increase in the number of phonemes (altus-altior-altissimus). The same tendency can be observed between singular and plural forms, because Jakobson, quoting Greenberg, points out that plural may be expressed by an additional morpheme, whereas, as compared to the plural form, no language expresses the singular by adding an morpheme.

Finally, Jakobson reflects on the possible iconic nature of linguistic sound patterns. After having considered a few examples in which such features may be existent, he concludes:

> Yet on a plain, lexical level the interplay of sound and meaning has a latent and virtual character, whereas in syntax and morphology (both inflection and derivation) the intrinsic, diagrammatic correspondence between the signans and signatum is patent and obligatory. (Jakobson SW II: 355)

It should be added, however, that, in another place, he points out a genuine example of the iconicity of sounds in what one could call iconic emphasis, namely the difference between [big] and the emphatic prolongation of the vowel [biːg] which is a "conventional, coded linguistic feature" (Jakobson, in Sebeok 1960: 354). The example is felicitous, because it illustrates the friendly cohabitation of iconic and symbolic features (or similarity and conventionality) within one and the same sign. The iconicity of linguistic sound, which plays a minor part in language as a system, plays a leading character in literature, especially in poetry.

The conclusion that Jakobson draws from his findings is far reaching, since it amounts to a showdown against two central dogmas of Saussurian linguistics:

> However, the "system of diagrammatization," patent and compulsory in the entire syntactic and morphological pattern of language, yet latent and virtual in its lexical aspect, invalidates Saussure's dogma of arbitrariness, while the other of his two "general principles" — the linearity of the signans — has been shaken by the dissociation of phonemes into distinctive features. With the removal of these fundamentals their corollaries in turn demand revision. (Jakobson SW II: 357)

No wonder Jakobson feels close to Peirce, and uses him to combat some of the extravagances of idealization and autonomization committed in certain quarters of structural linguistics. The following paragraph from Peirce shows an important reason for Jakobson's agreement. In the text preceding the quotation Peirce has claimed that iconic signs, e.g., diagrams in themselves, have no means of identifying the object to which they may be applied. Peirce continues:

> If a diagram cannot do it [i.e., identify an object, JDJ], algebra cannot: for algebra is but a sort of diagram; and if algebra cannot do it, language cannot: for language is but a kind of algebra. It would, certainly, in one sense be extravagant to say that we can never tell what we are talking about; yet, in another sense, it is quite true. The meanings of words ordinarily depend upon our tendencies to weld together qualities and our aptitudes to see resemblances, or, to use the received phrase, upon associations by *similarity*; while experience is bound together, and only recognizable, by forces acting upon us, or, to use an even worse chosen technical term, by means of associations by *continuity*. (3.419)

After having exemplified his point by letting two men, who meet on a country road, identify a house in the vicinity, he says:

> It is not the language alone, with its mere associations of similarity, but the language taken in connection with the auditor's own experiential associations of continuity, which determines for him what house is meant. It is requisite then, in order to show what we are talking or writing about, to

put the hearer's or reader's mind into real, active connection with the concatenation of experience or of fiction with which we are dealing, and, further, to draw his attention to, and identify, a certain number of particular points in such concatenation. (3.419)

In Peirce Jakobson rediscovers his own basic concepts of *similarity* and *continuity* linked to the concepts of iconicity and indexicality; and Peirce's implicit comparison between the concatenation of speech and the continuity of experience heightens the similarity between their points of view.

Neither Peirce nor Jakobson want to deny the tantamount part played by symbolic signs, and consequently, by conventionality, in language. They agree, however, in viewing the specific character of the symbolic structuration and partition effectuated by language as an operation carried out on other (perhaps simpler) modes of signifying, namely by similarity and by continuity. Peirce, using the parlance of the schoolmen, distinguishes between *first* and *second intentions* (the former being signs signifying objects and states of affairs, the latter signs signifying other signs, or thoughts). In trying to describe a part of a small number of opinions that, according to Peirce, the study of logic will never shake, he concentrates on "naive" opinions about assertions, and very interestingly, he begins with verbal and dialogical communication between a speaker/writer who emits signs to a hearer/reader. For the semiosis of dialogue to take place, Peirce presupposes the following:

> In any case, the deliverer makes signals to the receiver. Some of these signs (or at least one of them) are supposed to excite in the mind of the receiver familiar images, pictures, or, we might almost say, *dreams* – that is, reminiscences of sights, sounds, feelings, tastes, smells, or other sensations, now quite detached from the original circumstances of their first occurrence, so that they are free to be attached to new occasions. The deliverer is able to call up these images at will (with more or less effort) in his own mind; and he supposes the receiver can do the same. (3.433)

Such signs are iconic. These iconic signs may form a complexus, a composite image "of which the whole is not familiar," and in this way the composition of iconic signs may yield new information. To do so, however, in addition to iconic signs containing positive information, i.e., iconic signs of first *intention* (today we might say signs belonging to an object semiotics), another type of iconic signs is needed, expressing the form of the composition and modifying the first intentional iconic signs. Peirce mentions two kinds of such signs, *conjunctive* and *disjunctive* relations. These are called iconic signs of second intention, because they operate on the signs of first intentions, combining and modifying them (cf. the example given below).

In addition to the iconic signs making up the predicate of the assertion, an index is needed, forcing the attention to the subject of the assertion and indicating its continuous identity, its *thisness* (Peirce also uses the medieval term *hecceity*). According to Peirce, "the assertion represents a compulsion which experience, meaning the course of life, brings upon the deliverer to attach the predicate to the subjects as a sign of them taken in a particular way" (3.435). This compulsion takes on the nature of a law, because every time an appropriate occasion arises, i.e., whenever these hecceities and first intentions are called up, the speaker/hearer is compelled, or forced, to make the assertion, to combine the indexical and iconic signs in that way. To effectuate and communicate this combination another kind of sign is needed. Peirce says: "The deliverer thus requires a kind of sign which shall signify a law that to objects of indices an icon appertains as sign of them in a given way. Such a sign has been called a *symbol*. It is the *copula* of the assertion" (3.435). To make clear what Peirce is aiming at, I have to use the longest quotation in this book. It is from the unpublished Ms. 599, 1902, and it takes up the thread from the review, quoted above, "The Regenerated Logic" (of Schröder's *Exakte Logik*), from the *Monist, VII* 1896. Peirce talks about the nature of a proposition, and he defines it as follows:

It is the same proposition every time it is thought, spoken, or written, whether in English, German, Spanish, Tagalog, or how. A proposition consists in a meaning, whether adopted or not, and however expressed. That meaning is the meaning of any sign which should signify that a certain iconic representation, or image (or any equivalent of it), is a sign of something indicated by a certain indexical sign, or any equivalent thereof. To illustrate this, any sentence will answer. Take this:

"Go your way into the village which is over against us, in the which as ye enter, ye shall find an ass tied and a colt with her whereon no man ever yet sat."

As this was said by Jesus to two of his disciples, it created in their imagination the picture of an ass tied and accompanied by a young colt. That picture was the icon which the definition mentions. What was this a picture of? He attaches a legend to it in this way. They were standing looking at the village. Now, says Jesus, you cannot see the colt from where we stand, but go there, and as you enter the village, look about; and you will see what I describe. That injunction put a force upon them which tended to direct their attention to what Jesus was talking about. It acted as an indicating sign or indication. The passage will furnish two further illustrations of the sense of the definition, since two other propositions are contained in it. One of these is that no man had ever yet sat upon that colt. Here the iconic sign is any diagram representing negation. Probably every person has his own way, or ways, of picturing negation to himself. A proposition never prescribes any particular mode of iconization, although the form of expression may suggest some mode. Here, however, the two disciples are left to picture negation in their own fashions. That method might have been to think one transparent image overlying another and not matching it. Or two separate dots might be pictured as a diagram of non-identity, and each dot might be pictured as having a thread running from it to an image of anything identical with it. They were now to think that they would be allowed to select any instant of the colt's life they liked, and get information of what its situation was at that instant, to get a photograph of it, at that instant, or anything equivalent. Then taking this picture and the picture of a colt with a man on its back, to those two the icon of negation would be applicable. Such a complicated idea was expressed by the few words "whereon no man ever yet sat." The other illustration is afforded by the proposition "you will go your way into the village which is over against us." Jesus does not *assert* this proposition, that is, does not make himself responsible for it. On the contrary, he *enjoins* or commands it, that is, makes the two disciples responsible for it. But that does not affect the proposition itself. The icon, or picture excited in the imagination is here that of two men walking to a village. There are two indices, or labels, to show what this is a picture of. One of these is their eye-sight, as Jesus spoke of "that there village over against us." That label is attached to the village in the icon. The other label is the pronoun "you" (in the Greek merely the termination — ετε of ὑπάγετε) taken in connection with the look on their master's countenance, which would have been quite sufficient to show them who the two men of the icon were; for in very many languages the second person of the imperative mood dispenses with all terminations or special indications of the person addressed. These explanations render the nature of a proposition sufficiently clear for our present purpose. It has, I hope, been made tolerably plain to the reader who thinks the matter over carefully for himself, without allowing himself to be disturbed by perplexities as to details (which are endless), that no matter in what other way a proposition may be comprehended, and whether we are going to the very heart of the matter or not, yet it is true (and a significant truth) that every proposition is capable of expression either by means of a photograph, or composite photograph, with or without stereoscopic and cinetoscopic elaborations, together with some *sign* which shall show the connection of these images with the object of some index, or sign or experience forcing the attention, or bringing some information, or indicating some possible source of information; or else by means of some analogous icon appealing to other senses than that of sight, together with analogous forceful indications, and a sign connecting the icon with those indices. (Ms. 599, 1902: 4-9)

Here Peirce in detail attempts to describe the interaction of iconic, indexical, and symbolic signs in the process of communication and interpretation, and thereby makes apparent the complexity of his theory of signs.

The point of departure is the claim that for symbolic signs to signify it must be attachable (not necessarily in fact be attached) to iconic and indexical signs. In the example, this condition is fulfilled by the supposed process of imagination (pictorialization) on the part of the disciples, and by the deictic indications within the situational context. It seems acceptable that to find the ass and the colt the disciples must be able to identify those animals in reality, and consequently in imagination, and probably this is effectuated by some kind of image based on memory. The disciples need not actually imagine such a composite iconic sign, at the time Jesus speaks, but they must be able to do it when they arrive in the village.

The proposition that "no man had ever yet sat upon that colt" certainly introduces complexities into the relationship between predominantly iconic and predominantly symbolic signs. In iconizing this proposition, Peirce modifies the concept of iconicity in two important respects. First, in saying that every person probably has his own way of picturing negation, he introduces an element of arbitrariness and conventionality. This, however, is not necessarily at variance with this kind of sign, because every selection of properties for comparison between sign and object is relative to a purpose and includes an habitual element (cf. pp. 101-107). Second, Peirce sees the iconic sign of negation as a second intentional distinctive sign relating to each other the iconic representations of a colt without a rider and one mounted by a rider, and negating the latter. The iconic sign of negation, then, is supposed to indicate the relation of the two images to each other. It is hard to see, however, that such a second intentional iconic sign fulfills the function of sharing properties with its object. In fact, such a sign is related to other signs. It is a sort of diacritical sign and only through such a sign does it mediately refer to an object. It seems, then, that a second intentional iconic sign, at least a sign of negation, answers the description of a symbolic sign far better than that of a first intentional iconic sign. Is it possible to represent negation by means of nothing but iconic signs, or is a symbolic sign necessary, i.e., a sign representing the judgment that a predicate (iconic representation) does not apply to a given state of affairs? If this is the case, as I think it is, we cannot fully translate symbolic into iconic signs. This is not surprising, because iconic signs are related to positive qualities, or to relations between entities that are defined positively, and negation is related to non-identity, to difference. We can illustrate the point by looking at the difference between the following two signs:

Fig. 39

The first sign is iconic. It is only symbolic in the weak sense of presupposing the ability to distinguish figure and ground, and to be able to comprehend that the different elements constitute one image, i.e., that of a lit cigaret. The second sign contains an additional element which is symbolic in the strong sense of being arbitrary, because the sign of negation has no precedence in perception.

Even if the second sign (just as the first sign) as a speech act is a command that a certain state of affairs should prevail, and consequently refers to a given zone of validity, its understanding presupposes an act of abstraction and the reference to a sign-sign relationship. The second sign could make no sense without reference to the first sign, because the diagonal bar symbolizing negation constitutes an operation on the first sign.

Let us, however, return to the first iconic sign. This sign is a stylized and conventional stereotype with a standard translation into language. It is, however, not the only sign expressing that within a given area smoking is permitted. Another cultural stereotype was created for the Olympic games in Mexico, in 1968. Here it is next to the first sign:

Fig. 40

Both iconic signs should be translated as "smoking permitted," and within a given context this translation seems to be unproblematic. In certain, specific contexts the Mexican sign will, however, be absolutely misleading, because often in airplanes cigaret smoking is allowed within certain areas, whereas pipe and cigar smoking is not permitted at all (this is, for instance, explicitly said on SAS's transatlantic flights). This fact points to some interesting problems and limitations concerning iconic signs. First and foremost, an iconic sign is incapable of indicating its own level of abstraction or generality. The problem concerning the sign representing a stereotype of a lit cigaret is whether it represents a general permission to smoke or the permission to smoke cigarets only. In the first case the stereotyped cigaret is an iconic synecdoche (part for whole), in the second case it is a "literal" iconic sign, because it represents the only class of objects one is allowed to smoke.

Staying within the boundaries of iconic signs one might try to correct and clarify the situation by juxtaposing the following two signs:

Fig. 41

Cigar smokers would be left in the dark by this composite sign, but this might be helped by adding one more sign similar to the one representing a pipe, one showing a cigar. The real trouble is that this composite sign only functions by virtue of including the non-iconic sign of negation.

It seems, then, that there are three levels of symbolicity: The first, symbolicity in the sense of discrimination or differentiality, is present in any iconic sign whatsover, because the very notion of borders and relations presupposes a discrimination between what is part of an image and what is part of its background or frame. Symbolicity in this sense is, however, not dominant in the sign, but only a necessary presupposition that makes the sign-object relationship possible, i.e., recognizing something as an image or diagram of something else, because of shared and perceptible qualities or structures. Even on this level, however, the essential differentiating function of symbolicity is explored in what is, with a vague expression, called "style," which includes both principles of selecting features from the original or model in question and principles of organizing these features within the sign.

On the second level, we introduce elements of signification that do not in any way correspond to features of the original or model, but operate on the image or diagram itself. This means that symbolicity is liberated from its subservient function on the first level so that sign meaning becomes the effect of the interrelation between iconic and relatively independent symbolic elements of signification. Since, however, the symbolic part of the sign constitutes an operation on the iconic part, symbolicity on this level has not come completely into its own.

On the third level, e.g., the level of language and speech, symbolicity as arbitrarity and lack of a motivated relationship between sign and object comes into its own: *Smoking permitted* or *No smoking* have no features in common with a lit cigaret or pipe. This means that symbolicity has become the dominant organizing principle of both natural languages and many artificial semiotics. It does not mean, however, that iconic features are absent in predominantly symbolic semiotics, since near universal morphological and syntactical features of natural languages are iconic (cf. for instance Jakobson 1965), and the iconicity of many artificial semiotics, such as for instance notational systems for chemistry, is obvious (cf. the views of Jakobson, here pp. 225-227).

Both positive qualities and relations, and differentiation, are needed in any semiotic system. In other words symbolicity as a diacritical and syncategorimatic determination of the sign is not restricted to language, but is a dimension in sign interpretation in general. This objection to Peirce's example is in accordance with his own claim that the copula of an assertion is a symbolic sign (cf. p. 229).

## 7. Code and reference

The concepts of *universe of discourse* and *common ground* and the problems concerning the interaction of iconicity, indexicality, and symbolicity in perceptual judgment and in the assertion of a proposition are all parts of the question of how sign meaning is produced and realized. What is involved, in the sense of made explicit and/or being presupposed, in understanding a linguistic utterance (i.e., interpreting correctly)? Peirce's general answer to this question has already been given in chapter IV. The meaning of a sign is its *translation* into another equivalent or perhaps more developed sign (cf. p. 154). It should, however, also be remembered that Peirce states that "the meaning of the sign is not conveyed until not merely the interpretant but also this [i.e., its, JDJ] object is recognized" (Ms. 318, 1907: 34). Given the fact that the interpretant is defined as another sign representing the same object as the original sign, it is hardly surprising that Peirce gives a definition of meaning that includes the collateral experience (factual or imagined) of the object. As regards Jakobson's position, the definition is somewhat ambiguous, but since he succeeds admirably in stating the issue, we will comment on his reflections on translation and meaning (from "On Linguistic Aspects of Translation"). Jakobson starts his paper as follows:

> According to Bertrand Russell, "no one can understand the word 'cheese unless he has a nonlinguistic acquaintance with cheese." If, however, we follow Russell's fundamental precept and place our "emphasis upon the linguistic aspects of traditional philosophical problems," then we are obliged to state that no one can understand the word *cheese* unless he has an acquaintance with the meaning assigned to this word in the lexical code of

English. Any representative of a cheese- less culinary culture will understand the English word *cheese* if he is aware that in this language it means
'food made of pressed curds' and if he has at least a linguistic acquaintance
with *curds*. We never consumed ambrosia or nectar and have only a linguistic acquaintance with the words *ambrosia, nectar,* and *gods* — the
name of their mythical users; nonetheless, we understand these words and
know in what contexts each of them may be used. The meaning of [ . . . ] any
word or phrase whatsoever is definitely a linguistic or - to be more precise
and less narrow - a semiotic fact. (Jakobson SW II: 260)

In this paragraph Jakobson nicely delineates the two positions that confront each other: On the one hand the position that meaning is the effect
that results from the correlation of sign and object, and on the other
the position that the meaning of a sign is an effect of its relations to
other signs within the codes of a given language. Furthermore, he
delivers a devastating criticism of Russell's empiricist concept of
meaning, since obviously we know the meaning of "nectar" although
we have never tasted it. It would indeed be absurd to equate our
knowledge of sign meanings with personal, sense experience.

If we turn to Russell's text, the article "Logical Positivism" (1950,
in Russell 1956), to find what caused Jakobson's reaction, it is difficult
to see why he should start his own article by attacking Russell. Russell's paragraph about cheese runs as follows:

Absorption in language leads to a neglect of the connexion of language with
non-linguistic facts, although it is this connexion which gives meaning to
words and significance to sentences. No one can understand the word
'cheese' unless he has a non-linguistic acquaintance with cheese. The problem of meaning and significance requires much that is psychological, and
demands some understanding of pre-linguistic mental processes. Most logical positivists fight shy of psychology, and therefore have little to say
about meaning or significance. This makes them, in my opinion, somewhat
narrow, and not capable of producing an all-round philosophy. (Russell
1956: 381)

The paragraph justly objects to what Russell sees as the narrowness of
the logical positivists' approach to language, and it argues for the
necessity of studying the problem of linguistic meaning in the broader
context of pre-linguistic mental processes. Furthermore, Russell himself refers to nonexistent items from Classical Antiquity, not to nectar,
but to a winged horse, and he claims that the expression "winged
horse" is understandable, even if no winged horse ever existed (Russell

1956: 379). Another example from Russell's essay is this expression: "Mr. A had a father." This sentence, according to Russell, "is completely intelligible even if I have no idea who Mr. A's father was" (ibid.). He further claims that if Mr. B was in fact Mr. A's father, Mr. B, nevertheless, is not a constituent of the sentence, "Mr. A had a father," or of any statement containing the words "Mr. A's father," but not containing the name "Mr. B" (ibid.). From the above there seems little reason for a quarrel, but the real issue may be Russell's and Jakobson's different view on the role played by *ostensive definition* in the understanding of verbal utterances, and what preconditions must be fulfilled for this kind of definition to take place at all.

On the face of it, Jakobson's position is clear: ostensive definition is never sufficient. He says:

> The meaning of the word "cheese" cannot be inferred from a nonlinguistic acquaintance with cheddar or with camembert without the assistance of the verbal code. An array of linguistic signs is needed to introduce an unfamiliar word. Mere pointing will not teach us whether *cheese* is the name of the given specimen, or of any box of camembert, or of camembert in general, or of any cheese, any milk product, any food, any refreshment, or perhaps any box irrespective of contents. Finally, does a word simply name the thing in question, or does it imply a meaning such as offering, sale, prohibition, or malediction? (Jakobson 1971: 260-261)

In his article Russell states his position only generally: In fact he only says that "Experience is needed for ostensive definition and therefore for all understanding of the meaning of words" (Russell 1956: 379). In the two books on general philosophy that he wrote in the same period as the article, *An Inquiry into Meaning and Truth* (1940) and *Human Knowledge: Its Scope and Limits* (1948), he states what he regards as the characteristics and preconditions of an ostensive definition of a word. In the latter book he describes six fundamental conditions that make learning by ostensive definition possible:

> There must be a feature of the environment which is noticeable, distinctive, emotionally interesting, and (as a rule) frequently recurring, and the adult must frequently utter the name of this feature at a moment when the infant is attending to it. (Russell 1948: 65)

According to Russell, 1) noticeability, 2) distinctiveness, 3) emotional relevance, 4) frequent recurrence, 5) copresence of verbal utterance and object, and 6) attention are necessary for the learning of a word, or rather of a one word sentence. It is interesting, however, that Russell recognizes these conditions are insufficient to ensure the right association between object and word, and he argues along the same lines that Jakobson does. Russell gives the following very elementary example: a child is presented with a bottle of milk, and the parent says "milk." The child could take the expression to refer to the bottle as well as to the milk, and, consequently, the parent has to vary the linguistic expression (e.g., "bottle of water" and "glass of milk") to ensure the correct predication.

Russell's insistence on the necessary part played by ostensive definition (or as I would prefer to call it *ostensive identification*) in the understanding of language meaning leads to the insight that to be understandable any verbal utterance has to be correlated, immediately or mediately, with a nonlinguistic context, a life-world of perception and action that constitutes the common ground that makes communication possible. In claiming this, Russell is in accordance with Peirce's insistence of the necessity of collateral experience for the understanding of signs.

Jakobson's position on this point is somewhat ambiguous. If he, in attacking Russell (an attack which seems rather poorly founded), is only making the point that the meaning of linguistic signs necessarily involves their (paradigmatic) relations to other signs within the same language, then there is no reason for objection. If, however, he thinks that this relation is not only a necessary, but a sufficient precondition for linguistic meaning, then according to Peirce, Russell, and the point of view advocated in this study, he is wrong. The main reason why it is doubtful Jakobson really holds this restricted and intrinsic view of meaning is because he adopts Peirce's view on meaning as interpretation by virtue of translation, which he systematizes as follows:

1) Intralingual translation or *rewording* is an interpretation of verbal signs by means of other signs of the same language.
2) Interlingual translation or *translation proper* is an interpretation of verbal signs by means of some other language.
3) Intersemiotic translation or *transmutation* is an interpretation of verbal signs by means of signs of nonverbal sign systems. (Jakobson SW II: 261)

Let us consider translation proper for a moment, because sometimes it is claimed that interlingual translation has problems of its own, especially as regards so-called *radical translation,* as Quine calls it, i.e., "translation of the language of a hitherto untouched people" (Quine 1960: 28), where neither the structural similarity between the language translated and the translating language nor a shared culture facilitate the understanding. Quine is cruel enough to deny the imaginary anthropologist the help of a native interpreter or still better of a bilingual. Quine imagines the anthropologist starting from scratch: "A rabbit scurries by, the native says 'Gavagai'; and the linguist notes down the sentence 'Rabbit' (or 'Lo, a rabbit') as tentative translation, subject to testing in further cases" (Quine 1960: 29). According to Quine such a case is favorable for translation since such *occasion sentences* seem to relate a *stimulation,* the appearance of the rabbit, and the so-called *stimulus meaning,* the uttering of the sentence "Gavagai." This leads the anthropologist to equate "gavagai" and "rabbit," because they have the same stimulus meaning for natives and English speaking people respectively. To make such an equation likely the anthropologist has to test the use of "gavagai" in different contexts, and Quine presupposes that the anthropologist also has learned the linguistic, or semiotic, expression for "yes," and "no," for affirmation and negation. Quine's description of the intricacies of *radical translation* is thorough and rich. The main thrust of his argument, however, may be exemplified by his claim that even the translation of "gavagai" as "rabbit" is uncertain:

Who knows but what the objects to which this term applies are not rabbits after all, but mere stages, or brief temporal segments, of rabbits? In either event the stimulus situations that prompt assent to "Gavagai" would be the same as for "Rabbit" or perhaps the objects to which "gavagai" applies are all and sundry undetached parts of rabbits; again the stimulus meaning would register no difference. (Quine 1960: 51-52)

On the basis of such reflections Quine rests his case for the principle of *indeterminacy of translation,* which means that the linguist's finished jungle-to-English manual contains "an *infinite semantic correlation* of sentences: the implicit specification of an English sentence . . . for every one of the infinitely many possible jungle sentences" (Quine 1960: 71).

Is there any way to escape these difficulties and uncertainties? The most obvious way, that the anthropologist turns himself into a child, and learns the native language as he once learned his mother

tongue, Quine rejects. He argues that "going bilingual" does not solve
the problem of indeterminacy of translation, because "another bilingual could have a semantic correlation [between sentences in the two
languages, JDJ] incompatible with the first bilingual's without de-
viating from the first bilingual in his speech despositions within either
language, except in his disposition to translate" (Quine 1960: 74).

    This observation seems valid. Translations are often made by bi-
linguals, and two translations of a given text into the same language
will rarely be identical; especially not if the text in question is complex, e.g., a novel, not to speak of a poem. This observation basically
flaws Quine's case for the specificity of the difficulties which confront
us in *radical translation*. Indeed, the indeterminacy of translation
seems to be a basic condition for translation in general, even for
intralingual translation. This point has also been made by the Danish
philosopher Niels Ole Bernsen:

> "The principle of indeterminacy in translation" is, however, of such a na-
> ture that it must apply to all language learning, and must therefore also be
> incident to any attempt to understand what other people say in our own
> mother tongue. At the same time this question is not confined to
> translation, but affects the possibility of any kind of understanding of, and
> sympathetic insight into, the world horizon of other individuals or cultures
> and societies, as a condition both for every kind of inter-human relationship
> and for every humanistic and social science. (Bernsen 1978: 202)

Bernsen is correct in pointing out that Quine's *indeterminacy principle*
covers any understanding between individuals whatsoever. Quine
himself, of course, is aware of this perspective, since he mentions the
"domestic analogue" to radical translation. He makes, however, a distinction between the two situations:

> In language learning there is the multiplicity of individual histories ca-
> pable of issuing in identical verbal behavior. Still one is ready to say of the
> domestic situation in all positivistic reasonableness that if two speakers
> match in all dispositions to verbal behavior there is no sense in imagining
> semantic differences between them. It is ironic that the interlinguistic case
> is less noticed, for it is just here that the semantic indeterminacy makes
> clear empirical sense. (Quine 1960: 79)

One wonders whether Quine will ever meet two speakers matching in
"all dispositions to verbal behavior." What we do meet, rather, are

people (compatriots, or people who master foreign languages), who share certain basic parts of a linguistic competence, i.e., the ability to encode and decode a number of utterances in a given language, and who are able on the basis of such a competence to negotiate the meaning of a given utterance. To Quine's point that two bilinguals may offer different translations of the same sentence, it has to be added that the two bilingual translators are able to discuss their respective translations. Even if each prefers his own translation, both are able to give reasons for their choices. In so doing they  engage in both metalinguistic and contextual specifications and explanations, i.e., they situate the sentence in question both within a wider linguistic framework, and within the context of the sentence regarded as an utterance, a speech event. Doing the latter means embedding shared linguistic competence in the wider semiotic competence characterizing the two cultures of the bilingual. Furthermore, a part of this semiotic competence must be common to both cultures in its capacity as a species specific way of experiencing the world (cf. here pp. 211-213), because otherwise bilingualism itself would not be possible.

The point of view advocated here accords with Jakobson's position, since he claims translatability as a dogma:

> Both the practice and the theory of translation abound with intricacies, and from time to time attempts are made to sever the Gordian knot by proclaiming the dogma of untranslatability. "Mr. Everyman, the natural logician," vividly imagined by B. L. Whorf, is supposed to have arrived at the following bit of reasoning: "Facts are unlike to speakers whose language background provides for unlike formulation of them." In the first years of the Russian revolution there were fanatic visionaries who argued in Soviet periodicals for a radical revision of traditional language and particularly for the weeding out of such misleading expressions as "sunrise" or sunset." Yet we still use this Ptolemaic imagery without implying a rejection of Copernican doctrine, and we can easily transform our customary talk about the rising and setting sun into a picture of the earth's rotation simply because any sign is translatable into a sign in which it appears to us more fully developed and precise. (Jakobson SW II: 262)

Jakobson declares as an article of faith that, given the selfreflexivity, or metalinguistic potential of any natural language, "all cognitive experience and its classification is conveyable in any existing language" (Jakobson SW II: 263). Jakobson is right, because there is no reason to distinguish between the intralingual and interlingual translation in this respect (cf. above pp. 239-240). If it is possible to communicate the same cognitive import in a variety of sentences, different as to their linguistic expression, within one language, there is no reason why it should be impossible interlingually. In both cases it is decisive that two linguistic expressions are considered equivalent as regards the purpose of the communication. Just as iconic signs are judged to be similar to their objects in some relevant respect (cf. III, 4), so two symbolic signs, either within one and the same language or in two different languages, are equivalent if they are different expressions of the same proposition. As Jakobson says, "Translation involves two equivalent messages in two different codes" (ibid. p. 262). If the codes are different, however, how do we know that the messages, or rather their cognitive import, are equivalent? By intersemiotic translation, by transmutation, i.e., by referential and communicative contextualization. Intersemiotic translation means the correlation between two or more different semiotics, for instance perceptual, gestural, and linguistic. Peirce's description of the scene from *Matthew* 21:2 (cf. pp. 229-231) shows precisely such an interaction (and Peirce is translating from the Greek).

Leaving aside interlingual translation for a moment, the meaning of a linguistic utterance can be defined as the outcome of an interpretative process involving both metalinguistic and intersemiotic activity, silmultaneously. As these two activities are interrelated in the process of interpretation, they modify and correct each other, they mutually define each other, and they keep, so to speak, each other in place, because elements within the different semiotics are identified and defined by their correlation to elements within the others.

Metalinguistic activity by itself, which, according to Jakobson, means the correlation of equivalent linguistic elements in order to explain the one by its identity, or near-identity, to the other, is clearly not a sufficient condition for the establishment of sign meaning. In Jakobson's article there is ambiguity concerning this question, but I think it worth reading the last part of the paragraph (quoted here p. 236) closely: "The meaning of [ . . . ] any word or phrase whatsoever is definitely a linguistic or — to be more precise and less narrow — a semiotic fact" (Jakobson SW II: 260). According to this statement linguistic facts, e.g., linguistic meaning, are a subset of the wider set of semiotic facts, and he utilizes this insight in his distinctions between *intralingual, interlingual,* and *intersemiotic* translation. In my opinion, intersemiotic translation is the *conditio sine qua non* of linguistic meaning, because no meaning can possibly be established by intralingual translation, unless the language is known beforehand. To take Russell's own example and Jakobson's rejoinder. Jakobson claims that "any representative of a cheese-less culinary culture will understand the English word *cheese* if he is aware that in this language it means 'food made of pressed curds' and if he has *at least* [my italics, JDJ] a linguistic acquaintance with *curds*" (Jakobson 1971: 260). This process could go on endlessly, supposing that the person in question does not understand words such as *curds, milk, drink, food* and so on and so forth. In fact you could neither teach an infant the mother tongue nor a stranger a foreign language by this method, because it would be pointless to load somebody with synonyms and definitions just as unknown to him as the original word. The reason why this procedure is hopeless is that this synonymic expansion takes place within one and the same semiotic system, i.e., as a homogeneous process. Intersemiotic translation, on the contrary, is characterized by heterogeneous expansion, since the linguistic utterance is correlated with non-linguistic signs. Percepts are the most important of these non-linguistic signs, but by no means the only ones.

It would be just as naive to go to the other extreme, and restrict meaning to the identification of the object or state of affairs to which the linguistic utterance refers, and it is certainly not the point I am making here. The point is rather that in addition to the linguistic coding of a given sign (a coding that can be made explicit either by componential analysis or intralingual translation leading to a synthetic definition) it is necessary to identify the object(s) of the sign within the universe of discourse. Furthermore, the universe of discourse, whether it be historical, fictional, or a possible universe of some other kind, will, in the last analysis, have to be related either to the common universe of experience of the parties of a dialogue, or at least to the life-world of the interpreter. This universe of common experience is the only universe which unites perception, action, symbolization, and interpretation. To relate and to mediate between these different activities intersemiotic translation is necessary. It is erroneous to suppose that meaning is only created by linguistic codes. Even if they are indispensable in making it explicit.

I claimed above that if meaning were constituted by nothing but the translation of a given sign into other "equivalent or perhaps more developed signs" within the same semiotic system, then the process of signification could go on infinitely without leading to an understanding between the parties. Since in many cases people reach an understanding as to the meaning of signs, we can ask the positive question: What conditions have to be fulfilled so that people agree on the meaning of a sign? Leaving aside for the moment, the intentional and rhetorical aspects, that are always involved in an utterance, there are two: agreement about *identification* and *signification*. Both can be immediately given, as for instance, when somebody says: "Pass me the cheese, please," and the other party knows the signification and identifies the object. The same would of course apply to the exclamation and response: "Oh, this is nectar!" if the other party replies: "Yes, the wine is excellent, really, a drink fit for gods." Agreement, however, can also necessitate both directions for identification and metalinguistic explanation. Meaning, then, is not a question of code or reference, it is a question of code *and* reference, because meaning comes into being through the interplay of intralingual and intersemiotic translation, through the interplay of rewording and transmutation. Linguistic meaning is neither an entity nor is it the outcome of a homogeneous process of signification. It is a process of correlation between heterogeneous systems, between different semiotics.

According to Peirce, this basic heterogeneity as a precondition for the production of meaning, the interconnectedness of the non-symbolic and the symbolic, is at the root of even symbolic semiotics such as language: "Every symbol is, in its origin, either an image of the idea signified, or a reminiscence of some individual occurrence, person or thing, connected with its meaning, or is a metaphor" (2.222).

# VI. A Dialogic Model of Semiosis

The relationship between utterer and interpreter, Peirce's concepts of the *common ground* and of the *universe of discourse,* and the description of the interplay between the iconic, indexical, and symbolic aspects of the sign make up the foundation for reflections on sign meaning, its production, transmission, and interpretation.

## 1. The semiotic pyramid

The diagrammatic model in Fig. 42, which I call *the semiotic pyramid,* represents graphically the relations between the different elements of the semiosis that have been described in the preceding parts of the study. The diagram has two purposes: it is a heuristic device which should enable us to recognize the multiple relationships of each element; and it should further inquiry into the nature of the signifying process by calling attention to interrelations between meaning, production, and interpretation, and, of course, by provoking objections.

The diagram represents a *dialogue* between two parties. The solid line represents the semiosis seen from the utterer's point of view, the dotted line the interpreter's point of view. In a dialogue the verbal sign will be instanced as a token emitted by the utterer, but to understand it the interpreter must identify it as a replica of a representamen, and this involves the interpretation connecting it with object and interpretant. If understanding between parties is perfect (at least with regard to the purpose of the dialogue, and meaning implies reference to a purpose), utterer and interpreter will identify the token as an instance of the same type; the immediate object or "idea" referred to would be (for the purpose) sufficiently similar. Among the possibilities given by the immediate interpretant, the interpreter would choose the one intended by the utterer, and each would understand and recognize their respective roles within the semiosis, accepting each other as per-

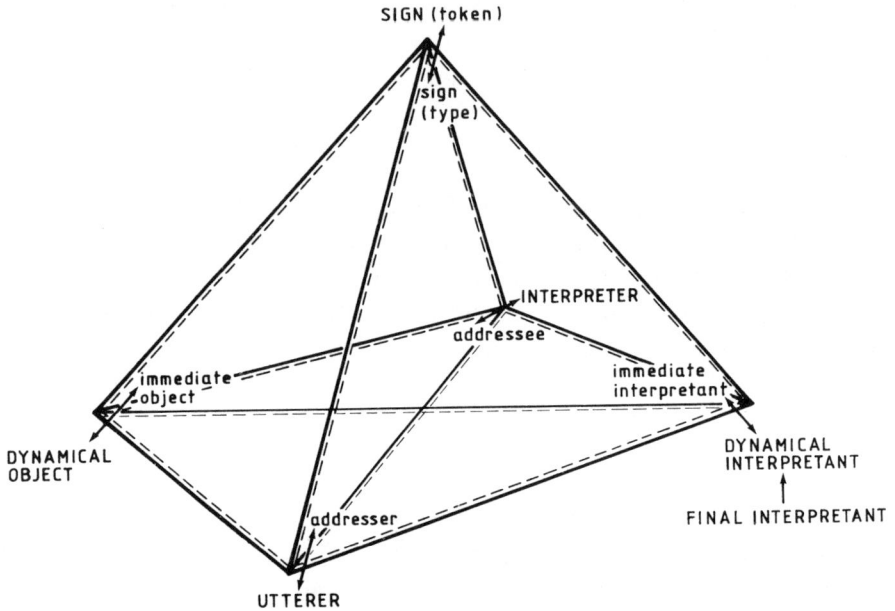

Fig. 42

sons. Moreover, explication can correct dialogical communication by metalinguistic activity, by reference to a common universe (e.g., ostensive identification), by stating intentions and purposes and by questioning.

The elements at the vertices of the semiotic pyramid are divided into two, and the relation between the pairs has been notated as an interdependence. This determination is heavy with semiotic and philosophical problems, and in all five cases there may be objections. I will make my position clear from the beginning, and will argue for it in what follows. The case of the interpretant is special because it has three rather than two elements. No interdependence exists between the dynamical and the final interpretant because as a rule a dynamical interpretant is not final. A final interpretant, however, necessarily implies a dynamical, because the final interpretant *is* a dynamical interpretant that has been confirmed by sufficient study.

The semiotic pyramid might exemplify the perfect dialogue and we have seen that the dialogic situation offers opportunities for sorting out misunderstandings concerning the sign's meaning although the goal of understanding is not guaranteed. It is obvious, however, that a *lack of understanding leads to* the need for interpretation. Either the parties of a dialogue feel a lack of understanding or an observer finds that understanding is missing; even if the parties believe they understand each other, an observer may be able to point out that there is only pseudo-understanding.

The study of written texts is more complicated than face-to-face communication because we are not engaged in real dialogue but in *quasi-dialogue.*The utterer is not present in person. The interpretation of written as well as verbal texts, however, rests on a dialogic understanding, and the constructive aspect of the study of written texts consists precisely in framing them in a dialogic context. This concept of the interpretation of written texts is corollary to the view that utterances in general call for such framing, and it follows that the methodology and analytic procedures must be the same as, or derived from, those of a general semiotics of the text. The foundation of such a semiotics is Peirce's concept of the semiosis, and there are two ways in which the semiotic pyramid can be used to inquire into the relation between the sign and the other elements of the semiosis: (1) by analyzing the dyadic relations between the elements of the semiosis connected by one axis; (2) by analyzing the triadic relations of the semiosis, i.e., the planes made up by the different triangles of the pyramid.

The problem of understanding the sign can simply be the quality of the token. The utterer may be mumbling, or the written or printed copy may be defective. If we cannot make the utterer speak louder or we lack a fair copy, we will have to conjecture about the missing part of the text. Philologists base their conjectures on inferences from the co-text and context, and this means constructions of missing parts rest on explications of what is left by relating preserved texts to the other elements of the semioses.

As regards the *linguistic* sign, the relation between replica (token) and representamen (type) is an interdependence. While any materially manifested linguistic sign has to be interpreted as an instance of a type to be meaningful (Peirce would say that the actual *sinsign* was an instance of a *legisign*), it is not possible to imagine a linguistic symbol

other than instanced as a token. We may doubt that some phenomenon is a linguistic symbol, but this means precisely that we hesitate
to identify it as a token of a linguistic type.

The problems of interpreting a fair text (or of disagreement with
the argument of the text) can be specified according to the following
points, with regard to the dyadic relations of the semiosis:

1. Concerning the relation between *sign and object:*
   Questions concerning:
   a)   how the sign applies to an object (icon, index, symbol).
   b)   the identification of the object.
   c)   the mode of being of the object.
   d)   the relation between the object as it is represented in
        the sign and the object as it is otherwise known.
   e)   the attribution of qualities to the object by the sign.

2. Concerning the relation between *sign and interpretant:*
   Questions concerning:
   a)   the identification of the sign system to which the sign be-
        longs.
   b)   the comprehension of the sign.
   c)   how the sign signifies the interpretant (rheme, propo-
        siton, argument).
   d)   the problem of the indeterminacy of the sign with re-
        gard to its translation into an interpreting sign.

3. Concerning the relation between *sign and utterer:*
   Questions concerning:
   a)   the identification of the addresser.
   b)   the mode of the utterance (kind of speech act).
   c)   the relation between the actual utterance and its textual
        and situational context (e.g., its institutional context).
   d)   the identity or non-identity between addresser and utterer.
   e)   the purpose of the utterance.

4. Concerning the relation between *sign and interpreter:*
   Questions concerning:
   a)   the identification of the addressee.

b)    the qualities attributed to the addressee in the utterance.
c)    the identity or non-identity between addressee and in-
      terpreter.
d)    the relation between the actual utterance and the semiotic
      competence of the interpreter.
e)    the interpreter's reaction to the utterance.

Previous parts of this study have already mentioned questions and
problems concerning these dyadic relations. Therefore, a few remarks
about each dyadic relation between the sign (or representamen) and
the other elements of the semiotic pyramid should suffice.


## 2. The axes

1. Let us call the axis connecting the representamen and the immediate object the *indexical axis,* because taking the representamen
as the point of departure, the relation between the two factors is
*referential,* and starting with the immediate object the relation is one
of *determination.* This relationship creates problems from the point of
view of philosophy, linguistics, and semiotics, because questions concerning how we *refer* or *designate* play fundamental parts in the theory of knowledge. In view of all the difficulties described in the literature on reference, it is no small wonder that we actually succeed in
referring to objects or states of affairs, and even make ourselves understood. We might do so because the act of referring presupposes all
the other relations of the semiosis, or, in other words, that the preconditions described in Peirce's definition of the *common ground* are fulfilled. Nevertheless, it may be fruitful to isolate this aspect of the
semiosis, because if we misunderstand a sign, the reason may be we
do not understand its reference. Typical questions concerning the object of the sign will be about its identification within the universe of
discourse, its mode of being, i.e., which universe of discourse does it
belong to, and the additional question of whether the specific sign
refers its object to the "proper" universe. This last question leads to
two others: what is the relation between the object and the sign as the
sign represents it; and what, if anything, is known about the object
from other sources, including other sources of knowledge, e.g., percep-

tion. The talk about the "proper" universe can be exemplified by this question: Is an object referred to by a given sign dependent or independent of an individual mind (e.g., Macbeth's dagger)?

While questions b, c, and d emphasize the object pole of the indexical axis, questions a and e stress the sign pole. In case of the linguistic sign, it is fruitful to analyze the relative strength of the iconic and indexical elements within the text, although both aspects are mediated by the basic symbolic function of language. Question e concerns matters on the borderline between the sign's relation to its object and to its interpretant. In Peirce's view a sign denotes by connoting, and this means that the depth of a sign is explicated in its interpretant. In an absolutely basic sense, however, the attribution of qualities by the sign to the object concerns the indexical axis, because the question may be asked, whether the sign rightfully attributes the qualities to the object, or whether it is false to refer a certain sign to a certain object. In fact, what is involved in this relationship are questions about truth and falsity.

2. Let us name the axis linking sign and interpretant the *conventional axis* of the semiotic pyramid, because if no specific information is added in the co-text and context, the sign will not change its meaning potential. Although a linguistic sign ultimately acquires meaning by being an element in an argument, it is important for text analysis whether the sign is presented as a collection of rhemes, e.g., a pile of signs signifying qualities, as is sometimes the case in modernist poetry, or as a collection of propositions, or as arguments, as in a proof of something. In the last analysis, text interpretation consists in framing the text in such a way that it becomes a manifestation of an argument; in other words, if the argumentation of the (dynamic) interpretant is accepted, then the sign's appearance and nature becomes a matter of fact because it can be inferred from what is explicated in the interpretant. All the other questions under point 2 concern the identification of possible interpretants and the determination of the sign's latitude of interpretation. Identification of the sign system to which the sign belongs means not just to which natural language, but to which sub-system within a given language, e.g., to which type of discourse. The difference between explicating the sign's comprehension, or immediate interpretant, and translating it into another sign, its dynamical interpretant, is that the context may rule out some significations usually connected with the sign to the effect that the trans-

lation of the sign into another sign can be viewed as the selection, in the dynamic act of interpretation, among the possibilities offered by its comprehension.

3. Let us term the axis between sign and addresser the *symptomatic axis*. In linguistic communication the topic of an utterance is the object of the sign, i.e., the indexical relation between the sign and its immediate object, but in addition to this reference to the universe of discourse, the sign refers back to its own act of enunciation, and functions as a symptom of the enunciator. Obviously, the enunciator himself may be the topic of discourse, as when Richard III in Shakespeare's play introduces himself:

> And therefore, since I cannot prove a lover,
> To entertain these fair well-spoken days,
> I am determined to prove a villain
> And hate the idle pleasures of these days. (I, 1, 28-31)

There is of course, a difference between referring to oneself as the object of the sign and the fact that the sign becomes a symptom of the utterer, or of the circumstances of the process of uttering. In the above example, Richard's definition of himself might be taken as a symptom revealing a deeply disturbed personality. Consequently, the distinction between the sign's indexical and the symptomatic aspects has to be maintained even if the utterer is referring to himself. The importance of the distinction between utterer and addresser occurs in cases of a forgery, e.g., when someone signs a document with someone else's signature. Likewise, fictional discourse offers interesting differences between addresser and utterer. In the example quoted above, Richard III is clearly the addresser of the soliloquy, but is he the utterer? Is the utterer the author of the play? Within the fictitional universe it seems sensible to claim that Richard is both addresser and utterer, whereas Shakespeare, being the author, is the non-fictitious utterer of the whole text.

The other questions concern the relation between the act of uttering a sign as a kind of rule-governed behavior (e.g., studied in the theory of speech acts) and the act of uttering a sign as an individual action taking place within a specific context, and determined by the circumstances producing it. Interpreting texts necessitates recognizing the interplay between the rule-governed and historical aspects of the production of the text. Linguistics (at least before pragmatics) and text interpretation differ precisely in this respect, because linguistics lacks the contextual and historical aspect. Consequently, linguistics can only be one tool among others in the interpretation of texts.

4. A sign is necessarily directed to somebody even if it is only, as Peirce says, the ego of the next moment. Consequently, the identification of the addressee is important. Is the addressee humanity, some well-defined community, some individual existent person, etc.? In identifying the addressee as he is represented in the sign we have no clues other than the qualities explicitly attributed to him in the sign and what has to be presupposed about him to make the sign meaningful (cf. Peirce's concept of the *common ground*). There is, however, a difference between the receiver of the sign as a represented element within the sign, the addressee, and the actual receiver, the interpreter. This is true not only in the sense that it is doubtful whether love letters from a bachelor to a charming housewife would be appreciated in the same way if her husband were the interpreter, but also in the sense that the woman herself might react to the letters differently from the way the signs represented her as doing. Since the relation between the sign and the addressee/interpreter is bound up with the signifying process considered as an action, let us borrow a term from speech act theory and name this axis the *perlocutionary axis*. Just as the sign refers back to its utterer, as a symptom points to its cause, so the sign in its capacity of symbolic action refers to its addressee and attempts to exert a perlocutionary force. A rather elementary non-linguistic sign, the traffic light, illustrates these relations: as a symptom, it refers to the traffic regulations that permitted the legal authorities to put it up; but as a sign, or rather a small system of signs, endowed with a perlocutionary force it confronts road users as a small series of commands (cf. the analysis of this micro-system in the last chapter of this book).

In addition to the axes radiating from the sign pole of the semiotic pyramid, there are six more axes at the bottom. Even if we are able to discuss them only through the production and interpretation of conventional signs (e.g., language), they are just as fundamental as the other ones in making the signifying process possible.

5. Let us call the axis relating addresser/utterer with the immediate interpretant the *axis of semiotic competence*, because it links the subject of an utterance with the semiotic code necessary to produce

and interpret the sign. Even if the utterer tries and is successful in changing the code through the signifying process, he must still, if he wants to communicate at all, refer to and rely on socio-cultural systems of signification that are, at least to a considerable degree, public. That is, they are intersubjectively shared and accepted. If a relationship between individual and public systems does not exist, or if it is severely damaged, as occurs in some neurological illnesses, the possibility of communication by conventional means does not exist. Other semiotic codes have to be used, e.g., communication by means of sign language, the language of the deaf and mute. The possession of linguistic or semiotic competence is, however, a matter of degree, at least as regards complex semiotic structures like natural languages. It is doubtful whether it makes sense to claim that any individual person masters a language in *toto* or if we should only claim that somebody masters a given sociolect. One important source of misinterpretation occurs precisely when utterer and interpreter only partially share a given semiotic code, or rather interpretive network.

6. We will identify the axis linking utterer/addresser and immediate object as the *experiential axis,* because, according to Peirce, it is through collateral experience that we obtain information about the object. Just as the relationship between addresser/utterer and immediate interpretant can be non-existent or damaged, so can the one between utterer and immediate object if, for instance, the perception of sense qualities is injured. Furthermore, the nature of the immediate object itself may be such that it is impossible to perceive it directly; this is the case if the object of discourse is a past event, an object supposed to have existed, etc. In these cases we get information about the objects through conventional sign systems (e.g., written testimonies and documents) or through indices of part-objects (e.g., postholes indicating the past existence of a house). On the basis of these symbols and/or indices the immediate object is constructed in the imagination of the utterer. The importance of the experiential axis is due to the fundamental fact that without the possibility of perceptual or *experiential* acquaintance with objects, no content at all could be attached to conventional sign systems. Two preconditions have to be fulfilled for the semiosis of speech to take place: (1) the symbol must denote an object and signify its characters, and (2) the denoted object must be known through collateral experience, at least in the sense of imagi-

native construction. Such imaginative constructions are based on the collateral and direct experience of other objects (cf. below).

7.-8. The utterer's intended addressee is linked with object and interpretant through a similar pair of axes, but not necessarily in exactly the same way. If the communication is directed toward reaching mutual understanding, the utterer has to presuppose it is possible by means of his utterances to bring the addressee in the same relation to interpretant and object that he himself is. He may, of course, fail to do so.

9. The axis between immediate object and immediate interpretant could be called the *informational axis* because Peirce defines information as the product of extension and comprehension. Obviously, only a sign has extension and comprehension, but the existence of synonymity is sufficient reason to insulate this axis for consideration, because this relation may remain constant, even if the sign is changed.

10. The axis linking utterer and interpreter should be named the *contractual axis* because communicating with somebody means to enter into some kind of contractual relationship. This relationship is often represented in the sign itself as an explicitly stated, specific relation between addresser and addressee (e.g., requests and orders of command), but, in fact, it is presupposed between the parties actually taking part in a dialogue. This axis is important for the analysis of meaning because to interpret a given utterance, the utterance must be framed within a wider communicative context of social interaction. Actual linguistic communication is always already structured and controlled by social relations of power, norms, and values.

## 3. The triangular planes of the pyramid

The way the ten axes are connected with each other means that the semiotic pyramid is made up of ten triangular planes.

a. The *proposition plane, a,* is delimited by the *indexical,* the *conventional,* and the *informational* axes (Fig. 43).

The relation among the three poles of this plane measures the information of a sign in a given semiosis, or the propositional content of an utterance. I have claimed that the relationship between the internal and external elements at the vertices of the semiotic pyramid is one of interdependence; this point of view, however, seems absurd

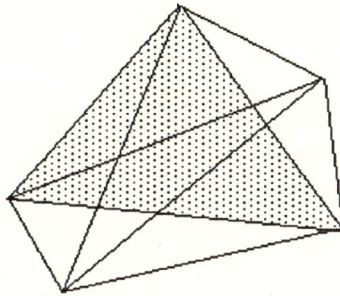

*a*

Fig. 43

as regards the relation between immediate object and dynamical object because a sign may very well refer to a non-existent object created by the signifying process itself. In this case an immediate object exists as an element within a universe of discourse, but there is no dynamic object existing in a material and social universe of action. Mr. Pickwick or the Little Mermaid certainly have a fictitious extension, namely their place within the universe of Dickens' novel and Hans Christian Andersen's tale, but they neither have, have had, nor will have any extension within a physical universe of social interaction. What is important for a semiotic theory of meaning is this: even if a given sign does not refer to something existent, somewhere in the chain of interpretants there will be references to an object that does exist. A sign like "mermaid" does not denote something real; it has no dynamical object. But one of its interpretants would be "woman with a fishtail," and this more developed sign, as Peirce would say, refers to something real and even something existent, although not existing in this combination, since no women endowed with fishtails as organic parts of their bodies have ever been encountered. This relationship is represented in Fig. 44.

The sign "mermaid'" and its interpretant "woman with a fishtail" are, for some purposes, synonymous or equivalent, i.e., they refer to the same immediate object. "Woman with a fishtail" is, however, a complex sign in Peirce's terminology, and this means that each part sign of this complex sign has interpretants that at some point in the semiotic regress will denote something existent. In this sense the in-

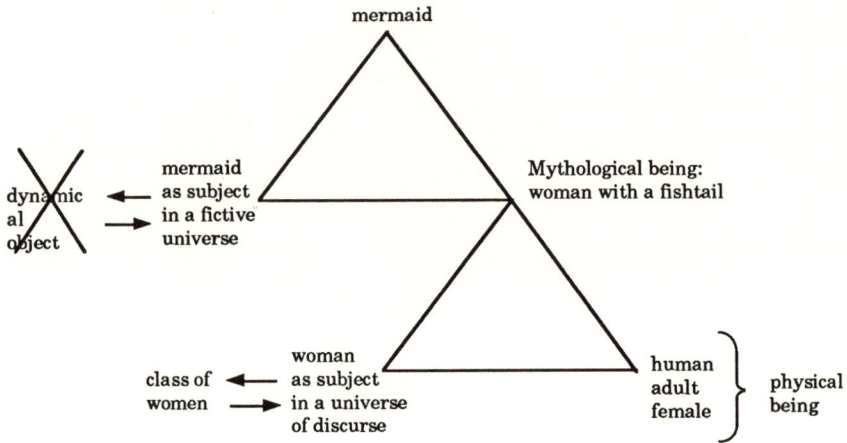

mermaid

dynamical object

mermaid
as subject
in a fictive
universe

Mythological being:
woman with a fishtail

class of
women

woman
as subject
in a universe
of discurse

human
adult
female
} physical
being

Fig. 44

terdependence between immediate and dynamical object holds true, not as a direct relationship, because this is clearly false, but as a relationship mediated through the process of semiotic regress.

The interpretation of the relationship between immediate and dynamical object might also be helpful in interpreting Peirce's *pragmatic maxim*. In one of its best-known versions from "How to Make Our Ideas Clear" (1878) it runs as follows:

> I only desire to point out how impossible it is that we should have an idea in our minds which relates to anything but conceived sensible effects of things. Our idea of anything is our idea of its sensible effects; and if we fancy that we have any other we deceive ourselves, and mistake a mere sensation accompanying the thought for a part of the thought itself. It is absurd to say that thought has any meaning unrelated to its only function. It is foolish for Catholics and Protestants to fancy themselves in disagreement about the elements of the sacrament, if they agree in regard to all their sensible effects, here and hereafter.
>
> It appears, then, that the rule for attaining the third grade of clearness of apprehension is as follows: Consider what effects, that might conceivably have practical bearings, we conceive the object of our conception to have. Then, our conception of these effects is the whole of our conception of the object. (5.401-5.402)

The additional material printed in the *Collected Papers* indicates that Peirce is eager to avoid any concept of meaning as the outcome of an individual action; on the contrary, he sees action as collective and as the outcome of a continuing process. Furthermore, he states explicitly that the pragmatic maxim applies to *conceived action* as well as to action proper: "Pragmaticism makes thinking to consist in the living inferential metaboly of symbols whose purport lies in conditional general resolutions to act" (5.402, note 3). Here Peirce is close to defining intellectual purport not as individual action but as habit-formation, and this is in accordance with his definition of the *ultimate logical* interpretant. If, however, action includes conceived action, and if it has to be understood as a habit rather than as individual action, what, then, does the "practical bearings" of a concept mean? Joseph Ransdell has suggested (personal communication) that it might be interpreted as a demand that icons can be attached to the concept in question. Some of Peirce's remarks seem to contradict this interpretation because he says he wants to "avoid all danger of being understood as attempting to explain a concept by percepts, images, schemata, or anything but concepts" (5.402, note 3). This statement is, however, contradicted by Peirce himself, such as where he talks about an iconic sign as the interpretant of a symbolic sign (cf. p. 218), and where the iconic, the indexical, and the symbolic are inextricably connected in the percipuum which is the fundamental source of knowledge.

By including *conceived action* in a definition of *action,* and especially including quasi-experimentation in the sense of mental operations on the icons, we avail a reductionistic and simplistic definition of action. At the same time we keep the necessary connection between signifying and perceiving. *The view presented here allows the pragmatic maxim to be interpreted as a demand. If a sign has any meaning at all, then it must be possible through semiotic regress at some point in the chain of its interpretants to attach to it icons and indices; it must also be possible to carry out mental operations on these icons; finally, it must be possible to trace these icons back to their foundation in perception, i.e., to point out the part played by firstness and secondness in the process of signification.*

b. The *communication plane* of the semiotic pyramid is delimited by the *symptomatic,* the *perlocutionary,* and the *contractual* axes (Fig. 45).

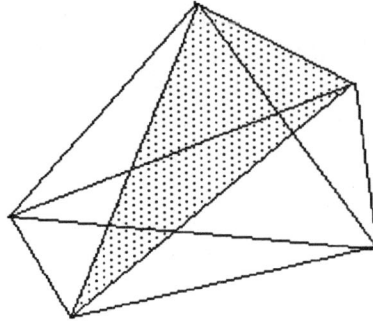

*b*

Fig. 45

Most of its characteristics can be inferred from the description of the axes by which it is delimited. It should be noted, however, that since the signifying process is something dynamic, there will be a constant interplay between the contractual relationship between utterer and interpreter and their intercommunication through the production and interpretation of signs. Through the sign process, people are engaged in defining and redefining their relationships. Normally, a redefinition is only possible within certain limits because such a process will be restricted by social constraints. Since, however, uttering signs imply some kind of purpose, this aspect of symbolic interaction deserves attention, and beyond doubt it is a basic function of linguistic communication to preserve or change interpersonal and/or social relations. It is also through social interaction and communication that individuals delimit themselves as persons and subjects. In other words, it is through semiosis, through sign action, that the subject, and subjectivity, is created as a position within the semiotic network.

*c, d, e, and f. There are* four more planes radiating from the sign-pole of the pyramid: (1) the *convention plane, c,* delimited by the *symptomatic,* the *conventional,* and the *competence axes;* (2) the *representation plane, d,* delimited by the *symptomatic,* the *indexical,* and the *experiential axes;* (3) a *supposed, convention plane, e,* delimited by the *perlocutionary,* the *conventional,* and the *competence axes;* and (4) a *supposed representation plane, f,* delimited by the *perlocutionary,* the *indexical,* and the *experiential axes* (Figure 46, c, d, e, f).

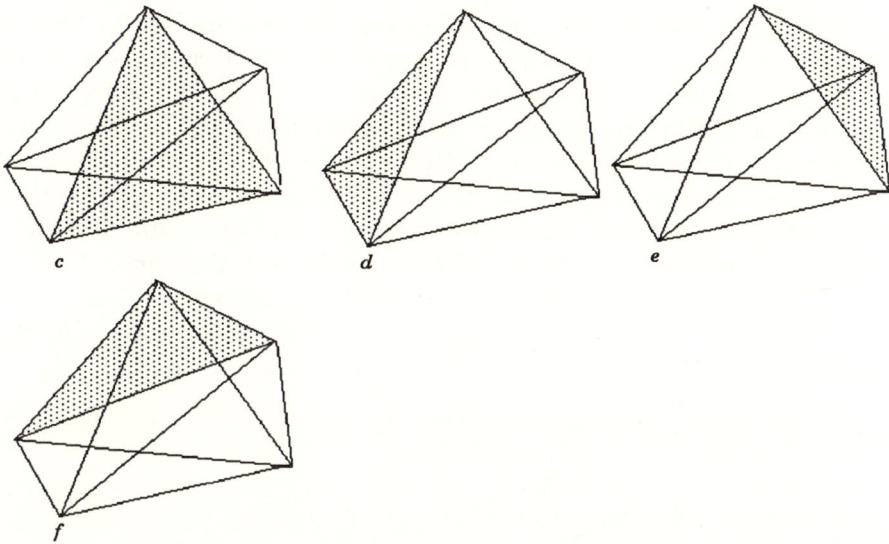

Fig. 46

In *c*, the sign's double reference to addresser and immediate interpretant will often permit us to infer the relation between addresser and interpretant because the use of certain signs characterizes the text both as belonging to a certain type or genre, and as a specific kind of symbolic action related to the intention and purpose of the addresser. One could say that the relation between the elements of this plane in a specific semiosis would be a measure of the sign's, or text's, accordance with or deviation from a set of codes and norms, and thereby indicates as well a measure of its individuality.

In *d* the double reference to the addresser and the immediate object will, likewise, often permit us to infer the relation between addresser and immediate object. A trivial example would be a person who repeatedly called objects green that everyone else would designate as red. In this case we would infer that the person was colorblind, at least if certain conditions were satisfied, e.g., that the person in other respects mastered the linguistic code. The representation plane, then, characterizes the relation between addresser and the universe of discourse.

*e* and *f* represent similar planes as *c* and *d* but in relation to the addressee, i.e., the way that the addresser supposes these relations to be, and this supposition determines partly the nature of the signifying process. That this is the case has been convincingly demonstrated by speech act theory and by the analysis of the so-called *conversational implicaturs* by H. P. Grice (1975) (see also Searle 1969 and 1979), but Peirce was already fully aware of the importance of the addressee in the intentions of the utterer for meaning analysis (cf. p. 200). Furthermore, it should be mentioned that this relationship is a cornerstone in the teaching of classical rhetoric, the art of persuasion.

*g and h.* In addition to the six planes radiating from the semiosis sign-pole four planes are at the basis of the pyramid (Fig. 47):

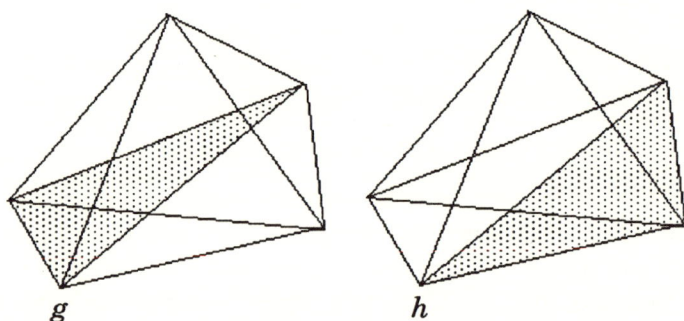

Fig. 47

These two planes represent two important aspects of what constitutes the common ground of utterer and interpreter, or rather the utterer's hypothesis about this common ground. The first plane is delimited by the *contractual* axis, the *experiential* axis, and the *supposed* or *hypothetical experiential* axis (of the addressee), and the plane represents a common universe of interaction in the understanding of the utterer. A similar plane exists in the understanding of the interpreter. Without being connected with the sign pole, the immediate object cannot be defined as an object in a universe of discourse, but that does not prevent it from being an object in a universe of action, and presupposed in social interaction. The immediate object could, in this capacity, be a percept that the parties engaged in the interaction mutually presupposed the other perceived, without making it an object of discourse. Only an inference from signs can ensure that the parties realize they are dealing with the same object. Only through the interpretation of verbal communication or through the interpretation of the other party's nonverbal behavior are there signs of the fact that he perceives and understands the object in a certain way. Nevertheless, to presuppose an experiential relation between the immediate object and the other party which is equivalent, or at least similar, to one's own, is a necessary *initial* step in reaching understanding, because the very notion of "different from" presupposes a concept of something positive. In what sense and to what degree the parties do have the same experiential relation to the object can, of course, only be revealed through verbal communication or through their nonverbal collaboration.

The other plane, delimited by the *contractual* axis, the *competence* axis, and the *supposed* or *hypothetical competence* axis represents a common set of coded significations in the understanding of the utterer. Most of what has been said about the first plane, which could be named the *interactional* plane, applies to this plane as well. To presuppose a common language means to assume that the addressee possesses a repertoire of significations and rules for their combination, in Peircean terms, immediate interpretants, identical or similar to the utterer's repertoire. Again, the validity of this presupposition can only be tested in the dialogical interplay of the signifying process, the semiosis. Since this plane represents the presupposed relation of the parties to a common repertoire of significations and their combinations, it shall be called the *intersignificational* plane.

Together these two planes constitute the presupposed *semiotic competence* upon which the signifying process is founded. This competence is only revealed through the concrete signifying process, or rather through a large collection of semioses. In this perspective it can be regarded as an idealized construction. It is a necessary construction, however, because it would not be possible to explain meaning without referring to such a concept. Without the capability of storing significations as possible sign meanings, and without the ability to form an unlimited number of utterances in accordance with basic syntactic rules, no dialogue could be carried out in natural language. It should be noted, however, that even if the power and range of the semiotic competence may be specific to the different species, this competence is developmental and historical within mankind. First, this means the individual acquires his semiotic competence through a learning process, and seen in this perspective, it is a trivial although fundamental fact that he has a species-specific semiotic learning capability. Second, this learning process is dependent on interaction with the environment and on social interaction. Consequently, from the view presented in this study, it follows that linguistic competence is a subspecies of semiotic competence and that the former could not exist without the latter.

Semiotic competence must be regarded as the outcome of social interaction, and with regard to human speech, it is certainly a necessary precondition. There is, however, one more way of looking at the relationship between the elements at the bottom of the pyramid. Diagrammatically the last two planes are represented in Figure 48:

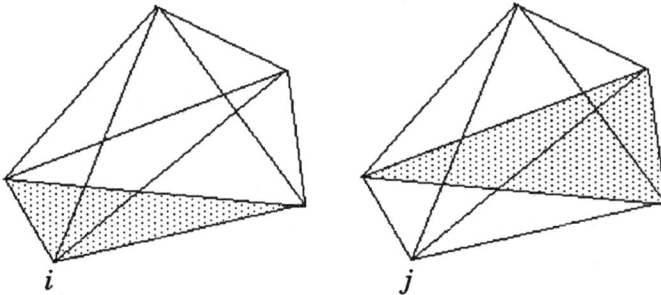

Fig. 48

*i* and *j*. The first plane is delimited by the *competence,* the *experiential,* and the *informational* axes; since this plane connects object, utterer, and interpretant without any communicative aspect, it may be called the *informational* plane. An unconditioned reflex is a good example of a semiosis without any intervention of conventional signs, i.e., instinctual behavior, such as responses invariably triggered by certain stimuli. Since such behavior is goal-directed, it cannot be described as dyadic, because any presence of intention, in these cases intentional effort, implies the relation between three distinct elements, even if this behavior is both subconscious and outside volitional control.

If the foregoing triadic relation is regarded as a semiosis, then it might be objected that the addresser/utterer pole will function as a sign. In view of Peirce's tentative identification of utterer with object and interpreter with interpretant (cf. pp. 192-194), the above identification of subject and sign may seem to complicate the matter. It should be remembered, however, that a sign is relatively defined as a position within a triadic action. Furthermore, ample evidence exists that Peirce himself analyzed *man as a sign*. An example is the following famous passage from "Consequences of Four Incapacities" (1868):

> For as the fact that every thought is a sign, taken in conjunction with the fact that life is a train of thought, proves that man is a sign; so, that every thought is an external sign, proves that man is an external sign. That is to say, the man and the external sign are identical, in the same sense in which the words homo and man are identical. Thus my language is the sum total of myself; for the man is the thought. (5.314)

If Peirce's statement is accepted, sign, addresser, addressee, and interpretant are all regarded as signs. The only element not yet included in this all-encompassing sign definition seems to be the object, but the object, or rather the immediate object, is no exception. Peirce states the sign character of the object in this way:

> Let us talk about yonder chair. "Chair" is a word. It is a sign. The *Vorstellung* chair is a *sign*. What will you have? Get down to the very impressions of sense, and there is no chair there. *The life we lead is a life of signs.* Sign under Sign endlessly. (Ms. 1334, 1905: 46)

This last addition means that all poles of the semiotic pyramid may be regarded as signs, as shown by Figure 49:

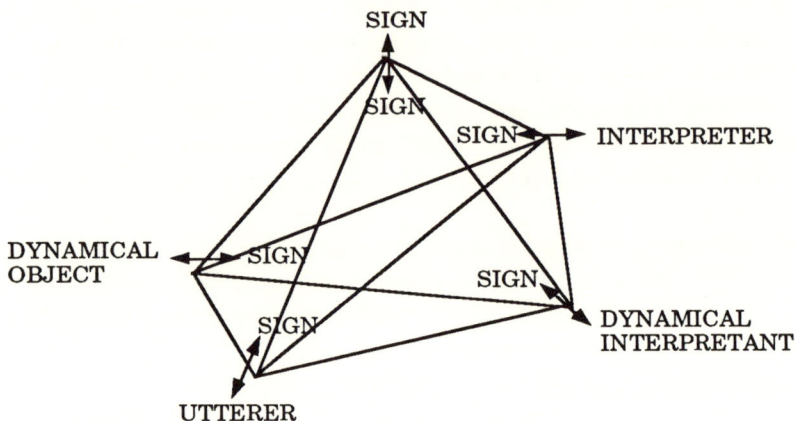

Fig.49

Such an idea may elicit serious objections, but in a way it is both fruitful and in accordance with common sense. In perceiving an object, we are often conscious that it is a phenomenal manifestation both of something external and of ourselves (as Peirce says, cf. p. 77), especially when we are uncertain what we are in fact looking at. In such cases we think of the percept as an appearance, as a sign of something else, but we are hesitant as to what it is a sign of. There may be more than one possibility. So we become acutely aware that we are dealing with a sign (an image) whose referent is indeterminate. Probably we will look more attentively at the phenomenon to perceive other aspects that may function as more determinate signs, identifying the object with greater certainty.

In dialogue we also perceive other people as signs. We read them, so to speak, symptomatically to understand the import of what they are saying. Peirce repeatedly points to the deictic function of the utterer's body which links the linguistic utterance to the perceptual and interactional field of the interlocuters. We are also attentive to the interplay between the different semiotic systems used in communication, in addition to language: the paralinguistic features of speech, facial expressions, gestures, postures, etc. Furthermore, the other party of the dialogue not only takes what is said to refer to the object, but also understands it as something linked to the beliefs, norms, and attitudes of the utterer, to his very being as a complex, multilayered system of systems that incessantly produces intra-organismic and interorganismic signs.

It is of the utmost importance to realize that defining and analyzing something as a sign does not mean it ceases to be something else, an organism, an object, an event, etc. It means that it is considered as occupying a specific position within a sign action, a signifying process.

Since this study is about human communication, and consequently primarily about linguistic signs, it may be worthwhile to reflect on the reason why immediate object, addresser, addressee, and immediate interpretant may be considered to be signs themselves, when the linguistic utterance is taken as the point of departure. If we here disregard the replica–representamen distinction, we see these elements of the semiosis all occupy a mediating position, marking a precarious differential threshold between what is inside and outside a particular sign action. Looking at the semiosis in this way, we see the four following triadic structures:

1) Linguistic sign – immediate object – dynamical object
2) Linguistic sign – addresser – utterer
3) Linguistic sign – addressee – interpreter
4) Linguistic sign – immediate interpretant – dynamical interpretant

Fig. 50

In all four cases the middle position is, so to speak, posited by the linguistic sign, but it presupposes itself the third element in the structure (fiction is, of course, a special case, but in the view presented here fiction presupposes non-fiction). The signs' threshold positions are due to their indexical function (or potential). The *I* and *you* of a linguistic utterance point to addresser and addressee, but the latter point themselves to the real or supposed parties engaged in a dialogue. Likewise, the linguistic sign posits the immediate object as the topic or theme of the utterance, but this immediate object becomes in its turn a sign indicating something in its own right, not only existing by virtue of being posited by discourse. Finally, the immediate interpretant is determined by the sign, but it is a meaning potential that has to be realized in the dynamical interpretant. In this way each of the four terminal points of the semiotic pyramid possesses a potential signhood. That signhood may remain latent, but may easily be made explicit and thematized through further sign action.

According to the view presented here, we can define the generation of language meaning as the effect of the interaction of two different semioses, the *informational* at the pyramid's basis and the *communicative* going from top to basis. The former does not, unlike the latter, presuppose any communication between two parties by means of a codified system of signs, but it does presuppose an interaction between a subject and an environment through which information is processed and stored. The following simple example illustrates a course of sign action, and the successive involvement of the poles and planes of the semiotic pyramid: a person grasps a wire without realizing it is electricfied. He gets shocked, and spontaneously pulls his hand back from the wire. A spontaneous pulling of the hand from an electric wire represents an energetic, dynamical interpretant; it is a reaction based on an emotional, dynamical interpretant, the feeling of pain; the body is, so to speak, coded to react in that way. It is, however, through the dynamic reaction and the subsequent cessation of the pain that the object, in the understanding of the subject, is constructed as something independent of the subject. This means that even on an elementary informational level Peirce's idea that denotation presupposes connotation holds true. This kind of semiosis can be represented as in Fig. 51.

Even in this elementary case of spontaneous action we distinguish two interpretants, an emotional and an energetic. Both belong, however, to the same order of interpretants, the dynamical, because the immediate interpretant is better defined as stored information existing prior to a given semiosis and partly governing the content of the dynamic interpretant. This difference can be illustrated by supposing the subject of the first example has learned from his unpleasant experience to avoid touching the wire. In this case the sight of the wire will be interpreted as a sign of a danger or pain to be avoided. Figure 52 illustrates the process.

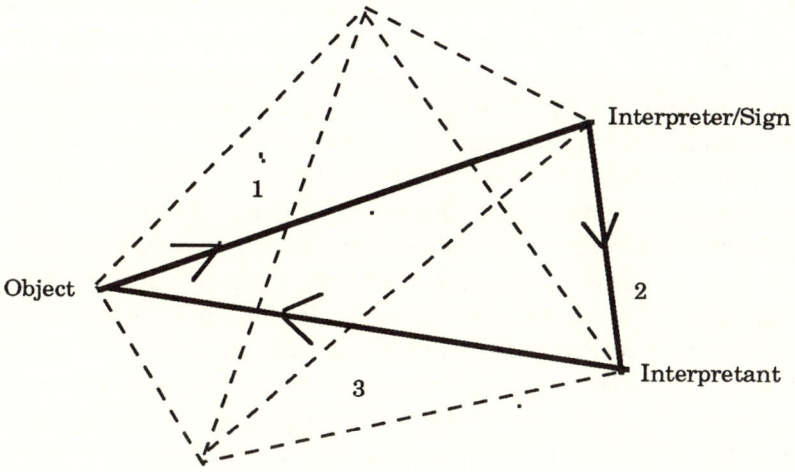

Fig. 51

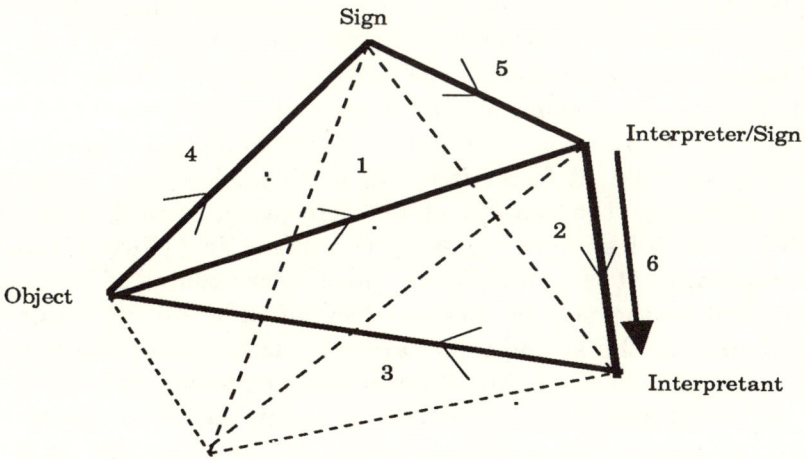

Fig. 52

The first three steps in the semiosis are the same as in the first example, but through the immediate interpretant, which means the interpretability of the sign, the object becomes a sign (step four) of an anticipated danger to which the interpreter (step five) reacts by avoiding the wire (step six). In this case it would be reasonable to assume that the immediate interpretant is a memory of an iconic-indexical nature, whereas the dynamical interpretant is the action of avoiding the wire, an action governed by the immediate interpretant.

No communication, so far, has taken place between two parties. That is why the two examples have been represented as a process involving only one subject, or subject pole. There is, however, yet another way of interpreting the latter example, namely, as a *dialogic* or *intracommunicative* process within the subject. If this interpretation is chosen, the steps may be represented as they are in Figure 53.

The only difference is in steps five and six, because in this interpretation the subject is split into two functions, interpreter and utterer. The merit of looking at the process this way is that it brings the informational and the communicative processes nearer to each other. Furthermore, the interplay between memory and anticipation in the semiosis, in such cases, justifies splitting the subject. Finally, this interpretation is preferable because it indicates the proto-dialogic nature of the process. In this way internal dialogue *sensu strictu,* which clearly needs two subjects, can be given a double foundation, the informational semiosis described above and the internalization of speech, which according to psychologists such as Vygotsky and Piaget is supposed to play a foundational role in the language aquisition.

In the first informational semiosis of our example the object has a triple function. First, it forces itself upon the subject, i.e., it brings about a change in the content of his perception; second, it is interpreted through feeling and possibly through action; third, through the interpretation it is posited as an independent source of information external to the subject, here in fact an independent, exterior source of pain. In the second informational semiosis we add a fourth step because the stored information of the immediate interpretant initiates the interplay between memory and anticipation (cf. above) so that the interpreted object becomes a sign of something else, in this case the danger of a painful experience. Consequently, the dynamical interpretant is an action determined by the object in its capacity as sign.

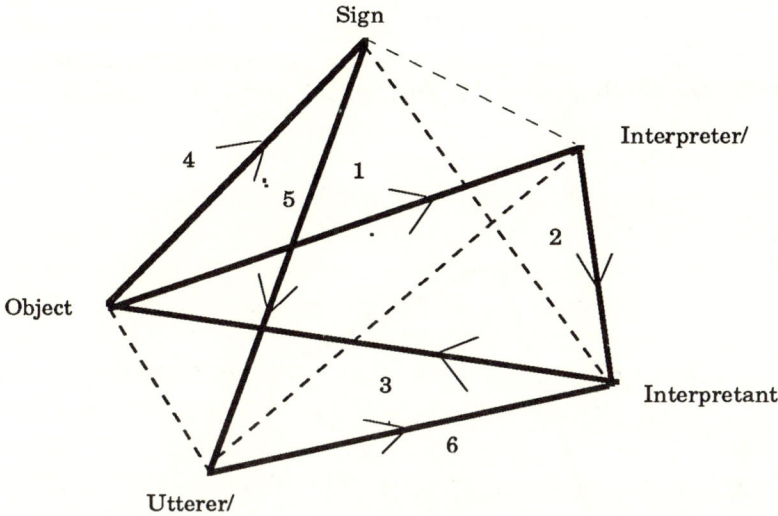

Fig. 53

These four functions of the object in the informational semiosis are not only necessary for the establishing of preverbal experience, but also a precondition for the establishing and the functioning of speech, for it is the capacity of an object to refer to something else, its sign function, that is the decisive step that makes possible the use of conventional symbols. This is not to say that the ability to use conventional sign systems, e.g., language, does not constitute tremendous progress, since it means a new categorization of the world; but through the function of an object as a sign, the semiosis becomes independent of the presence of the *signified object*. The signified object is inferred through the interpretant by the presence of a *signifying object* (cf. also Piaget, here quoted on pp. 133).

In contradistinction to informational semiosis, which logically only presupposes the interaction of an individual subject and an environment, language is social and public. It presupposes the existence, or sometime existence, of a community. The concept of communicative semiosis is broader than human language, since it extends coverage to the sign systems used for communicative purposes by animals. Let us, however, define speech as the creation and transmission of information (in an extremely broad sense) between an utterer and an interpreter by means of language. According to this definition, the route of the signifying process will differ from the one in the informational semiosis. Figure 54 illustrates the route of the semiosis of speech.

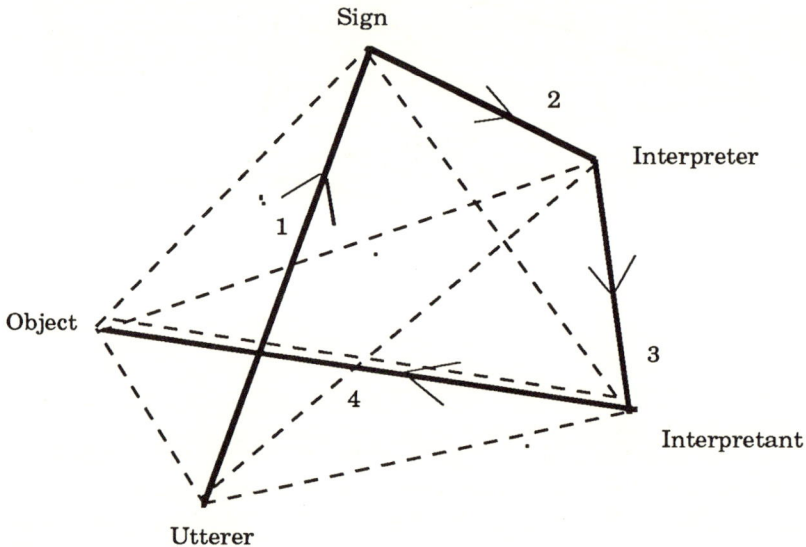

Fig. 54

Since most information is conveyed by symbols, in Peirce's sense of the word, an utterer, not an object, starts the semiosis (but, according to Peirce, the utterer represents the object). But as has been repeatedly pointed out, conventional signs have no signification unless connected to the informational semiosis, and this means that for the communicative semiosis to work, both parties, or at least one of them, must have achieved the correlation of the two semioses. That this is the case can be seen in language acquisition, because teaching a child the mother tongue means, among other things, directing its attention towards certain objects, events, or states of affairs, i.e., trying to bring about certain informational semiotic processes in the child and to correlate them with the communicative semiosis (cf. Russell, here pp. 237-238).

At the same time two other processes start: the building up of verbal structures (elements and combination rules on the phonological, the syntactic, and the semantic levels and their interrelations), and the establishment of patterns of social interaction partly governed by verbal utterances (language as symbolic action). Just as the building up of the propositional aspect of language is related to the informational semiosis and its dependence upon a historical environment, so is the actional aspect of language embedded in other semiotic interactional systems which historically are dependent on the group, class, and culture to which the parties belong.

# VII. Beliefs, Rhetoric, and the Validity Basis of Speech

because there has been implanted in us the power to persuade each other and to make clear to each other whatever we desire, not only have we escaped the life of wild beasts, but we have come together and founded cities and made laws and invented arts; and, generally speaking, there is no institution devised by man which the power of speech has not helped us to establish. For this it is which has laid down laws concerning things just and unjust, and things honourable and base; and if it were not for these ordinances we should not be able to live with one another. It is by this also that we confute the bad and extol the good. Through this we educate the ignorant and appraise the wise; for the power to speak well is taken as the surest index of a sound understanding, and discourse which is true and lawful and just is the outward image of a good and faithful soul. With this faculty we both contend against others on matters which are open to dispute and seek light for ourselves on things which are unknown. . . . (Isocrates: *Antidosis* 254-256, Loeb 1929: II, 327)

In practice, a language is a semiotic into which all other semiotics may be translated – both all other languages, and all other conceivable semiotic structures. This translatability rests on the fact that languages, and they alone, are in a position to form any purport whatsoever; in a language, and only in a language, we can "work over the inexpressible until it is expressed." . . . It is an all but obvious conclusion that the basis lies in the unlimited possibility of forming signs and the very free rules for forming units of great extension (sentences and the like) which are true of any language and which, on the other hand, make it possible for a language to allow false, inconsistent, imprecise, ugly, and unethical formulations as well as true, consistent, precise, beautiful, and ethical formulations. The grammatical rules of a language are independent of any specific purpose. (Hjelmslev 1953a: 70)

Logic ought to rest directly on the phenomena of life which nobody doubts. Nobody really doubts that there is such a thing as Truth, which every sentence we utter takes for granted. . . . (Ms. 313, 1903: 21)

The preceding chapter argues that, at least in a certain sense, we are always fixed in a threshold position vis-à-vis semiosis (cf. Figure 50). As utterers and interpreters we emit and receive signs; in fact, we only become visible and intelligible to one another, and to ourselves, through and as signs. This liminal mode of being may cause existential problems, because even if through constant interpretation we attempt to become diaphanous to ourselves and others, as signs we will always point to something else, and parts will always remain unexplored. Furthermore, the social and physical environment, as the object of inquiry, assumes sign character as well, because even if our concept of them as immediate objects becomes more and more rich, we cannot be certain that they, as dynamical objects, will ever stop surprising us by revealing new dimensions.

Confronted with this predicament two different stances are possible: The first stresses "the reign of the signifier," and claims that we are imprisoned in an infinite and unstable process of signification which is both unpredictable and ungovernable. Furthermore, the interaction between sign production and reality has become so intense and complex that it blurs the borderlines between the imaginary, the fictional, and the real. Late industrial society has created a fuzzy universe in which distinctions between artifact and nature are attenuated, as they are between manufactured fictional worlds and social reality, in short the very relation between sign and object. Man is now creating dynamical objects on a large scale, in the sense of changing the natural forces operating in the environment (ecological catastrophes, etc.). These new natural conditions are mind-independent, and they confront us; they are, however, caused by our own activity. In addition to our using technological skills in changing nature, minds are influenced, and polluted, by the construction and confusion of reality and fiction in mass media; and as voters and consumers we are shaped and modelled by campaigns exploiting the findings of social psychology and rhetoric. The relationship between signs and meanings, which is always unstable, is now in a constant state of flux to the effect that social intercourse is impaired and people are left to themselves in a fragmented universe. Consequently no general ways of communicating and settling opinions exist. At best local language games regulate belief systems, which are just as local. The different parts of communities are at odds with each other, and the eventual

settlement of opinion is a result of the use of power, rhetorical sub-
terfuges, or, at best, unholy compromises. Having demonstrated that
such is the actual human condition, at least in the Western world,
people holding this view may either despair or rejoice in the multi-
farious and exciting adventures which such a disintegrated universe
offers.

The other stance recognizes the imperfection, misery, and wicked-
ness of the present world. It holds, however, that this condition is not
inescapable, it is neither due to our species specific nature nor to a
constitutional deficiency in the semiotic systems we use to interpret
and communicate. Even if it is true that we lead a life as, and among,
signs, it does not imply that we are helplessly at the mercy of self-
generating sign processes. On the contrary, sign systems and sign
processes are at our service, they are means of knowledge and understanding. Isocrates' beautiful panegyric which opens this chapter
stresses the pivotal role and the potential emancipating force in the
process of civilization of man's most important semiotic. The san-
guinity of Isocrates' claim is moderated, however, by Hjelmslev's remark that natural languages, as systems, are ethically and epistemo-
logically neutral. If they were incapable of expressing both truth and
falsity, they could not fulfill their office as pass-key languages. Their
inbuilt capacity for producing an infinite number of sentences is at
variance with ethical and epistemological restrictions.

Isocrates' and Hjelmslev's claims do not contradict each other. The
one concerns speech; the other concerns language. Hjelmslev's remark
warns us, however, not to look for intrinsic and systematic features of
language that guarantee right reasoning. In the quotation from Peirce
truth is not seen as a systematic property of a given semiotic, but
rather as a presupposition for communication. A recognition of its
existence as an operative force is implicit in every utterance, because
without making this presupposition dialogue and interaction would
break down and become senseless. This recognition of truth as a force
operative in social action does not mean that we already know the true
answers to every question. On the contrary, we know that our knowledge is imperfect, in many respects perfunctory. This is why, according to Peirce, truth functions both as a presupposition for and the end
of inquiry, i.e., the only valid way of fixing beliefs.

## 1. The fixation of belief

Peirce constantly stresses the cooperative nature of the process of inquiry. Even his complex definition of truth poses consensus as one condition that has to be fulfilled, namely the consensus among an unlimited community of researchers. Furthermore, Peirce links semiotics (i.e., speculative grammar, logic proper, and speculative rhetoric) to ethics and aesthetics. It will be remembered that, according to Peirce, the ideal that should guide our actions is to make the universe more rational (cf. pp. 194-195). This ideal has far-reaching implications for the moral (and scientific) conduct of individuals, because, according to Peirce, it demands that they identify themselves with the objective of this unlimited community and if necessary sacrifice themselves (cf. 5.354). Indeed, one man alone is not even considered to be a unified whole. Peirce says this in a note from about 1898 in "How to Make Our Ideas Clear":

> When we come to study the great principle of continuity and see how all is fluid and every point directly partakes the being of every other, it will appear that individualism and falsity are one and the same. Meantime, we know that man is not whole as long as he is single, that he is essentially a possible member of society. Especially, one man's experience is nothing, if it stands alone. If he sees what others cannot, we call it hallucination. It is not "my" experience, but "our" experience that has to be thought of; and this "us" has indefinite possibilities. (5.403, note)

Indeed, the social and communicative nature of the process of inquiry is at the heart of Peirce's reflections on how to settle opinion in "The Fixation of Belief" (1877, but constantly revised until 1910). Here he distinguishes four methods of obtaining beliefs, all of which are characterized by a different kind of communicative process. Two of these methods are primarily individualistic, only intradialogic, while the other two are social, interdialogic.

The first, the "method of tenacity," is in fact even hardly intradialogic, because it simply consists in sticking to a belief at any cost by using the strategy of an ostrich: to avoid any confrontation with experiences or arguments that may contradict the belief. This method, which is indeed widespread, is, however, unable to hold its ground when seriously challenged, because it, in Peirce's words, is "against the social impulse":

> This conception, that another man's thought or sentiment may be equivalent to one's own, is a distinctly new step, and a highly important one. It arises from an impulse too strong in man to be suppressed, without danger of destroying the human species. Unless we make ourselves hermits, we shall necessarily influence each other's opinions; so that the problem becomes how to fix belief, not in the individual merely, but in the community. (5.378)

Another method of fixing beliefs is the metaphysical or a priori method. Compared to the method of tenacity it certainly means a tremendous step forward, because it constitutes a reflection on the nature of the universe, and on the laws that are thought to be operative within it. According to Peirce, however, metaphysical systems have one basic flaw, namely that they are founded on what is "agreeable to reason" instead of what is discovered by experimental inquiry (an example offered by Peirce of this way of reasoning is Plato's idea "that the distances of the celestial spheres from one another should be proportioned to the different lengths of strings which produce harmonious chords"). Consequently, despite its much higher level of reflection, and despite its communicative intent, traditional metaphysics is only quasi-dialogic, because it develops its systems from individual preferences and avoids both the experiential dialogue with nature and a dialogue with other philosophical positions. Whereas the method of tenacity refuses to look at all, metaphysics looks, but it only sees what seems to substantiate its own position.

The method of authority seems to be contrary to the metaphysical because it is public and does not leave the fixation of belief to the individual choice of a thinker's imagination. It teaches what is to be believed, and it forces members of a community to believe its teachings, or at least to pretend to do so. Its combination of a more or less systematic exposition of the "laws" governing both man and the universe, and political and ethical rules regulating the life of a society with power and the determination to use them (often ruthlessly), makes it a formidable instrument for settling opinion, and in the history of man a method always used.

Nevertheless, according to Peirce, the method of authority necessarily breaks down for both internal and external reasons. Authority is subverted from the inside, because no authoritarian system is capable of fixing beliefs concerning every question which may arise. It will constantly be threatened by discoveries of inconsistencies and contradictions which will eventually make it unworthy of credence. From the outside an authoritarian system is constantly threatened as well. No such system is universally accepted. The knowledge of other beliefs cannot be prevented, and neither can the influence of such alien beliefs be totally suppressed. Although authoritarian belief systems certainly are public, Peirce's point is that they are not dialogic, but pseudodialogic. Questions are only allowed within very narrow limits, and the only valid answers are provided by the system itself.

All three above mentioned methods of fixing beliefs do in fact block the road of inquiry, because they inhibit the search for unforeseen answers to problems that question traditional beliefs, whether they be cherished ideas or enforced dogmas. The scientific method of fixing beliefs, which Peirce favors, is different from the other three in two highly important respects, because it is founded on a double dialogue: a discursive dialogue between researchers and an experiential one between researchers and their object of study.

As a scientist Peirce points out the extreme importance of the experiential dialogue with nature: "To satisfy our doubts, therefore, it is necessary that a method should be found by which our beliefs may be determined by nothing human, but by some eternal permanency - by something upon which our thinking has no effect" (5.384). It has to be pointed out that this non-human permanence does not prevent a dialectic relationship between researcher and nature. Permanence means public, what is in principle accessible to everybody:

> Our external permanency would not be external, in our sense, if it was restricted in its influence to one individual. It must be something which affects, or might affect, every man. And, though these affections are necessarily as various as are individual conditions, yet the method must be such that the ultimate conclusion of every man shall be the same. Such is the method of science. (5.384)

The other kind of dialogue, the one between members of a community, both a scientific community and community at large, is just as important to the fixation of beliefs on scientific principles, indeed even more so, because the "concept, that another man's thought or sentiment may be equivalent to one's own . . . arises from an impulse too strong in man to be suppressed, without danger of destroying the human species."

On this principle of equality, which precludes the use of authority, the search for methods both of discovery and of represention of arguments becomes necessary. In Peirce the third part of logic, speculative rhetoric or methodeutic, is designed to fulfill this need, because it "would treat of the formal conditions of the force of symbols, or their power of appealing to a mind, that is, of their reference in general to interpretants" (1.559). In Peirce the names *speculative rhetoric* and *methodeutic* point to the fact that this discipline has several aspects. It is, simultaneously, conceived as "the art of inquiry," as "the general theory of how research must be performed" (2.106), and as "a method of discovering methods" (2.108).

In Ms. 774 (probably 1904), where Peirce names his trivium, *speculative grammar, speculative critic,* and *speculative rhetoric,* he also provides a feast of distinctions and classifications of speculative rhetoric. He begins by stating his concept of it:

> Evidently, our conception of rhetoric has got to be generalized; and while we are about it, why not remove the restriction of rhetoric to speech? What is the principal virtue ascribed to algebraical notation, if not the rhetorical virtue of perspicuity? Has not many a picture, many a sculpture the very same fault which in a poem we analyze as being "too rhetorical." Let us cut short such objections by acknowledging at once, as an *ens in posse,* a universal art of rhetoric, which shall be the general secret of rendering signs effective, including under the term "sign" every picture, diagram, natural cry, pointing finger, wink, knot in one's handkerchief, memory, dream, fancy, concept, indication, token, symptom, letter, numeral, word, sentence, chapter, book, library, and in short whatever, be it in the physical universe, be it in the world of thought, that . . . causes something else, its interpreting sign, to be determined to a corresponding relation to the same idea, existing thing, or law. . . . There ought, at any rate to be (. . .) a science to which should be referable the fundamental principles of everything like rhetoric, – a *speculative rhetoric,* the science of the essential conditions under which a sign may determine an interpretant sign of itself and of whatever it signifies, or may, as a sign bring about a physical result. (Ms. 774, ca. 1904: 3-5)

This description of rhetoric is indeed inclusive, and it leads to many subdivisions of the discipline. From our point of view the most interesting one is the division "according to the special nature of the ideas to be conveyed" (ibid. 14), which results in the following three classes:

> A rhetoric of fine art, where the matter is of feeling mainly, a rhetoric of practical persuasion, where the chief matter is of the nature of a resolve; and a rhetoric of science, where the matter is knowledge. The rhetoric of science would be subdivided into a rhetoric of the communication of discoveries, a rhetoric of scientific digests and surveys, and a rhetoric of the applications of sciences to special kinds of purposes. (Ms. 774, ca. 1904: 14)

Consequently, a part of this branch of semiotics, or logic, is linked with Peirce's scientific and logical work, and especially with his existential graphs, because he claims that they give a moving picture, an iconic representation of thinking (cf. 4.8). Another part of it is bound up with communication between speaker and listener (Peirce also named this branch *transuasional logic,* cf. 2.93), and it is concerned with the ways of bringing a listener to share the opinion of the speaker. Peirce regards, for instance, the making of an assertion from this point of view:

> The assertion consists in the furnishing of evidence by the speaker to the listener that the speaker believes something, that is, finds a certain idea to be definitively compulsory on a certain occasion. There ought, therefore, to be three parts in every assertion, a sign of the occasion of the compulsion, a sign of the enforced idea, and a sign evidential of the compulsion affecting the speaker in so far as he identifies himself with the scientific intelligence. (2.335)

Peirce goes on to explain that this implies an assertion must contain indexical elements to represent the compulsory aspect of the assertion. For the problems concerning the fixation of beliefs the force of an argument consists precisely in its compelling power, its ability to ensure that listener accepts it. As mentioned in chapter II, 1, Peirce holds that meaning implies some reference to a purpose, and he further holds that "the professed purpose of an argument is to determine an acceptance of its conclusion" (5.175). This is why he defines *meaning* technically "to denote the intended interpretant of a symbol" (ibid). As should be clear in chapter IV, the *intended interpretant* is only one out of nine; however, from the point of view of settling opinion it is certainly not the least important, because to ensure its acceptance is a necessary step on the way to reaching agreement. Peirce himself had valuable insights concerning the presuppositions of understanding and of the forces operative in the fixation of beliefs. He did not, however, carry out a specific investigation into this part of speculative rhetoric, because his main interest was in scientific rhetoric, or logic of discovery (for this aspect of speculative rhetoric see the study by Tursman, Tursman 1987). This is why it may be fruitful to turn briefly to a systematic study of practical rhetoric, as Peirce calls it, by a thinker in no way inferior to Peirce, namely Aristotle.

## 2. The presuppositions of rhetoric

In the diagrammatic reconstruction of semiosis (Fig. 42, chapter VI) the splitting of the vertices of the pyramid marks the opposition and interaction between the internal and external aspects of the sign process. These splits make semiosis problematic, uncertain, and liable to error and confusion, and offer the possibility of progress in knowledge. The analytical necessity of splitting these elements, and especially the splitting of both addresser and addressee to study human communication, is, at the same time, both a formal and a practical precondition of persuasive discourse, because this split makes possible the planning of strategic communication. The addresser is divided into an addresser, which is the image of the utterer as he appears within the sign, i.e., the utterer as he wishes to appear to the addressee, and the utterer, i.e., the producer of the sign, including the motives he may have in producing it. The very existence of such a phenomenon as a lie makes this distinction necessary. Whenever we lie, we not only pass on what we believe to be false information, but also appear otherwise to the addressee than we would, if we had told the truth. Furthermore, it is also necessary to distinguish between the addressee on the one hand and the interpreter on the other. The addressee is the image created by the sign of the interlocutor. Normally this image of the addressee will be produced on the basis of the utterer's notions of the person he is talking to. The addressee, then, is a semiotic (or rhetorical) construct effectuated by the sign, whereas the interpreter is the one who actually interprets the sign. The utterer may sometimes intentionally use the split between addressee and presumed interpreter by addressing the latter as if he were somebody else. The orator may, for instance, address his audience as a collection of noble, intelligent, and discriminating men who are never to be beguiled, while he is in fact addressing a mob that he is leading by the nose.

In general what is inside the pyramid are *addresser, addressee, immediate interpretant,* and *immediate object.* They, at least to some degree, are controlled by the sign, and by the utterer of the sign. By virtue of embodying a number of codes (constituting the immediate interpretant), the sign governs to a certain extent its actual interpretation. Furthermore, implicitly or explicitly, it structures the relationship between addresser and addressee and characterizes both positions. Finally, it also governs the concept of the object by foregrounding the features and qualities relevant to its message. What is outside the pyramid, but inextricably connected to it, namely *utterer, interpreter, dynamical object,* and *dynamical interpretant,* is only partly controllable. The utterer may try to appear as a friendly addresser, but may be unable to control his anger or disgust. Through the image of the addressee the sign seems to ascribe certain attitudes and qualities as appropriate for the interpreter to assume. It is obvious, however, that any actual interpreter, consciously or unconsciously, may reject the offered image. The concept of the object, and the way in which we interact with it, may be belied by hitherto unknown properties. Finally, by its argumentative structure, the specific combination of codes, the sign seems forcefully to suggest a certain interpretation, i.e., to determine and select a predicted response in the audience. It is, however, impossible for any sign to obtain absolute command of codes and context, and consequently a certain unpredictability is always inherent in the process of human communication.

Certain means exist, however, that may be used to reduce this unpredictability, and rhetoric is precisely the study of how to reduce the unpredictability of communication by controlling message and context: As regards the split between utterer and addresser, and the eventual betrayal of the latter by the former, the rigor of self discipline and the art of role-playing suggest themselves. Consequently, any training that controls the heterogeneity of attitudes, unifies them, and makes them subserve an overruling purpose will tend to diminish this source of uncertainty. This goes only for the created impression of the addresser in the mind of the interpreter. In fact, such strategies of dissimulation deepen the split between addresser and utterer. As regards the split between addressee and interpreter, any sociological and socio-psychological knowledge of the audience may serve to adjust the image of the addressee to well-founded hypotheses about the in-

tended receiver and interpreter of the sign. As regards the split between immediate and dynamical object, the same holds true. Depending upon the nature of the object different types of research will try to
minimize the surprises (in part unwelcome) that ignorance of the
properties of the object may incur. Any intentionally produced sign,
however complex it may be, selects and foregrounds a certain range of
the object's properties. This selection is governed by criteria of relevance as regards some purpose. It is, however, also due to a lack of
knowledge, and more specifically to a lack of answers to questions that
are usually raised in connection with the kind of object in question.
Any investigation of an object is, then, an attempt to control the object
and to provide answers that may be integrated in its representation.
These efforts to reduce the unpredictability of the interpretation of the
sign are united and manifested in the sign by means of its coding, i.e.,
articulated through a set of semiotic systems available to the parties
of the dialogue. The sign may itself change the codes in question in
some respect; it must, however, be related to and explicable by a stock
of common knowledge in order to govern the actual interpretation, at
least partially.

The ways in which an utterer tries to control the interpretation of
the sign, and thereby the interpreter's concept of the object, brings us
right into the heart of rhetoric. It should be stressed, however, that
such an effort is common to other kinds of discourse. In fact most
kinds of discourse attempt to govern the interpretation of their texts
as strictly as possible according to their purposes and objectives. According to Aristotle, what distinguishes rhetoric from other crafts and
sciences is its generality. He defines it as follows:

> Rhetoric then may be defined as the faculty of discovering the possible
> means of persuasion in reference to any subject whatever. This is the
> function of no other of the arts, each of which is able to instruct and
> persuade in its own special subject. (*Rhetoric,* 1355b, I, II, 2, Loeb 1959: 15)

According to this definition a sign may, or rather will, manifest both
rhetorical and technical codes, and it will be *informative,* or as Aristotle would say, *instructive* and *persuasive,* simultaneously. This duplicity of the instructive and the persuasive will also be manifest in the
orator's representation of the object. The district attorney will not only
present what he believes to be the facts of the course of events, he will

also interpret the legal and ethical significance of the act, inquire into its motives, claim that it was done intentionally for the defendent's own good, although he was well aware that it was harmful to others, etc., etc. The politician who recommends a specific course of action will eloquently point out that we know from experience there is no better remedy available, and he will stress the legitimacy and moral nature of his proposal. If the sign in question is an ad, the object of the sign, which is an artifact, will be characterized by the same duplicity as the sign. We may distinguish between its *utility* and its *aesthetic appeal*. These two values may vary independently of each other. The utility value of a given product is the outcome of its technical capacity to fulfill a function adequately within a given context according to a given purpose. The aesthetic appeal of an object is due to its accordance with accepted standards of the beautiful or agreeable, or to its creative reshapening of such standards. As to the utterer and interpreter, they will in this case be related to each other as manufacturer and seller to buyer and consumer. In advertising a given merchandise the manufacturer and seller will, however, also fulfill the function of an orator informing, arguing, and persuading the interpreter about the excellency of his cause. This means that the potential buyer and consumer becomes a judge of the message contained in the sign, consciously or inconsciously estimating its claims and promises.

Classical rhetoric stresses the communicative and interactive aspects between utterer and interpreter to an almost extreme extent. In Aristotle we read for instance as follows:

> Now the proofs furnished by the speech are of three kinds. The first depends upon the moral character of the speaker, the second upon putting the hearer into a certain frame of mind, the third upon the speech itself, in so far as it proves or seems to prove. (*Rhetoric*, 1356a, I, II, 3, Loeb 1959: 17)

This tripartition of the proofs makes sense, when the communicative context of classical rhetoric is taken into account, because it was used in face to face verbal communication on primarily three occasions, in forensic, deliberative, and epideictic speeches (speeches of praise or blame). Thus the orator's objective is to create a common bond between himself and his audience. Furthermore, since rhetoric concerns not what is necessarily true, but what is probable, the trustworthiness of the speakers becomes important. Aristotle writes:

> The orator persuades by moral character when his speech is delivered in
> such a manner as to render him worthy of confidence; for we feel confidence
> in a greater degree and more readily in persons of worth in regard to
> everything in general, but where there is no certainty and there is room for
> doubt, our confidence must be due to the speech itself, not to any pre-
> conceived idea of the speaker's character. (*Rhetoric*, 1356a, I, II, 4, Loeb
> 1959: 17)

This precondition for persuasive communication is by no means out-
dated, and consequently *credibility, reliability,* and *benevolence* are
the essential ingredients in the utterer's construction of his own image
in the sign. Credibility and reliability need no comments. Benevolence
is just as essential, however, because the audience ought to be per-
suaded that what is advised and prescribed is in its own interest. The
orator, because of his credibility and uprightness, or, as Aristotle says,
"good sense, virtue, and good will," is thus to be thought of as the
benefactor of the addressee.

The second kind of proof is, according to Aristotle, the rousing of a
certain emotional state in the hearers, "for the judgments we deliver
are not the same when we are influenced by joy and sorrow, love or
hate" (*Rhetoric*, 1356 a, I, II, 4, Loeb 1959: 17). This task is triple. It
consists of gaining the audience's attention and sympathy, of eliciting
a certain emotional attitude towards the object of the speech, and of
persuading the audience that the recommended decision will further
their happiness or pleasure.

It may seem presumptuous for the utterer to evoke the happiness
of his audience as the theme of his speech; but its involvement, its
willingness to act, and its preference of one thing or one course of
action over another are often caused by considerations concerning its
own happiness and well-being. Aristotle puts it as follows: "Men, in-
dividually and in common, nearly all have some aim, in the attainment of which they choose or avoid certain things. This aim, briefly
stated, is happiness and its component parts" (*Rhetoric*, 1360b, I, V, 1,
Loeb 1959: 47). He holds further that, in fact, "all who exhort or
dissuade discuss happiness and the things which conduce or are de-
trimental to it. For one should do the things which procure happiness
or one of its parts" (ibid.). He goes on to define what is commonly
thought to constitute happiness:

> Let us then define happiness as well-being combined with virtue, or in-
> dependence of life, or the life that is most agreeable combined with se-

curity, or abundance of possessions and slaves, combined with power to protect and make use of them; for nearly all men admit that one or more of these things constitutes happiness. If, then, such is the nature of happiness, its component parts must necessarily be: noble birth, numerous friends, good friends, wealth, good children, numerous children, a good old age; further, bodily excellences, such as health, beauty, strength, stature, fitness for athletic contests, a good reputation, honour, good luck, virtue. (*Rhetoric,* 1360b, I, V, 3-4, Loeb 1959: 47-49)

Except for the possesions of slaves, this list, which does not reflect Aristotle's own concept of happiness, but public opinion of his time, also seems valid from our point of view. It might serve us as a description of commonly shared values and motives for action. In "The Fixation of Belief" Peirce also claims that "it is certainly best for us that our beliefs should be such as may truly guide our action so as to satisfy our desires" (5.375).

The object of the sign, e.g., the past, present, or future state of affairs it refers to, will explicitly or implicitly be represented as an object of praise or blame, either being claimed to subserve the happiness of the audience, or as something to be avoided. However factual and unbiased a text may be, however removed it may seem from the interests and desires of its audience, or readers, and those of its author for that matter, it nevertheless implicitly claims some sort of existential relevance, claims to subserve someone's happiness.

According to classical rhetoric there are three principal means of making a cause, or an object, convincing: through examples, maxims, and arguments. An example (the rhetorical equivalent of induction) may compare a present case with a previous and well-known case to make probable the conjecture that since the cases are alike in many respects they will also be alike in the decisive respect which interests the audience. In such a case you use singular past events to predict a future course of events.

Aristotle's second way of presenting a cause in a persuasive manner is to show that it falls within the class of cases covered by a generally accepted maxim. He defines a maxim in this way:

A statement, not however concerning particulars, as for instance, what sort of man Iphicrates was, but general; it does not even deal with all general things, as for instance that the straight is the opposite of the crooked, but with the objects of human actions, and with what should be chosen or avoided with reference to them. (*Rhetoric,* 1394a, II, XXI, 2, Loeb 1959: 279)

Among other examples Aristotle gives this line as a beautiful example of a maxim:

Being a mortal, do not nourish immortal wrath.

This maxim may be used when we advise somebody to stop showing immoderate anger and hatred, and to forgive an injustice. According to Aristotle, the use of maxims has two advantages: first to generalize the particular experiences of the individual members of the audience, and he adds, "the hearers are pleased to hear stated in general terms the opinions which they already formed" (*Rhetoric*, 1395b, II, XXI, 15, Loeb 1959: 287).

The second advantage is the fact that a maxim

> makes speeches ethical. Speeches have this character, in which the moral purpose is clear. And this is the effect of all maxims, because he who employs them in a general manner declares his moral preferences; if then the maxims are good, they show the speaker also to be a man of good character. (*Rhetoric*, 1395b, II, XXI, 16, Loeb 1959: 289)

Another feature of maxims is their ability to express experiential stereotypes and accepted values in a proverbial manner. Furthermore, a maxim, being a kind of quasi-universal statement, may serve as one of the premises in an argumentation (a syllogism). Very often the maxim establishes the link between the narrative and the argumentative modes of the sign, and at the same time expresses the point of view that the utterer wants the interpreter to accept as his own. Cassius, for example, urges Brutus to free Rome of Caesar with the following maxim (which in itself is a rhetorical syllogism, an enthymeme):

> Men at some time are masters of their fates:
> The fault, dear Brutus, is not in our stars,
> But in ourselves, that we are underlings.
> (*Julius Caesar*, I, II, 139-141)

Whereas the maxim mediates between the sign's, or text's, discursive and narrative modes, the narrative, the example, either quotes experience or invents a story, or both, or becomes an illustration of a probable course of action, of a moral precept, of human nature as it is generally thought to be, or of all of such illustrations at once.

Besides the discursive and narrative strata of the rhetorical text, the phenomenal surface consists of what is inherent in the sign itself, the arrangement of its perceived material qualities (euphony, meter, rhyme, composition, etc.). The phenomenal surface is the material and perceptual qualities and their arrangement in space and time. This surface is itself coded, music, choreography, scenography, and the patterning of space, shapes and colors. The design becomes vital to the structuring of this dimension of the sign. The narrative, the example, mediates itself between the logical structure and phenomenal surface of the sign in question. Sometimes it is held that the deep level of logic determines the narrative structure, that the latter determines the phenomenal surface level. It is more correct to say, however, that in a complex sign all three components will mutually determine each other, all of them being at least partly determined by the *telos* of the sign, its communicative intent. The more heterogeneous and complex the sign the more interplay between the different means of expression. The orator's voice, facial expressions, gestures, dress, movements, etc., all the elements of what classical rhetoric calls *actio,* all contribute to its impact on the audience. If the text is a work of art, for instance in the performance of an opera, or in a modern commercial, the signs' expression, or surface, becomes even more eminent. Figure 55 shows the elements and relationships of rhetorical communication displayed on the semiotic pyramid.

For reasons of clarity and space this diagram lists only the internal relations. In addition to the ethos of the *addresser* (the way in which he wants to appear to the interpreter in his speech) we have the *utterer* who wants to influence the interpreter. In addition to the attempted construction of the pathos of the *addresser* by means of the speech, we have the (maybe different) response of the actual *interpreter.* The *immediate object* is presented as one of praise or blame, but the *dynamical object* may certainly belie it by revealing other effects. A few comments on the last pole of the semiotic pyramid, the *immediate interpretant,* is needed: The point is that the different codes of expression and content rearticulate our already preformed life-world, impregnated with significations, desires, and values. Consequently, the images, examples, maxims, and arguments in which the object of praise or blame is represented will reflect the audience's culturally formed values and aspirations. Because of the mastery of these codes,

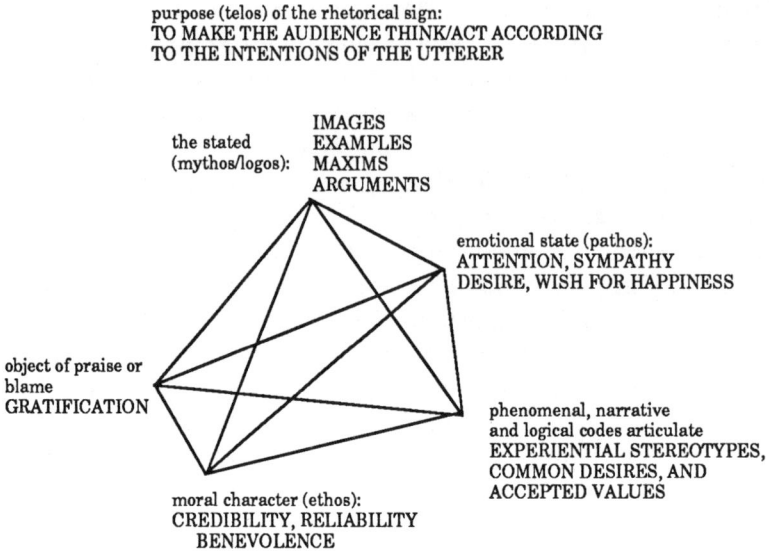

purpose (telos) of the rhetorical sign:
TO MAKE THE AUDIENCE THINK/ACT ACCORDING
TO THE INTENTIONS OF THE UTTERER

the stated       IMAGES
(mythos/logos):   EXAMPLES
                  MAXIMS
                  ARGUMENTS

emotional state (pathos):
ATTENTION, SYMPATHY
DESIRE, WISH FOR HAPPINESS

object of praise or
blame
GRATIFICATION

phenomenal, narrative
and logical codes articulate
EXPERIENTIAL STEREOTYPES,
COMMON DESIRES, AND
ACCEPTED VALUES

moral character (ethos):
CREDIBILITY, RELIABILITY
BENEVOLENCE

Fig. 55

however, the rhetorical sign will often get a degree of articulation and an expressive force beyond the audience's articulatory power. For this and other reasons the *dynamical interpretant,* the significant effect of the speech or text, may be different from the one intended.

According to Cicero (*De Oratore,* II, XXXVIII, 160, Loeb 1959: 313-315), Aristotle himself disdained rhetoric, and a certain reservation is indeed traceable in his treatment of the subject. Nevertheless, Aristotle claims that rhetoric may be useful:

> Because the true and the just are naturally superior to their opposites, so that, if decisions are improperly made, they must owe their defeat to their own advocates; which is reprehensible. Further, in dealing with certain persons, even if we possessed the most accurate scientific knowledge, we should not find it easy to persuade them by the employment of such knowledge. (*Rhetoric,* I, II, 32, 1855a, Loeb 1959: 11)

It is interesting that Aristotle's defense of rhetoric stresses its non-dialogical nature, since it is defined as a means to impress and persuade "certain persons" who would not be convinced by scientific arguments, even if such were available.

Even if classical rhetoric stresses that the orator should be a most ethical character, and that credibility, reliability, and benevolence are listed among his most eminent qualities, as a craft it is itself morally neutral. Basically it is associated with strategic action. As an investigation into the conditions of the successful settling of opinion from the orator's point of view, it does, however, point to the necessity of intentionally creating, at least seemingly, an ideal speech event in which the truth of the matter, the justice of the cause, the credibility of the speaker, and the understanding of the audience are all presupposed.

This attempt to create and evoke ideal communication and its presuppositions signifies two things. First, it points to the social significance of this ideal as a guiding principle of public debate in which the equality of the speakers is presupposed, at least in principle. To cherish such a principle in legal action and political deliberation is important in itself, although one may often despair that only lip service is paid to it. Second, however, it may be asked whether dialogue in itself is necessarily founded on the principles which for better or worse classical rhetoric explores? The next section will inquire into this question.

## 3. The validity claims of speech

Peirce's sets up an opposition between authority and science in "The Fixation of Belief" and in other writings. These have inspired contemporary philosophers such as Jürgen Habermas and Karl-Otto Apel, who wrote an admirable book on Peirce (Apel 1975). In addition to a strong inspiration from Kant, they have used Peirce's points of view and arguments in an attempt to found theories of discursive ethics and communicative action. Despite certain differences and nuances in their points of view, the works of Apel and Habermas are animated by the same general ambition, namely to argue for a communicatively founded and cognitivistic ethics. In doing so they try to work out an alternative to philosophical and ethical relativism. It is, however, only a part, albeit an important one, of their impressive and laudable work that will be discussed here, namely the project of a universal pragmatics. I have chosen to expound important points in Habermas' version, but it should be stressed that it is worked out in an ongoing dialogue with the works of Apel.

According to Habermas, universal pragmatics belongs to the reconstructive sciences (like, e.g., the linguistic theory of Chomsky). Their objective, unlike the empirical-analytic sciences, is not to form hypotheses and make predictions about states of affairs in the external world based upon observations that, in the last analysis, rest upon perceptions. Instead these reconstructive sciences aim at explicating the pre-theoretical knowledge of the subjects by what is called a process of rational reconstruction. These sciences have their data, but data that belongs to the symbolically preformed life-world of individuals. There is no way to avoid taking the self-understanding of individuals into account. The judgments of the participants in communicative action are thought to be fundamental, whether it is a question of the grammaticality of sentences or of the legitimacy of norms and actions. This does not mean that the explication of the reconstructive sciences cannot go beyond the self-understanding of the members of a given community (their objective is precisely to formulate the conditions and rules which govern communication and action); it means that the essential part of these sciences is made up by an analysis, not of facts, but of interpretations. If perception is regarded as interpretation, the difference between empirical-analytic sciences of facts and reconstructive sciences of interpretations becomes lesser; still, it is certainly not negligible.

More specifically, Habermas conceives the objective of universal pragmatics to be "the identifications and reconstruction of the universal conditions of understanding," or as he expresses it elsewhere, "the conditions of every communicative action directed towards understanding." According to Habermas every person who wants to participate in a dialogue, the objective of which is to establish a reciprocal understanding, will have to respect four fundamental validity claims. He says:

> The goal of coming to an understanding [Verständigung] is to bring about an agreement [Einverständnis] that terminates in the intersubjective mutuality of reciprocal understanding, shared knowledge, mutual trust, and accord with one another. Agreement is based on recognition of the corresponding validity claims of comprehensibility, truth, truthfulness, and rightness. We can see that the word understanding is ambiguous. In its minimal meaning it indicates that two subjects understand a linguistic expression in the same way; its maximal meaning is that between the two there exists an accord concerning the rightness of an utterance in relation

to a mutually recognized normative background. In addition, two participants in communication can come to an understanding about something in the world, and they can make their intentions understandable to one another. (Habermas 1979: 3)

The four fundamental validity claims are these: 1) *comprehensibility* for the linguistic expression of an utterance, 2) *truth* for the state of affairs referred to in a given utterance, 3) *truthfulness* on the part of the utterer, and 4) *rightness* in relation to a given norm. The first claim, comprehensibility for the linguistic expression, seems intuitively to be a *conditio sine qua non* for participating in a dialogue whose objective is to reach understanding. The problem, however, is to indicate the conditions of comprehensibility of an utterance.

In "What Is Universal Pragmatics," Habermas thought that comprehensibility is the only validity claim that can be analyzed intrinsically by linguistics, although he was well aware of the problems of delimiting an immanent semantics. In his later work, *Theorie des kommunikativen Handelns* (1981, Eng. trans. 1989), he does not mention comprehensibility but concentrates on the three other validity claims. Now, however, he seems to have given up this claim, and at present subscribes to the view (proposed among others by Searle) that even literal meaning is based on deep-rooted presuppositions about the world. In other words there can be no linguistic competence without a pragmatic competence. This position implies that linguistics, or at least semantics, is embedded in pragmatics.

The remaining three validity claims presuppose the well-known distinction between propositional content and illocutionary act (or as Peirce says between a proposition and the act of affirming it). An obvious reason for this has already been given in the quotation from Peirce, where he claims that the same proposition can be asserted, denied, questioned, etc. (cf. p. 198). It is certainly also obvious that any given propositional content of an utterance can be replaced by another without changing the type of illocutionary act in question.

If the speaker wants to participate in a dialogue directed towards understanding he has, according to Habermas, to relate the linguistic expression to three different domains of reality in the following ways:

By "communicative competence" I understand the ability of a speaker oriented to mutual understanding to embed a well-formed sentence in relations to reality, that is:

1. To choose the propositional sentence in such a way that either the truth conditions of the proposition stated or the existential presuppositions of the propositional content mentioned are supposedly fulfilled (so that the hearer can share the knowledge of the speaker);

2. To express his intentions in such a way that the linguistic expression represents what is intended (so that the hearer can trust the speaker);

3. To perform the speech act in such a way that it conforms to recognized norms or to accepted self-images (so that the hearer can be in accord with the speaker in shared value orientations). (Habermas 1979: 29)

To redeem the claim to truth or rather to make a rational discussion of this claim possible, the speaker has implicitly or explicitly to satisfy three suppositions: 1) The presupposition of existence, meaning that the object or fact indicated by (the indexical aspect of) the proposition is supposed by the speaker to exist and that he can give reasons for his assertion. 2) the speaker can identify what he is referring to, meaning that he gives directions that permit the hearer to identify the object or state of affairs. 3) The predication, or attributive act, must be justified in the sense that the speaker can give reasons for his attribution of specific characters to the object or state of affairs referred to.

The condition that the speaker has to satisfy with regard to veracity is similar to the so-called sincerity rule that figures in John Searle's speech act analysis:

Whenever there is a psychological state specified in the sincerity condition, the performance of the act counts as an expression of this state. This law holds whether the act is sincere or insincere, that is whether the speaker actually has the specified psychological state or not. (Searle 1969: 65)

According to Habermas, then, in communication directed towards understanding the speaker is obliged to express his real psychological state, or in other words no difference will be allowed between his individual intention and the intention ordinarily associated with the performance of a given illocutionary act, if the speaker wants to redeem the claim to truthfulness.

In *Theorie des kommunikative Handelns,* Habermas makes a strict distinction between the intentions of the speaker and the illocutionary act. The ultimate reason for this distinction can be found in Habermas' concept of social interaction. Here the basic distinction is the one between communicative and strategic action. In another place. he presents his classification in the diagram shown here as Fig. 56:

Social Action

Communicative Action  Strategic Action

Action Oriented to    Consensual   Openly Strategic   Latently Strategic
Reaching Understanding  Action      Action             Action

Action  Discourse    Manipulation   Systematically
                                     Distorted
                                     Communication

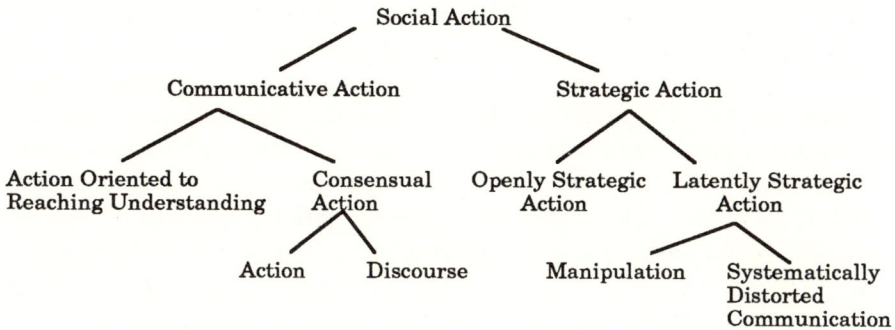

(Habermas 1979: 209)

Fig. 56

Strategic action is action directed towards success that follows rules of rational choice and that can be appraised in terms of its efficiency. Communicative actions, on the contrary, take place "when social interactions are co-ordinated not through the egocentric calculations of success of every individual but through cooperative achievements of understanding among participants" (Habermas in Thompson and Held 1982: 264). The dialogue directed towards achieving understanding is evidently the principal means to reach an agreement about cooperation or communicative actions, but the realization of individual intentions certainly does not imply the achievement of understanding between the parties taking part in a dialogue. This is the reason why Habermas sees a connection between teleological action, intentions, and the perlocutionary effect of an utterance in contradistinction to the illocutionary act which is related to communicative action. In making this distinction Habermas is referring to Austin, who defines the perlocutionary act as the production of "consequential effect upon the feeling, thoughts or actions of the audience, or of the speaker, or of other persons" (Austin 1962: 101). According to Habermas' point of view it is important that the illocutionary act implies that the speaker states (or at least can state) the kind of act he is uttering without destroying the purpose of his utterance, while the perlocutionary effect (Habermas thinks) would be destroyed if the intention of the utterance was revealed. According to Habermas, another difference between illocution and perlocution is that in uttering an illocutionary act the speaker is announcing the way in which he wants the hearer to understand the utterance. Thus, his communicative intention is said to be fulfilled when the hearer understands the manifest type of speech act he is expressing. This is not the case in uttering a perlocutionary act. This distinction between illocutionary acts understood as acts that establish interpersonal agreement and perlocutionary acts as acts that are subspecies of strategic action intended to achieve success by changing a state of affairs in the world needs clarification, but the more profound reasons for justifying it are related to the fourth validity claim.

The fourth universal pragmatic condition the speaker has to satisfy in participating in communicative action is the accordance of his utterance with recognized norms. This implicit (or explicit) reference to a normative background constitutes the *acceptability* of a given speech act. Habermas defines the understanding of a speech act as the understanding of what makes it acceptable; by acceptable he means the speech act, or its normative basis, can be intersubjectively recognized. In Habermas' view there is a difference in type between, on the one hand, naked imperatives that are based on the power of the speaker and his possibilities of applying sanctions, and on the other hand, commands and requests based on recognized norms. The latter case implies an intrinsic relation between a claim to rightness and the reasons justifying this claim, whereas in the former case justification by reason is contingent.

If the parties of a dialogue refer to a well-known state of affairs that they identify and describe in the same way, if both parties truthfully state what kind of speech acts they are uttering, and if both parties share a common system of norms and values, then there will exist a common ground of communicative action. It can be objected that this situation is ideal and that it is impossible to be certain that its conditions are ever satisfied. It might be argued that it is probable they are never completely satisfied, because of differences in background knowledge and world views, not to speak of particular interests and power-relations. This objection has not escaped Habermas' notice. He offers an intriguing counter-argument, stating that even if this ideal speech situation has, at least for the past and present, seldom been realized, it is nevertheless anticipated every time we engage in a dialogue. Habermas argues as follows:

The ideal speech situation is neither an empirical phenomenon nor a mere construct, but rather an unavoidable supposition reciprocally made in discourse. This supposition can, but need not be, counterfactual; but even if it is made counterfactually, it is a fiction that is operatively effective in the process of communication. (Habermas 1973: 258)

This argument has certainly a *prima facie* plausibility, because if we did not in fact presuppose these validity claims our communication would break down.

To explicate what is involved (and at stake) concerning the acceptance and presupposition of these validity claims in verbal communication, let us begin by quoting a well-known joke told by Freud in *Jokes and Their Relation to the Unconscious:*

Two Jews met in a railway carriage at a station in Galicia. "Where are you going?" asked one. "To Cracow," was the answer. "What a liar you are!" broke out the other. "If you say you're going to Cracow, you want me to believe you're going to Lemberg. But I know that in fact you're going to Cracow. So why are you lying to me?" (Freud {1905}, S. E. VIII, 1960: 115)

According to Freud this joke belongs to the rarer species of skeptical jokes; and this particular joke brings forth the following reflection:

Is it truth if we describe things as they are without troubling to consider how our hearer will understand what we say? Or is this only jesuitical truth, and does not genuine truth consist in taking the hearer into account and giving him a faithful picture of our own knowledge? (ibid.)

Freud's reflection, despite its value, misses an important point, namely that the joke's absurdity stems from the strange rule that is presupposed in order to make the conversation meaningful. This rule could be stated as follows: *any assertion that something is the case counts as an expression that it is not the case.* It is, however, important to realize that this rule of interpretation is not just an inversion of the claim to truth and truthfulness. If, for instance, you ask somebody when the next plane leaves for New York City, and the other party says at 10 am, to know that the validity claims are inverted would not help the person who asks, because the only thing he could infer would be that his interlocutor did not believe that the flight left at 10 am. Consequently, although truth and falsity are opposites, they do not function in the same way as presuppositions of dialogue. Furthermore, this example brings out the distinction between truth and truthfulness, because the answer is a prediction stating a belief that the plane will leave at 10 am. The person answering the question may be wrong for several reasons. He may simply be mistaken. According to the schedule, the plane really leaves every week day morning at 9.30, or it is Sunday, and on Sundays the morning plane leaves at 11 am, not at 10, or the timetable may have changed without his noticing it, etc. It may also happen that the flight is scheduled for 10 am, but it is delayed (such things do happen), or that it is simply cancelled. In these cases the answer (prediction) will prove false, but it will have been made in good faith. The person to the best of his knowledge will have answered truthfully.

Despite the fallibility of memory and uncertainty of prediction, in innumerable cases we act according to the presupposition that the other party of the dialogue tries to tell the truth. This example has been presented as a prediction, because predictions, despite their inherent uncertainty, play an important role in our actions. In a sense, however, asking when a flight leaves is more complicated than presumed above, because when we ask about it, what we are asking normally means: "When is the flight scheduled to leave?" This question is not answered with a prediction, but with a statement of fact, and if the interlocutor is mistaken, then he is mistaken about a fact, because his indication of time disagrees with the timetable.

The function of the timetable itself is rather interesting, because it is debatable what kind of speech act it utters. According to the above, it seems relevant to consider it a table of predictions, since it can be read as a series of statements to the effect that something is going to happen in the future at a specified time and place. This definition really does not do justice to what is involved in setting up a timetable. According to Searle's taxomy of speech acts, in which he distinguishes between *assertives, directives, commissives, expressives,* and *declarations* (including the important subcategory *assertive declarations,* cf. Searle 1979: 12-20), a timetable seems to manifest a commissive speech act, because it functions not only as a prediction, but also as a promise that the utterer, the airline, will make the flight leave at a certain time. The timetable commits or obligates the utterer to attempt to act in a certain way (in Habermas' classification it would be classified as a *regulative,* cf. below). That this is so can also be seen by the fact that airlines, on the tickets, disclaim any legal responsibility for delays and cancellations caused by incidents beyond their control.

Commissives (or regulatives) are clearly related to the fourth validity claim, *rightness*, because they, in Habermas' formulation, refer to a common social world, and represent a legitimate recognized, interpersonal relationship. In uttering a commissive (regulative) speech act the utterer obliges himself to act in a certain way, and it is judged morally wrong if he does not meet the expectations which he has himself created, unless, of course, something unforeseen prevented him from doing so. In our case, even if it is not possible to sue the airline in question for delays and cancellations, the airline would get a bad reputation, and eventually lose customers.

Until now, we have only considered cases in which false information about the time of departure, or delay and cancellation of the flight itself, is due to lack of proper information, or caused by incidents beyond control. It might happen, however, that a person intentionally would give false information about departure time, for instance, to make the other party stay longer. In this case, the claim to truthfulness (Searle's sincerity rule) would be covertly violated, and, in Habermas' theory, the action would change from *communicative* to *strategic*, since the purpose would no longer be to share knowledge and objectives, but to further the success of the utterer's intentions.

The distinction between *communicative* and *strategic* action is basic to Habermas and influences his way of analyzing and classifying speech acts. The following table (Fig. 57) from *Theory of Communicative Action* (Habermas 1989: I, 329) shows how he links the analysis of actions to the analysis of speech acts.

This is one typology of speech acts among others (e.g., the one by John Searle), and I do not intend to analyze it in detail. One thing seems puzzling, however: the fact that Habermas places perlocutions together with imperatives as the two typical speech acts belonging to strategic action. His reason is that he defines perlocutions as speech acts that are used to promote covertly strategic actions, just as imperatives express overtly strategic action. This definition of perlocutions as a means to effect covertly strategic action does not seem useful. The most general definition of perlocution offered by Austin is the effect of or the consequent of an utterance, and he goes on to distinguish between intentional and unintentional consequences. This distinction is important, since, for instance, it is fundamental within the philosophy of law. Consequently, we have to distinguish between the intention of the utterer and the reaction of the interpreter, and, to

## Pure Types of Linguistically Mediated Interaction

| Types of action \ Formal Pragmatic Features | Characteristic Speech Acts | Functions of Speech | Action Orientation | Basic Attitudes | Validity Claims | World Relations |
|---|---|---|---|---|---|---|
| Strategic Action | Perlocutions Imperatives | Influencing one's opposite number | Oriented to success | Objectivating | (Effectiveness) | Objective world |
| Conversation | Constatives | Representation of states of affairs | Oriented to reaching understanding | Objectivating | Truth | Objective world |
| Normatively Regulated Action | Regulatives | Establishment of interpersonal relations | Oriented to reaching understanding | Norm-conformative | Rightness | Social world |
| Dramaturgical Action | Expressives | Self-representation | Oriented to reaching understanding | Expressive | Truhtfulness | Subjective world |

Fig. 57

complicate things a little, we must further distinguish *the reaction of the interpreter in the intention of the utterer* from *the actual reaction of the interpreter,* and in the same way *the intention of the utterer in the interpretation of the interpreter from the actual intention of the utterer.* In talking about intentions and reactions we understand utterances as purposive actions. In saying something we are not only doing something, but we are doing something to some purpose, and doing it to bring about a change in some state of affairs, at least in the sense of affecting the mind of the addressee. If by perlocutionary act is meant the intended effect of the utterance upon the addressee, then perlocutionary acts are performed in every utterance and are not confined to being a subspecies of strategic actions. If semantics is embedded in pragmatics, because sentences to be meaningful have to be analyzed as utterances, and there is every reason to suppose so, then some idea of the purpose of the communication is intrinsic to the understanding of utterances. Utterances that do not violate the sincerity rule are characterized by identity between the utterer's intention and the intention presupposed in the type of speech act in question. Furthermore, understanding what kind of speech act a given utterance expresses presupposes the identification of the context that makes it sensible. If someone, for instance, in the middle of the Sahara comes

across a *no parking sign,* it will not be easy to interpret it as an utterance expressing a regulative speech act. One would rather interpret it
as a joke. It could be objected that one cannot understand it as a joke,
if it is not understood in the former way, and that it proves that one
can identify speech acts out of context. However, it points rather to the
fact that understanding a given type of speech act presupposes a
reference to a standard context that makes it understandable.

Both Austin and Habermas point out that speech acts are themselves intrinsically connected to consequences. If you make a promise
you are supposed to keep it, if you advise somebody it is supposed to be
your intention that he will act accordingly, when the no-smoking sign
is on in the plane you are supposed not to smoke, etc., etc.

In view of what has been said about intentions, reactions, and
consequences in relation to utterances it seems reasonable always to
ask the following question in trying to interpret a text: What is the
purpose in uttering it? This question can be subdivided into two: 1)
What is the intention of the utterer? 2) How am I in the capacity of
addressee supposed to react to the utterance? Consequently, I find it
to be more correct and fruitful to speak of the locutionary, illocutionary, and perlocutionary aspects of an utterance than about lo-
cutions, illocutions and perlocutions as separate acts, and to suppose
that the interpretation of every utterance, at least in principle, calls
for an analysis of all three aspects. Consequently, a perlocution should
not be considered as an independent kind of speech act allied to strategic action. A covert strategic action, in the form of an utterance,
might, however, be defined as an utterance in which the illocutionary
force (which is to a great extent given in the standard meaning of
many illocutionary verbs) and the perlocutionary effect (in the sense of
utterer's intention) are at variance with each other. For instance, in
lying about the time of departure of a flight a person may pursue a
certain perlocutionary effect, maybe that the other party stays with
the liar for another day. This would be the covertly intended effect, the
perlocutionary aspect which is sought, achieved by knowingly uttering
a false propositional content (the locutionary aspect of the utterance)
as an (affirmative) assertion (the illocutionary aspect of the utterance). We also have to distinguish between the intended perlocutionary effect and the consequences an utterance may in fact have. If we
adhere to our story about a false departure time, the other party may
believe the lie, but may decide to rent a car to get to another airport to

catch a flight, or may call the airport anyway, to check the time of departure.

The examples given above are trivial, but this is exactly the point, because they illustrate how our most simple actions involve procuring reliable information from others, how we act according to expectations about the behavior of others, and how we suppose that interpersonal relations within a given community are governed by norms considered legitimate. Examples to the contrary abound, but as Habermas argues (cf. p. 295), it seems impossible to avoid presupposing these validity claims, even if we want to catch a certain flight to New York City.

The quotation on logic and truth at the head of this chapter strongly suggests that Peirce would agree with Habermas, and Russell gives expression to an analogous belief. In admitting that uncompromising empiricism is untenable because general propositions cannot be inferred from any finite number of observations (cf. Peirce's suggested solution to this problem p. 81), he reflects on the stances philosophers take when faced with this problem:

> Some hold that truth does not consist in conformity with fact, but only in coherence with other propositions already accepted for some undefined reason. Others, like Reichenbach, favor a posit which is a mere act of will and is admitted to be not intellectually justified. Yet others make attempts — to my mind futile — to dispense with general propositions. For my part, I assume that science is broadly speaking true, and arrive at the necessary postulates by analysis. But against the thoroughgoing skeptic I can advance no argument except that I do not believe him to be sincere. (Russell 1956: 381-382)

According to Habermas, and to the point of view put forward here, the insincerity of the skeptic may, among other things, express itself in an inconsistency between his explicit denial and implicit acceptance of the validity claims of universal pragmatics. This inconsistency may be revealed by the fact that skeptics in dialogue and action behave according to presuppositions that they refuse to recognize. Also, skeptics catch flights.

There is, however, a way to counter this accusation of inconsistency, namely by pointing out that such presuppositions work when they work, but that they have no universal binding force. To put it in a less circular manner, as long as people agree on what is comprehensible, true, truthful, and right, communication directed towards understanding may function unimpeded and make communal action possible.

What we have in this case, the skeptic might point out, is a factual agreement about a set of beliefs, and nobody will deny that people within a community have many beliefs in common. Furthermore, both parties in a dialogue can claim to comply with these claims and at the same time disagree as to the truth or rightness of a given utterance.

In this case, according to Habermas, the parties have to leave the level of communicative action and shift to the level of discourse, i.e., the level on which the rational discussion of these claims takes place. Whereas communicative action is located within the constraints of social interaction in general (e.g., a pressure to find practical solutions to problems and to act within a certain span of time), discourse is characterized by what Habermas calls a virtualization of the constraints of action. One of the clearest statements of what he understands by discourse is given in the book *Legimation Crisis* within the context of a discussion of ethics:

> Discourse can be defined as that form of communication which is liberated from experience and relieved from the pressure to act. By its structure it is guaranteed that only virtualized validity claims for assertions or recommendations and warnings are discussed. It is further guaranteed that there will be no restrictions as to participants, subjects, and contributions except maybe with regard to the examination of problematized validity claims, that no force except that of the better argument is exercised, and that, as a result, all motives except that of the cooperative search for truth are excluded. If under these conditions a consensus about the recommendation to accept a norm arises argumentatively, that is, on the basis of hypothetically proposed, alternative justifications, then this consensus expresses a "rational will." Since all those affected have, in principle, at least the chance to participate in the practical deliberation, the "rationality" of the discursively formed will consists in the fact that the reciprocal behavioral expectations raised to normative status afford validity to a common interest ascertained without deception. The interest is common because the constraint-free consensus permits only what all can want; it is free of deception because even the interpretations of needs in which each individual must be able to recognize what he wants become the object of discursive will-formation. The discursively formed will may be called "rational" because the formal properties of discourse and of the deliberative situation sufficiently guarantee that a consensus can arise only through appropriately interpreted, generalizable interests, by which I mean needs that can be communicatively shared. (Habermas 1975: 107-108)

This long quotation contains the most important elements of Habermas' concept of discourse and at the same time a synopsis of his early ideas of communicative ethics. Whereas the ideal speech situation is unavoidable supposition in communicative action, it is so to speak thematicized on the level of discourse. In addition to *practical discourse* which examines claims to rightness, Habermas mentions *theoretical discourse* which examines claims to truth.

This is not the place to go into the flourishing debate about the possibility of reaching a rational consensus on the level of theoretical and practical discourse, i.e., an agreement about universally acceptable criteria of truth and rightness, especially since, at the moment, Habermas' position seems to hinge on a distinction between *norms,* which can be rationally discussed, and *values,* which are culturally grounded, and consequently may not be universalized.

Values, Habermas says, are candidates for being embodied in norms, but people seem unable to take up a hypothetical attitude towards values that form a part of their own identity. Furthermore, it is of no small interest that Habermas claims that the ethical discourse of norms gets its material from the "softer" discourses of esthetics and therapy (cf. Habermas 1983: 113-119).

The uncertainty as to the range of the area to which cognitivistic ethics apply need not, however, invalidate the necessity of presupposing the four validity claims in order to participate in the discussion on the level of discourse. Even a skeptic, in arguing on the level of discourse, implicitly recognizes the force of the better argument, because participating means an attempt to redeem the stated position through argumentation. A proponent and opponent are obliged to formulate their points of view in a non-contradictory way both on the level of propositional content and on the level of illocution. On the latter level what must be avoided is the so-called *performative contradiction* which takes the form of an inconsistency between the act of uttering and the content of the utterance (such as for instance *I do not exist here and now*).

The objective of Apel and Habermas is to show the relevance of the minimal logic necessarily presupposed in rational discourse, and particularly to ethics in an attempt to counter ethical skepticism. Whether their attempts will finally prove successful is at present hard to tell, especially because what will count as a "success" not only depends on the soundness of the argument, but also on what one expects a theory of ethics to do. Is a formal and procedural ethics satisfactory, or should a cognitivistic theory of ethics contain general principles on the basis of which it is possible to evaluate cultural values?

## 4. Semiotics and universal pragmatics

The relevance of the four validity claims of speech (in linguistic communication directed towards understanding), and the distinction between the level of communicative action and discourse for a semiotic theory of text interpretation is obvious. One all-important reason, as Habermas points out, is that this mode of speech may be considered as original, in the sense of having logical priority, and so other modes of speech are dependent on it (Habermas 1981: I. 388-389). A lie is only successful if the other party is in fact deceived, i.e., recognizing the utterance as a truthfully uttered belief. Irony works only if it is recognized that the utterance expresses conflicting attitudes that might be unambiguously stated in separate utterances. Many jokes are dependent for their effect on the tacit understanding between speaker and hearer that the obligations to which a speaker normally is committed are suspended. These examples all point to the privileged position of speech directed towards understanding within linguistic communication. Methodologically the validity claims function as principles of interpretation. Even if these claims are in fact violated or suspended in innumerable cases, interpretations of linguistic utterances must necessarily take them into account (explicitly or implicitly) and inquire into the relations of a concrete utterance to these claims, because they are decisive for the pragmatico-semantic dimension of speech, and consequently for meaning analysis.

The methodological necessity of inquiring into the compliance or non-compliance of linguistic utterances with these claims is based on the fundamental function of speech in society and in relation to the individual. Habermas summarizes the nature and function of speech as follows:

> Language can be conceived as the medium of interrelating three worlds; for every successful communicative action there exists a threefold relation between the utterance and (a) "the external world" as the totality of existing states of affairs, (b) "our social world" as the totality of all normatively regulated interpersonal relations that count as legitimate in a given society, and (c) "a particular inner world" (of the speaker) as the totality of his intentional experiences.

We can examine every utterance to see whether it is true or untrue, justified or unjustified, truthful or untruthful, because in speech, no matter what the emphasis, grammatical sentences are embedded in relations to reality in such a way that in an acceptable speech action segments of external nature, society, and internal nature always come into appearance together. Language itself also appears in speech, for speech is a medium in which the linguistic means that are employed instrumentally are also reflected. In speech, speech sets itself off from the regions of external nature, society, and internal nature, as a reality sui generis, as soon as the sign-substrate, meaning, and denotation of a linguistic utterance can be distinguished. (Habermas 1979: 67-68)

In conclusion to this part of the study, let us compare Habermas' definition of speech with the model of dialogical semiosis worked out on the basis of Peirce's theory of signs and let us map the validity claims on the model itself.

The four realms, worlds, or domains (as Habermas calls them) are represented in the semiotic pyramid by the vertices at the bottom and the relations between them and by their relation to the sign. One important difference should be noted. Habermas distinguishes three (or four) worlds, "the" external, "our" social, and the "inner" worlds (and language itself). On the semiotic pyramid, however, the object pole must not be identified with the reference of speech to outer reality, even if this is indeed often the case. The object pole is a position within the semiosis that may be occupied by whatever the sign or text identifies, within some universe of discourse, and posits it as the topic of speech. The distinction between immediate and dynamical object is, so to speak, designed to make the analysis of the signifying process applicable to ontologically different universes (although the perceptual, experiential, and social universe of the interpreter necessarily is the point of departure). In the utterance "Beware of the pink elephants!" uttered by a person suffering from delirium tremens, the object of speech is these pink elephants, even if they exist only in the hallucinatory universe caused by his intoxication. To such an utterance we do, however, apply the validity claims, because we may judge it to be a truthfully uttered statement about a state of affairs experienced in the imaginary universe of the utterer, or on evidence from the context, we may conclude that he is trying to fool us, that the elephants do not exist with hallucinatory force in his imagination.

The specification of the dialogical model of semiosis to represent linguistic communication directed toward understanding would yield the following diagram (Fig. 58).

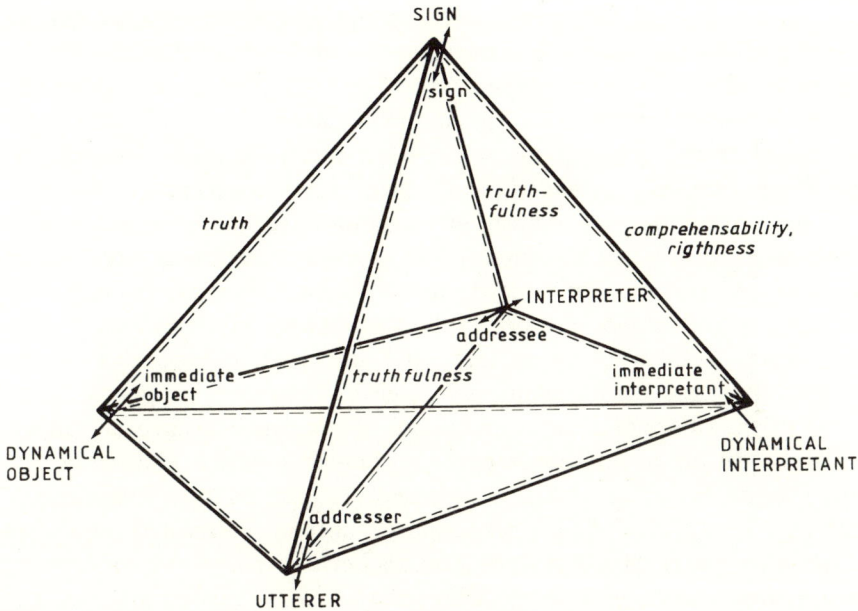

SIGN

sign

truth-
fulness

truth

comprehensability,
rigthness

INTERPRETER

addressee

immediate
object

truthfulness

immediate
interpretant

DYNAMICAL
OBJECT

DYNAMICAL
INTERPRETANT

addresser

UTTERER

Fig. 58

The claim to truth concerns the relationship between the immediate object indicated by the sign and the (supposedly existent) dynamical object. If an accordance between the two objects are established through further inquiry (further semioses), then this claim will be redeemed.

Being a model of dialogue, the claim to truthfulness concerns both parties, both because they are supposed to take turns, and because the truthfulness of the other is presupposed in the intention of the utterer (otherwise the utterer would switch to strategic action). At each pole this claim concerns the relationship between the representation of the subject within the semiosis and the utterer's status as its producer or receiver. If accordance exists between the intrinsic and extrinsic aspects of the parties, then the claim to truthfulness is redeemed.

Both the claim to comprehensibility and the claim to rightness concern the interpretant pole of the semiosis. This is not surprising because in different ways both cases concern normativity. For a linguistic utterance to be comprehensible means that the immediate interpretant, indicated by the sign, can be translated into a dynamical interpretant. This is only possible if the sign is generated according to the rules of the semiotic in question, or if a violation of these rules are accompanied by co- or contextual specifications that make up for the "non-grammaticality" of the sign. As in the cases of the claims to truth and truthfulness, a comparison between intrinsic and extrinsic aspects of the semiosis is needed, and in this case the utterance is judged as to its accordance with linguistic competence. Judging the rightfulness of an utterance also means comparing it to norms extrinsic to it. If the utterance is in accordance with such norms, its claim to rightness is redeemed. I have placed questions of rightness at the interpretant pole of the semiosis, and not with the parties of the dialogue, because such norms are social. They are supposed to be shared by members of a community and to govern their interaction.

The addition of the universal pragmatic validity claims to the dialogical model of semiosis is rather a revelation and precision of what is already implicitly presupposed (and in Peirce's thought we find *in nuce* much of what Apel and Habermas point out concerning the presuppositions of speech). Nevertheless, the contribution of the pragmatic philosophy of language and communicative and social interaction to the semiotics of text and speech is invaluable, regardless of whether one finds that its argument is sound and its program feasible. The value of this approach is due to the basic questions it raises concerning the preconditions of the understandability of speech and of text meaning. By positing an ideal speech situation and showing its double status as simultaneously extrinsic and intrinsic to actual speech and text production, we are given a methodological tool by virtue of which we may be able to analyze actual communication and different types of discourse.

According to the preceding the dialogic semiosis of human speech does not necessitate, indeed does not even favor, a skeptical and nihilistic attitude towards the possibility of reaching understanding, and validly fixing beliefs. The difference and possible conflicts between the internal and external aspects of semiosis offer multiple ways of misunderstanding and manipulation. This fact is simply beyond dispute. These splits, however, are also preconditions for the advancement of knowledge. A semiotic in no way capable of processing an input from the outside would not augment our knowledge of the environment and ourselves.

In the very purposiveness and function of speech, however, it is reasonable to presuppose the operative force of the validity claims pointed out by universal pragmatics. Concerning this question, the testimony of classical rhetoric is precious, because of its complexity. On the one hand, rhetoric may certainly be seen as an art instrumental in making strategic action, manipulation through persuasion, successful. On the other, it pays tribute to communication directed towards understanding by presupposing its principles and putting them to use. It is not by accident that Aristotle, Cicero, and Quintilian all stress that the orator should be concerned with the well being of his audience and attempt to make them understand the nature and the moral issues of the case. Quintilian goes so far as to claim that an orator should be, and even *must* be, a good man:

> The orator then, whom I am concerned to form, shall be the orator as defined by Marcus Cato, "a good man, skilled in speaking." But above all he must possess the quality which Cato places first and which is in the very nature of things the greatest and most important, that is, he must be a good man. This is essential not merely on account of the fact that, if the powers of eloquence serve only to lend arms to crime, there can be nothing more pernicious than eloquence to public and private welfare alike ...
>
> But this conviction of mine goes further. For I do not merely assert that the ideal orator should be a good man, but I affirm that no man can be an orator unless he is a good man. For it is impossible to regard those men as gifted with intelligence who on being offered the choice between the two paths of virtue and of vice choose the latter, nor can we allow them prudence, when by the unforeseen issue of their own actions they render themselves liable not merely to the heaviest penalties of the laws, but to the inevitable torment of an evil conscience. (*Institutio Oratoria*, Book XII, 1-3, Loeb 1922: IV, 355-357)

In other words, it is only by the trustworthy attempt to establish, or by simulating, the speech directed towards understanding that rhetoric achieves its objectives.

The fundamental distinction between attempted realization and simulation strongly indicates that speech, like other semiotics, e.g., animal communication systems, is adapted to serve purposes of survival and cooperation, because the systematic flouting of its presuppositions (as they are studied by semiotics speech act theory and universal pragmatics) endangers the survival of society. The possibility of exploiting them for other purposes by simulation, however, clearly shows that, because these sign processes are produced and used by human agents, and to a large extent controlled by them, speech's adaption to cooperation may easily be misdirected. Consequently, it is "up to us," as Peirce says, to make speech serve the attempt to realize understanding. Peirce defined the *summum bonum* as the effort to make the universe more rational (cf. pp. 194-195), and he found that logic was rooted in the *social principle.* However, one need not necessarily agree with Peirce's definition of the ultimate good to subscribe to his view that long term survival is possible only by sacrificing self-interest to the wider interests of community, and even to those of an unlimited community. In fact, according to Peirce, we have no choice:

> We are in the condition of a man in a life and death struggle; if he have not sufficient strength, it is wholly indifferent to him how he acts, so that the only assumption upon which he can act rationally is the hope of success. So this sentiment is rigidly demanded by logic. If its object were any determinate fact, any private interest, it might conflict with the results of knowledge and so with itself; but when its object is of a nature as wide as the community can turn out to be, it is always a hypothesis uncontradicted by facts and justified by its indispensableness for making any action rational. (5.357)

# PART III. LIGHT

# VIII. Light

The subject of this concluding part and chapter is light. It is not the light as a founding metaphor for beauty and truth in Platonism and Christianity so beautifully described by Gadamer (Gadamer 1960: 457 ff), nor the *lume naturale* of Galileo that Peirce often mentions and on which he comments as follows:

> Galileo appeals to *il lume naturale* at the most critical stages of his reasoning. Kepler, Gilbert, and Harvey — not to speak of Copernicus — substantially rely upon an inward power, not sufficient to reach the truth by itself, but yet supplying an essential factor to the influences carrying their minds to the truth.
>
> It is certain that the only hope of retroductive reasoning ever reaching the truth is that there may be some natural tendency toward an agreement between the ideas which suggest themselves to the human mind and those which are concerned in the laws of nature. (1.80-1.81)

The light I will analyze is much humbler, although eminently useful, indeed indispensable, in contemporary industrialized societies. It is the traffic light.

I may be accused of revealing a bent for the trivial, but if so, I share the inclination with many other semioticians, since articles and textbooks on semiotics abound in references to it, and since they sometimes even contain short analyses of the phenomenon. Normally, semioticians seem to regard it as so humble they mention it merely in passing; they do not stop to reflect on its elements, structures, and presuppositions. One notable exception is Louis Hjelmslev. Like Saussure, Hjelmslev was primarily a linguist, although he tried to found a general semiotics and to describe analytic procedures that should be valid for semiotic systems other than language. His own work and especially his concrete analyses, however, were almost exclusively linguistic. One of his few non-linguistic exemplifications of semiotic analysis is the traffic light (Hjelmslev 1973:119-153 [orig. 1947]).

## 1. The traffic light as a system: Hjelmslev's analysis

Hjelmslev explains the semiotician's attraction to the traffic light convincingly. In search of the fundamental characteristics and the basic structure of language, Hjelmslev says, it may be useful to widen the traditional field of research, and in addition to natural languages (or as Hjelmslev prefers to call them *unrestricted* or *pass-key languages*) to include *restricted languages*, i.e., languages that only serve specific purposes, whereas "an unrestricted or 'linguistic' language can be used to convey any possible meaning" (Hjelmslev 1973: 122). He goes on to state that among the restricted languages such as the traffic light,

> There will be languages of so simple a structure that the basic structure is, so to speak, the only structure existent, so that this basic structure can easily be laid bare without the interference of any complications due to the superstructure found in more highly developed languages. The basic structure detected in this way seems so fundamental that we can hardly conceive anything which would deserve the name of language and which is not based on this structure. (Hjelmslev 1973: 123)

While the first part of this study describes glossematics and Hjelmslev's understanding of semiotics in greater detail, it would be useful, here, to quote Hjelmslev's own summary of his position four years after the completion of *Prolegomena* in an address to an audience unfamiliar with his theory. The four fundamental features are these:

1) It has two sides (or planes), an *expression side* and a *content side* that together make up the sign function but which have to be analyzed seperately.
2) It is possible to distinguish between a *succession* (or a *text*) and *system* (or *language*).
3) *Commutation*, i.e., the solidarity between *expression* and *content* in the sign function, means that a change of sign component on one side (expression or content) implies a change on the other side as well. Exceptions to this principle are the so-called *variants*.
4) *Relations, combinations* and *government*, within the succession (text) and within the system (language). According to Hjelmslev these relations between sign components (figurae) or signs can be specified as follows:

a) *Determination*, i.e., unilateral or one-sided government.
b) *Interdependence*, i.e., mutual government.
c) *Constellation*, i.e., combination without government.

This enumeration of the basic features of language concludes Hjelm-slev's lectures, and he has reached this conclusion inductively (at least as regards his presentation) by analyzing the traffic light, the clock chime, and the telephone dial, all restricted languages in his ter-minology. Consequently, let us follow his exemplification of these basic features by the traffic light. We will, however, feel free to add to and complete his analysis, although, at first, we remain within the bound-eries of classical structuralism.

The following diagram by Hjemslev (Fig. 59) presents some of the basic features of the traffic light.

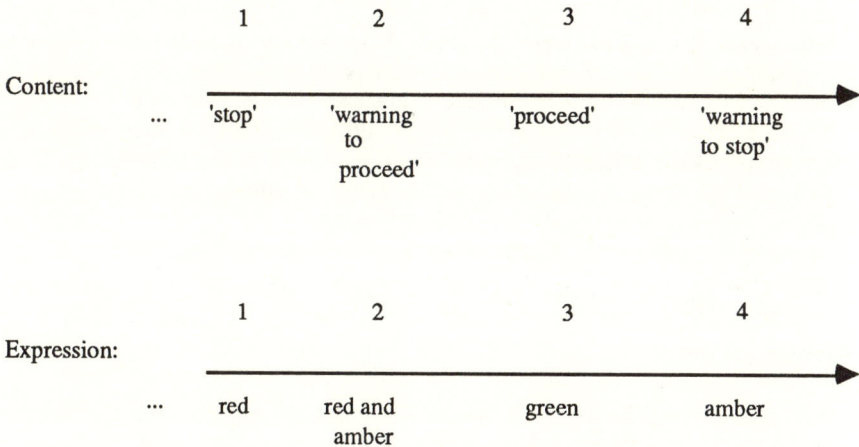

|          | 1      | 2                        | 3         | 4                    |
|----------|--------|--------------------------|-----------|----------------------|
| Content: |        |                          |           |                      →|
|   ...    | 'stop' | 'warning to proceed'     | 'proceed' | 'warning to stop'    |

|             | 1     | 2                | 3       | 4       |
|-------------|-------|------------------|---------|---------|
| Expression: |       |                  |         |        →|
|   ...       | red   | red and amber    | green   | amber   |

(Hjelmslev 1973: 132)

Fig. 59

The diagram, which shows the constantly repeated succession of the traffic light's signs, its *text*, illustrates some of the basic features of his concept of sign and structure. If we do not restrict ourselves to Hjelm-slev's analysis and terminology, we may distinguish between the level of sign components conceived as an inventory and the level of signs. On the expression plane there are two sets of minimal units: the distinction between the three colors, *red, amber,* and *green;* and a positional distinction between *upper, middle,* and *lower.* These two inventories are invariably correlated as follows: *red: upper, amber: middle,* and *green: lower.* Eco's distinction between s-code (or code as system, cf. Eco 1976: 38) and code proper defines the sequence of the different states of the expression plane (as depicted in Hjelmslev's diagram) as the coupling of two s-codes. The criterion for regarding the sequence as coded is that a finite inventory of elements form a sequence governed by a combination rule (syntax).

According to Hjelmslev the traffic light satisfies (already on this level) the fourth basic feature of language, *the existence of definite relations* between linguistic units (Hjelmslev 1973: 149). Hjelmslev explicitly mentions the traffic light, saying:

> The proper characteristic of a succession, and consequently, of a text, is that it is submitted to a general rule of positional order: it consists of units whose components are arranged in a definite way so as to take up definite positions. This positional order is nearly always essential, so that any change in it would have the effect of disturbing or changing the fundamental idea. Thus the colours of the traffic lights *must* follow each other in the order indicated: red, red and amber, green, amber, and any change in this order would mean a fundamental distortion. (Hjelmslev 1973: 128)

Another fundamental distinction is also exemplified by the diagram: the distinction (and correlation) between *expression* and *something expressed,* i.e., *content.* Hjelmslev states the importance of this distinction as follows:

> For purely logical reasons it seems obvious that any conceivable language involves two things: an expression, and something expressed. There simply cannot be an expression without something expressed, and there cannot be something expressed without an expression. These two things taken together are fundamental to all languages. (Hjelmslev 1973: 126)

Whereas the sign components (at least according to Hjelmslev) can be analyzed seperately, the sign is by definition a correlation between an expression s-code and a semantic s-code. Hjelmslev's analysis of the content plane of the traffic light consists in a partition into a binary opposition, *stop* vs. *proceed,* and a positional modifier, *warning to* whose completion is determined by the succeeding content element. The semantic code (as explained by Hjelmslev) can be depicted in a kind of Greimasian model as shown in Fig. 60.

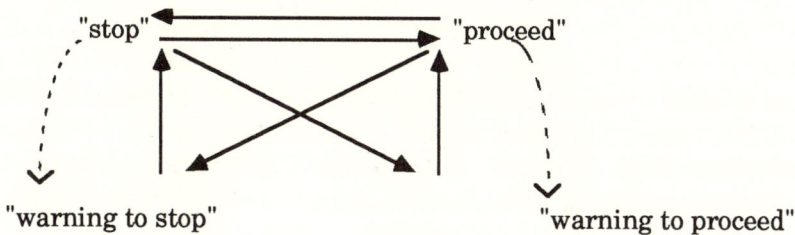

Fig. 60

Although Hjelmslev's analysis of the content plane seems convincing, it is not quite in accordance with the Danish Road Traffic Act, but this point will have to be discussed at the sign level.

Hjelmslev says nothing about the expression s-code presumably because of his general unwillingness to analyze substance (whether of expression or of content). This code, however, deserves a few comments.

Since the traffic light is a conventional and institutionalized sign system, the expression s-code is the outcome of a deliberate decision. Historically, the first traffic light (placed on the corner of Bridge Street and Palace Yard in London, 1868) had only two expression units, *red* and *green*. These two colors are complementary, and easily distinguishable to normal sight (cf. below). The main reason for the color choice, however, is probably their already existing semantization, *red* connoting *blood* and *danger* while *green* connotes *nature* and *hope*. The intermediate expression unit, amber, was introduced fifty years later (in New York City, 1918). *Amber* (or *yellow*) is situated in the spectrum between *red* and *green*, and it is the only spectral color that cannot be mistaken for either of the others.

The one serious drawback of *red* and *green* is that color-blind people will experience difficulties in distinguishing them. The red-blind will experience *red* more or less as *black*, whereas the green-blind will experience *green* as *gray* and *red* as *olive*. The fact that between 6% and 8% of all males suffer from some sort of colorblindness could have damaged the efficiency of the expression s-code. This draw-back is remedied by the copresence of the other expression s-code, the positional one, in which not a specific color, but the presence or ab-sence of light is decisive.

The interchangeability of the two expression s-codes is a strong argument in favor of the structuralist (and glossematic) claim that the sign components of language or other semiotic systems has to be con-ceived formally and analyzed differentially, relatively, and negatively. The differences manifested by *red, amber,* and *green,* and by the cor-relative positional sequence *upper, middle,* and *lower,* could (at least from a formal point of view) just as well be manifested by numbers or letters, for instance by the numbers 1, 2, and 3 and a negation mark (Fig. 61).

| | | | |
|---|---|---|---|
| red: | 1 | $\overline{2}$ | $\overline{3}$ |
| amber: | $\overline{1}$ | 2 | $\overline{3}$ |
| green: | $\overline{1}$ | $\overline{2}$ | 3 |
| red + amber: | 1 | 2 | $\overline{3}$ |

Fig. 61

From the point of view of the expression plane certain possible com-binations will arbitrarily be excluded, not allowed by the code (Fig. 62):

| | | | |
|---|---|---|---|
| red + amber + green: | 1 | 2 | 3 |
| neither red nor amber nor green: | $\overline{1}$ | $\overline{2}$ | $\overline{3}$ |
| red + green: | 1 | $\overline{2}$ | 3 |
| amber + green: | $\overline{1}$ | 2 | $\overline{3}$ |

Fig. 62

The reason why the content s-code disallows these combinations will become apparent the moment the traffic light is analyzed as sign system (Fig. 63).

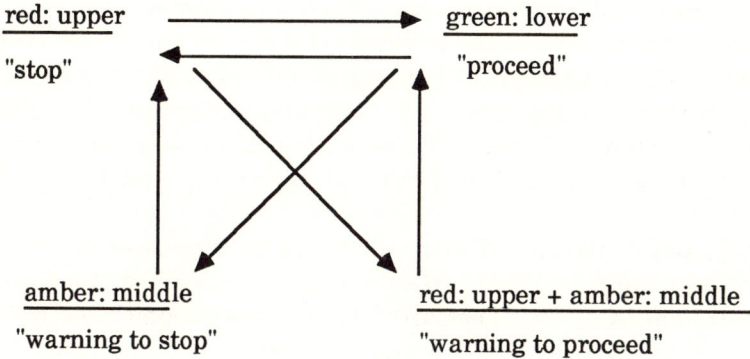

Fig. 63

In this diagram the double coding of the expression plane is marked.

The diagram exhibits all four features that, according to Hjelmslev, are basic to language or other sign systems. In addition to the distinction between succession (text) and system (language) and to the relations (positional order) mentioned earlier, it demonstrates the distinction between expression and content and their being tied together in the sign function. This correlation between expression and content is, so to speak, proven by the *commutation* that obviously is operative in the traffic light: if the expression changes from *green* to *amber,* then the content changes from "proceed" to "warning to stop." Even the concept of *variant* is, according to Hjelmslev, exemplified by the traffic light. He says:

> Within one and the same paradigm, units which are not mutually commutable may be called *variants.* In principle, we shall have to recognize a positional variant for each position; in the traffic lights, *amber* in *red and amber* with preceding *red* and subsequent *green* is not in all respects the same *amber* as the one which is preceded by *green* and followed by *red;* in one respect, however, the two instances of *amber* are identical: they have no mutual commutation. They are positional variants of one and the same commutable. Further, we shall have to state in principle a free variant for each occurence in one and the same position; the *amber* which is present in this moment in position no. 2 is not in all respects necessarily the same *amber* as the one which was in the same position some minutes ago. But the two ambers have no mutual commutation. They are free variants of one and the same commutable. (Hjelmslev 1973: 146)

Hjelmslev's analysis of the traffic light is successful in laying bare the
basic features and structural principles of this semiotic system, and in
bringing forth its value as an example of a simple, *restricted*, language
structure. His description of the traffic light is, however, deficient in
certain, highly important, respects. It leaves out preconditions necessary for the function of the traffic light, and it rests on presuppositions
that not only are not analyzed but also explicitly dismissed as irrelevant.

Hjelmslev's deficient description is by no means accidental; it is
inextricably bound up with the way glossematics (and continental
structuralism in general) constitutes its research object and with its
concept of its objective, an objective defined by Hjelmslev as follows:
"One of the main tasks of science must be that of finding a standpoint
from which things look less complicated. A scientific approach means
an approach towards simplification" (Hjelmslev 1973: 120). According
to Hjelmslev, this general principle applied to the study of language
ought to result in concentrating on its formal, or structural, aspects:

> My endeavour will be to make you look upon language as a structure, to
> help you to unravel the fundamental framework which underlies the be-
> wildering multiplicity of language, and to make you understand the various
> aspects of language with the help of a few general principles of great
> simplicity. If I succeed to some extent, I shall feel happy to know that I
> have been overestimating the difference between ease and simplicity.
> (Hjelmslev 1973: 121)

This concentration means that he neglects certain aspects of language
(in a broad sense), namely the question of meaning and speech considered as an event. Hjelmslev faces a kind of dilemma, since his
reason for including the traffic light, the clock chime, and the telephone dial operates within a wider concept of language. He says:

> The first fact we shall consider is the most striking one. It is obvious that
> these structures, just like ordinary language, convey what we are accus-
> tomed to call "meanings." This, no doubt, is the capital fact which induces
> us to call them languages. They are, as it were, made up of signs or
> symbols, and their function is that of expressing something. We might even
> go further and say that, in a sense, the traffic lights speak to the road users
> in words or in sentences, or even in imperatives, urging them to behave in
> certain ways. (Hjelmslev 1973: 124)

This quotation proves beyond doubt that expressing something, "meaning," is considered to be the "capital fact" that allows us to count the traffic light among the languages. Nevertheless, Hjelmslev puts the expression *meanings* within quotation marks. The reason for his reluctance to accept the concept of meaning wholeheartedly is that he does not want to commit himself to any of the theories of meaning that he mentions: the mentalistic and the behavioristic. He sketches this alternative as follows:

> we may roughly say that mentalists mostly emphasize the speaker and behaviourists the listener (or the reader) involved in the speech situation. To come back to our examples, mentalists will have it that behind the traffic lights, the telephone dialling and the clock chime there is a thought, a will, an idea, a conscience or the like, and that this is the "meaning," whereas behaviourists would hold that meaning is nothing but the constant relation between the utterance and the behaviour it evokes; in our examples, the meaning of the traffic lights would be the conduct of the road users. . . . (Hjelmslev 1973: 125)

Consequently, Hjelmslev prefers the term "content" to   the   term "meaning," using the following argument:

> Since we are not sure that a meaning is necessarily involved, whether in the mentalistic or in the behaviourist sense, I shall not make use of the term "meaning" to denote the something which is expressed. I shall call it the *content*, a term which is designed to be perfectly non-committal, thus reserving for later discussion the problem of meaning proper. (Hjelmslev 1973: 126)

At first glance this maneuver sounds unconvincing. A mere change of name does not solve the question. From Hjelmslev's other writings, e.g., from *Prolegomena*, we know, however, that Hjelmslev does distinguish between "content" and "meaning" (see this study p. 36).

According to Hjelmslev, a text to be meaningful has to satisfy stricter criterea than just to possess a content. In English the following string of letters, *kvai dinqli litud dorug,* would be void of content, whereas we may wonder whether Chomsky's famous example, *colorless green dreams sleep furiously,* makes sense at all, although nobody would deny that it possesses a content.

*Meaning,* then, implies that a string of sounds or letters can be interpreted in such a way that, taken as a whole and provided it meets a certain, unspecified number of contextual requirments, is acceptable as an understandable utterance, a text. *Content* is ascribed to signs, i.e., to minimal units of signification, on the basis of the existing dictionary of a given language and its phonological, morphological, and syntactical structures. These definitions ought to be explained more fully, but for my immediate purpose, they have to suffice. The point here is that *meaning* and *content* are mutually dependent, because to say that a given expression has a content is a shorter way of stating that it can be placed as a significational unit in a meaningful text. Conversely, to declare a string of signs meaningful is to ascribe a content to the expression. Consequently, Hjelmslev's maneuver, talking of *content* and not of *meaning,* is unsatisfactory because there is no way to escape the question of meaning (cf. below).

Hjelmslev thinks that the problem of meaning, which he refuses to consider, is bound up with speaker and listener; therefore neither does he consider relevant the complete speech event, in which speaker and listener are included. He says:

> My point is that, whereas speaker and listener (reader) are relevant to the complete speech event, they are hardly relevant to every speech event, and they are not relevant to language structure. A speech event may be incomplete, in so far as speaker or listener (reader) or both may be missing. I may talk on the telephone or over the radio without anybody listening to me, and I may write a book without ever having any readers. . . .
>
> To turn to traffic lights again, these may go on and on indefinitely without anybody passing and without any human will or command behind them. . . .
>
> It may be well here to point out that from a logical point of view speech is a necessary condition of speaker and listener, whereas the reverse is not true. A speaker becomes a speaker, and a listener becomes a listener, only because of the speech,whereas the speech, as we have seen, may take place without any speaker or listener. (Hjelmslev 1973: 125-126).

Again a certain tension is apparent in Hjelmslev's text, because he has previously included the traffic light among languages, in a wider sense, because it expresses something. Indeed, in the last part of the passage (quoted above) he says: *"In a sense, the traffic lights speak to the road users in words or in sentences, or even in imperatives, urging them to behave in certain ways"* (Hjelmslev 1973: 124, italics mine).

It might be argued that Hjelmslev does not contradict himself, because he only claims that meaning, speaker, and listener are irrelevant to the study of language structure. The objection to this argument is that these three categories are necessarily involved as soon as the study of content is carried out. To use Hjelmslev's own example, how can we study imperatives without taking into account the relationship between speaker and listener and the illocutionary force with which the former try to influence the latter concerning a certain topic? Furthermore, one is tempted to accuse Hjelmslev of bad faith when he speaks about the traffic lights going on indefinitely "without any human will or command behind them." These two points, however, bring us back to the traffic light, and instead of discussing these matters on a general level, it might be more fruitful to argue about them concretely.

## 2. A pragmatic interpretation of the traffic light

In Hjelmslev's interpretation there is a certain dissymmetry, and a certain tension, between the traffic light's expression s-code and its semantic s-code. The Danish traffic light has no congruence, or merging, between component and sign, since on the expression plane three sign components exist, whereas there are four signs (the fourth sign "warning to proceed" being a combination of two components). Consequently, the traffic light is an excellent illustration of the necessity and usefulness of this distinction.

On the content plane Hjelmslev analyzed the two positional modifiers as "warning to — " plus either "proceed" or "stop," depending on the subsequent sign in the sequence. This view means the complete semantic system is built on a double dichotomy:

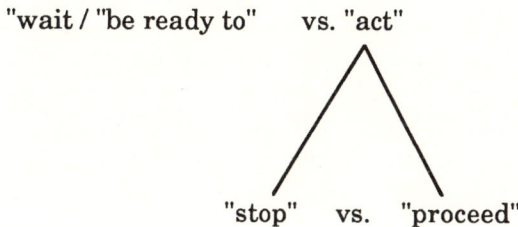

"wait / "be ready to"     vs. "act"

"stop"     vs.     "proceed"

Fig. 64

This double content dichotomy requires only three signs to be communicated, *amber*, *red*, and *green*, and the syntactic rule governing the succession, the text, would be even simpler than the Danish version of the traffic light, namely that red must never succeed green.

Another version, in which sign components and signs merge, is actually used in the United States. This version has no intermediary sign between *red* and *green*, and consists in the succession of three signs in the following order:

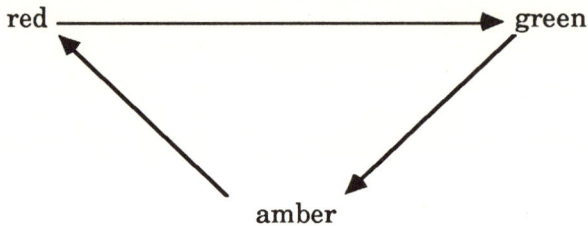

Fig. 65

As the traffic light (in Denmark) is designed to function, the two intermediate signs are, however, clearly differentiated, and what is more, Hjelmslev's interpretation of the intermediate sign between red and green, i.e., *red and amber*, is slightly but significantly at odds both with its literal and the legal interpretation. Hjelmslev correlates the sign components *red + amber* with the compound content "warning to proceed," anticipating the action of the road user as soon as the traffic light changes to green. Literally, however, this expression is correlated with the compound content "stop + be ready to. . . ." In other words, the expression signifying "proceed," namely *green,* is absent, while the expression signifying "stop," namely *red,* is present. To accuse Hjelmslev of a mentalistic reading of this sign seems fair. What he really does is to put himself in the ordinary, well-informed road user's place: Since I, the ordinary road user, know, by teaching and by experience, that this sign will be followed by *green*, I anticipate in thought my future action. I have no quarrel with this way of deciding the content of the sign. I will, however, firmly contest that it is a literal interpretation. As a matter of fact, if we look closer at the sequence on the expression plane, we have this:

|        | 1    | 2     | 3     | 4     |
|--------|------|-------|-------|-------|
| Upper  | red  | red   | –     | –     |
| Middle | –    | amber | –     | amber |
| Lower  | –    | –     | green | –     |

Fig. 66

This means the upper position, *red,* is constantly lit in both segment 1 and 2 and the transition from the former to the latter consists in the lighting of *amber.* Interpreted semantically, this means: *stop still in force, but be ready to . . .*

In contradistinction to Hjelmslev's interpretation, the determination of the intermediary unit of expression, *amber,* stems from the precedent and still valid unit, *red,* not from the subsequent, and absent, unit, *green.*

The legal, the only authorized, interpretation of the traffic light in Denmark can be found in a Goverment notice on road signs published as supplementary rules to the Danish Road Traffic Act. The paragraphs concerning the traffic light and the meaning of the four signs are interesting, because they differ from intuitive interpretations like Hjelmslev's and because of the complexity of the text.

The notice reads as follows (§ 55):

Red light means stop. The road users, other than pedestrians, must stop at the stop line or, where no stop line exists, within adequate distance from the intersection or road section. . . .

Red and amber lights together mean stop. On the whole they mean the same as red light. They also indicate, however, that the signal shortly will change to green. . . .

Green light means go. . . .

Amber light means stop. It indicates that the signal will shortly change to red, but otherwise it means the same as red. Road users, other than pedestrians, should not stop, however, if they, the moment the light changes from green to amber, have gone so far that stopping would cause danger. (Due, Christensen, et al. 1979: 855-856)

The interesting fact concerning the notice is the clearcut distinction between "meaning" and "indication," or between the imperative (normative) and the indicative aspects of the sign system. As regards their meaning, i.e., their normative purport, three of the four signs, *red, red + amber, amber,* are equivalent and opposed to the fourth, *green.* Furthermore, for these signs, *red* is the semantic point of reference, because it is defined as "stop" and *red + amber* and *amber* are said to be semantically equivalent to red. From the forensic point of view the basic opposition is the one between *red*: "stop" vs. *green*: "go," because as to normative purport *red + amber* and *amber* are positional variants of *red.* Concerning what could be called the *indicative import* of the sign system no differentiation exists between it and the *normative purport* in the basic opposition (*red* vs. *green*), whereas the two intermediary signs are clearly differentiated. According to the authorized interpretation the sign system can be depicted in the following diagram:

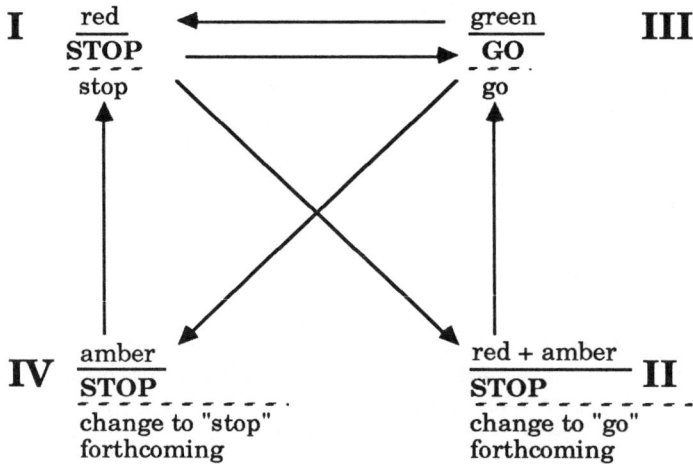

Fig. 67

Position IV (normative purport: **STOP**, indicate import: change to "stop" forthcoming) may seem pleonastic, but only as long as functional and pragmatic considerations are unconsidered. In fact, the notice itself mentions a case in which a vehicle has to continue in order to avoid danger.

The above calls attention to the rather unsurprising fact that the traffic light is a system designed to transmit behavioral imperatives according to preestablished rules for traffic regulation. Unsurprising or not, it links together three different, in this case, interdependent codes: the actual expression s-codes of traffic light, its linguistic interpretation as laid down in the Government notice, and the actual behavior of the road users. This is why it has been, strictly speaking, an inadmissable simplification to employ the dyadic sign concept (and models) of glossematics and structuralism, because this concept, by only distinguishing between expression and content, does not account for the referential and communicative function of the sign system.

It is, however, an indisputable fact that the very *raison d'être* of the traffic light is to invoke a certain behavioral pattern in road users. In the traditional triadic concept of the sign a distinction is made between signification and denotation (or referent). Applied to the traffic light this would mean that the signification of *green,* for instance, would be the meaning that in language is expressed by "go" and its denotation would be the action "to go," i.e., a set of behavioral patterns, such as setting the vehicle in motion or continuing to drive it, to the effect of crossing the intersection. Since the sign is imperative, a command to act in a certain way, it is obviously not referring to an object, and not even, *sensu strictu*, to a state of affairs; rather, it is bringing about a state of affairs, provided the road users obey it. The traffic light, then, is imperative in the sense that it prescribes the proper action. An argument in favor of interpreting the signs of the traffic light as prescribing certain actions is that a person violating the prescription, e.g., by crossing on *red,* is liable to be prosecuted by law.

Peirce's concept of semiosis better accounts for the meaning and function of sign systems such as the traffic light.

According to Peirce, any given sign in the traffic light's text (its succession) should be interpreted as an irreducible triadic action that can be diagrammatically presented as shown in Fig. 68.

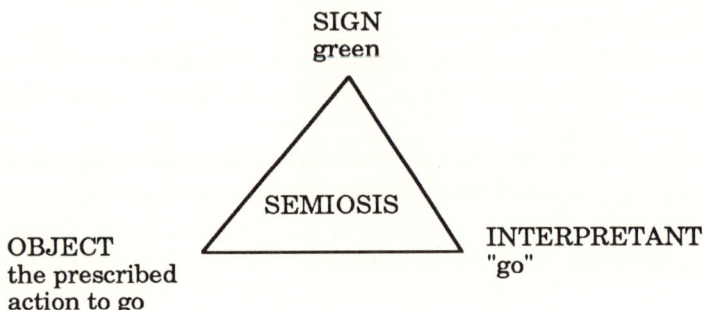

SIGN
green

SEMIOSIS

OBJECT                                      INTERPRETANT
the prescribed                              "go"
action to go

Fig. 68

Peirce considers the semiosis to be triadic because the equivalence between interpreted and interpreting sign (sign and interpretant) is referential in the sense that they are signs of the same object. Considered from this point of view, the object determines the relationship between sign and interpretant. In conventional sign systems, however, the interaction of the three poles of the semiosis is, in fact, reciprocal, because one could as well look upon the sign as linking together object and interpretant, or see the interpretant as the mediating element uniting sign and object.

In the diagram the interpretant is a linguistic translation of the sign green. This means that the interpretant of a sign is another sign. Peirce calls such an interpretant a "logical interpretant." As we know from chapter IV, however, he distinguishes between three different interpretants, the "emotional," the "energetic," and the "logical," saying they "consist respectively in feelings, in efforts, and in habit-changes" (Ms. 318, 1907: 35).

For a road user facing a traffic light the proper interpretant would certainly be energetic, namely the act of stopping or going. In order for the road user to respond to the sign with the proper action, however, it is necessary that he knows the signification of the signs. In other words he should (in Eco's terminology) acquire the habit of relating an expression s-code, a semantic s-code, and a behavioral s-code to each other, or as Peirce would say, to relate sign, object, and interpretant. Thus the energetic interpretation of green could be considered as a procedure involving two steps, shown in Fig. 69.

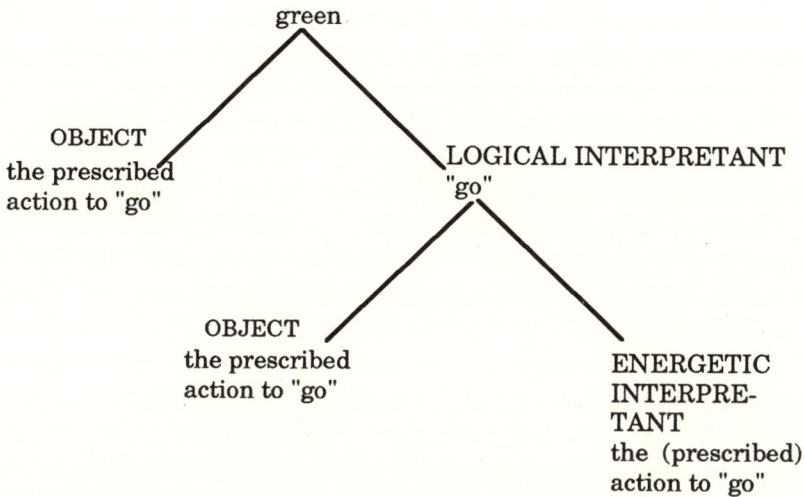

green

OBJECT
the prescribed
action to "go"

LOGICAL INTERPRETANT
"go"

OBJECT
the prescribed
action to "go"

ENERGETIC
INTERPRE-
TANT
the (prescribed)
action to "go"

Fig. 69

There are several reasons for presenting the semiosis in this way. Some road user may, for instance, disregard the sign even if he is able to interpret it correctly (cf. below). The main reason, however, is that in the second step of the semiosis this presentation illustrates the equivalence between object and interpretant. The object of *green* is a command to go and the energetic interpretant is the actual going; consequently, the energetic interpretant is a realization of the object, the object being the normative purport that a given state of affairs should occur.

By defining the object of the traffic light's signs as an intention, or command, that certain actions will occur, the communicative aspect of this kind of semiosis is already implied. But who are communicating? The addressee of the traffic light is obviously the road user, and the addresser the lawful authorities. I accused Hjelmslev of bad faith, because he talked about traffic lights going on forever without any human consciousness or will behind them. I find it hard to believe he was unaware that placing a traffic light at an intersection is a deliberate action that rests on an official procedure.

In Denmark, for instance, the authorities use certain criteria to decide whether to put up a traffic light. The two main criteria are safety and the assurance of an adequate flow of traffic. A notice from the Danish Road Administration announces that if an intersection is passed in any direction by 750 cars per hour (as a mean) for eight hours per day, and if at least 175 cars pass per hour on the less frequented road, then there should be a traffic light.

The figures cited here may only interest highway engineers and the traffic police, but the general point, that traffic lights owe their existence to deliberation and conscious action, concerns us as semioticians. Hjelmslev's concepts of *consciousness* and *will* are simply too narrow, because he relates them to the idea of an individual person. A law or a notice, however, expresses the intentions of an institution regardless of any of its individual officials. It seldom can be related to an individual. A valid regulation need not have a specific human consciousness and will constantly occupied with it; on the contrary, until it is explicitly revoked, it is, at least in principle, still in force.

Suppose, for instance, that in some deserted village there is a traffic light still working at an intersection nobody has used for the last fifteen years. Suddenly two cars collide in the middle of the intersection, one car having crossed on green and the other on red. If this accident is taken to court, the driver who transgressed the red command would certainly be at fault, regardless of the claim that nobody used the roads for years. Only if society had invented some other way of regulating traffic would he be discharged. In that case, the notice concerning traffic lights would have been revoked.

Defining the addresser of the traffic light as the lawful authorities (a definition supported by the fact that [in Denmark] anybody else is explicitly forbidden to put them up on public roads), stresses the *institutionalized intertextuality* of this sign system. That there is the authorized interpretation of the traffic light as it is laid down in the Road Traffic Act and supplementary notices implies that it is part of a much wider system of traffic regulations involving different agencies, police, and courts. Here intertextuality should be taken in a strong sense, not as informal dialogue, allusions, or quotations going on between separate texts, but as a codified relation between a specific and limited sign system on the one hand and a wide network of related texts and institutions on the other. There are texts, for instance, that state that under certain circumstances the normative purport of the sign may be disregarded (cf. below).

I have said that the addressee of the traffic light is the road user. That is, however, too vague. If I am driving on the road and I see a traffic light ahead, it need not concern me at all if I turn right onto another road before the intersection. This points to the inextricable relationship between sign system, location, and direction, in short to the relationship between *text and context,* a relationship that is instrumental not only in ensuring the proper function of the traffic light but also indispensable for its very meaning. Suppose we were driving in the Sahara desert when suddenly, in the middle of nowhere, we encountered a traffic light. Since no roads exist in this part of the desert, we would simply be confused. We have learned the sign's meaning, but in a context that does not exist here.

The notice (but not Hjelmslev's analysis) says that "on red the road user must stop at the stop line or at an adequate distance from the intersection." In this way the validity of the sign is delimited. In his article "Traffic Signs" Franciszek Studnicki talks about the "deicticity of the TS system" and about what he calls "the section of validity," and he explains the importance of these concepts as follows:

> By the term "the section of validity of a certain sign" I mean the section of a road to which the information carried by that sign (R-sign) refers. . . .
> The peculiar property of the TS system, consisting in the fact that each of the signs: (a) carries information referring to a certain section of a road and, at the same time, (b) indicates by its geographical position the section of the road to which that information refers, I shall call "the deicticity of the TS system."
> The deicticity of the TS system is decisive for the occasionality of its utterances. By this I mean that the elementary as well as the compound utterances of that system can be regarded as utterances having fully defined meanings only when the geographical positions of the signs of which they are composed are taken into consideration. (Studnicki 1970: 155)

Studnicki's observation is absolutely essential to the understanding and analysis of the preconditions for the traffic light's ability to produce meaningful utterances. In fact, it is a sign system superimposed upon another system, the system of roads, that facilitates and regulates the traffic. The road system is itself governed by behavior rules of a general nature (e.g., the duty [at least in northern Europe] to give way to traffic entering from the right), rules that are modified precisely by the traffic light. Furthermore this context, the road system, has the same triple character as the traffic light itself. It is 1) a physical reality; 2) it has been designed and built to fulfill specific human communicative purposes (the transportation of people and commodities); and 3) this communication functions according to rules laid down to ensure that the traffic flows safely, smoothly, and swiftly (an ideal it has become increasingly harder to realize). In other words, the traffic light as a semiotic micro system is embedded in another system, and this latter system has a double impact upon the traffic light: 1) it functions as a wider and more general institutional code, or system of interpretants, that ensure the meaning of the restricted micro system; 2) it makes up the concrete physical context of the traffic light and especially a vectorization of the traffic without which the lights would lose their signification.

In addition to the indispensable context of the traffic light, it is important to realize that it is also a co-textual phenomenon, its very function and meaning dependent on the coded relation between two texts. For some reason or another semioticians tend to place themselves only in front of the light and read the succession of signs from this position. Normally, however, a traffic light has no front and back; it has four sides, and these sides are synchronized two and two. The road user only sees one side of the light, but *he acts on the assumption* that the sides facing the intersecting road communicate a different, contrary message. This idea indicates the essential spatio-temporal nature of the traffic light, and the necessary interplay between simultaneity and succession. Two texts, each one the co-text of the other, are simultaneously unfolded in time, and at the same time have a definite spatial relationship to each other. If we look at a traffic light from above, we can mark the two pairs of synchronized sides as A+A' vs. B+B' as shown in Fig. 70.

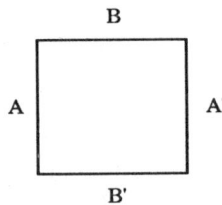

Fig. 70

The sequences of signs in the two texts can be presented as shown in Fig. 71.

|   | A+A' | vs. | B+B' |   |
|---|------|-----|------|---|
| 1 | red | | ..... | |
|   | | | green | 1 |
|   | | | amber | 2 |
| 2 | red + amber | | | |
|   | | | red | 3 |
| 3 | green | | | |
| 4 | amber | | | |
| 5 | red | | | |
|   | | | red + amber | 4 |
|   | | | green | 5 |
|   | | | amber | 6 |
| 6 | red + amber | | | |
|   | | | red | 7 |
|   | ..... | | ..... | |

Fig. 71

The two texts are displaced in proportion to each other to the effect that at one moment (in Denmark for at least two seconds) both pair of sides command "stop." The reason for this correlation is obviously to avoid collisions by clearing the intersection before each change of direction in the flow of traffic.

Before concluding, a few words should be added on three topics: text and context, i.e., the traffic light and the road system; interpretation; and the development of the traffic light.

The system of interconnected traffic lights regulating the flow of traffic in a big contemporary intersection may be very complicated, but there are four principal types of traffic lights (Fig. 72).

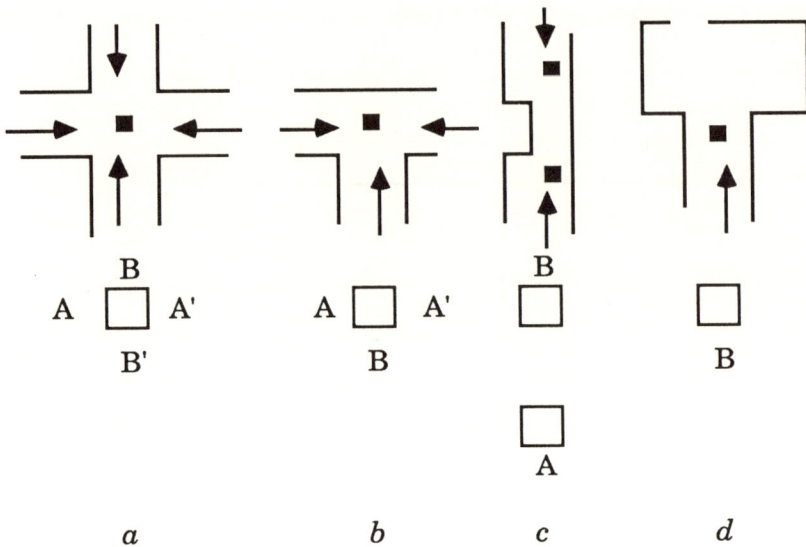

Fig. 72

In the preceding only *a* has been analyzed, because it represents the normal crossroad type of traffic light. The road user is here presented with one side of the light, but he acts on the presupposition that the four sides of the light are correlated as described above. The function of this type of light depends on the double interplay between presence and absence, in the light he actually sees between lighted: present vs. non-lighted: absent, and between the signs present in his field of perception and the signs he supposes to function in the fields of perception of his fellow road users, although he cannot see them himself. *b* is only a variation of *a* representing a simpler system of co-texts. *c*, which is used in some section if the road is contracted, is different from *a* and *b* in one essential respect: the two opposite sides that in *a* function as pairs here communicate contrary information. Indeed this is the whole point. *d* is not very much used, and often *amber* is left out. It regulates normally the inflow of traffic from a road into a delimited space, and often the outflow need not be regulated by a light.

The point in describing these different types of lights, is, however, that their differences are functions of their use in contexts. Given the fact that a traffic light in *a, b,* and *c* presupposes invisible co-texts, the very number of these co-texts and the relationship between them (cf. *c*) are determined by the context, the interrelations between the roads. Even *d,* where the visible text is the only one, depends for its function on the nature of the vectorized space on which it is imposing temporal regulations. Hjelmslev commits a serious simplification in isolating the minimal syntagma from considerations of its function and use in a context!

In describing these four different traffic lights I have, however, simplified matters myself, because the diagrams (Fig. 72) showing the direction of the flow of traffic are inaccurate. In a crossroad intersection the light confronting any driver will regulate not one but three possible directions:

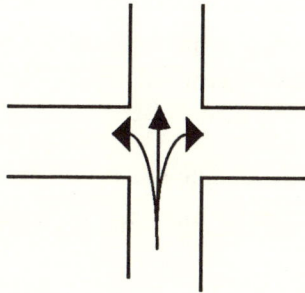

Fig. 73

"Green" means always that it is allowed, if safe, to cross or to turn right or left. "Red," however, is differently interpreted in different national road traffic acts. In Denmark it means a total stop for the traffic facing it, whereas in the United States a right turn is permitted, if it can be done safely (and is not specifically interdicted). This national difference illustrates once more the dependence of the system on the context, both the material context of the roads, and the existence of interpreting texts.

The traffic light may be unable to coordinate traffic by failing to emit reliable and meaningful signs for three principal reasons:

1) *Malajustment between context and semiotic system:*
    a) The context does not provide the necessary vectorization of the traffic flow for the light to emit sufficiently univocal signs (e.g., the traffic light in the desert).
    b) The context is too complex for the traffic flow to be regulated by a traffic light (maybe a traffic circle would solve the problem better).
    c) Inadequate adjustment between context and system (for instance, the angle between the traffic light and the intersecting roads is wrong and causes confusion concerning the section of validity of the different sides of the light).

2) *Maladjustment between text and co-text:*
    a) One pair of sides works, the other pair does not.
    b) The same message in simultaneously emitted by both pairs.
    c) The speed with which the signs change is not adjusted between the two pairs of sides.
    d) The synchronization of the two sides of one pair is defective.

3) *The coding of the text is defective:*
On p. 316 the following combinations were shown to be technically possible but uncoded:

| | | 1 | 2 | 3 |
|---|---|---|---|---|
| Case 1: | red + amber + green | 1 | 2 | 3 |
| Case 2: | neither red nor amber nor green | $\overline{1}$ | $\overline{2}$ | $\overline{3}$ |
| Case 3: | red + green | 1 | 2 | $\overline{3}$ |
| Case 4: | amber + green | $\overline{1}$ | 2 | 3 |

The appearance of any of the above listed combinations would damage the code and thereby destroy the coordinating power of the traffic light.

    Case 1 would carry too much and contradictory information, because it would simultaneously command "stop" and "go." Case 2 would carry no information at all, and consequently the road user could use only general traffic regulations. Case 3, cf. case 1. Case 4 is interesting because this sign would logically be possible, its meaning being "stop, change to green forthcoming." It is, however, unnecessary, because the meaning is already expressed by *red* + *amber,* and this sign fulfills the function better, because the prohibition to go is strongly expressed by the presence of *red.*

Violations of the traffic light's commands will, if detected, be punished by law. This fact shows the institutional enforcement of this kind of traffic regulation. Here, however, the interesting point is another question, namely whether the traffic light's signs allow some latitude of interpretation? With the exception of *amber,* the answer is "no." This answer may seem surprising considering that some road users are acquitted even if they have violated a *red* signal. It should be noted, however, that the meaning of the sign is never questioned, acquittals occur for others reasons, and they all have to do with the specific circumstances of the violation (the condition of the road, the behavior of the other road users, cases of emergency, etc.). Even *amber* has a limited latitude of interpretation because you are allowed to cross only if you are already in the intersection when the light changes from *green* to *amber.* Consequently, the alternative "stop" vs. "go" is decided then by position and velocity. This lack of interpretive latitude together with the legal enforcement of the rules ensures its general validity. Another way of ensuring validity is by teaching. All adult members of Danish society are not only supposed to know how to interpret the lights, they are obliged to know because they have learned it in school. Furthermore, to get a driver's license road users have to pass an examination about traffic regulations.

The development of the traffic light is characterized by *differentiation* and *adaption.* An example of differentiation is the use of separate lights for pedestrians, cyclists, and motorists. The adaption of the traffic lights to the flow of traffic is exemplified by using detectors, placed in the road surface, to govern the frequency of the change of signs according to the number of vehicles passing, whereas the usual traffic light is governed by a fixed program (or by three different ones, for morning, day, and night traffic).

## 3. Basic properties of an intentionally produced semiotic

The point in this attempt to give a reasonably full acount of a seemingly simple semiotic system like the traffic light is double: I have tried to show that this system is less simple than even semioticians generally suppose; and I think it is possible to generalize the results of this analysis, and thereby acquire a certain knowledge of the requirements of text semiotics in general.

Being a public sign system designed to ensure and coordinate the traffic, the traffic light is characterized by fifteen points:

1) *Purposiveness:*
Since the traffic light is especially designed to fulfill a function that is considered necessary and important, its purposiveness is self-evident. Any cultural semiotic should be analyzed with a view to its possible purposiveness, although its purpose is likely to be less explicit in most semiotic systems and also will probably serve multiple purposes (e.g., language).

2) *Utterer:*
The utterer is the agent, or agency, who in fact produces the sign, or text. In contradistinction to the addresser, he, or it, is the actual emitter of the message, whereas the addresser is a position within the semiosis. A Road Traffic Act, for instance, may be carried through parliament by a majority consisting of individual MPs who may be named and eventually, in some way or another, also be made responsible for the Act. The passing of the bill may have been preceded by a fierce debate, where a minority of MPs have fought against it with all their strength, disclaiming all responsibility for the Act. Finally the Act may be signed by an individual, e.g., a minister, who will be the final utterer making the proposed bill into a law. In doing so, he is, however, impersonating the will of the majority; and the addresser will be parliament which authorizes him to act.

In a certain sense both utterer and interpreter (cf. point 12) are external and accidental to the signifying process, because it is only by assuming the position of addresser and addressee that they become related to the semiosis, but on the other hand in their capacity as agents they are obviously realizing a process of signification which might never have taken place without them.

3) *Addresser:*
A given semiotic system, or a text, may have an explicit addresser responsible for its communicative function. The addresser may be col-

lective or individual, known or anonymous. The addresser of the traffic light is collective and known: the legal authorities, agencies, etc. It may very well be the case, however, that it makes little sense to attempt to identify an addresser in the traditional sense of the word, because the system in question is the work of tradition. If in some society a woman is wearing the traditional costume of the unmarried, she will only be an addresser in an attenuated sense. She will address others and communicate her status by wearing it; she will, however, not be the originator or producer of its signification.

### 4) *Communicative intent:*
The purposiveness of a semiotic system may, as in the case of the traffic light, be directly communicated in utterances (directed to people that fulfill the criteria of addressees), utterances that state the intentions of the addresser concerning a certain subject matter.

### 5) *Mode of the semiotic system or text:*
Concerning cultural semiotic systems, modality has to be considered in a rather broad sense, meaning the way it addresses the recipients. Even the traffic light has both an imperative and an indicative mode; and the more complex the system the more modes it will probably possess. The modality of the system will be decisive for the proper way of responding to it (cf. the imperative mode of the traffic light commanding a certain behavior).

### 6) *Elements and combination rules of the sign system:*
a) Has the system a double articulation (as, for instance, language), i.e., is there a distinction between sign components and signs? The Danish version of the traffic light has this distinction, whereas in the American system they merge.

b) What are the positive qualities of the signs (or sign components), and how are they differentiated from each other?

c) The system's syntax, i.e., its combination rules (cf. Hjelmslev's distinction between "determination," "solidarity," and "independence"). It should be noted that combination rules exist on different levels of complexity, dependent on the nature of the inventories they govern.

### 7) *Correlation between sign systems and interpreting sign systems, its immediate interpretants:*

The traffic light is characterized by a one to one correspondence between its expression s-code and a restricted inventory of utterances that function as the linguistic translation. Normally, semiotic systems are, however, less simple, both in cases when the interpreted system, or text, is non-verbal and when it is linguistic.

8) *Object and context of the sign system or text:*
The traffic light prescribes a certain behavior within a contextual space specified as the section of validity of its signs, pointed out by their deicticity. In general the context of a sign system cannot be disregarded. Its universe of discourse and/or action is not a phenomenon exterior to semiotics. On the contrary, it constitutes a part of the necessary presuppositional network that endows the signs with signification.

9) *Co-textual relations between sign systems, texts, and codes:*
Not only functionally, but as a precondition for its imperative purport and indicative import, the traffic light is dependent on the pairing of two contrary texts (both manifestations of the same system). Within semiotics the co-text should be understood as concurrent codes making up the text in a wider sense (for instance, costume, makeup, and style of hairdressing all signifying a certain status within society).

10) *Intertextuality of the semiotic system or text:*
The traffic light is primarily intertextually related to the Road Traffic Act and its supplementary notices. Generally the intertextual relations of a system or text have to be decided by extensive historical studies. There are two main problems, one of extent, or range, and one of specifying the exact place of the linkage between the systems, or texts, in question. As an example of the first problem, most Western literature from the Middle Ages until the close of the eighteenth century stands in an intertextual relationship to Christianity (e.g., to the Bible); yet, in each case the extent and significance of this relationship has to be assessed. Furthermore, the nature of intertextuality is truly Protean, and there is a big difference between a link through reference on the one hand and through the sharing of one or more codes on the other.

11) *Addressee:*
The traffic light's addressee is the road user within (or entering) its
section of validity. He is supposed and obliged to understand the system's signification correctly and to act according to its imperative
instructions. Generally, the addressee of a text is a position and role
pointed out and endowed with certain presupposed qualities by the
text itself (e.g., the ability to understand the text and the good sense to
agree with it). The addressee, then, is an element of the presuppositional network of the text in much the same way as the context (cf.
that the traffic light's addressee is somebody moving in a certain
direction within its contextual space).

12) *Interpreter*
Whereas the addressee is an internal and presupposed position in the
network on which the process of signification is founded, the interpreter is the concrete agent which confronts the sign or text. The position
of addressee may be looked on as a role offered, or prescribed, to the
interpreter who is the accidental, unpredictable, and in principle ungovernable agent who realizes the dynamical interpretant through his
response to the sign event; thereby – for the moment – bringing it to a
conclusion. In purposive, but non-intentional semiotics, such as for
instance the mating behavior of the Three-spined Stickleback (cf. III,
7), the agents are preprogrammed to act their roles, but individual
agents may, for some reason or another, fail to do so. If, however, on a
grand scale, the biological keys failed to fit their locks, the result
would be a Stickleback-free universe. If road users in general failed to
comply with the orders of command of the traffic light, the result
would be traffic chaos. However, since this micro-semiotic is the result
of deliberation and decision, and because its violation would also be
the outcome of deliberation and decision, a dialogue between the authorities (utterer, addresser) and the offenders (interpreters) might take
place, and eventually result in the creation of a new system.

This example points to the decisive role played by the interpreter
in intentionally produced semiotic systems. In his capacity as the
agent addressed by the sign, or text, and as its user, his response will
eventually influence the other element of the semiotics and signifying
process itself.

13) *Dynamical interpretant of a semiotic system or text:*
The usefulness of Peirce's distinction between immediate interpretant, more or less equivalent to the semantic s-code of a system or text, and the dynamical interpretant, i.e., the actual interpretation of it, becomes obvious the moment the code allows the interpreter to choose between several possibilities. That the traffic light allows only one choice, or shadow of choice, namely whether to stop or go for *amber,* illustrates this point, and the dynamical interpretant will be the road users' actual choice. This dynamical interpretant may, of course, be contested by the authorities. The dynamical interpretant is, however, not only a choice between the possibilities of the semantic s-code, or codes; it is rather an interpretation founded on the total network of the semiosis, taking addresser, reference, and addressee into account.

14) *Historicity of the semiotic system or text:*
Culturally designed semiotic systems such as the traffic light cannot be fully understood and make sense outside a wider historical context. Furthermore, changes within the system itself (such as the introduction of *amber* in 1918) are not explicable without taking into account the development of neighboring areas and systems (in our case the development of the size and the speed of traffic). Two kinds of historical developments seem to be of great importance to semiotic analysis:
     a) Technological development of the means of communication: This development is, of course, a part of the development of the means of production in general. In any case the possibilities offered by a given technology are, directly and indirectly, decisive for the development of sign systems, and even within the short history of the traffic light this is true. Of greater general interest is, however, the present development of information technology at large that results in a different mixing of semiotic systems (e.g., the impact of iconic systems through the mass media).
     b) The development of the institutions responsible for the production and diffusion of semiotic systems and texts and the interrelations of these institutions: Changes in the status and function of the institutions producing and maintaining semiotic systems influence the systems themselves. When, for instance, an institution that produces sets of differences and distinctions decays, then the semiotic systems manifesting such differences will tend to dissolve or become simplified.

15) *Final or infinite interpretation of a semiotic system or text:*
Most often Peirce himself (cf. chapter IV) and the literature on him
look at the final interpretant as an eternally valid interpretation that
is conceived of as the result of an unending process of inquiry. This
interpretation is conceived as an ideal limit that is approached, but
may never be reached. In an optimistic vein Peirce describes this
process in the Berkeley review (1871):

> There is, then, to every question a true answer, a final conclusion, to which
> the opinion of every man is constantly gravitating. . . .
> There is a definite opinion to which the mind of man is, on the whole and
> in the long run tending. On many questions the final agreement is already
> reached, on all it will be reached if time enough is given. (8.12)

The point here is not whether his optimism is well-founded (in many
other places Peirce is more cautious), but his claim that concerning
many issues agreement already exists. This claim points to the important fact that final interpretants of signs mean two very different
things in Peirce: they are the outcome of the scholarly and scientific
quest for truth mentioned above; and they are the stably formed
habits that govern interpretations and actions within a given culture.
Every time we stop on *red* and go on *green* our dynamical interpretants are also final. Final interpretants in this sense are vital to the
survival of a society, and to the sanity of individuals, because unless
its members agree on the interpretation of a great many sign systems,
society will disintegrate and eventually collapse, and if individuals are
unable to form habits they go insane.

It makes no sense to inquire into the truth or falsity of such
regulatory signs systems as the traffic light. If they are abandoned
and replaced by other systems, it will  probably be for reasons of
efficiency. Such an inquiry is essential for other types of systems or
texts. In these cases final interpretants, meaning final answers to
questions concerning signs and objects, are sought for. The process of
inquiry, however, will necessarily contain premises that, at a certain
stage, are unquestioned, because they are regarded as true. This is
why Peirce talks about agreement having been reached on many questions, although his recognition of fallibility prevents him from claiming that they may never be questioned. Consequently, every process of
interpretation in the sense of inquiry will contain a dialectic between
using unquestioned interpretants as presuppositions and premises

and the questioning of specific points in search for solutions to other problems. Among the unquestioned presuppositions and premises some will be considered as practically certain, because the community of scholars or scientists cannot find reasons to doubt them.

The conclusion of this study maps the elements and interrelationships of a semiotic micro system such as the traffic light on the semiotic pyramid as shown in Fig. 74.

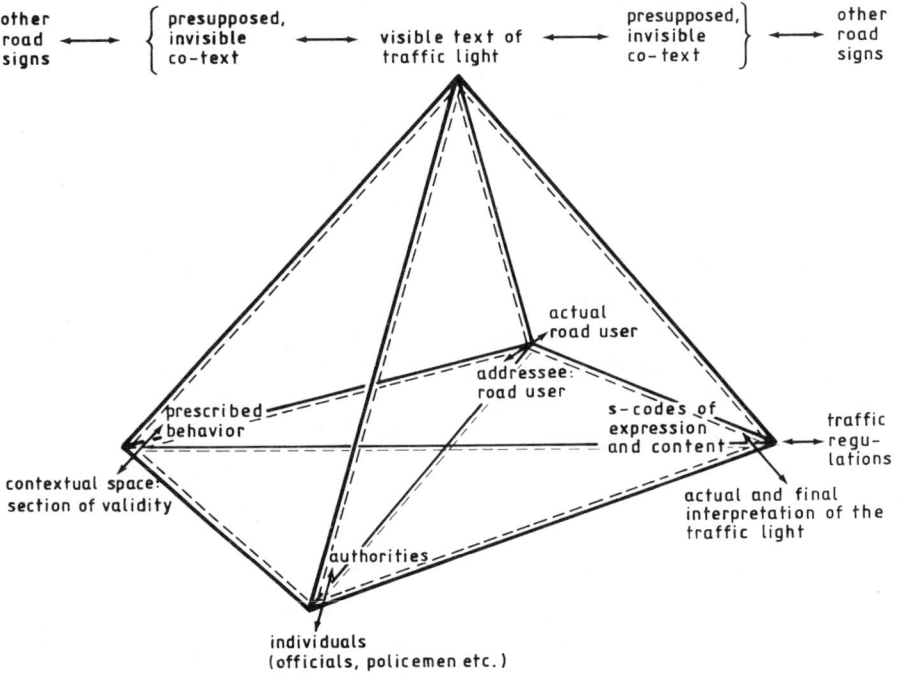

Fig. 74

In this view the traffic light has to be analyzed not only as a intrinsic system that is manifested successively as a text, but also as a cultural semiosis designed to fulfill a purpose, i.e., as a truly communicative and dialogical phenomenon!

# Bibliography

Apel, Karl-Otto (1975). *Der Denkweg von Charles S. Peirce*. Frankfurt am Main: Suhrkamp.

———(1980). "C.S. Peirce and the Post-Tarskian Problem of an Adequate Explication of the Meaning of Truth: Towards a Transcendental-Pragmatic Theory of Truth, Part I." In *The Monist* 63, pp. 386-407.

———(1982). "C.S. Peirce and the Post-Tarskian Problem of an Adequate Explication of the Meaning of Truth: Towards a Transcendental-Pragmatic Theory of Truth, Part II." In *Transactions of the Charles S. Peirce Society*, pp. 3-17.

Aristotle (1926). *"Art" of Rhetoric* (transl. J.H. Reese). London: Heinemann, Loeb Classical Library.

Austin, J.L. (1962). *How to Do Things with Words*. Oxford: Oxford University Press.

Ayer, A.J. (1968). *The Origins of Pragmatism. Studies in the Philosophy of Charles Sanders Peirce and William James*. San Francisco: Freeman, Cooper & Company.

Benveniste, Emile (1966). *Problèmes de linguistique generale* I. Paris: Gallimard.

Bernsen, Niels Ole (1978). *Knowledge. A Treatise on Our Cognitive Situation*. Odense: Odense University Press.

Boler, John F. (1963). *Charles Peirce and Scholastic Realism*. Seattle: University of Washington Press.

Bouissac, Paul (1986). "Iconicity and Pertinence." In *Iconicity. Essays on the Nature of Culture* (P. Bouissac, M. Herzfeld, R. Posner, eds.). Tübingen: Stauffenburg Verlag, pp. 193-214.

Bozorete, Jerry (1979). "The Internally Real, the Fictitious, and the Indubitable." In *Peirce Studies* I, Studies in Peirce's Semiotic. A Symposium by Members of the Institute for Studies in Pragmaticism. Institute for Studies in Pragmaticism, Lubbock TX, pp. 77-88.

Braga, Lucia Santaella (1989). "From pure icon to metaphor: Six degrees of iconicity" (forthcoming).

Brask, Peter (1979). "Model Groups and Composition Systems," in *Danish Semiotics* (J. Dines Johansen & Morten Nøjgaard, eds.), *Orbis Litteratum*, Supplement no.4, pp. 177-272. Copenhagen: Munksgaard.

Bruner, Jerome S. (1966). "On Cognitive Growth." In *Studies in Cognitive Growth* (J.S. Bruner, R.R. Olver & P.M. Greenfield, eds.). New York: John Wiley, pp. 1-67.

Buchler, Justus (1966). *Charles Peirce's Empiricism.* (1st ed., 1939). New York: Octagon Books.

Buczyńska-Garewicz, Hanna (1978). "Sign and Continuity." In *Ars Semiotica* no. 2, pp. 3-15.

———(1979). "Peirce's Method of Triadic Analysis of Signs." In *Semiotica* 26, pp. 251-259.

———(1979). "The Degenerate Sign." In *Semiosis* no. 13, pp. 5-15.

———(1983). "Sign and Dialogue." In *American Journal of Semiotics*, vol. 2, nos. 1-2, pp. 27-43.

*Danish Semiotics* (J. Dines Johansen & M. Nøjgaard, eds.) *Orbis Litterarum*, Supplement no. 4. 1979. Copenhagen: Munksgaard.

Deely, John (1982). *Introducing Semiotic: Its History and Doctrine.* Bloomington IN: Indiana University Press.

———(1990). *Basis of Semiotics.* Bloomington IN: Indiana University Press.

Ducrot, O. & Todorov, T. (1972). *Dictionnaire encyclopédique des sciences du langage.* Paris: Le Seuil.

Due, Christensen et al. (1979). *Kommenteret færdselslov* (The Annotated Danish Road Traffic Act). Copenhagen: Juristforbundet.

Eco, Umberto (1976). *A Theory of Semiotics.* Bloomington IN: Indiana University Press.

———(1979). *The Role of the Reader.* Bloomington IN: Indiana University Press.

Ege, Niels (1949). "Le signe linguistique est arbitraire," in *Recherches structurales.* Copenhagen: Nordisk Sprog og Kulturforlag.

Engler, Rudolf (ed.), (1968). *Ferdinand de Saussure: Cours de linguistique générale. Edition critique,* I. Wiesbaden: Harrasowitz.

———(1974). *Ferdinand de Saussure: Cours de linguistigue générale. Edition critique,* II. Wiesbaden: Harrasowitz.

———(1975). "European Structuralism: Saussure," in Thomas Sebeok (ed.), *Current Trends in Linguistics* 13: Historiography of Linguistics, fasc. 2. The Hague: Mouton, pp. 826-866.

Feibleman, James K. (1946). *An Introduction to the Philosophy of Charles S. Peirce,* Cambridge MA: MIT Press.

Fischer-Jørgensen, Eli (1966). "Form and Substance in Glossematics." In *Acta linguistica* X, pp. 1-33. Copenhagen.

———(1975). *Trends in Phonological Theory.* Copenhagen: Akademisk Forlag.

Fitzgerald, John J. (1966). *Peirce's Theory of Signs as a Foundation for Pragmatics.* The Hague: Mouton.

Freud, Sigmund (1953). *The Interpretation of Dreams* I-II (1900a), *The Standard Edition of the Complete Psychological Works of Sigmund Freud,* vols. IV-V. London: Hogarth Press.

———(1955). "Some Neurotic Mechanisms in Jealousy, Paranoia, and Homosexuality" (1922b), in *The Standard Edition of the Complete Psychological Works of Sigmund Freud,* vol. XVIII, pp. 221-234. London: Hogarth Press.

———(1960 (1905c)). *Jokes and Their Relation to the Unconscious. The Stan-*

*dard Edition of the Complete Psychological Work of Sigmund Freud,* vol. VIII. London: Hogarth Press.

Gadamer, Hans-Georg (1960). *Wahrheit und Methode,* Tübingen: J.C.B. Mohr.

Godel, Robert (1957). *Les sources manuscrites du Cours de linguistique générale de F. de Saussure.* Genève: Droz.

———(ed. 1969). *A Geneva School Reader in Linguistics.* Bloomington IN: Indiana University Press.

Gombrich, E.H. (1960). *Art and Illusion.* London: Phaidon.

———(1963). *Meditations on a Hobby Horse.* London: Phaidon.

Goodman, Nelson (1969). *Languages of Art.* London: Oxford University Press.

———(1970). "Seven Strictures on Similarity." In Goodman, *Problems and Projects.* Indianapolis/New York: Bobbs-Merrill 1972, pp. 437-446.

Goudge, Thomas A. (1950). *The Thought of C.S. Peirce.* Toronto: University of Toronto Press.

———(1965). "Peirce's Index." In *Transactions of the Charles S. Peirce Society* 1965:1, pp. 52-70.

Greenlee, Douglas (1973). *Peirce's Concept of the Sign.* The Hague: Mouton.

Greimas, A.J., (1966). *Sémantique structurale,* Paris: Larousse.

———(1970). *Du sens.* Paris: Le Seuil.

——— et Courtés, J. (1979). *Sémiotique. Dictionnaire raisonné de la théorie du langage.* Paris: Hachette.

Grice, H. P. (1968). "Utterer's meaning, sentence-meaning, and word-meaning." In *Foundations of Language* 4, pp. 225-242.

———(1969). "Utterer's meaning and intentions." In *Philosophical Review* 78, pp. 147-177.

———(1975). "Logic and Conversation." In *Syntax and Semantics* (P. Cole and J.L. Morgan, eds.), vol. 3. *Speech Acts.* New York: Academic Press, pp. 41-58.

———(1978). "Further Notes on Logic and Conversation." In *Syntax and Semantics* (P. Cole, ed.). vol. 9. *Pragmatics.* New York: Academic Press, pp. 113-128.

Habermas, Jürgen, (1973). *Legitimationsprobleme im Spätkapitalismus.* Frankfurt am Main: Suhrkampf.

———(1975) *Legitimation Crisis.* Boston: Beacon Press.

———(1979). *Communication and the Evolution of Society* (transl. & introd. by Thomas McCarthy). Boston: Beacon Press.

———(1981). *Theorie des kommunikative Handelns I-II.* Frankfurt am Main: Suhrkamp.

———(1982). *Habermas – Critical Debates* (John B. Thompson & David Held, eds.). Cambridge MA: MIT Press.

———(1983). "Interpretative social science vs. hermeneuticism." In *Social Science as Moral Inquiry* (N. Haan, R.N. Bellak, P. Rabinov, and W.M. Sullivan, eds.). New York: Columbia University Press.

———(1983). *Moralbewusstsein und kommunikatives Handeln.* Frankfurt am Main: Suhrkamp.

———(1987). *The Theory of Communicative Action* I-II (transl. Thomas

McCarthy). Boston: Beacon Press.

Hall, Edward (1959). *The Silent Language.* New York: Doubleday.

———(1966). *The Hidden Dimension.* New York: Doubleday.

Harris, Frank (1963). *My Life and Loves.* New York: Grove Press.

Hjelmslev, Louis (1928). *Principes de grammaire générale,* Copenhagen: Det Kgl. Danske Videnskabernes Selskab. Historisk-filologiske Meddelelser XVI, 1 (Høst & Søn).

———(1936). "Sprog og Tanke" (Language and Thought). In *Sprog og Kultur* V, 1, pp. 24-33.

———(1943). "Langue et parole," in *Essais linguistiques* 1959: 69-81, TCLC XII. Copenhagen: Nordisk Sprog og Kulturforlag.

———(1953a). *Prolegomena to a Theory of Language* (transl. by Francis J. Whitfield, Danish orig.: *Omkring Sprogteoriens Grundlæggelse,* 1943). Baltimore: Waverly Press.

———(1953b). "The Content Form of Language as a Social Factor" in *Essais linguistiques,* 1959, 89-95, TCLC XII. Copenhagen: Nordisk Sprog og Kulturforlag.

———(1954). "La stratification du language," in *Essais linguistiques,* 1959: 36-68. TCLC XII, 1959: 36-68, Copenhagen: Nordisk Sprog og Kulturforlag.

———(1957). "Pour une sémantique structurale," in *Essais linguistiques,* 1959: 96-112, TCLC XII. Copenhagen: Nordisk Sprog og Kulturforlag.

———(1959) *Essais linguistiques* TCLC XII. Copenhagen: Nordisk Sprog og Kulturforlag.

———(1961). "Some Reflections on Practice and Theory in Structural Semantics." In *Language and Society. Essays Presented to Arthur M. Jensen on His Seventieth Birthday.* Copenhagen: Det Berlinske Bogtrykkeri, pp. 56-64.

———(1973). *Essais linguistique* II TCLC XIV. Copenhagen: Nordisk Sprog og Kulturforlag.

———(1973/1947). "The Basic Structure of Language," in *Essais linguistique* II, pp. 119-156. Copenhagen: Nordisk Sprog og Kulturforlag.

*Iconicity. Essays on the Nature of Culture. Festschrift for Thomas A. Sebeok on His 65th Birthday* (P. Bouissac, M. Hezfeld, R. Posner, eds.), 1986. Tübingen: Stauffenburg Verlag.

Isocrates (1928). *Antidosis.* In *Isocrates,* II, 181-368 (transl. G. Norlin). London: Heinemann, Loeb Classical Library.

Jakobson, Roman (1956). " Metalanguage as a Linguistic Problem." In *Selected Writings* VII: 113-121. The Hague: Mouton.

———(1957). "Shifters, Verbal Categories, and the Russian Verb." In *Selected Writings* II: 130-147. The Hague: Mouton.

———(1959). "On Linguistic Aspects of Translation." In *Selected Writings* II: 260-266. The Hague: Mouton.

———(1960). "Linguistics and Poetics." In *Selected Writings* III: 18-51. The Hague: Mouton (also in T. Sebeok, ed., *Style in Language,*1960, Cambridge MA: MIT Pres, pp. 350-377).

————(1961). *"Linguistics and Communication Theory."* In Selected Writings II: 570-579. The Hague: Mouton.

————(1963). "Implications of Language Universals for Linguistics." In *Selected Writings* II: 580-592. The Hague: Mouton.

————(1965). "Quest for the Essence of Language." In *Selected Writings* II: 345-359. The Hague: Mouton.

————(1966-1988). *Selected Writings.* 8 vols. The Hague and Berlin: Mouton de Gruyter.

————(1968). "Language in Relation to Other Communication Systems." In *Selected Writings* II: 697-708. The Hague: Mouton.

————(1977). "A Few Remarks on Peirce, Pathfinder in the Science of Language." In *Selected Writings* VII: 248-253. The Hague: Mouton.

Johansen, Jørgen Dines (1980). "Sémiotique et pragmatique universelle." In *Communication et sujet, Degrès* VIII, 21, printemps 1980: 1-33.

————(1985). "Prolegomena to a Semiotic Theory of Text Interpretation." In *Semiotica* 57, 3/4: 225-288.

————(1986). "Umberto Eco's Platform. Sign and Object in the Theatre." In *Approches de l'opéra.* Actes du colloque AISS (A. Helbo, ed.). Paris: Didier, pp. 183-190.

————(1986). "The Place of Semiotics in the Study of Literature." In *Semiotics and International Scholarship: Towards a Language of Theory* (J. Evans & A. Helbo, eds.). Dordrecht: Martinus Nijhoff, pp. 101-126.

————(1986). "Semiotics and Comparative Literature." In *Sensus Communis. Festschrift für Henry Remak.* Tübingen: Günter Narr Verlag, pp. 23-38.

————(1988). "What Is a Text? Semiosis and Textuality: A Peircean Perspective." In *Livstegn* nr. 5 1/1988. Bergen, pp. 7-32.

————(1989). "Hypothesis, Reconstruction, Analogy: On Hermeneutics and the Interpretation of Literature." In *Semiotica* 74 -3/4: 235-252.

Krampen, Martin (1986). "The Development of Children's Drawings as a Phase in the Ontogeny of Iconicity." In *Iconicity. Essays on the Nature of Culture* (P. Bouissac, M. Herzfeld, R. Posner, eds.). Tübingen: Stauffenburg Verlag, pp. 141-192.

Lieb, Irwin C. (1977/1953). "On Peirce's Classification of Signs," in *Semiotics and Significs* (Charles S. Hardwick, ed.), pp. 160-166, Bloomington IN: Indiana University Press.

Lyons, John (1977). *Semantics 1-2.* Cambridge: Cambridge University Press.

Martinet, André (1964). *Elements of General Linguistics.* Chicago: University of Chicago Press.

Morris, Charles (1971) *Writings on the General Theory of Signs.* The Hague: Mouton.

Murphey, Murray G. (1961). *The Development of Peirce's Philosophy.* Cambridge MA: Harvard University Press.

Parret, Herman (1974). *Discussing Language.* The Hague: Mouton.

Pavel, Thomas G. (1986). *Fictional Worlds.* Cambridge MA: Harvard University Press.

Peirce, Charles Sanders (1931-1958). *Collected Papers* I - VIII (C. Hartshorne,

P. Weiss, and A. Burks, eds.). Cambridge MA: Harvard University Press.
———(1975-1979). *Contributions to The Nation* I - III (K. Ketner and J. Cook, eds.). Lubbock TX: Texas Tech Press.
———(1976). *The New Elements of Mathematics* I - IV (C. Eisele, ed.). The Hague: Mouton (four volumes in five, here referred to as NEM).
———(1977). *Semiotics and Significs: The Correspondence between Charles S. Peirce and Victoria Lady Welby* (Ch. S. Hardwich, ed.). Bloomington IN: Indiana University Press (here referred to as SS).
———(1982). *Writings of Charles S. Peirce: A Chronological Edition* (M. Fisch, C. Kloesel, E. Moore, et al., eds.). Bloomington IN: Indiana University Press (so far four volumes of this monumental and critical edition have been published, here referred to as WP).
Piaget, Jean (1962). *Play, Dreams and Imitation in Childhood.* New York: Norton.
Plato (1961). *Thaetetus, Sophist* (transl. H.N. Fowler). London: Heinemann, Loeb Classical Library.
Posner, Roland (1986). "Iconicity in Syntax." In *Iconicity. Essays on the Nature of Culture. Festschrift for Thomas A. Sebeok on His 65th Birthday* (P. Bouissac, M. Herzfeld, R. Posner, eds.). Tübingen: Stauffenburg Verlag, pp. 305-338.
Potter, Vincent (1967). *Charles S. Peirce. On Norms and Ideals.* Amherst MA: University of Massachusetts Press.
Quine, Willard van Orman (1960). *Word and Object.* Cambridge MA: MIT Press.
Quintilian (1920-22). *Institutio Oratoria I-XII* (transl. in four volumes by H.E. Butler). London: Heinemann, Loeb Classical Library.
Ransdell, Joseph M. (1966). "Charles Peirce: The Idea of Representation" (Dissertation, Columbia University, New York).
———(1977). "Some Leading Ideas of Peirce's Semiotic." In *Semiotica* 19: 157-178.
———(1979). "The Epistemic Function of Iconicity in Perception," in *Studies in Peirce's Semiotic: A Symposium by Members of the Institute for Studies in Pragmaticism* (K.L. Ketner & J. Ransdell, eds.). *Peirce Studies* I. Lubbock TX: Institute for Studies in Pragmaticism 1979: 57-66.
———(1979). "Semiotic Objectivity." In *Semiotica* 26: 261-288.
———(1980). "Semiotic and Linguistics." In *The Signifying Animal: The Grammar of Language and Experience* (I. Rauch & G.F. Carr, eds.). Bloomington IN: Indiana University Press, pp. 135-185.
———(1983). "Peircean Semiotics" (Incomplete draft of a work in progress). Department of Philosophy, Texas Tech University, Lubbock TX (photocopy).
———(1986). "On Peirce's Conception of the Iconic Sign," in *Iconicity. Essays on the Nature of Culture. Festschrift for Thomas A. Sebeok on His 65th Birthday* (P. Bouissac, M. Herzfeld, R. Posner, eds.) Tübingen: Stauffenburg Verlag.
Rescher, Nicholas (1978). *Peirce's Philisophy of Science: Critical Studies in*

*His Theory of Induction and Scientific Method.* Notre Dame IN: University of Notre Dame Press.

Ricoeur, Paul (1984/1988). *Time and Narrative* I - III (transl. K. McLaughlin & D. Pellaur). Chicago: University of Chicago Press.

Robin, Richard S. (1967). *Annotated Catalogue of the Papers of Charles S. Peirce.* Amherst MA: University of Massachusetts Press.

Russell, Bertrand (1940). *An Inquiry into Meaning and Truth.* London: Unwin.

———(1948). *Human Knowledge: Its Scope and Limits.* New York: Simon and Schuster.

———(1956/1950). "Logical Positivism," in *Logic and Knowledge. essays 1901-1950* (R. C. Marsh, ed.). London: Allen & Unwin, pp. 365-382.

Sanders, Gary (1970). "Peirce's Sixty-Six Signs?" in *Transactions of the Charles S. Peirce Society,* Winter 1970, vol. VI, no.1: 3-16.

Savan, David (1976). *An Introduction to C. S. Peirce's Semiotics, Part 1,* in *Toronto Semiotic Circle: Monographs, Working Papers and Prepublications,* no. 1. Victoria University, Toronto. 1976.

———(1977). "Questions Concerning Certain Classifications Claimed for Signs." In *Semiotica* 19: 171-195.

———(1980). "Abduction and Semiotics." In *The Signifying Animal* (I. Rauch & G. F. Carr, eds.). Bloomington IN: Indiana University Press, pp. 252-262.

———(1980). "La séméiotique de Charles S. Peirce." In *Langages* 14: 9-23.

———(1981). "The Unity of Peirce's Thought." In *Pragmatism and Purpose: Essays Presented to Thomas Goudge* (L.W. Summer, J. G. Slater, F. Wilson, eds.). Toronto: University of Toronto Press, pp. 3-14.

Saussure, Ferdinand de (1959). *Course in General Linguistics* (transl. Wade Baskin). Glasgow: Fontana/Collins.

———(1967). *Cours de linguistique générale* (Bally, Sechehaye, et Riedlinger, eds.). Paris: Payot.

Searle, John R. (1969). *Speech Acts.* Cambridge: Cambridge University Press.

———(1979). *Expression and Meaning.* Cambridge: Cambridge University Press.

Sebeok, Thomas (1960, ed.). *Style in Language.* Cambridge MA: MIT Press.

———(1976). *Contributions to the Doctrine of Signs.* Bloomington IN: Indiana University Publications, *Studies in Semiotics,* vol. 5.

———(1979). *The Sign, Its Masters,* Austin: University of Texas Press.

Sechehaye, Albert (1940). "Les trois linguistiques saussuriennes." In Godel (ed., 1969), pp. 138-181.

Short, Thomas L. (1980). "Peirce and the Incommensurability of Theories." In *The Monist* 63: 316-328.

———(1981). "Peirce's Concept of Final Causation." In *Transactions of the Charles S. Peirce Society* 17: 369-382.

———(1981). "Semeiosis and Intentionality." In *Transactions of the Charles S. Peirce Society* 17/3: 197-223

———(1982). "Life among the Legisigns." In *Transactions of the Charles S. Peirce Society* 18/4: 285-310.

Siertsema, Bertha (1954). *A Study of Glossematics. Critical Survey of Its Fundamental Concepts.* The Hague: Martinus Nijhoff.

Sonesson, Göran (1989). *Pictorial Concepts.* Lund: Lund University Press.

Studnicki, Francizek (1970). "Traffic Signs," in *Semiotica* II, 2, pp. 151-172.

Sørensen, Holger Steen (1958). *Word Classes in Modern English,* Copenhagen: G.E.C. Gad Publisher.

Thompson, Manley (1953). *The Pragmatic Philosophy of C.S. Peirce.* Chicago: University of Chicago Press.

Tinbergen, Niko (1953). *Social Behaviour in Animals.* London: Chapman and Hall.

Turley, Peter T. (1977). *Peirce's Cosmology.* New York: Philosophical Library.

Tursman, Richard (1987). *Peirce's Theory of Scientific Discovery.* Bloomington IN: Indiana University Press.

Uexküll, Thure von (1986). "From Index to Icon. A Semiotic Attempt at Interpreting Piaget's Developmental Theory." In *Iconicity. Essays on the Nature of Culture* (P. Bouissac, M. Herzfeld, R. Posner, eds.). Tübingen: Stauffenburg Verlag, pp. 119-140.

Van Gennep, Arnold (1960, paperback 1977). *The Rites of Passage.* London: Routledge and Kegan Paul.

Weiss, P. & Burks, A. (1947). "Peirce's Sixty-Six Signs," in *The Journal of Philosophy,* vol. XLII, no. 14: 383-388.

# Index

JØRGEN DINES JOHANSEN is Professor of General and Comparative Literature at the Center for Literature and Semiotics, Odense University, Denmark. He is Vice President of Sémiologie du spectacle, a member of the Executive Council of the *International Association for Semiotics* and secretary of the *Nordic Association for Semiotic Studies*. He is author of a number of books on literary theory, semiotics, psychoanalysis and literature, and the history of European literature.